THE NEOLIBERAL LANDSCAPE
AND THE RISE OF ISLAMIST CAPITAL IN TURKEY

DISLOCATIONS

General Editors: August Carbonella, *Memorial University of Newfoundland,* Don Kalb, *University of Utrecht* & *Central European University,* Linda Green, *University of Arizona*

The immense dislocations and suffering caused by neo-liberal globalization, the retreat of the welfare state in the last decades of the twentieth century and the heightened military imperialism at the turn of the 21st century have raised urgent questions about the temporal and spatial dimensions of power. Through stimulating critical perspectives and new and cross-disciplinary frameworks, which reflect recent innovations in the social and human sciences, this series provides a forum for politically engaged, ethnographically informed, and theoretically incisive responses.

For full volume listing, please see pages 298–299.

The Neoliberal Landscape and the Rise of Islamist Capital in Turkey

Edited by

Neşecan Balkan, Erol Balkan, and Ahmet Öncü

berghahn
NEW YORK · OXFORD
www.berghahnbooks.com

First edition published in 2015 by
Berghahn Books
www.berghahnbooks.com

English-language edition
© 2015, 2017 Neşecan Balkan, Erol Balkan, and Ahmet Öncü
First paperback edition published in 2017

Turkish-language edition
© 2014 Yordam Kitap
Neoliberalizm, İslamcı Sermayenin Yükselişi ve AKP

Library of Congress Cataloging-in-Publication Data

Neoliberalizm, İslamcı Şermayenin Yükselişi ve AKP. English
The neoliberal landscape and the rise of Islamist capital in Turkey / edited by
Neşecan Balkan, Erol Balkan, and Ahmet Öncü.
   pages cm. -- (Dislocations ; volume 14)
   Includes bibliographical references.
   ISBN 978-1-78238-638-4 (hardback: alk. paper) -- ISBN 978-1-78533-527-3
(paperback) -- ISBN 978-1-78238-639-1 (ebook)
   1. Turkey--Economic policy. 2. Capitalism--Religious aspects--Islam. 3.
Neoliberalism--Turkey. 4. Islam--Economic aspects--Turkey. 5. Islam and
politics--Turkey. 6. Turkey--Politics and government. I. Balkan, Neşecan. II. Balkan, Erol M. III. Öncü, Ahmet F. IV. Title.
   HC492.N4613 2015
   306.309561--dc23

2014029068

British Library Cataloguing in Publication Data
A catalogue record for this book is available from the British Library

ISBN 978-1-78238-638-4 (hardback)
ISBN 978-1-78533-527-3 (paperback)
ISBN 978-1-78238-639-1 (ebook)

Dedicated to the memory of those who lost their lives fighting the forces of repression during the 2013 popular revolt in Turkey widely known as the Gezi Park protests.

CONTENTS

TABLES

ABBREVIATIONS

AKP   Adalet ve Kalkınma Partisi
              (Justice and Development Party)

AKSİAD   Afrika Ülkeleri Kültürel Sosyal ve Ekonomik
              İşbirliği Derneği
              (Turkey-African Countries Cultural, Social, and
              Economic Development Association)

ANAP   Anavatan Partisi
              (Motherland Party)

AP   Adalet Partisi
              (Justice Party)

ASEAN   Association of Southeast Asian Nations

ASKON   Anadolu Sanayicileri Konfederasyonu
              (Association of Anatolian Businessmen)

BDP   Barış ve Demokrasi Partisi
              (Peace and Democracy Party)

CHP   Cumhuriyet Halk Partisi
              (Republican People's Party)

CMB   Capital Markets Board

CU   Customs Union

ÇUSİAD   Çukurova Sanayicileri ve İşadamları Derneği
              (Çukurova Industrialists' and Businessmen's
              Association)

DEİK   Dış Ekonomik İlişkiler Kurulu
(Foreign Economic Relations Board)

DİSK   Türkiye Devrimci İşçi Sendikaları Konfederasyonu
(Confederation of Progressive Trade Unions of Turkey)

DTP   Demokratik Toplum Partisi
(Democratic Society Party)

DYP   Doğru Yol Partisi
(True Path Party)

EANICs   East Asian Newly Industrializing Countries

FP   Fazilet Partisi
(Virtue Party)

HAK-İŞ   Türkiye Hak İşçi Sendikaları
(Confederation of Turkish Real Trade Unions)

IFBs   Interest free banks

ISE   Istanbul Sock Exchange

İŞHAD   İşhayatı Dayanışma Derneği
(Business Life Cooperation Association)

İSO   İstanbul Sanayi Odası
(Istanbul Chamber of Industry)

İTO   İstanbul Ticaret Odası
(Istanbul Chamber of Commerce)

MHP   Milliyetçi Hareket Partisi
(Nationalist Action Party)

MNP   Milli Nizam Partisi
(National Order Party)

MSP   Milli Selamet Partisi (National Salvation Party)

MÜSİAD	Müstakil Sanayici ve İşadamları Derneği (Independent Industrialists' and Businessmen's Association)
PASİAD	Pasifik Ülkeleri ile Sosyal ve İktisadi Dayanışma Derneği (Association for Social and Economic Cooperation between Pacific Asian Countries)
PKK	Partiya Karkerên Kurdistan (Kurdistan Workers' Party)
PLO	Profit-loss sharing
RP	Refah Partisi (Welfare Party)
SFIs	Special Finance Institutions
SMEs	Small- and medium-scale enterprises
SPK	Sermaye Piyasası Kurulu (Capital Markets Board)
TBMM	Türkiye Büyük Millet (Grand National Assembly of Turkey)
TİM	Türkiye İhracatçılar Meclisi (Turkish Exporters' Assembly)
TOBB	Türkiye Odalar ve Borsalar Birliği (Union of Chambers and Commodity Exchanges of Turkey)
TOKİ	Toplu Konut İdaresi Başkanlığı (Housing Development Administration of Turkey)
TSK	Türk Silahlı Kuvvetleri (Turkish Armed Forces)
TÜMSİAD	Tüm Sanayici ve İşadamları Derneği (All Industrialists' and Businessmen's Association)

TÜPRAŞ   Türkiye Petrol Rafinerileri A.Ş.
(Turkish Petroleum Refineries Corporation)

TÜRK-İŞ   Türkiye İşçi Sendikaları Konfederasyonu
(Confederation of Turkish Trade Unions)

TÜRKONFED   Türk Girişim ve İş Dünyası Konfederasyonu
(Turkish Enterprise and Business Confederation)

TÜSİAD   Türkiye Sanayici ve İşadamları Derneği
(Turkish Industrialists' and Businessmen's Association)

TUSKON   Türkiye İşadamları ve Sanayicileri Konfederasyonu
(Turkish Confederation of Businessmen and Industrialists)

PREFACE

Turkish politics has experienced many dramatic conjunctures since preparations for this book first began in 2012. Mentioning some of these developments will be helpful since many of the assessments and predictions in the following chapters are directly related to them. The crisis of confidence brought on by the Gezi Revolts had not yet abated when the country was rocked by a corruption scandal in December 2013 that implicated top ranking party officials and family members of the governing *Adalet ve Kalkınma Partisi* (Justice and Development Party, henceforth AKP). The scandal and political witch-hunt that ensued led many to anticipate a decline in the party's legitimacy and future electoral success. Subsequently, the results of the local elections of March 2014 came as a great surprise. As in all elections since its establishment in 2001, the AKP had won a clear victory! The electoral results showed that despite allegations of corruption and cronyism, Prime Minister Recep Tayyip Erdoğan remained popular through the widespread use of police force and political intimidation. After its victory, the AKP intensified its attacks on its former ally, Fethullah Gülen and the Gülen movement, portraying them as a fifth column that ran a parallel state within the state. In April 2014, scores of high-level police officers were arrested and accused of releasing fabricated evidence to the press that chronicled corruption within the government. These arrests were followed by a massive reshuffling of tens of thousands in the civil service and political purges that continue to this day.

The spring of 2014 saw the entire country absorbed by what would be the first presidential election by popular vote in its history. On 10 August, Erdoğan sailed to victory in the first round of voting, garnering nearly 52% of all votes cast. He was caricaturized in regal robes on the cover page of *The Economist*, whose editorial "The Next Sultan?" asserted that "The result has bolstered Mr. Erdoğan's increasingly tight grip on power and prompted further worries about the future of Turkey's shaky democracy."[1] It was not an unfair assessment. The manner by which Foreign Minister Ahmet Davutoğlu was instilled as prime minister of the AKP, filling the lacuna caused by Erdoğan's ascent to the presidency, put to shame even the feeble standard that Turkish democracy has upheld. The reason that Erdoğan made this appointment was probably because Davutoğlu had gained his trust during the war against the Gülenists. Erdoğan did not hesitate to vocalize this point in his speeches to the party and elsewhere. Meanwhile, Davutoğlu launched a concerted attack on the Gülen movement as soon as he became prime minister.

Alongside these developments in the domestic sphere, Turkey is faced with a growing crisis on its border owing to territorial advances made by the armed Islamist group ISIL (The Islamic State of Iraq and the Levant). In October 2014, ISIL took new positions in Syria and laid seige to the Kurdish town of Kobane on the Syrian/Turkish border. As news of its massacres spread, Kurds in Turkey demonstrated in many cities to protest Davutoğlu's passive stance and draw public attention to the situation in Kobane. Forty people died during these demonstrations as the police did little to prevent violence by some people against the protestors. Following these protests, the government introduced a bill to strengthen the power of the police force. Though questionable in terms of international human rights standards, we believe that this dubious bill will pass into legislation and lead to further intrusion into the judicial system. As this book goes to press, most Turks express concern that the judiciary is already under government control and that Turkey is rapidly deteroriating into a police state.

The Editors
October 2014

Notes

1. http://www.economist.com/news/europe/21612237-recep-tayyip-erdogans-plans-p
residency-next-sultan

INTRODUCTION

Neşecan Balkan, Erol Balkan, and Ahmet Öncü

Over the past ten years, Turkey has been held up by the global media as an exemplary country for successfully reconciling Islam with democracy and a market economy. In reports published by both private banks and international financial institutions like the International Monetary Fund (IMF), World Bank, and World Trade Organization (WTO), the Adalet ve Kalkınma Partisi (Justice and Development Party, AKP) was praised for its economic miracles and political victories. Peter Boyles, chief executive of global private banking at HSBC, recently characterized Turkey as the new rising star of the world economy, adding that its startling economic success is not accidental and should be attributed to the government's strong commitment to "fiscal discipline" and a "well-regulated banking and financial system" (Boyles 2012). Similar statements can be found in the World Bank Group's "Turkey Partnership: Country Program Snapshot," published in the spring of 2013. The opening line of this report resolutely proclaims that "Turkey's rapid growth and development over the past ten years is one of the global economy's success stories." During the same period, internationally prominent publications like the *Economist*, the *New York Times*, and *Der Spiegel* regularly referred to Turkey's rare ability to combine Islam and capitalism, and the idea that Turkey could serve as a model for other countries in the Islamic world was widely circulated. However, the well-known events of June 2013 threw this much-lauded "success story" into serious doubt for both Turkish and international audiences.

What lay hidden behind the so-called economic miracle was in reality a structural transformation in the mode of capital accumulation that was achieved through undemocratic means. This process was initiated in the 1980s with the free-market economic policies of the Özal government. At the time, the political environment was devoid of any serious opposition because of the restrictive legal order established by the military following its coup of 12 September 1980. The structural transformation was a typical case of "accumulation by dispossession" resulting in the redistribution rather than the generation of wealth and income. Its main pillars were privatization, financialization, the management and manipulation of economic crises, and the redistribution of state assets. Under the regime of privatization, public utilities of all kinds, most state enterprises, public institutions, and the provision of social welfare were gradually privatized to some degree. Financialization meant the deregulation of the financial system and its emergence as one of the main centers of redistribution through speculation. The Istanbul Stock Exchange and many mutual funds and investment banks were established. This all led to the development of a financial market in which both domestic and foreign investors participated. The management and manipulation of crises were carried out through a series of structural adjustment programs for trade liberalization, liberalization of interest rates, and deregulation of property rights. Under pressure from the IMF, the Turkish state reduced public spending on services such as education, health care, and social security, resulting in their deterioration. The neoliberal state also redistributed wealth and income through tax reforms in favor of both domestic and foreign capital, which included revisions in the tax code to benefit returns on investment for owners of capital.

The transition to a relatively more open and democratic order in the 1990s allowed for the reemergence of oppositional groups. Nonetheless, this decade saw the continuation of "market-oriented policies" and the creation of attendant institutions. Under Erdoğan governments in the 2000s, economic policies became increasingly neoliberal, leading to further consolidation of this mode of capital accumulation. By the end of this journey, Turkey had completed its transition from a mode of capital accumulation driven by import-substituting industrialization to a regime based on global flows of goods and capital, popularly known as neoliberalism.

This structural transformation in the economy, which was achieved over a thirty-year period, brought with it a series of important changes in the social and political arenas. First and foremost in the social realm was the appearance of an Islamist[1] bourgeoisie whose cultural formation was markedly different than the laic[2] bourgeoisie of an earlier period. Ideological divisions in the Islamist movement were reflected in the development of a new dominant class faction whose interests conflicted with the laic bourgeoisie. A new Islamist faction emerged in the early 2000s, splintering off from the Milli Görüş (National Vision) movement, which had since the 1970s adopted a distinctive "anti-Western" position and served the interests of small-scale capital. The new Islamists supported a number of political initiatives that were not easily reconcilable with Islamism, such as deeper integration into the world market, greater openness to capital flows (and the interest-based profits that came with them), further integration with the European Union, and a willingness to serve as the strategic partner of the United States and the North Atlantic Treaty Organization (NATO) in the Middle East. Presenting themselves as "conservative democrats," these metamorphosed Islamists founded the AKP and eventually came to power.

Several economists had predicted that the neoliberal policies implemented by the AKP would result in a fragile economy that was vulnerable to external shocks. Up until the summer of 2013, however, these critiques were not taken seriously outside of a small circle of observers. Regardless, it would be unfair to suggest that there were no material bases for the practically superstitious faith in the miraculous power of neoliberal policies. During the 2000s, Turkey appeared to be one of the fastest-growing economies in the world. Yet this growth, which had the effect of stifling any critique of the neoliberal agenda, was primarily predicated upon short-term capital inflows. Investment and consumption rose through external financing, which in turn stimulated the growth of the national income. The current account deficit reached record levels. Upon closer inspection of the sources of capital accumulation during this period, it becomes evident that the process was driven not by profitable new investments in the productive sectors of the economy, but by revenue obtained through the privatization of public assets. This rapid and astonishing accumulation spurred on by privatization was in reality nothing but large-scale dispossession. From late May 2013 onward, large-scale capital outflows exposed the fragile structure of the Turkish economy. The Turkish lira rapidly lost value. Mainstream media outlets began to voice critical viewpoints that had previously been marginalized. In September, the *Economist* wrote that Turkey was one of the most fragile economies in the global market. According to the magazine, future economic growth in Turkey depended on access to new loans, that is, new capital inflows. If these could not be secured, a crisis loomed on the Turkish horizon.

The eruption of the Gezi Park protests, a broadly inclusive social movement that marked a turning point in Turkish history, coincided with the economic free fall of June 2013. These events, which received a great deal of international attention, can be analyzed from a variety of different angles. At their root, however, lies widespread discontent over urban transformation, a continuation of accumulation by dispossession. These urban renewal projects were premised on the argument that gentrification would lead to the creation of globally attractive centers. In fact, they were nothing more than the private enclosure of public spaces. Areas that had previously been open to public use, such as parks and forests, were being transformed into large hotels, residential buildings, and shopping centers. The plan to turn Taksim Square's Gezi Park into a shopping center was the tipping point. With the eruption of the June protests to take back the park, Pandoras box was thrown wide open. People from all classes and walks of life, particularly the middle class, which was most affected by the enclosure of city spaces, poured into public squares across the country to express their disapproval of the AKP's increasingly authoritarian posturing. Though the flames of protest appeared to be extinguished by August—owing in large part to the onset of the holiday season—they were rekindled in September. This time masses of people spilled into the streets to demonstrate against a project to build a highway through the forests of the Middle East Technical University (ODTÜ), one of Turkey's most prominent universities. Shortly thereafter large-scale protests erupted triggered by Alevi citizens over the construction of a *cemevi* (house of worship) in Ankara's Tuzluçayır neighborhood, a project conceived by the Gülen movement, a behind-the-scenes partner of the AKP government. Just as it had during the earlier Gezi protests, the Erdoğan government set aside constitutionally guaranteed democratic rights and responded to the "September revival" with a level of police brutality rarely seen in the democratic world.

While the subject and content of this volume was established well before the ongoing popular uprisings that overlap with the undeniable manifestation of the vulnerability of Turkey's economy, its completion coincides with this historical turn of events. As such, this book has gained a new significance that its editors had not anticipated. We hope that it will help readers make sense of the extraordinary events that took place throughout the summer of 2013 by providing an overview of the historical developments that led to this current conjuncture.

During the writing of this introduction, a new surprising series of events unfolded in Turkey. On 17 December 2013, the country was shaken by a bribery and corruption scandal that included several ministers and their families. These scandals have raised questions about the AKP's involvement in high levels of corruption. It appears as if government officials are attempting to cover up charges through new appointments in the Ministries of Justice and Interior Affairs, who in turn have replaced the prosecutors and high-level police officials involved in this inquiry. On the other hand, the AKP government claims that the Gülen movement has formed a "parallel state" within the state. If this claim is true, it puts the AKP in a very difficult position, because for many years, and despite similar claims by AKP critics, the party tried to cover up and protect the symbiotic relationship between the AKP and the Gülen movement. Ironically, the recent events have turned this partnership into an open struggle for hegemony.

The power struggle between these two partners is actually the tip of the iceberg. The Gezi Park protests have deeply damaged Erdoğan's credibility, which had already been eroding due to a series of domestic and foreign policy decisions. Erdoğan and the AKP can no longer convince their partners and supporters that they are able to govern the country with stability. The conflict between the AKP and the Gülen movement and the resulting crisis is an extension of these unfolding events.

It is clear by now that this power struggle has triggered a process that will largely weaken both sides. To this we need to add the ongoing fragility of the economy. Given the uncertainties in the political environment, this fragility may reach unmanageable levels. As we write this introduction at the end of January 2014, the Turkish lira continues to depreciate despite Central Bank interventions into the currency market and a sharp increase in interest rates. This puts a tremendous burden on the economy, where the private sector has borrowed heavily abroad. All these developments place Turkey at the top of the list of "the fragile five" countries. The future is highly unpredictable, and may lead to a collapse of the strongest government that the Islamist bourgeoisie in Turkey ever controlled.

The book focuses on different aspects of neoliberalism and the rise of Islamist capital. While previous works have analyzed these phenomena separately (see, e.g., Buğra 1998, 2002 for the rise of Islamist capital; see, e.g., Bekmen 2013; Balkan and Savran 2002a, 2002b; Harvey 2005; Rutz and Balkan 2009 for neoliberalism in Turkey), the contributions to this volume represent an approach that brings them together for the first time. In doing so, they examine the relationship between neoliberal policies, processes of Islamist capital accumulation, and the emergence of new class factions. In this context, we are especially concerned with the rise of the Islamist bourgeoisie and the Islamist middle classes.

The collection begins with an overview of Islamism. In chapter 1, Gürel explores the meaning of Islamism and defines it as a political ideology that perceives current socioeconomic problems of the Muslim world to be the result of alienation from Islam. As a solution to this problem, Islamism proposes the creation of a state and society in line with Islamic principles. Gürel describes how in various countries the devout, conservative bourgeoisie seeks to be the dominant class by establishing hegemony over the working class. According to Gürel, the emergence of Islamist movements of various sorts in Muslim countries can be attributed to the crisis of secular and nationalist movements since the mid-1960s, and subsequent disillusionment in these societies. He describes how the Islamist movement in Turkey, as represented by the AKP, has become a model for some Islamist movements around the world because of its ability to acclimatize itself to neoliberalism while simultaneously establishing hegemony over labor. Gürel concludes with a less than optimistic account of the future success of Islamist movements considering the ongoing revolt in the Middle East against this ideology.

In chapter 2, Savran conducts an analysis of the AKP phenomenon by situating it in a long-term historical perspective of Turkey's relationship to Islam and Islamism. He starts out with a discussion of what he terms the exceptionalism of Turkey in the Islamic world, defining this in terms of the radical purging of the influence of Islam not only in the political and legal orders, but in the sociocultural and educational spheres as well. This separation was achieved in the early republican period under Kemal Atatürk in the second quarter of the last century. He stresses that this purge, unequalled in any other Muslim country, was part of a wider process that could be defined as a civilizational shift from the Islamic world to the Western world. Having thus set the background, Savran then proceeds to analyze the different stages through which Islam and Islamism regained prominence in sociopolitical life. Following the revival of social Islam in the form of religious orders in the quarter of a century after World War II, the half century that extends from the 1970s to the present saw the ascendance of Islamism as a political current, with two interludes in the early 1980s and the late 1990s. Savran points to the ironic contrast between the early twentieth and the early twenty-first centuries with respect to the fortunes of Islam in Turkey. The central questions that the author poses for this more recent period are, first, the dynamics behind the rise of Islamism and, second, the reasons for the success and resilience of the AKP, given that earlier attempts by the Islamist movement had been frustrated mainly through the intervention of a Western-looking coalition with the hitherto all-powerful army acting as a battering ram. The explanation Savran provides for the first question relies on class analysis, emphasizing a bifurcation within the Turkish bourgeoisie and the rise of a specifically Islamist wing. As for the second, Savran relates this to the acceptance by the AKP of the Western alliance as an anchor for Turkey, whereas the movement had previously staunchly refused to cooperate with Western nations. In the end, though, Savran points to the limits of the AKP's resilience, as manifested by two outstanding events that occurred in the course of 2013: the Gezi Park protests and the internecine war that resulted in an open conflict between two groups that had historically worked in tandem—the forces headed by Prime Minister Erdoğan and those led by the imam Fethullah Gülen, in voluntary exile in the United States. Savran suggests that these historic events may even signal the opening up of a period of secular decline for political Islamism in Turkey and beyond.

In chapter 3, Tanyılmaz demonstrates that the objective bases of the polarization within the bourgeoisie and the contemporary contradictions in Turkish capitalism are not simply superstructural, but are rooted in a qualitative transformation in the structure of the capitalist class. His discussion shows that the present-day conflict within the ruling class cannot be explained in solely political or cultural-ideological terms. In this context, he first provides an overview of the various conflicts taking place among the two capitalist factions and the ways in which these processes have been analyzed. Next, he explains that the class basis of this differentiation is rooted in the separation of political and economic interests (markets, incentives, technology transfers, etc., and the political means by which changes in these domains are realized). Using statistical evidence, he then compares the economic strength and influence of the Westernized, laic bourgeoisie and the Islamist bourgeoisie. For Tanyılmaz, Islamist capital is the economic force behind the political ascendancy of the AKP and its "conservative democrat" political position. In his account, this faction of the bourgeoisie appears to be the one that has gained strength after the military coup of 12 September 1980.

In chapter 4, Öztürk focuses on the formation and development of Islamic big business—a topic usually neglected in discussions about Islamic capital in Turkey. After clarifying the reasons as to why identifying a big business group as Islamic remains debatable, he argues that the two variants of Islamic big business, Anatolian holding companies and conservative finance capital, have constituted the basic forms of Islamic big business in Turkey up until today. He then provides a compelling historical narrative about how the growth and progressive development of political Islamism has been implicated in the conflict between the monopolist big business groups and smaller capital formations, which became increasingly visible at the end of the 1960s. According to Öztürk, as industrial monopolies internalized various economic activities (commerce, production, and finance) within their "holdings," they effectively blocked the growing potential of smaller capitalists, unless this latter group accepted a junior partnership in the commercial hierarchy (as commercial distributers, vendors, subcontractors, etc.). With respect to the case known as the "Erbakan event" in Turkish political economy, he shows how the conflict between big and small businesses not only initiated the mobilization of political Islam in connection with the interests of small businesses, but also led to the formation of a separate business organization to defend the interests of big business in the 1970s. In this context, Öztürk argues, the "conservative" faction of Turkish finance capital emerged in collaboration with the "secular" one. Moreover, there was no visible difference between the two in terms of organization and business characteristics (such as diversification). Although conservative groups were definitely a part of Turkish finance capital from the beginning, Islamist big bourgeoisie as a whole was not very effective until the 1980s, when Turkey moved from import-substituting industrialization to export-oriented neoliberalism. In the neoliberal era, Islamist business associations created platforms for Islamic capital clusters of various sizes, including conservative finance capital, Anatolian holding companies, small- and medium-scale enterprises (SMEs), and the companies of religious orders. For Öztürk, these organizations formed the most dynamic elements behind political Islam at a time when Turkish capitalism was becoming increasingly integrated with the world capitalist system, especially during the reign of the AKP.

   In chapter 5, Hoşgör critically reviews the current literature on Islamic capital in Turkey. Instead of a culturalist account that primarily focuses on conservative lifestyles and religious orientations of entrepreneurs as the main indicator of class formation, she tries to develop a criterion that will identify "Islamic capital" as a separate capital faction that can pursue a distinct and collective agenda. To this end, she first highlights different stages of capital accumulation in the Anatolian region. She interprets their growth and success as the product of multiple determinants that only became possible thanks to the neoliberal transformation from the 1980s onward, and to the export-orientation strategy and its specific forms of promoting SMEs. Second, she discusses the symbiotic relationship between interest-free banks, firms, religious networks, and communal linkages in order to understand this peculiar way of capital accumulation in relation to Islamic motifs. She demonstrates the limits of communal, religious, and other nonmarket networks in pursuing further economic development, and the possible solutions these capitals have pursued to solve their dilemmas. Lastly, she reviews their present situation, with a particular reference to the process of internationalization of capital accumulation and to the emerging multiple power relationships among different capital factions in the present environment. In doing so, she attempts to go beyond simplistic analyses that merely differentiate capital groups in terms of distinctions based on Islamic/Anatolian versus Istanbul-based capitals or based upon the size of the enterprise (big vs. SMEs). Hoşgör also provides guidelines to understand what the future may hold for this specific capital faction and assesses the explanatory capacity of the term "Islamic capital" under present conditions.

In chapter 6, Balkan and Öncü focus on the middle class in general and the Islamic middle class in particular to help better understand the peculiarities of contemporary Turkish society. The authors first introduce the premises of their analytic framework, which sees class as a theoretical concept that provides a useful lens to analyze three interrelated social and political processes. These are: (1) the underlying material bases of ideological formations, competitions, and conflicts; (2) the structural roots of social inequality and social mobility; and (3) the economic factors involved in the emergence and prevalence of a set of social practices at work in processes of social reproduction. Next, they provide a brief historical account of the bifurcation of Turkish society into laic and Islamic social sectors, and the ramifications of this process for state formation and class dynamics in different eras of capital accumulation, namely, national developmentalism (1923–80) and neoliberalism (1980–present). Then, they turn to the question of the middle class in order to explain the ongoing social formation driven by the emergence of an Islamic bourgeoisie in the neoliberal era. Here, they first take up the theoretical puzzle concerning the difficulties involved in conceptualizing the middle class, and clarify their position in this debate by drawing on the work of Pierre Bourdieu. Following this, they present some of the major findings of their survey of middle-class households in Istanbul in a comparative manner to specify differences and similarities among the "new" laic and Islamic middle-class factions that have benefited economically, socially, and culturally from the neoliberal regime. Based on their analysis of the findings of the survey concerning the cultural capitals of these middle-class factions, Balkan and Öncü suggest that in each faction a new middle class reflecting neoliberal values and lifestyles emerges and separates itself from the rest. Thus, although they have had different ideological and cultural histories and orientations, both the laic and the Islamic factions of the new middle class converge into a new status group as the "winners" of the neoliberal landscape.

In chapter 7, Hoşgör critically assesses the key features of the AKP's hegemonic appeal. She offers a class-theoretical account of the power bloc and explains multiple (and contradictory) power relationships behind this hegemonic conquest from a Gramscian perspective. She argues that although the AKP's hegemonic project allows for cooperation among different social forces within a coalition against a "common enemy," it also leads to a series of contradictory and unequal power relationships among the partners of this alliance. She devotes the first two parts of the chapter to different moments of hegemony (i.e., economic development and political reforms) and discusses how a relatively unified coalition/a temporary balance behind AKP rule has emerged in a specific historical context as a result of constant negotiations and concessions among various contradictory interests. In the third part she focuses on the role of cultural hegemony, thereby exploring the means with which the AKP succeeded in establishing its intellectual, moral, and cultural leadership by winning the hearts and minds of the people. In the final section she problematizes the existing difficulties in dealing with multiple power relationships and discusses the intensification of such conflicts and the resulting problems for the institutional unity of the state. She elaborates on how contradictions among different social forces create tensions between the government and certain state apparatuses (namely, the military and the judiciary) and particular strategies of the government to control strategic state capacities. She concludes with a discussion of the transformations within the institutional architecture of the state and the wider political system in tandem with the pursuit of particular strategies and tactics in wars of position and/or maneuver.

In chapter 8, Hendrick draws from multisided ethnographic fieldwork in Turkey and the United States to illustrate how Muslim networks have taken advantage of economic globalization in an effort to passively transform the contours of social hegemony in contemporary Turkey. As a case study, he presents the Turkish Gülen movement, a globally expansive, Islamist movement that is rooted in education, media, and business. Hendrick argues that in coalition with the AKP, the Gülen movement, with its market orientation, its of the AKP's "conservative democratic" political platform, its focus on education and civil society, and its global reach, indicates a move to mount a Gramscian "war of position" vis-à-vis rival factions in Turkey's elite. Unique within the field of Islamist activism, however, the Gülen movement works in the interests of domestic social transformation by striving to outperform rivals in the market, rather than to overcome them in political battle. The Gülen movement's attempt to wage a "passive revolution" thus appears to focus more on "increasing the Muslim share" than it does on "Islamizing" the secular institutions of the Turkish republic.

In chapter 9, Oğurlu and Öncü approach the question of hegemony in light of the schism that has developed in the dominant class between laic and Islamist factions in relation to neoliberal transformations, resulting in an intraclass struggle. Their focus is the media sector, particularly newspapers. Their discussion is divided into two parts. In the first part, they develop a theoretical argument concerning the implications of the schism in the dominant class for the "dominant ideology" of the capitalist class as a whole. By drawing from Althusser's concept of the ideological state apparatus, Herman and Chomsky's propaganda model, and Gramsci's conception of hegemony and its relation to the media sector, Oğurlu and Öncü emphasize that the mainstream media in Turkey is divided along the lines of laic and Islamist interests, and thereby fails to represent the interests of the capitalist class with a "single voice." Thus, neither dominant class faction can gain full "consent," nor do they lose their reputation in the public eye. In the second part, they focus on the Turkish mainstream media space and attempt to illustrate how the schism in the dominant class is reflected in what has come to be known as "media wars." Oğurlu and Öncü conclude that media wars in Turkey, like in other ideological state apparatuses, are signaled by a heavy focus on the struggle for hegemony. Each side of the dominant class, Islamist and laic, aims to be supreme in the commanding heights of the economy, and sees the media as an important power basis for gaining the consent of the masses by controlling their ideas and emotions.

In closing, we would like to emphasize our belief that this volume will add a new perspective to the theoretical and empirical debates of what we feel is an understudied phenomenon in Turkey, namely, the middle class. Greater attention to this perspective in future work on Turkey will provide a critical resource for the class-based analyses and solutions that are revived in politically salient moments like the Gezi Park protests and beyond.

Notes

1. Although the meaning differs considerably, the terms "Islamic" and "Islamist" have been used interchangeably in the literature. In this text the usage of these terms has been left to the preference of the authors, and we have respected their choice in the introduction where we present their chapters.
2. "Laic" derives from the French laïcité, which is often mistranslated as "secular" or "secularism." As Andrew Davison (2003: 333) has observed, "secularism and laicism are not two different words for the same institutional arrangement, but rather, two distinct, complex, varied, contested, and dynamic possibilities in the range of non-theocratic politics. ... As concepts, secularism and laicism have different etymologies, institutional histories and normative theoretical implication." Laïcité is an institutional arrangement that involves not the separation of church and state, but the subordination of religious affairs to the state. In other words, the state determines the limits of religious belonging in the public and political spheres. For a historical overview of the Turkish case, see Berkes (1998). In this text the usage of these terms has been left to the preference of the authors.

References

Balkan, Neşecan, and Sungur Savran. 2002a. *The Politics of Permanent Crisis*. New York: Nova.
_____. 2002b. *The Ravages of Neoliberalism*. New York: Nova.
Bekmen, Ahmet (ed). 2013. *Turkey Reframed: Constituting Neoliberal Hegemony*. London: Pluto Press.
Berkes, Niyazi. 1998. *The Development of Secularism in Turkey*. New York: Routledge.
Boyles, Peter. 2012. "Turkey Earns Its Place on the Trade Map." HSBC, News and Insight, 16 November. Accessed 13 September 2013. http://www.hsbc.com/hsbc-com/news-and-insight/2012/turkey-earns-its-place-on-the-trade-map.aspx.
Buğra, Ayşe. 1998. "Class, Culture and State: An Analysis of Interest Representation by Two Turkish Business Associations." *International Journal of Middle East Studies* 30, no. 4: 521–39.
_____. 2002. "Labor, Capital, and Religion: Harmony and Conflict among the Constituency of Political Islam in Turkey." *Middle Eastern Studies* 38, no. 2: 187–204.
Davison, Andrew. 2013. "Turkey, a 'Secular' State? The Challenge of Description." *South Atlantic Quarterly* 102, nos. 2–3 (Spring/Summer): 333–50.
Harvey, David. 2005. *A Brief History of Neoliberalism*. Oxford and New York: Oxford.
Rutz, Henry, and Erol Balkan. 2009. *Reproducing Class: Education, Neoliberalism and the Rise of the Istanbul New Middle Class*. New York and Oxford: Berghahn Books.
World Bank Group. 2014. "Turkey Partnership: Country Program Snapshot." April. Accessed 10 February 2014. http://www.worldbank.org/content/dam/Worldbank/document/eca/Turkey-Snapshot.pdf.

– Chapter 1 –

ISLAMISM
A Comparative-Historical Overview
Burak Gürel

⌇

Islamism has been one of the most hotly debated political ideologies of the world for more than three decades. A series of significant political developments have kept Islamism in the headlines during the 1980s and 1990s, such as the Iranian Revolution (1979), the war between the Soviet Union and the Afghan mujahideen (1979–89), the emergence of Hezbollah in Lebanon (1982) and Hamas in Palestine (1987), the Algerian Civil War (1992–97), and the Taliban's takeover in Afghanistan (1996). Younger generations' first encounter with Islamism was the suicide attacks in the United States on 11 September 2001 and the subsequent US invasion of Afghanistan. Islamism continues to be an important political subject in the twenty-first century. The war between the Taliban and the US-led coalition in Afghanistan is continuing. Different Islamist actors, ranging from the Islamic Republic of Iran to al-Qaeda-linked groups in Eurasia, pose a significant challenge to the United States and other Western powers. The Palestinian question remains important, and Hamas continues to be a powerful force in the Palestinian national movement. Islamist movements have recently resurged in the Arab world in the process of the Arab Spring that started in December 2010. The electoral success of Ennahda in Tunisia in 2011, the victory of Al-Ikhwan al-Muslimeen (the Muslim Brotherhood) in the presidential elections in Egypt in 2012, the killing of the United States ambassador to Libya by Salafists in 2012, and the shockingly rapid rise of the Islamic State of Iraq and the Levant in 2014 are different manifestations of this recent revival. Finally, cultural and political problems experienced by the Muslim minorities in Western Europe introduce a new spatial dimension to Islamist politics.

Islamism appeared with a new face in Turkey at the beginning of the twenty-first century. The Adalet ve Kalkınma Partisi (Justice and Development Party, AKP), founded by Recep Tayyip Erdoğan and his associates in 2001, gained an immediate electoral victory in the parliamentary elections on 3 November 2002 and became the ruling party with a clear parliamentary majority. The AKP successfully defeated the Turkish military's memorandum on 27 April 2007, a clearly secularist backlash against the AKP, by gaining nearly half of the votes in the parliamentary elections on 22 July 2007. The AKP's hegemony over the working masses since the 2002 elections is the peak of Turkish Islamism. This hegemony has led to hot debates in political, media, and academic circles about the character of the AKP (whether it is an Islamist or semi-Islamist party, or simply a conservative party like the Christian Democrats in Western Europe) and its similarities with and differences from the National Vision movement. The globally strong Islamist network headed by Fethullah Gülen, which had supported Erdoğan's AKP until recent years and then entered into a serious conflict with it recently, has also been an important theme of research and debate.[1]

Islamist Ideology

In this chapter, I define Islamism in line with Guilain Denoeux, as "a form of instrumentalization of Islam by individuals, groups, and organizations that pursue political objectives" (2002: 61). For Denoeux, Islamism "provides political responses to today's societal challenges by imagining a future, the foundations for which rest on reappropriated, reinvented concepts borrowed from the Islamic tradition" (2002: 61).[2] Therefore, instead of focusing on Islam as a religion, it makes more sense to focus on the political actors who have constantly reinterpreted Islam in different ways in order to achieve their particular cultural, economic, and political objectives in the twentieth and twenty-first centuries (Ayoob 1979: 535–36; Mamdani 2005: 148–49; Bayat 2008: 105). Reinvention of the Islamic tradition to address modern problems is the basis of Islamist politics of all brands:

> It is the invention of tradition that provides the tools for de-historicizing Islam and separating it from the various contexts in which it has flourished over the past fourteen hundred years. This decontextualizing of Islam allows Islamists

in theory to ignore the social, economic, and political milieus within which Muslim communities exist. It provides Islamists a powerful ideological tool that they can use to "purge" Muslim societies of the "impurities" and "accretions" that are the inevitable accompaniments of the historical process, but which they see as the reason for Muslim decline. (Ayoob 2004: 1)

This sort of invention of tradition lies at the heart of the political theory of all major Islamist theorists. They view the pre-Islamic history of the Arabs as an age of "ignorance" (*jahiliyya*) in which injustice and barbarism prevailed, and the history of the Arabs in the seventh century, when the prophet Mohammad (570–632) founded the first Islamic state, as an age of happiness. According to Sunnis, the age of happiness includes the period of the rule of the four caliphates after the Prophet, while Shiites limit this age to the period of the prophet Mohammad and the fourth caliph, Ali (599–661). Despite this significant disagreement on the history of Islam, since all Islamists see (at least parts of) the seventh century as an age of happiness, they all propose a "return" to the essence of Islam as experienced in its purest form in the seventh century. For instance, Mawlana Mawdudi (1903–79) argued for the necessity of a radical break from the past, which he saw as not Islamic enough, and the foundation of a truly Islamic state similar to the first one established in the seventh century. Famous Egyptian Islamist theorist and activist Sayyid Qutb (1902–66) took this call for a radical break from the not so Islamic past very seriously. He argued that the Muslim world was currently living in the age of the modern *jahiliyya* in which new ungodly idols such as nationalism and socialism had replaced the idols of the pre-Islamic past (Kepel 2002: 25–26, 34). The leader of Iran's Islamic revolution, Ayatollah Khomeini (1903–89), interpreted the concept of the return to *jahiliyya* within a conceptual framework of Shiism. He argued that the history of the Muslim world after the death of the prophet Mohammad is an era of uninterrupted injustice and alienation from the real Islam (Harman 1994).[3] In short, the definition of *jahiliyya* and the goal of overcoming it by returning to an essentialized version of Islam is the basis of Islamist ideology.

It is necessary to emphasize two issues regarding the idea of returning to the essence of Islam. First of all, with the exception of a few individuals and marginal groups, Islamist intellectuals and movements have never advocated wholly mimicking the Islamic practices of the seventh century. This type of an extremely antimodern interpretation of Islam has not received much credit, even in Saudi Arabia, where the Wahhabi branch of Islam, which—

at least on paper—advocates such a practice, is the official ideology. Thus, Wahhabism could be incorporated into the Saudi regime, which is deeply integrated into the capitalist world system. Similar to other religious ideologies, Islamism takes a selective approach toward modernity in which it keeps a certain distance from a number of modern ideas and practices without rejecting modern technology and capitalism, both of which lie at the core of modernity.[4]

Second, despite viewing the seventh century as a century of happiness, some Islamist movements depart from Khomeini's radical approach by embracing more recent experiences as political references. For instance, in Turkey the AKP and other Islamist parties view the Ottoman Empire as a positive historical reference. They advocate neo-Ottomanism, which aims to make Turkey an Islamic superpower that can act as a big brother of non-Turkish Muslims outside Turkey.

Mawlana, Qutb, and Khomeini proposed using state power to overcome *jahiliyya* and revive Islam. Putting the question of political power forward is as radical an intervention as the conceptualization of ignorance and has enabled Islamism to turn into a modern political movement. The question of political power inevitably brought the question of political organization to the agenda. Mawdudi, who founded the Jamaat-e-Islami (Islamic Community) in India in 1941, referred to the "vanguard" role of the first Muslims who accompanied the Prophet when he was moving from Mecca to Medina in 622. Qutb saw the solution to the question of political power in the organized struggle led by the "new Koranic generation." Finally, Khomeini advocated the foundation of an Islamic state ruled by a leading Islamic jurist, for which he started an organized struggle (Kepel 2002: 26–40). Thus, Islamism is an ideology that attributes to *jahiliyya* responsibility for all the economic, social, and political problems that Muslims face in modern times and defines the return to the essence of Islam as a political project that can be realized through organized political struggle.

Leading Islamist theorist-activists like Qutb and Khomeini defined Islamism as an opposition movement against secular regimes. For this reason, despite all their differences regarding the strategy for taking political power, the political movements they inspired have aimed to change the status quo in secular countries. On the other hand, "Islamism in power" is as important as "Islamism in opposition." As the cases of Iran, Pakistan, Saudi Arabia, and (north) Sudan demonstrate, "Islamism in power" politicizes Islam for the sake of defending the status quo. Interestingly, "Islamism in power" may encounter opposition not only from secularists but also from Islamists.

In contemporary Iran, a significant part of the opposition movement contains groups claiming to be the true heirs of Khomeini and utilizing Islamic themes and discourses. Today there are Islamist groups who aim to topple the Saudi kingdom, which claims to be an Islamic regime. Ironically, in the case of Saudi Arabia the ideological apparatuses once utilized by the regime to reinforce its political hegemony were later utilized by opposition groups in order to discredit the regime. Radical Islamist groups, whose leaders became familiar with the works of Ibn Taymiyya (1263–1328) due to the enormous Wahhabist propaganda campaign generously funded by the Saudi regime in the 1970s and 1980s, quoted his works in order to call for overthrowing the Saudi kingdom in the 1990s due to its alliance with the United States (Kepel 2002: 72).

The complexity and contradictory character of Islamist ideology and politics require us to define the concept of Islamism broadly. Therefore, my definition of Islamism includes all (mainstream and radical) political movements and regimes that make politics with reference to Islam and state their aim as reviving Islam regardless of their differences in terms of political positions (in opposition or in power), strategies of power (reformist or revolutionary), and means to make politics (armed or unarmed).

Class Dynamics of Islamism

Although there have been numerous intellectuals and political movements that interpret Islam in an anticapitalist framework, the great majority of Islamist movements do not aim to destroy capitalist relations of production. Regardless of the weight of state-owned enterprises in their national economies, all Islamist regimes have large private sectors in which the bourgeoisie owns the means of production.[5] Even in the distinctive case of Iran, in which the strong mass appeal of the leftist interpretation of Islam had forced Khomeini to adopt a more leftist rhetoric, the Islamist revolution did not destroy the capitalist relations of production. It only eliminated the secular bourgeoisie around the shah and assisted the devout bourgeoisie[6] in increasing its economic power. Islamist movements' ability to establish (complete or partial) hegemony over the working class in spite of their bourgeois character requires us to understand the class dynamics of the mass support behind these movements very well.

Islamist movements are products of an alliance of the devout bourgeoisie and the working class. The hegemonic force of this alliance is the devout bourgeoisie, and the subordinate force is the working class.[7] Similar to other capitalist states, all nation-states founded in the Muslim world in the twentieth century were based on a power bloc that included certain factions of the capitalist class while excluding others. Islamist movements, which emerge as opposition movements demanding a regime change in secular countries, politicize the demands of the capitalists outside the power bloc with religious rhetoric. For instance, in Iran before the Islamic revolution, the big bourgeoisie, which had close connections and shared the same secular culture with the Pahlavi dynasty, was well positioned to obtain significant economic opportunities due to its inclusion in the power bloc. On the other hand, the small and medium-sized bourgeoisie (which were known as the bazaaris, since most of their businesses were located in the Tehran marketplace called the bazaar) outside the power bloc became the hegemonic force of the Islamist opposition against the Pahlavi dynasty. In Turkey, the Islamist movement represented the devout bourgeoisie of Anatolia, which consisted of small-scale, nonmonopolistic capitalists who were outside the power bloc, which was dominated by the monopolistic and secularist capital of Istanbul and İzmir (Gürel 2004: 88–91).

Similar to all bourgeois political movements, the success of Islamism depends on the devout bourgeoisie's capacity to establish hegemony over the lower classes. Despite their historical differences, the successes of Khomeini in Iran in the 1970s and the AKP in Turkey in the 2000s are both products of the devout bourgeoisie's ability to win the support of the lower classes. Conversely, the defeat of Islamists in Algeria in the 1990s stemmed from the devout bourgeoisie's loss of hegemony over the lower classes (Kepel 2002: 67). For this reason, it is critical to understand what circumstances lead the lower classes to support the devout bourgeoisie.

In all successful cases in the last and the current century, the Islamist bourgeoisie won the support of two groups within the working class: the informal sector workers and the white-collar workers with a high school or university degree. In order to understand the political behavior of these groups, we need to examine the economic and demographic indicators of the Muslim world for the second half of the last century. Between 1955 and 1970, the population of the Muslim world increased by 50 percent. By 1975, 60 percent of this population was under the age of twenty-four. The development of capitalist relations of production in the rural areas and the industrial and service sectors in the urban areas increased the pace of rural to urban migration. Unemployment increased as the speed of employment creation fell behind the speed of population growth. Since urban infrastructure could not be improved to the extent needed to provide decent-quality housing to the new urbanites, the number and the population of the shantytowns increased rapidly (Kepel 2002: 66). Although a part of the shantytown population could find jobs in the formal sector, the majority were employed in the informal sector, with low wages, without access to social security, and under constant threat of unemployment. In fact, the majority of the people who are counted as unemployed in national statistics constantly oscillate between informal sector employment and unemployment. The informal proletariat, which is often called the "urban poor" in the academic literature, is the most important target population of the Islamist movements due to its numerical strength and mobilization capacity.

A significant source of the militant cadres of Islamist organizations is the workers and the unemployed who have received relatively higher education. Some commentators call them the "educated middle class" (Bayat 2008: 101) or the "new middle class" (Denoeux 2002: 62; Harman 1994), but it seems more proper to classify this group as the "educated proletariat" because of its economic distance from the higher echelons of white-collar workers and the middle class. Another significant transformation in the Muslim world in the second half of the twentieth century was the expansion of the middle and higher education so as to encompass lower classes. This transformation created a large educated segment within the proletariat composed of people who follow the outside world, popular lifestyles, and consumption patterns more closely than the less educated segments of the proletariat. This segment expected to find high-wage jobs providing the comfortable living standard that they think they deserve due to their higher educational credentials. However, since the speed of employment creation fell behind the speed of population growth, the unemployment rate of this group also increased rapidly. Moreover, most of the educated workers could find jobs that did not provide enough to let them achieve the high living standards they expected. The big disparity between the expectations and the actual results laid the groundwork for the crisis of hegemony of the secular (or partially secular) regimes in the Muslim world and ripened the conditions for the Islamist movements to gain the support of the educated proletariat (Harman 1994; Kepel 2002: 66; Bayat 2008: 101). On the other hand, these circumstances were no less advantageous for the Marxist organizations to win the informal and educated proletariat. In fact, Islamists were able to win the support of the working masses only with the decline of the radical left. Moreover, Islamist influence among the blue-collar workers in the formal sector is often much more limited than among the two groups mentioned above. This applies to the case of Iran, in which the Islamists had to carry out massive purges to eliminate Marxist influence among the factory workers (Poya 2002: 156–62).

In order to establish hegemony over the informal and educated sections of the proletariat, Islamist movements adopted leftist themes as part of their political discourse. They blamed the *jahiliyya* as responsible for the existing economic problems and social injustice and argued that complete Islamization of the society and the state was the only way to bring welfare and social justice. Furthermore, they effectively utilized anti-imperialist and anti-Zionist slogans, which are always appealing to the masses. By doing this, they prevented the Marxists from becoming the only political actor representing anti-imperialism and anti-Zionism.

The Crisis of Secular Ideologies and the Rise of Islamism

The national liberation movements in the Muslim world in the twentieth century were led mostly by secular elites. It was these elites that determined the developmental path of their countries after independence. These postcolonial states promised the masses economic welfare and independence from imperialism. In the 1950s and 1960s, many countries in the Middle East and North Africa, both of which have central importance for the subsequent development of Islamism, were ruled by secular and nationalist parties that declared themselves "socialist." These parties promised economic development and distributive justice to gain the support of the masses. The second important source of their mass support was their propaganda against imperialism, which retained its existence in the region both economically and militarily during the Cold War, and against Zionism, which became a strong regional actor after the foundation of Israel in 1948. The victory of the Egyptian president Gamal Abdel Nasser (1918–70) over Britain and France in the Suez Crisis (1956) was the pinnacle of the power of secular nationalism in the entire region. However, it did not take long for the secular nationalist regimes' decline from that pinnacle to begin. Their failure to bring economic welfare became apparent from the second half of the 1960s on. Growing mass disillusionment was due not only to economic failure but also to the awareness of a rising capitalist class well connected with the so-called socialist regimes. The demagogic nature of the socialist rhetoric of these regimes became more visible. As the struggle against imperialism and Zionism failed, this disappointment turned into anger. The quick and disastrous defeat of the Egyptian, Jordanian, and Syrian armies, which joined together under the leadership of Nasser, against Israel in the Six-Day War in 1967 was the second biggest trauma for the Arab world after the foundation of Israel. That trauma directly determined the course of the rise of Islamism in Arab countries and also made a less direct but still profound impact upon the masses in Iran, Turkey, and other non-Arab, Muslim countries.

The Islamist movement was not the only potential beneficiary of the crisis of the secular regimes. Indeed, radical leftist movements gained some power in countries like Algeria, Egypt, Iraq, and Syria, while they experienced a considerable rise in Iran and Turkey in the 1970s. However, these movements were soon defeated due mainly to their lack of a coherent strategy of taking political power that could end the bourgeois hegemony over the working class. Hence, the radical left in Muslim countries entered into a long-lasting crisis about a decade earlier than the collapse of the Eastern bloc. In short, the crisis of the secular regimes and the radical left laid the groundwork for the rise of Islamism.

A Brief History of Islamism

The great trauma of 1967 not only benefited the Islamist groups in opposition, but also Saudi Arabia, which was the most prominent Islamist regime at that time. The Saudi kingdom, whose economic power increased astronomically thanks to its increasing oil exports, became a rising star almost simultaneously with the decline of secular nationalism. As mentioned above, the Suez Crisis of 1956 symbolizes the rise of secular nationalism, while the Six-Day War of 1967 symbolizes its decline. It is possible to explain the rise and fall of Saudi prestige in the Muslim world similarly, with reference to two other wars. The Organization of the Petroleum Exporting Countries (OPEC) started an oil embargo to protest the support of the United States and Western European countries given to Israel during the Arab-Israeli War in 1973. Saudi Arabia, a key member of OPEC, gained twofold from the embargo. First, it increased its economic power thanks to increasing oil prices due to the embargo. Saudi capital effectively used the petro dollars to establish the system of Islamic banking. The second gain from the embargo was political. The effectiveness of the embargo created an image that the Saudis could find more effective political solutions to the Palestinian question than the secular Arab regimes.

The new international landscape after the oil embargo appeared as a golden opportunity for the Saudis, who intensified their propaganda campaign, already begun in the 1960s, to spread Wahhabi ideology in the Muslim world. During the 1970s and 1980s, generous Saudi funds helped establish numerous Islamic institutions wherever there was a sizeable (Sunni) Muslim population, from Southeast Asia to Western Europe. Among many activities, these institutions distributed a vast amount of Wahhabi literature for free. Saudi influence among the Sunnis thus increased considerably. However, given the continuation of the US-Saudi alliance and the remaining severity of the Palestinian question, the resilience of the Saudis' prestige remained contested. The Iranian Revolution of 1979, which quickly enabled the new Islamist regime of Iran and its revolutionary discourse to earn high prestige among Muslims, increased that uncertainty. It soon became clear that the Saudis could not easily break Iranian influence only by anti-Shia propaganda.

The occupation of Afghanistan by the Soviet Union in the same year as the Iranian Revolution gave the Saudis an opportunity to divert the attention of the Muslim masses from Iran and Palestine to Afghanistan. They quickly seized that opportunity by establishing a triple alliance with Pakistan and the United States in order to start an anti-Soviet jihad in Afghanistan.[8] In addition to vast economic and military aid given to different groups in Afghanistan, commonly referred to as the Afghan mujahideen, the Saudis effectively mobilized their global Wahhabi network in order to recruit volunteers to join the Afghan mujahideen. As a result, Saudi Arabia succeeded considerably in portraying the Soviet Union as the greatest enemy and the Afghan war as the greatest jihad. This success translated into the peaking of Saudi prestige in the Muslim world in the 1980s.

Everything seemed pretty positive for the Saudis by the year 1989. The Afghan jihad had finally succeeded. Islamic banks and the Wahhabi network, which played important roles in that outcome, were strengthened. However, Iraq's invasion of Kuwait in 1990 turned the Saudi project of hegemony in the Muslim world upside down. The Saudi elite could find no other option but to seek the support of the United States and accept the deployment of tens of thousands of foreign troops in their country. Although Iraq's disastrous defeat in January 1991 relieved Saudi Arabia, deployment of Western troops on the holy lands of Islam played into the hands of Iran, which attacked the Saudi regime for its alliance with imperialism. More importantly, the alliance of the Sunni jihadists and the Saudi regime received a serious blow from the presence of foreign troops in Saudi Arabia. Many jihadists who fought in Afghanistan started to question the legitimacy of the Saudi regime. The most prominent figure among them was Osama bin Laden (1957–2011), the leader of al-Qaeda, who left Saudi Arabia and declared the Saudi regime illegitimate in 1991. In short, Saudi Arabia's star, having risen during the Arab-Israeli War in 1973, quickly fell after the First Gulf War in 1991. The Arab Spring that started in December 2010 has already approached the shores of Saudi Arabia, and the Saudi elites are extremely nervous about the unfolding of those events. They are currently implementing a variety of policies in order to defeat the Arab Spring. They have increased the level of economic aid given to ordinary citizens in order to prevent the radicalization of the masses. Saudi Arabia is currently providing military assistance to other countries like Bahrain in order to crush the revolution outside its borders. Finally, it is trying to transform the ongoing revolutions into sectarian bloodshed by playing into the Shia-Sunni divide, as clearly seen in the ongoing civil war in Syria.

Pakistan is an example of semi-Islamism in power. It is a product of the partition of the Indian subcontinent in 1947 on the basis of the Hindu-Islam divide. Two of the most popular (and competing) Sunni Islamic currents in contemporary Pakistan, the Barelvi and the Deobandi schools, are all rooted in the prepartition period. While the Barelvi school embraces popular devotion and mysticism and is closely associated to Sufism (White 2012: 182), the Deobandi school represents an interpretation of Islam that has certain similarities with Wahhabism in the sense of a strong emphasis on the return to seventh-century practices and a strong hostility toward heterodox interpretations of Islam such as Sufism (Kepel 2002: 58). Mawdudi, one of the principal ideologues of modern Islamism, was a member of the Deobandi school. Although Deobandis are numerically weaker than Barelvis, they have dominated Islamist politics in Pakistan (White 2012: 184).

Pakistan's character as an extremely diverse country both in terms of ethnicity and language forced the founders of the country, most of whom were secular, to construct the national identity mainly around religion. Although the creation of Bangladesh in 1971 after a national liberation war against Pakistan showed the limits of religious identity to maintain Pakistan's national/territorial unity, without any other effective tool to serve this end, emphasis on Islam was reinforced even further after 1971.[9] Islam continues to be the only unifying element in Pakistan, which lives in a state of permanent crisis.[10] That is why the secular elites did not repress the Islamists in Pakistan as harshly as they did elsewhere, for instance, in Egypt (Kepel 2002: 59). Similarly, the religious establishment, which is made up of religious scholars (the *ulema*), personnel, and institutions, preserved its power relatively better than in many other secular countries in the Muslim world. For these reasons, the Islamization of Pakistan progressed on a different path. In 1977, the pressure exerted by the Islamist parties forced Zulfikar Ali Bhutto (1928–79), a secular politician by Pakistani standards, to accept their demands to make a number of sharia laws part of the legal system.

General Mohammad Zia ul-Haq (1924–88), who overthrew and executed Bhutto, put several Islamic policies into practice. Zia supported the Afghan mujahideen enormously. He made *zakat* (a religious rule that requires better-off Muslims to give 2.5 percent of their wealth to poor people as alms at the end of the month of Ramadan every year) official by taxing 2.5 percent of all bank deposits during Ramadan every year. Those taxes funded the madrassas (schools where classes on religion make up the bulk of the curriculum), which provide meals and accommodation to their students, most of whose families were displaced and lost their sources of livelihood during the process of agrarian transformation (Alavi 2009). Zia also changed the laws to allow madrassa graduates to take teaching posts in public schools (Kepel 2002: 59). These policies of Islamization aimed to decrease the further radicalization of the poor and strongly tie the religious establishment to the regime. However, the Pakistani ruling elite did not entirely eliminate secularism in the country. For this reason, despite the significant erosion of secularism in daily life and politics, the Pakistani regime should be defined as semi-Islamist. This is one of the reasons why alongside the secular and semisecular parties there are still many Islamist parties in opposition in Pakistan today.

The case of Iran makes possible the analysis of the transition of Islamism from opposition to state power. The Iranian Revolution (1979) is so far the only case in which an Islamist movement took power through a revolutionary overthrow of a secular regime by the masses. Although the revolution was a joint product of many Islamist, liberal, and radical leftist groups, the supporters of Khomeini succeeded in establishing hegemony over the liberal and the leftist opposition right before the revolution and destroying them after the revolution. For this reason, without forgetting the heterogeneity of the opposition that overthrew the Pahlavi monarchy, it is possible to define the period between 1979 and 1982 as a process of Islamic revolution.

The secular prime minister of Iran, Mohammad Mosaddeq (1882–1967), was overthrown in 1953 by a military coup backed by Britain and the United States. Shah Mohammad Reza Pahlavi (1919–80) returned to Iran after the coup and ruled the country on the basis of a secular monarchy until 1979. During the 1960s, Pahlavi implemented fundamental reforms, popularly known as the "White Revolution," which triggered Iran's capitalist transformation. Pahlavi faced opposition from three different social groups during the reform process. First, the religious establishment, led by prominent religious scholars, felt uneasy about the erosion of their cultural and economic power by the shah. For instance, the Iranian clergy fiercely opposed the Land Reform Law of 1962 that threatened to undermine the economic power of the landowning clergy and the religious institutions, which are financed by land-based income (Keshavarzian 2007: 238–39). Khomeini, the leader of the clergy, was sent into exile in 1964 after giving a speech condemning the shah for destroying national sovereignty by allowing US military presence in Iran. After that point, the religious establishment became a major force of opposition. The second major opposition group was the small and medium-sized bourgeoisie (the bazaaris), which started to feel alienated from the monarchy because of its nurturing of the big (and secular) bourgeoisie at their expense. In addition to this discriminatory treatment of the bazaaris, the Pahlavi regime also took openly hostile measures against them. For instance, in 1963, the state started stricter tax audits against the merchants who were refusing to pay taxes and threatened to launch an antispeculation campaign (Keshavarzian 2007: 240). These policies forced the small and medium-sized bourgeoisie to join the opposition almost simultaneously with the religious establishment under Khomeini. The continuing expansion of the Iranian economy until the mid-1970s prevented further radicalization of the bazaaris, whose income kept increasing despite their decreasing share in the national economy. However, following the sudden decrease in oil prices and rising inflation in 1975, the shah started a massive antispeculation campaign that hit the bazaaris hard: two hundred and fifty thousand businesses were fined or closed down, eight thousand businessmen were jailed, and twenty-three thousand businessmen were expelled to remote areas of Iran (Keshavarzian 2007: 242). After that point, the bazaaris became increasingly radicalized and enormously supported Khomeini.[11]

Finally, all parts of the working class were antagonized by the Pahlavi regime during the 1970s. While Marxist groups such as the Tudeh (the Iranian Communist Party; the name means "masses" in the

Persian language) became stronger among the formal workers than other parts of the proletariat, Khomeini's movement won the support of the informal workers in the shantytowns of Tehran and other big cities. In addition to liberals and leftists, Islamists also gained ground among the well-educated proletariat, whose expectations rose during the White Revolution but were not fulfilled in the subsequent period. As mentioned above, the Iranian Revolution is the historical period in which the Islamists utilized leftist discourses and slogans to the utmost. The situation was not born in a vacuum. Tudeh and the leftist guerilla organizations such as the People's Fedayeen were strengthened in that period. This overall rise of the radical left in Iranian society gave way to an Islamist-leftist hybridization. By reinterpreting concepts in the Koran such as *mostakberin* (oppressors) and *mostazafin* (oppressed) with reference to Marxist concepts of "exploitation" and "class struggle," the Iranian intellectual Ali Shariati (1933–77) became the leading theorist of the leftist version of Islamism. Shariati's works inspired groups like the People's Mujahideen, which played a crucial role in the Iranian Revolution (Kepel 2002: 72).[12] After recognizing the strong influence of this leftist interpretation of Islam in Iran in the late 1960s and early 1970s, Khomeini also used the concepts of *mostakberin* and *mostazafin* quite often until his death (Abrahamian 1993: 47–51; Harman 1994; Kepel 2002: 39–41). The leftist turn in Khomeini's political discourse did not scare the devout bourgeoisie much because it was instrumental in channeling the anger of the proletariat only toward the secular bourgeoisie and saving the Islamist bourgeoisie from that anger (Kepel 2002: 122; Poya 2002: 138).

Khomeini was equally careful when dealing with the secular opposition against the shah. He refrained from using a strictly religious language in order not to alienate the liberal opposition, which led the first big wave of protests against the shah in 1977. In November 1978, the leaders of the liberal opposition visited Khomeini in France and expressed their support to him. At that moment, Khomeini was declaring his goal as founding "an Islamic republic which would protect the independence and democracy of Iran." A few months later, political circumstances changed in his favor to such an extent that the liberals' support became less useful than before. Khomeini then declared democracy as "alien to Islam." Similarly, the Tudeh leadership declared Khomeini to be their guide before the revolution (Kepel 2002: 122). Khomeini was careful to preserve this support from the left until the revolution, but did not wait long to attack the leftists after the revolution. The ability to encourage secular political actors to participate in the revolution under an Islamist leadership while preparing to crush them when the circumstances ripened demonstrates Khomeini's political genius.

After the fall of Pahlavi in February 1979, Khomeini at first allied with the liberals to attack the radical left. After getting the first successful results, he then turned against the liberals. In fact, the taking of the US embassy personnel hostage by Khomeini supporters was a well-crafted tactical move against the liberals. Challenging US power with such a bold act was enough to convince the majority of the Iranian left once again to support Khomeini, who had attacked them only a few months ago, and made discrediting the liberals easier. The hostage crisis, which lasted 444 days, was the turning point in the transformation of the heterogeneous revolution into an Islamic revolution. After the end of the hostage crisis, Khomeini made another move, this time against the left, and destroyed all leftist organizations in the country, many of which backed him during his campaign against the liberals.

The Islamic revolution destroyed the secular bourgeoisie associated with the shah. The devout bourgeoisie filled the vacuum left behind. The state sector, which expanded by expropriating the wealth of the Pahlavi family and the secular bourgeoisie, became another key actor in the Iranian economy. The private sector, controlled by the devout bourgeoisie, and the state sector, controlled by the Islamist bureaucrats, some of whom became capitalists later by acquiring significant amounts of personal wealth, determined the capitalist character of the Islamist regime. The regime consolidated itself during the Iran-Iraq War between 1980 and 1988. In addition to the United States, Saudi Arabia also supported Iraq during the war in order to weaken the influence of the Iranian model in the Muslim world. Hundreds of thousands of Iranian soldiers died in the war. During the war, the Islamist regime established an extensive social security system, including numerous foundations and social aid organizations. The biggest of these organizations was the Foundation of the Oppressed and War Veterans (Bonyad-e Mostazafan va Janbazan; its current name is the Mostazafan Foundation of Islamic Revolution), a hybrid of a state-owned corporation and a social assistance organization, whose name itself shows the goal of the Islamist regime to establish hegemony over the lower classes. These organizations put the families of the soldiers who died or were wounded in the war on salary and distributed scholarships to their children. Today, young people from such backgrounds constitute the human source of the Revolutionary Guards and the Basij organization (Basij-e Mostazafin; Mobilization of the Oppressed).

The first period of the Islamist regime ended with the death of Khomeini in 1989. Despite all its efforts to export its model to the Muslim world during the 1980s, the Iranian regime ended up in relative isolation. Moreover, serious economic problems and the coming of a new generation who did not witness the revolution and the war challenged Islamist elites in their quest to preserve their hegemony over a rapidly changing society. Policies of privatization and opening up the economy started to be implemented under the presidency of Hashemi Rafsanjani between 1989 and 1997. Efforts to democratize the political system took place during the presidency of Mohammad Khatami between 1997 and 2005. However, those efforts failed to solve Iran's economic and political problems or bind younger generations to the system. The failure of those two politicians, considered the liberal faces of the Islamist regime, paved the road to the election as president of Mahmoud Ahmadinejad, an economically more populist and politically more authoritarian figure, in 2005, with the support of the lower classes. However, Ahmadinejad also failed to come up with any permanent solution for the problems of the regime. This failure became visible immediately after the presidential elections of 2009. The Basij militia attacked mass protests carried out by the supporters of Mir Hossein Mousavi, the candidate of the alliance known as the Green Movement, who claimed that Ahmadinejad got reelected through a massive election fraud. The regime managed to repress the protests, but its crisis of hegemony became more difficult to hide. The landslide victory of Hassan Rowhani, a centrist figure between Ahmadinejad's authoritarianism and the Green Movement's reformism, in the presidential election in June 2013, with the support of Khatami, Rafsanjani, as well as many supporters of the Green Movement, is another indication of the Iranian regime's crisis of hegemony. It remains to be seen whether Rowhani will be able to overcome or at least alleviate this crisis and protect the regime from a popular revolt similar to (or even stronger than) the revolt in 2009.

In contrast to the successful revolutionary takeover of political power by Islamists in Iran, Islamists' attempts to take power in Algeria failed in the 1990s. Similar to the Khomeini movement in Iran, the Islamic Salvation Front (Front Islamique du Salut, FIS), founded in Algeria in 1989, quickly grew in strength by establishing an alliance between the lower classes and the devout bourgeoisie (Kepel 2002: 168). The FIS received 48 percent of the votes in the parliamentary elections in December 1991. A military coup aiming to stop the FIS's march to power took place in January 1992. A bloody civil war between the Islamists and the military started. More radical elements within the FIS, which were less assertive before the civil war, suddenly became more active and independent. While the Islamic Salvation Army (Armée Islamique du Salut, AIS) fought as the military front of the FIS, radicals who split from the FIS fought under the banner of the Armed Islamic Group (Groupe Islamique Armé, GIA). Militants who previously fought in Afghanistan played leadership roles within the GIA. In its initial period, the GIA gained the support of the shantytown population who voted for the FIS in the elections. The class alliance that underpinned the FIS's success thus crumbled. The horror of the bloody civil war, which took one hundred thousand lives within only five years, and the GIA's increasing influence over the lower classes forced the Islamist bourgeoisie to recognize the fact that it could not gain anything from a continuing civil war. The military regime initiated a dialogue with the FIS leadership at that crucial moment, and the AIS finally quit armed struggle. The GIA, which faced increasing isolation thereafter, divided into different wings and became less effective.

Egypt has a long history of Islamist politics. The Muslim Brotherhood, which was founded by Hasan al-Banna (1906–49) in 1928, became a source of inspiration to the Islamists worldwide mainly due to Sayyid Qutb's theory and practice. Nasser's secular regime executed Qutb in 1966. Nasser's repression also led many members of the Muslim Brotherhood to leave Egypt and go to Saudi Arabia. Some of them assumed prominent positions in Saudi universities and contributed to the development of Islamist ideology. Others played key roles in the establishment of the Islamic banking system and accumulated capital (Kepel 2002: 51). Islamists started to reclaim their influence in Egypt after the trauma of 1967. That process quickened with the presidency of Anwar Sadat (1918–81), who took office after the death of Nasser. Sadat made peace with the Islamists in order to overcome the regime's crisis of hegemony and to counter the influence of the radical left, which was a result of that crisis.

Islamists started to organize openly on the university campuses in 1973. They assisted the state security forces in repressing the leftists on the campuses. At the same time, Muslim Brotherhood members who got rich in Saudi Arabia were allowed to return to Egypt and join the ranks of the Egyptian bourgeoisie (Kepel 2002: 83). Different Islamist groups soon went outside the campuses and started organizing in the shantytowns. The honeymoon of Sadat and the Islamists did not last long. Islamists declared Sadat a traitor when he signed the Egypt–Israel peace treaty (1979), by which Egypt gave diplomatic recognition to Israel. The Islamic Jihad organization assassinated Sadat in 1981.

The new president, Hosni Mubarak, started a witch hunt against radical groups. Although Mubarak put certain limitations on the activities of the Muslim Brotherhood, he refrained from completely repressing it because of the organization's strong influence in society and conciliatory attitude toward the regime. Groups more radical than the Muslim Brotherhood regained their strength in the shantytowns in the 1990s. The Imbaba shantytown, home to one-tenth of the population of Cairo, became a liberated zone for those radicals. While the civil war was continuing in Algeria, some groups resorted to armed struggle in order to start a similar war in Egypt. Similar to Algeria, the Islamist bourgeoisie of Egypt, having lost control over the radicals, made peace with the secular regime in the Nonviolence Initiative of 1997. Radicals tried to sabotage that initiative by massacring sixty-two foreign tourists in the Luxor Temple on 17 November 1997. Increasing unemployment caused by the damage to the tourism sector due to that incident led to the isolation of the radicals from the masses. Subsequent state repression weakened the radicals further.

The determined struggle of the masses gathered in Tahrir Square overthrew Hosni Mubarak, who ruled Egypt by dictatorship for thirty years, on 11 February 2011. Islamists, having at first refrained from participating in the revolution developing outside their control, joined the revolution when it became clear that Mubarak's downfall was inevitable. Islamists of all brands, from liberal Islamists and the Muslim Brotherhood to Salafis and the Gamaa Islamiya, have participated in the postrevolutionary political process and gained strength. Mohammad Morsi, the candidate of the Muslim Brotherhood, was elected president with 51.7 percent of the vote in the second round of elections in June 2012. Morsi's increasingly authoritarian rule and failure to meet the economic demands of the lower classes quickly led to mass disillusionment. Mammoth demonstrations that started on 30 June 2013 in Tahrir Square and the Ittihadiya district in Cairo as well as squares in major cities throughout Egypt demanded Morsi's resignation and opened up a new wave of the revolution. The Muslim Brotherhood did not give up and organized counterdemonstrations. On 3 July 2013, the Egyptian army staged a coup in order to prevent a popular revolution and to restore the power it lost in the post-Mubarak period by receiving the support of the revolting masses. The army's killing of more than one thousand Morsi supporters after the coup has increased the possibility of a civil war in Egypt. These recent events of historical proportions have brought

Egyptian Islamism to a very critical stage in its struggle for political power.

Islamism has been important for Turkish politics not only due to the relatively recent international context that is discussed throughout this chapter, but also because of Turkey's own experience with politics with Islamic references at least since the late nineteenth century. Islamism became a political alternative for the first time within the context of the existential crisis of the Ottoman Empire in the second half of the nineteenth century. Many intellectuals and political elites supported the idea of reorganizing the empire along more religious lines in order to overcome its apparent decline. Following the collapse of the Ottoman Empire and the foundation of the Republic of Turkey (1923), the relationship between Islam and politics quickly transformed into a hotly contested terrain involving the secularist elites ruling the new republic and the Islamist opposition. The contestation between the secularists and the Islamists increased especially during times of political reform, such as the abolition of the caliphate (1924), the abrogation of the constitutional provision that mentioned Islam as the religion of the state (1928), and the introduction of the principle of secularism into the constitution (1937). This contestation has evolved with the transition to a multiparty system after 1946, in which electoral competition between political parties made religious discourse and reforms related to religious education and practices crucial elements in Turkish politics. The legalization of the Arabic-language azan (Islamic call to prayer) is a prime example of this transformation. The Cumhuriyet Halk Partisi (Republican People's Party, CHP), then the ruling party of the single-party regime, had banned the Arabic-language *azan* in 1932 and replaced it with a Turkish-language *azan*. The Demokrat Parti's (Democratic Party, DP) election victory in 1950, which ended the 27-year-long single-party rule, ended the ban. Ironically, alongside the DP deputies, the deputies of the CHP, the party that had established the ban in the first place, also voted in favor of lifting the ban (Bardakçı 2006; 2010). This case demonstrates that even the CHP, the most secular establishment party in Turkish politics, could not ignore the mass appeal of religious motifs in the new political playground defined by electoral competition. The approach to Islam in public life retained its importance as a theme of political contestation between different (more or less) secular political parties in the first two decades of the multiparty system. There was not any Islamist mass party in Turkey in the 1950s and 1960s.

Necmettin Erbakan (1926–2011) turned Turkish Islamism into an independent and stable political movement in the 1970s.[13] Erbakan was elected to the presidency of the Union of Chambers in Turkey with the support of small and medium-sized capitalists from Anatolia, but was soon deposed from that post by the center-right Adalet Partisi (Justice Party, AP) government. Erbakan's subsequent application to the AP to present his candidacy for the 1969 parliamentary elections was also rejected. He then got elected to parliament as an independent deputy from Konya, a traditional stronghold of the Islamists. He founded the Milli Nizam Partisi (National Order Party, MNP) in 1970. The MNP and the subsequent parties founded by Erbakan are branded as the National Vision movement (Milli Görüş). The MNP soon became a representative of the small- and medium-scale, nonmonopolistic capitalists of Anatolia, who felt alienated from the AP's policy of supporting big capital against them. The party was banned in 1971 on grounds of its activities against the constitutional principle of secularism. Erbakan soon founded the Milli Selamet Partisi (National Salvation Party, MSP). The MSP won 11.8 percent of the votes in 1973 and 8.5 percent in 1977. It participated in coalition governments with the CHP in 1974 and with the AP and the Nationalist Action Party in 1975 and 1977.

Radical Islamism became more popular in Turkey after the Iranian Revolution. On 6 September 1980, six days before the military coup, radical Islamists turned the MSP's "Saving Jerusalem Meeting" in Konya into their own show of strength. That event demonstrated that Erbakan did not have total control over the more radical elements within the MSP.

The MSP was banned after the military coup of 12 September 1980. Nevertheless, the military junta made religion classes compulsory in secondary education and also dramatically increased the number of religious vocational middle and high schools known as İmam Hatip schools. By doing so, the military junta hoped to decrease the ideological influence of the Marxist left in Turkish society by utilizing religion. The generals thought that they would be able to keep the Islamization process under their control. They certainly did not expect that these policies would play into the hands of the Islamists in the long run. When the military junta allowed the establishment of political parties in 1983 as part of a controlled transition back to parliamentary rule, the supporters of Erbakan founded the Refah Partisi (Welfare Party, RP). The ban on the political leaders of the pre-1980 period was lifted in 1987, which allowed Erbakan to become the leader of the RP. The party benefited tremendously from the political vacuum in the shantytowns created by the repression of the Marxist left by the military dictatorship. It gradually won the support of the shantytown populations of the big cities like Ankara and Istanbul in the 1990s by effectively using populist slogans such as the "Just Order" and regularly distributing significant quantities of social assistance, including both cash and in-kind transfers. The RP successfully kept together the devout bourgeoisie and the proletariat as well as different types of Islamist activists. This success bore its first positive results in the municipal elections in 1994, when an Islamist party won the municipalities of Ankara and Istanbul for the first time. That was the first big shock to the secularists in Turkey, who eventually witnessed electoral victories of the Islamists in (almost) every election after 1994. In the parliamentary elections of 1995, the RP received the most votes (21 percent) of any party.

During the rise of the RP in the 1990s, Islamist capital underwent a significant transformation that is discussed in detail in several chapters in this volume. Some Islamic companies captured the opportunities that emerged out of the neoliberal transformation of the Turkish economy and transformed themselves from medium-scale capital to big capital. The term "Anatolian tigers," an analogy made between the East Asian tigers and the rising capitalists of Anatolia, became popular during that time. Müstakil Sanayici ve İşadamları Derneği (Independent Industrialists' and Businessmen's Association, MÜSİAD), was founded in 1990 as the representative of the Islamist bourgeoisie, which was able to compete somewhat with the secular bourgeoisie represented by Türkiye Sanayici ve İşadamları Derneği (Turkish Industrialists' and Businessmen's Association, TÜSİAD), albeit still much weaker than the secular bourgeoisie. The MÜSİAD supported the RP.

The RP formed a coalition government with the center-right party Doğru Yol Partisi (True Path Party, DYP) in 1996. Erbakan became the first Islamist prime minister of the Republic of Turkey. The secular capitalists and the military generals, who felt very uneasy about the political situation, soon started a coordinated attack against the RP. The decisions made during the meeting of the National Security Council on 28 February 1997 meant a military memorandum against the RP-DYP coalition. The coalition government was forced to resign six months after the 28 February memorandum. Soon after, the Constitutional Court shut down the RP and put a political ban on Erbakan for violating the constitutional principle of secularism.

Fazilet Partisi (Virtue Party, FP) soon replaced the RP. In the parliamentary elections of 18 April 1999, the FP took 15.4 percent of the popular vote and became the third largest party in the parliament. Recai Kutan and Abdullah Gül competed for party leadership in the first congress of the FP in 2000. That was the first leadership competition in the National Vision movement, which developed for almost thirty years under the undisputed leadership of Erbakan. The leadership competition was seen by many as a battle between the "traditionalists" (represented by Erbakan's close aide, Kutan) and the "reformists" (represented by Gül) within Turkish Islamism. It certainly reflected the Islamist bourgeoisie's search for an alternative leader. During the 1970s, when it lacked sufficient capital accumulation to transform itself into big, monopolistic capital, the Islamist bourgeoisie supported Erbakan. Erbakan's economic policy was to carry out "state-directed industrialisation whose benefits would accrue to the small businessmen of small towns" through "measures to disperse capital accumulation geographically and to reverse the tendency of economic concentration" (Keyder 1987: 213). As it started down the path of becoming monopolistic finance-capital through a deeper integration with the capitalist world economy in the late 1990s, the Islamist bourgeoisie started to view Erbakan's line as old-fashioned. It started searching for a younger and reformist leader who could represent their interests better than Erbakan.

Although Gül lost the leadership race in the FP, reformists soon prevailed in the entire movement. Recep Tayyip Erdoğan emerged as a perfect candidate for a new Islamist leadership. Erdoğan had enough charisma and political experience to gain the support of the masses living in the shantytowns. Moreover, partly due to his own business experience, he had a clear understanding of the Islamist bourgeoisie's new requirements in the age of neoliberalism. Erdoğan and his associates founded the AKP in 2001 and won a quick victory in the parliamentary elections of 3 November 2002, taking 34 per-cent of the popular vote. Erdoğan has been the prime minister of the country since 2003, winning significant victories in each new election. The AKP defeated the military memorandum of 27 April 2007 against Abdullah Gül's first bid for presidency by taking 47 percent of the to-tal vote in the parliamentary elections of 22 July 2007. Gül was elected to the presidency after the elections and became the first Islamist president of the Republic of Turkey. The AKP took 50 percent of the popular vote in the parliamentary elections of 12 June 2011.

Turkish economy and society has been experiencing a significant Islamization process, especially since the AKP's landslide victory in the elections of 22 July 2007. While supporting the Islamist capitalists generously by mobilizing all economic means within the reach of the state, the AKP government has used a series of punitive measures (such as handing down huge tax fines, reduction of state support, and exclusion from big government contracts) against secular capitalists such as the Koç and Doğan holdings. Although these policies have not ended the secular bourgeoisie's dominant position in the Turkish economy, they have nevertheless managed to dramatically improve the position of the Islamist bourgeoisie as opposed to the secular bourgeoisie. The government budget allocated to the Diyanet İşleri Başkanlığı (Directorate of Religious Affairs) has increased astronomically, and the institution has become increasingly assertive in cultural and political affairs (Peker 2012). The recent education reform that seemingly increased the years of schooling in fact allows students to pursue religious education after primary school. It also permits families to pull their children out of formal schooling after primary education, which could harm the educational attainment of girls from poorer sections of the Islamist constituency (Finkel 2012). Astronomical tax hikes on alcoholic beverages and administrative restrictions upon alcohol consumption are other manifestations of the ongoing Islamization process (Çağaptay and Ersöz 2010; Gürsel 2013).[14] Overall, as a successful case of an emerging Islamist bourgeoisie challenging the secular bourgeoisie by establishing a clear hegemony over the poorest segments of the proletariat, the AKP experience has gained a special place in the global history of Islamist movements.[15]

Despite this success, however, recent developments have indicated that the prospects of AKP rule are far from clear. A small-scale, local protest against the destruction of Gezi Park (near Taksim Square at the center of Istanbul) for the construction of a shopping mall designed like an Ottoman-era army barracks, a project designed by the Istanbul Metropolitan Municipality and the AKP government with close supervision and advocacy by Erdoğan himself, turned into a nationwide popular revolt on 31 May 2013 against the neoliberal, authoritarian, and Islamist policies of the AKP government. Although the revolt, which mobilized millions of people all over the country in June 2013, could not topple the AKP government, it nevertheless made clear that the AKP has lost the ability to rule Turkey with stability. The strengthening of the perception of Erdoğan as a source of instability has so far produced two important results. First, the United States, which already had disagreements with Erdoğan regarding his attitudes toward Israel and the crises in Syria and Egypt, distanced itself further from him and started to give stronger signals of support to the mainstream political actors that are alternatives to Erdoğan. The second outcome, related to the first one, is the worsening of the relations between the Erdoğan leadership and Fethullah Gülen's globally well-organized religious network. Gülen's network has been sharing the United States' criticism of Erdoğan's foreign policy for a long time. Moreover, there had been serious contradictions between Gülen and Erdoğan regarding important internal affairs, such as Erdoğan's plan to close down the private educational institutions that prepare students for university entrance examinations (which have provided a significant financial and organizational source for the Gülen network for a long time), Gülenist cliques within the police forces and the judiciary, as well as Erdoğan's negative stance toward capitalists who do not support the AKP. Erdoğan's weakening after the popular uprising encouraged and enabled the Gülenists to take a much firmer stance against Erdoğan. This has led to the giant anti-graft and anticorruption operations against the AKP government on 17 December 2013, which were carried out by Gülenists within the police and the judiciary. After the operation, Erdoğan declared the Gülen network an internal enemy and started using all means of the state to suppress it.[16] This is the largest split within Turkish Islamism in its recent history. Despite being weakened by the popular revolt and the antigraft operation, Erdoğan's AKP managed to take 43 percent of the total vote in the municipal elections on 30 March 2014, thus remaining the largest party in Turkey. On 10 August 2014, in the first round of Turkey's first presidential elections by a popular vote, Erdoğan was elected president with 51.7 percent of the vote.

Conclusion

Islamism is a political ideology that attributes the socioeconomic problems of the Muslim world in the modern era to an alienation from Islam and a return to jahiliyya. It proposes the establishment of a new state and society that are thought to fit Islamic principles. It is the political expression of the devout bourgeoisie's quest to become the dominant class by establishing hegemony over the proletariat. Islamists can take a revolutionary or a reformist stance while in opposition. They quickly become a force of the status quo after taking political power. The crisis of the secular regimes and the radical leftist movements that started in the mid-1960s provided the background to the rise of Islamist movements of different types. While Islamists successfully established hegemony over the proletariat and took power with a revolution in Iran, they lost their hegemony and the struggle for power in Algeria in the 1990s. Islamists have recently entered into a new struggle for political power in countries like Egypt, Tunisia,

Libya, and Syria in the wake of the Arab Spring, which started in December 2010. By simultaneously adjusting to neoliberalism and establishing hegemony over the proletariat, the reformed Islamist movement in Turkey, represented by the AKP, has become a model for some of the Islamist currents all over the world. However, the postelection revolt in Iran in 2009, the popular revolt and the military coup against the Muslim Brotherhood in Egypt, and the popular revolt against the AKP government in Turkey, both in the summer of 2013, indicate that the future prospects for the Islamist movements and governments are far from certain.

Notes

An earlier and much shorter version of this chapter was published in Turkish in *Siyaset Bilimi-Kavramlar, İdeolojiler, Disiplinler Arası İlişkiler* [Political science-concepts, ideologies, and interdisciplinary relations], ed. Gökhan Atılgan and E. Attila Aytekin (Istanbul: Yordam, 2012).

1. For detailed background information regarding Fethullah Gülen and his movement, see Yavuz (2013). It is necessary to caution the reader that my perspective on Islamism and the Gülen movement is entirely different from Yavuz's.
2. For another study following Denoeux's definition of Islamism, see Ayoob (2004).
3. The audiences of Khomeini, Mawdudi, and Qutb in the Muslim world are not isolated from each other. For instance, Khomeini influenced many Sunni Islamists in some countries, including Turkey, especially during the first few years following the Iranian Revolution. However, due to the historical significance of the Sunni-Shia divide within Islam, Mawdudi and Qutb had a much broader appeal among Sunnis, while Shiites remained as the main constituency of Khomeini's politics.
4. For a similar emphasis on Islamists' selective approach toward modernity, see Denoeux (2002: 58).
5. Afghanistan under the Taliban requires a more nuanced analysis, since it was entirely devastated by unending wars, neither the state nor the private sector had any significant production capacity, and the only commodity produced in significant quantities was opium.
6. In this chapter, I use the terms "devout bourgeoisie" and "Islamist bourgeoisie" interchangeably, referring to the section of the bourgeoisie that provides the backbone of the Islamist movements of the last and the current century.
7. Despite his recognition of the coalition of the devout bourgeoisie and the lower classes as the backbone of all successful Islamist movements, Kepel tends to present it as a coalition without any hegemon by arguing that Islamist ideology cannot be reduced to the interests of a single social group (Kepel 2002: 9, 29). As the vast literature on political hegemony indicates, different classes can join political movements that represent the core interests of another class. In fact, it is possible to read the entire political history of the world as the history of the formation and disintegration of alliances that represent the core interests of one class over others. Kepel's study itself provides enough material in-

dicating the devout bourgeoisie's quest to establish hegemony over the proletariat as the primary dynamic of the modern Islamist movements.

8. For a detailed analysis of the formative role of these three countries in the Afghan jihad, see Mamdani (2004).

9. In an essay written in 1973, Waheed-uz-Zaman, a well-known scholar of the time, illustrated well the logic of the renewed emphasis on Islam in Pakistan in the post-1971 period: "If we let go the ideology of Islam, we cannot hold together as a nation by any other means. … If the Arabs, the Turks, the Iranians, God forbid, give up Islam, the Arabs yet remain Arabs, the Turks remain Turks, the Iranians remain Iranians, but what do we remain if we give up Islam?" (quoted in Richter 1979: 550).

10. On the other hand, as the growing hatred and violence against the Christians and Shia Muslims by the Sunni extremists demonstrates, the Islamization process since the late 1970s has become a factor that threatens the national unity of Pakistan significantly.

11. This does not mean that all bazaaris were Islamists supporting Khomeini. There were three sections of bazaaris in the opposition before the revolution. One section was composed of Khomeini supporters; the other two supported, respectively, the Liberation Movement of Iran and the National Front (Keshavarzian 2007: 247). This shows that the Islamist small and medium-sized bourgeoisie and the religious establishment constituted the core of the Khomeini movement, which hegemonized the other sections of the bazaaris in the process of hegemonizing the entire opposition. Similar to other supporters of the secular organizations, many bazaaris were suppressed by the Islamist regime in the early 1980s (Keshavarzian 2007: 254–55).

12. For more detailed information on the People's Mujahideen, see Abrahamian (1989).

13. For a detailed investigation of different Islamist circles in Turkey before 1990, see Çakır (1990).

14. The existence of the Directorate of Religious Affairs since 1924 reflects the dominance of Sunni Islam and the incompleteness of secularism in Turkey. Within these limits, however, Turkey has remained a largely secular country up until today. The question of whether the ongoing Islamization process under the AKP rule might lead to the end of secularism in Turkey is a question that is yet to be answered. The argument that there is zero possibility of an end to the secular regime in Turkey no matter what happens in terms of the Islamization of society by government intervention is an extremely naïve proposition. The future of secularism in Turkey depends on the balance of power between different wings of the AKP on the one hand and between the AKP and the secular opposition against it on the other hand. Changes in the international context and the trajectory of the class struggle (both within the bourgeoisie and between the bourgeoisie and the proletariat) in Turkey could impact these two kinds of balance of power.

15. The devout bourgeoisie has always been the hegemonic force within the Islamist movement in Turkey from its time of inception in the early 1970s. The transition from the RP to the AKP reflects the transition of the devout bourgeoisie from small- and medium-scale capital to large-scale finance capital. Other chapters in this volume provide detailed analysis of this transition. My analysis is therefore entirely different from Cihan Tuğal's argument that the devout bourgeoisie became the hegemonic force within the Islamist movement only during the AKP period (2009: 8). The empirical material in Tuğal's study can be interpreted well within the framework that I propose here.

16. In these recent circumstances, the AKP government has increased the pace and intensity of the crackdown on the Gülen supporters within the police and the judiciary and started to implement punitive measures (similar to the ones that have been implemented against the secular bourgeoisie in recent years) against the Gülenist capitalists, who are organized under the umbrella of the Turkish Confederation of Industrialists and Businessmen (Türkiye İşadamları ve Sanayiciler Konfederasyonu, TUSKON).

References

Abrahamian, Ervand. 1989. *The Iranian Mojahedin*. New Haven, CT: Yale University Press.
_____. 1993. *Khomeinism: Essays on the Islamic Republic*. Berkeley: University of California Press.
Alavi, Hamza. 2009. "The Rise of Religious Fundamentalism in Pakistan." 10 March. Accessed 1 June 2013. http://secularpakistan.wordpress.com/2009/03/10/the-rise-of-religious-fundamentalism-in-pakistan-hamza-alavi/.
Ayoob, Mohammed. 1979. "Two Faces of Political Islam: Iran and Pakistan Compared." *Asian Survey* 19, no. 6 (June): 535–46.
_____. 2004. "Political Islam: Image and Reality." *World Policy Journal* 21, no. 3 (Fall): 1–14.
Bardakçı, Murat. 2006. "Adnan Menderes'i Suçlamaktan Vazgeçin! Arapça Ezanı DP ile CHP Beraber Serbest Bırakmışlardı!" [Stop blaming Adnan Menderes! The ban on azan in Arabic was lifted by the DP and CHP together!]. *Hürriyet*, 10 June.
_____. 2010. "Arabesk Ezanlar" [Arabesque azans]. *Habertürk*, 16 June.
Bayat, Asef. 2008. "Is There a Future for Islamist Revolutions? Revolution, Revolt, and Middle Eastern Modernity." In *Revolution in the Making of the Modern World*, ed. John Foran, David Lane, and Andreja Zivkovic, 96–111. London: Routledge.
Çağaptay, Soner, and Cansın Ersöz. 2010. "AKP, Alcohol, and Government-Engineered Social Change in Turkey." *Hürriyet Daily News*, 5 October.
Çakır, Ruşen. 1990. *Ayet ve Slogan: Türkiye'de İslami Oluşumlar* [The verse and the slogan: Islamic formations in Turkey]. Istanbul: Metis.
Denoeux, Guilain. 2002. "The Forgotten Swamp: Navigating Political Islam." *Middle East Policy* 9, no. 2 (June): 56–81.
Finkel, Andrew. 2012. "What Is 4 + 4 + 4?" New York Times, 23 March. Accessed 1 March 2013. http://latitude.blogs.nytimes.com/2012/03/23/turkeys-education-reform-bill-is-about-playing-politics-with-pedagogy/.
Gürel, Burak. 2004. "1970'ler Türkiye'sinde İslamcı ve Faşist Siyaset: Vaadler ve Sonuçlar" [Islamist and fascist politics in Turkey in the 1970s: Promises and results]. *Praksis*, no. 12 (Fall): 85–102.
Gürsel, Kadri. 2013. "'Moderate Political Islam' Leading Turkey to 'Moderate Sharia.'" *Al-Monitor*, 31 May. Accessed 1 June 2013. http://www.al-monitor.com/pulse/originals/2013/05/turkey-political-islam-sharia.html.
Harman, Chris. 1994. "The Prophet and the Proletariat." *International Socialism Journal*, no. 64. Accessed 1 February 2012. http://www.marxists.org/archive/harman/1994/xx/islam.htm.
Kepel, Gilles. 2002. *Jihad: The Trail of Political Islam*. Translated by Anthony F. Roberts. Cambridge: Belknap.
Keshavarzian, Arang. 2007. *Bazaar and State in Iran: The Politics of the Tehran Marketplace*. Cambridge and New York: Cambridge University Press.
Keyder, Çağlar. 1987. *State and Class in Turkey: A Study in Capitalist Development*. London and New York: Verso.
Mamdani, Mahmood. 2004. *Good Muslim, Bad Muslim: America, the Cold War, and the Roots of Terror*. New York: Pantheon.
_____. 2005. "Whither Political Islam? Understanding the Modern Jihad." *Foreign Affairs* 84, no. 1 (January/February): 148–55.
Peker, Efe. 2012. "Sahi, Laikliğe Ne Oldu?" [Really, what happened to secularism?]. *Birgün*, 1 February.
Poya, Maryam. 2002. "Long Live the Revolution! . . . Long Live Islam?" In *Revolutionary Rehearsals*, ed. Colin Barker, 123–68. Chicago: Haymarket.
Richter, William L. 1979. "The Political Dynamics of Islamic Resurgence in Pakistan." *Asian Survey* 19, no. 6 (June): 547–57.

Tuğal, Cihan. 2009. *Passive Revolution: Absorbing the Islamic Challenge to Capitalism*. Palo Alto, CA: Stanford University Press.

White, Joshua T. 2012. "Beyond Moderation: Dynamics of Political Islam in Pakistan." *Contemporary South Asia* 20, no. 2 (June): 179–94.

Yavuz, M. Hakan. 2013. *Toward an Islamic Enlightenment: The Gülen Movement*. New York: Oxford University Press.

– Chapter 2 –

CLASS, STATE, AND RELIGION IN TURKEY
Sungur Savran

Writing a chapter-length article that spans decades of history about a political movement currently in power in the very midst of a popular rebellion creates serious difficulties for the author. The enterprise is bound to be riddled with pitfalls of all kinds. It is true that at the time of writing, the popular revolt of June–July 2013, internationally known, somewhat misleadingly, as the Gezi Park protests, has subsided. But, given the international and domestic circumstances that fired the flames of the rebellion in the first place, it is highly probable that there will be a recrudescence of the movement in the short or medium term, whatever new forms it may take. Should that prove to be the case, then by the time this book has been published, an article on the current Adalet ve Kalkınma Partisi (Justice and Development Party, AKP) government would more aptly be cast as a postmortem. However, an equally likely scenario is a situation in which the Erdoğan government weathers the storm to reach calmer waters. And since the prospects for the government are not solely dependent on the domestic situation, either economically or politically, it should not be ruled out that Erdoğan could attain his much-coveted prize of being at the helm of the country in 2023, when the Republic of Turkey will be celebrating the centenary of its foundation. A postmortem written in 2013 would then raise eyebrows concerning the prescience of its author.

In this chapter, then, I will take a longer-term view of my subject matter and try to assess the significance, for Turkey, for the region, and for the international system at large, of the strength and resilience of the Islamist movement in Turkey, as well as its contradictions and resulting weaknesses, at the beginning of the twenty-first century.

The question is important for several reasons. The more obvious reason is that the future of the Islamist movement will be decisive for the politics and social life of Turkey itself domestically. Whether Erdoğan and the AKP remain in power for another decade or not will surely be of momentous importance for the people of this country. But beyond Turkey, the AKP's prospects will be of immediate importance for many countries in the Middle East and North Africa. Especially in the aftermath of the Arab revolutions, the AKP has become a pivotal force at the regional level and its fate will certainly create a serious impact on Islamist movements, in particular of the Muslim Brotherhood variety, in many countries, from Syria and Jordan to Morocco. Taking an even broader view, one can say that, given the rather exceptional position of Turkey in the Islamic world, with its close ties to Western institutions such as the North Atlantic Treaty Organization (NATO) and the European Union (EU), what lies in store for Erdoğan and the AKP will affect the delicate and intricate relations of the West with the Islamic world as well. So, whatever the scope of one's outlook, an analysis of the strengths and weaknesses of the Islamist movement in Turkey is of burning importance.

The main question this article will pose is the following: given that the AKP government under Erdoğan has already been in power for over a decade, what has caused the resilience of this government? This is a particularly apt question, not only because this whole decade has witnessed a full-scale tug-of-war between the government and its mighty opponents, starting with the country's armed forces, but also because a similar process had seen the demise of another Islamist government (that of Necmettin Erbakan, the historic leader of the Islamist movement in Turkey) in the space of a mere six months in 1997, only several years before the AKP took government in 2002. The same question could be cast in another form: how is it that the AKP government was able to reduce to submission what had always been considered by all observers to be the strongest actor on the Turkish political scene, that is, the armed forces, when all previous civilian governments that had been the target of the latter had almost instantly succumbed to its will?[1] We shall see that the question can be posed in still another manner, that is, as a question regarding the relative strength of one class fraction vis-à-vis another, but we should not anticipate the argument.

This central question begs another, more fundamental one regarding the dynamics behind the rise of the AKP to power. On this question the author of this chapter disagrees completely with overwhelming sections of the intelligentsia in Turkey. This is not to say that there is a single school of thought that is by itself dominant on this question. On the contrary, leaving aside what one might comfortably characterize as the "organic" intellectuals of the AKP, even in the so-called secular camp there are diverging, and at times diametrically opposing, views on what forces were behind the rise of the AKP to power. It is just that I find all of these wanting.

One very widespread view attributes this phenomenon, as well as its antecedents, to what is considered to be the driving contradiction that besets Turkish society, variously labeled as a rift between the *center* and the *periphery* or a conflict between a hapless *civil society* and an overpowering *state*, both sets of dualities characterizing Turkish society, so goes the argument, not only contemporaneously but from time immemorial. Erdoğan, quite in the same manner as earlier historic figures such as Adnan Menderes, prime minister in the 1950s, or Turgut Özal, prime minister and later president of the republic from the 1980s to the early 1990s, is seen as a leader that represents the revolt of the periphery or civil society against the shackles imposed on society by the behemoth that is the centralist state established and maintained by the Kemalist bureaucracy. The political stance that is deduced from this is to support Erdoğan in the face of a military-civilian bureaucracy which, apart from the periodic coups d'état it has staged, submits all other social and political forces to its ever-present tutelage. Thus, the AKP represents the democratization of Turkey. This position is best characterized as the liberal vision of Turkey past and present and has numerous subscribers on the left as well as, more predictably, on the center-right of the political spectrum.[2]

At the antipode of this position one can find, especially on the left and among various schools of thought that subscribe to Kemalism, an approach that considers the above-mentioned historic figures of the political right as well as others as representatives of a *counterrevolution* that has been sweeping aside the "gains of the republic." All history is interpreted through the lens of a dichotomy of secularism versus Islam. The "gains of the republic" are practically reduced to the extremely radical moves of the early republican period that made inroads into the domination of Islamic institutions and ideologies on Turkish society. Hence, all the policies pursued by the successive right-wing governments in the post–World War II era, and a fortiori those implemented by Islamist governments, are labeled counterrevolutionary and condemned. As the secular establishment, represented politically by the Republican People's Party (Cumhuriyet Halk Partisi, CHP) at the party level, was always weaker than these forces, with the exception of a period of several years in the 1970s, this camp usually deduced from this analysis the necessity of defending the "gains of the republic" through the vigilance of the armed forces, regarded, rather mistakenly, as we shall see, as staunch protectors of secularism.

A special variant of this outlook developed in the early 2000s during the rise of the AKP and has managed to survive intact up until today. This is the idea that the AKP was and is primarily a product of imperialist manipulation, a project prepared in Washington DC and marketed in Turkey. The motive behind this is said to be the United States' strategy of setting up bulwarks of moderate Islam against radical or fundamentalist Islam in the wake of the 9/11 attacks. The United States, so goes the story, paved the way for the setting up of the AKP in 2001 and, in the context of the deep crisis that had taken Turkey in its grip, manipulated Turkish politics so as to bring Erdoğan to power in 2002. This view is usually coupled with the idea that the United States wishes (or at least wished during the better part of the 2000s) to carve out a Kurdistan in the southeast of Turkey by siding, variously, with the Kurdistan Workers' Party (Partiya Karkerên Kurdistan, PKK), the guerrilla movement that has been waging war against the Turkish state since 1984, and/or Massoud Barzani's forces, which rule over the autonomous unit called the Kurdistan Regional Government in the new federal Iraq. The political position derived from this narrative is to look to the armed forces to protect, this time, both secularism and the territorial indivisibility of the Republic of Turkey (Bila 2007; Yanardağ 2007).[3]

There is also an influential theoretical characterization of what went on under the AKP as a passive revolution, a deflection of an Islamic challenge to capitalism. In the opinion of the author of this theory, the AKP experience represents the absorption of the Islamist movement into the system, whereas the movement had earlier posed a danger to the established order (Tuğal 2009).[4]

I believe that all the positions summarized above, necessarily somewhat schematically, are superficial and hence reductionist, empirically false, and/or internally inconsistent. It is interesting to note that, after a decade of history, when all these erroneous theories should have been abandoned in the light of practical developments that have clearly and unambiguously refuted them, people still cling to them. Of less immediate relevance to the purposes of this chapter, but nonetheless of burning importance for the future of the country, of the region, and, arguably, of the international system at large, the political attitudes derived from these analytic positions are, in my opinion, both counterproductive and dangerous, even bordering on being suicidal. I shall not engage, in this chapter, in a systematic critique of these theories. I shall only point to certain inconsistencies and defects of one or another theory as the occasion arises.

What I rather wish to do is to present my own account of the rise to power of the AKP and its consolidation of this power. This will also involve a characterization of the Islamist movement in general in Turkey and an account of its ascendancy in the second half of the twentieth century from the dismal situation in which it was placed in the early republican period. The AKP will then be situated in this overall account. The analysis will take its cue methodologically from the theory of class struggle. It would be useful to summarize my main propositions at the outset.

First, it is a firmly established fact, in my opinion, that the major driving force behind the rise of the Islamist movement is a dynamic of intraclass conflict at two levels at least. At the more fundamental level there is a conflict between two fractions of the bourgeoisie. Against the dominant fraction that was formed in the first half of the twentieth century and rose indisputably to dominance in the 1960s, concentrated in the major industrial and commercial centers of the country, most notably in Istanbul, İzmir, and Adana, there arose another fraction in the smaller provincial towns of Anatolia in the 1950s and 1960s. The previously hegemonic fraction was totally committed to Turkey's integration into and harmonization with the Western world (hence our characterization of this wing as Westernized-secular), whereas the new fraction, composed of small- and medium-scale enterprises (SMEs) in conservative small towns, took up Islamist ideology as almost a "natural" medium for the expression of its grievances. The entry into the Turkish political scene of the first serious Islamist party in 1970 was, as we shall see shortly, so indisputably tied to the strivings of this new fraction of capital that all commentators concur on this conflict as the prime motor of the rise of Islamism, albeit in widely varying idioms.

What seems obvious when one looks into the genealogy of the Islamist movement is more and more obscured as one moves away from this original moment, and by the time we arrive at the AKP, most of our theoreticians have forgotten the insight provided by the moment of birth. Furthermore, even those commentators who continue to ascribe the Islamist movement's main driving force to a rising fraction of the bourgeoisie equally in its subsequent stages nonetheless miss what I consider a *decisive metamorphosis* of this very fraction, or, rather, an alliance of fractions in this later moment of its evolution. Out of this fraction composed of the SMEs based in sleepy and dusty provincial towns, there arose in the 1990s a full-scale monopoly wing of conglomerates, organized in exactly the same form as the more powerful companies of the earlier Westernized-secular wing, that is, the form of holding companies whose activities range across diverse industries and all types of economic activity. Hence, it was no longer the large-scale companies of the Westernized-secular wing pitted against the SMEs of the Islamist one, but large against large; nor was it Istanbul versus the backwater of the provinces, but equally cosmopolitan units of capital vying for influence and advantage.[5] We shall see that this metamorphosis has proved to be decisive in the specific formation represented by the AKP as opposed to the earlier Islamist movement.

Alongside this struggle at the top, another one rages at the level of the intermediary classes represented by the professional, intellectual, and bureaucratic sections of the workforce. There is cutthroat competition between the formerly hegemonic intellectual and professional elites reared in well-to-do families in big cities and educated at the cream of Turkish universities or abroad, often polyglot and wielding a cosmopolitan outlook and lifestyle, on the one hand; and a newly rising layer with the same professional qualifications, but mostly coming from poorer families residing in small towns or even villages, some educated in the new provincial universities of Anatolia (although others at the best universities of Turkey and abroad), usually at a disadvantage when it comes to speaking foreign languages (though most manage to communicate in English) and with a more restricted outlook on the world and a more conservative lifestyle, on the other hand. The contest goes on both for mid- and senior-level posts within the state apparatus and for jobs in the private sector (although here companies discriminate according to typology, so that the job market is more segmented). To the former group, this contest looks like (we need not mince our words, but should call a spade a spade) barbarians taking over; to the latter, it looks like they are finally avenging the plight of their parents and overcoming age-old prejudices. This second dimension of intraclass struggle really converts what would otherwise have remained a friction within the class of capitalists into a more mass phenomenon, with high school and university students, future professionals and intellectuals as they are, also joining in the fray.

Second, I shall have occasion to show that the rise of Islamism has also received a thrust from class struggles between the bourgeoisie and the working class. The Turkish bourgeoisie, which made a very radical leap toward secularism in the initial stages of the foundation of a new state, found it necessary, under the whip of class struggle, to turn to religion as an ideology facilitating class rule in later stages of capital accumulation.

Third, Islamist ideology stands as a convenient candidate for the new expansionist urge that has taken the Turkish ruling class in its grip in the post-1980 stage. On the one hand, at least for the Islamist wing of the bourgeoisie, references to the *umma*, the world community of Muslims, greatly facilitate the penetration of Turkish interests into the Islamic world. On the other hand, the Islamic references and sensibility displayed by the AKP government (and its predecessors) project an image of Turkey that attracts greater sympathy in the countries of the Middle East and North Africa.

The fourth factor is simply a backdrop to all this. I take a Marxist view of religion. I believe that religion is not exclusively an outcome of a state of ignorance and superstition, as Enlightenment thinking and modernization theory would have us believe, but a product of class exploitation and oppression, both "the opium of the people" and "the heart of a heartless world." Hence the powerful attraction it exercises not only on the (now ever-decreasing) peasant population of Turkey, but on the urban industrial working class as well. Were it not for this fact, none of the factors invoked above would have been operational. The Islamist movement would not have been able to mobilize the support of the masses in its struggle against the Westernized-secular wing of the capitalist class. The Turkish bourgeoisie as a whole would not have been able to seek help in the calming effect that religion has on class struggle. And even the third factor would have been partially impaired, since Erdoğan's influence in the Arab world at least partially stems from the sympathy he enjoys within the ranks of the popular masses for his stance as a devout Muslim, much in the same fashion as he receives the sympathy of the poorer sections of the Turkish population.

These, then, are the major domestic factors that explain the rise of Islamism that Turkey has experienced within the last three or four decades. There is not a single shred of doubt that, in addition to these, international factors have also played their part. Chief among these are the ascendancy of Islamism in the Middle East and North Africa since the late 1970s (see Gürel, this volume), in particular the Iranian Revolution of 1979 and the jihad waged by the Afghan mujahideen against the Soviet Union around the same time, as well as the rise of the Gulf countries as centers of ground rent and finance since the formation of OPEC and the so-called oil crisis in the 1970s, thus exercising an attraction over other, resource-poor countries in the

Islamic world, in particular those, like Turkey, with a rapid rate of industrialization and a very poor level of savings.

It is only in this overall context that the reorientation of US policy to accommodate moderate Islam as a brake on more radical or fundamentalist versions of Islamism or on revolution in the Arab world (e.g., Tunisia and Egypt since 2011) has been effective. There is no doubt that the accommodationist stance of the United States has facilitated life for all moderately Islamist parties, including the AKP in Turkey (see, among many, Rabasa and Larrabee 2008: 96–99). But from here to the idea that the AKP was the product of a US machination there is a long way to go.[6] Moreover, it should not be forgotten that moderate Islamism is still Islamism and, given the appropriate circumstances, may very well come into contradiction with the aims of US policy. Witness the rejection by the Turkish parliament, dominated by an overwhelming Islamist majority, of the waging of military operations on Iraq through Turkey in 2003,[7] or the conflict between Erdoğan and the Israeli state that has put the United States in a very difficult situation for a long time.

In what follows, I will first look at the radical drive toward the reduction of the influence of religion over sociopolitical life in the first quarter of the twentieth century, which forms the backdrop to the more recent rise in Islamism in the country and generates both the peculiar dynamics of and the limits to the process. I will then survey the different stages through which Islamism went before it culminated in the decade-long supremacy of the AKP. This will set the stage for distinguishing between, on the one hand, the earlier stage of the Islamist movement, when it was called National Vision under the historic leader Necmettin Erbakan, and, on the other hand, the later and distinct stage formed by the AKP, both of which will form the subject matter of two sections each. The final section will then venture to understand the dynamics of the popular revolt that erupted in early June, trying to see what light this sheds on the future of the AKP government.

Historical Background: Turkish Exceptionalism

It is always dangerous to claim exceptionalism for a country, especially for one's own, for the enterprise may not only hide real similarities with others but also be accused of surreptitiously making a claim for privilege. But if the contours of the claim are defined clearly, then the operation may shed light on certain aspects of historical development. The Turkish exceptionalism that I am speaking of has to do with the special degree of inroad made by secularism in Turkey when compared to the rest of the Islamic world. The specific nature of bourgeois revolution in Turkey in the first quarter of the twentieth century left behind a legacy of an extreme form of secularism, or *laïcisme* in the French sense of the term, of which it is hard to find the like not only in the Islamic world, but also in the original home of bourgeois revolution, that is, Europe and, in particular, France. So my claim is not that Turkey was the only country that went through a bourgeois revolution in the Muslim world. There were many others, starting with the Iranian constitutional revolution of 1906, the Egyptian revolutions of 1919 and 1952, the Iraqi revolution of 1958, and so on. Nor is it that the other bourgeois revolutions did not encroach on and restrict the social space that Islam legislated and organized. The Tunisia of Habib Bourguiba, in particular, but also the Iran of the Pahlavis as well as many others did so too, and as for fighting Islamist movements, no one could match Gamal Abdel Nasser's record, under whose rule Sayyid Qutb, the then leader of the Egyptian Muslim Brotherhood was executed in 1966. My claim for exceptionalism is very clearly delineated: Turkey was the sole country in the Muslim world, or at least in the Middle East and North Africa, where political, social, educational, and civil relations were *all* completely removed from the sway of religion.[8] To understand the extent to which this was so and the rationale behind it, we first need to understand what stuff the Turkish bourgeois revolution was made of.

Bourgeois revolutionists in Turkey, the Young Turks in the beginning and Mustafa Kemal (Atatürk) later, had to solve several questions at once: they had to simultaneously provide for the survival of a country that was notoriously called the "sick man of Europe," build a modern (nation-) state out of a multinational empire, and overcome the resistance of the precapitalist structures of the ancien régime.[9] The revolution of 1908 tried to solve, in its first stage, the problems arising from the conflicts between national groups through a multiethnic alliance against the forces of the ancien régime, which itself sought refuge in Muslim religious reaction, thus forcing the revolutionaries to make inroads into the sway of religion over politics and society. But after the Balkan Wars of 1912–13, which resulted in substantial loss of territory, the Young Turks lost all hope of a multinational solution, becoming rabidly nationalistic, imposing policies in all spheres of social life that favored Turkification, and carrying out a policy of ethnic cleansing against the non-Muslim minorities during World War I, notably subjecting the Armenians to genocide. This went hand in hand with moves to suppress the religious bases of the power of the Sultan by downgrading, in 1916, the position of the *şeyhulislam*, the supreme mufti, by eliminating his post in the cabinet and transferring his powers over religious courts to the Ministry of Justice and over religious endowments to the Ministry of Finance (Zürcher and van den Linden 2004: 101–2). The latter was, of course, a fatal blow to the economic independence of all Islamic institutions, be they active in the domain of religion proper or education, health, and so forth. However, what the Young Turk revolution did in this area pales into insignificance compared to what was undertaken in the wake of the Kemalist revolution that established the republic in 1923.

The Kemalist revolution was radical and thoroughgoing in many senses except one very important domain. It avoided enlisting the masses and was totally oblivious to what would have been their specific class demands. This was dictated to it by the nature of the tasks to be solved: the so-called National Struggle of 1919–23 was not only a fight for the independence of the rump state that was once the Ottoman Empire, but also one against the non-Muslim nationalities of Anatolia, the Greeks and the Armenians (the Jews were not politically active, while other non-Muslim minorities were too weak to matter). In this endeavor, the Kemalist leadership could not afford to alienate either the provincial notables of the Turkish west or the landlords and religious leaders of the Kurdish east in favor of mobilizing the masses of poor peasants, nor, for that matter, the fledgling working class of the big cities. So all the radical measures taken were done so independently of the masses of the people, which was to prove mortal for the Kemalist reforms in the future. The French Revolution moved against the Catholic Church with the support of the masses. The Turkish revolution did the same to the Islamic establishment against their will.

The nineteenth century had seen the development of a commercial bourgeoisie, which, because it was tied to Western interests, was in the majority composed of the non-Muslim minorities, who had the prerequisite skills and connections to act as middlemen for European capitalists. This inequality of development, as well as the growing Islamization of the Ottoman state under the despot Abdülhamid II before the Young Turk revolution of 1908, led Turkish revolutionaries to conclude that Islam was the real impediment in the way of the progress of society. Hence, the Kemalist republicans attacked the religious bases of socioeconomic and political life in a radical manner. The onslaught was extraordinary in its sweep and tempo. The caliphate was abolished in 1924. In 1928 any reference to state religion was obliterated from the constitution and in 1937 a provision was inserted that explicitly characterized the state as "secular." In 1924, an educational reform turned over all schools to the Ministry of Education, thus ruling out a religious curriculum. Also in 1924, the institution of the *şeyhulislam* (supreme *mufti*) was replaced by the Directorate of Religious Affairs (Diyanet for short in Turkish), reporting directly to the prime minister. Over time this institution expanded, taking over the control of mosques, the appointment of their imams, and even interfering in the content of the Friday sermons. A civil code was adapted from the Swiss one in 1926, thus imposing civic marriage and all the paraphernalia of the Western system of family law, the only instance of its kind in the Islamic world to the best of my knowledge. Religious orders were banned in 1925, with dervish lodges and sacred tombs closed. The schools for training imams and preachers were shut down in 1930–31. The only School of Theology within the restructured University of Istanbul was also closed in 1935 (for details, see Zürcher and van den Linden 2004: 103– 4). The return of schools of theology to the Turkish educational scene would have to wait until the postwar period, more precisely, 1949, when the School of Theology within Ankara University was formed (Öcal 1986).

One feature of this radical secular model should be highlighted. The Turkish model has often been likened to the French model and rightly so. It was even inspired by the French case. But it spread its net even farther than the notorious French *laïcité*. In the French case, the church had been deprived of the means to intervene in public life, including most notably in the educational sphere. The Turkish practice copied all of this, but also added a supplementary feature. Whereas the church in France retained its autonomy from the state through its affiliation to the Roman Catholic Church in hierarchical order, the religious establishment in Turkey was brought directly under the control of the state through the Diyanet. So the classical separation between state and church (a general appellation for the religious establishment in the classical definition of secularism, justifying the use of the word "church" in a Muslim context) was fully achieved in the classical French model, but displayed an asymmetry in the Turkish case. The state did separate, indeed even firmly insulate, itself from religion, but religion was not separated from the state. At first sight, this looks like a more radical type of secularism than even the French *laïcité*, but in effect it had the paradoxical consequence of creating a surreptitious state religion. The Diyanet was and still is through and through a Muslim Sunni (even Hanafite) institution, which means that the state keeps pouring billions of dollars each year (close to three billion at the last count)[10] into the functioning of the Sunni religious establishment. Even if we disregard all the non-Muslims and the atheists, agnostics, and other nonbelievers, given the fact of the existence of a sizeable Alevi minority (anywhere between 10 to 20 percent of the population of Turkey), we have to conclude that under this model, from the very beginning until today, the state really brought the religious establishment under control at the cost of propagating Sunni Islam. It should be noted that with the Islamization of social and political life in recent decades, the budget of the Diyanet has swollen beyond all proportion, surpassing the appropriations for many a ministry.

But this was not simply an attempt to control religion in public life. It was an attempt to shift Turkey's civilizational basis from its roots in the Islamic world to the West. The dress code was radically rewritten and headgear symbolic of religious affiliation was banned for men (though not the traditional headscarves that almost all women of all walks of life wore at that time). The Latin alphabet replaced the Arabic one. Republican balls were organized with Western-style dancing, led by Mustafa Kemal Atatürk himself in person. The conservatory for classical Turkish music was shut down and remained so for years. The broadcasting of this music was banned on state radio (which was the only option for listeners at that time). In short, the Turkish bourgeois revolution relied as heavily on *civilizational cleansing* as it did on ethnic cleansing.[11]

This wholesale onslaught on the privileges of religion did lead to a radical change in ideology, outlook, and lifestyles in the big cities, not only Istanbul or the new capital city of Ankara, but also all others that underwent a certain level of socioeconomic modernization. The results were uneven, with the Western part of Turkey and coastal cities (with the exception of the Black Sea region) assimilating the new lifestyle and mentality much more rapidly and in its entirety than the internal provinces and the Kurdish region. And although in the big cities people of all walks of life adopted the new mores and lifestyles, there was an area in which class distinction made a visible difference. It was not only the haute bourgeoisie, but also the professional classes, intellectuals, and the new petty bourgeoisie that adapted rapidly to the new secular culture. Among these social classes and strata, going to pray in the mosque is a rare phenomenon even on Fridays. The hajj, the pilgrimage to Mecca, is unthinkable.

This was no passive adaptation, but one undertaken with missionary revolutionary zeal by the teachers and the doctors and the engineers of the early republican generations. However, among the more plebeian classes, the proletariat and the urban poor, but also and perhaps most markedly the traditional petty bourgeoisie, the opposite was the case. So all in all, Westernization and secularization had a clear class character until the rise of the new Islamist bourgeoisie. In addition to the peasantry and small town folk, where all classes clung quite conservatively to both old, "oriental" ways of life and to religion, the laboring classes of the big cities, with the notable exception of public employees, remained devout Muslims, as opposed to the higher classes and strata (although they did Westernize to a certain extent in their lifestyle; it is not unusual to find people who get infatuated with *raki*, the favorite alcoholic drink in Turkey, but still visit the mosque on Fridays). We see here once again a consequence of the distance that the Kemalist revolution established between itself and the masses. The new republic was to pay a high price for this from the 1970s, and more markedly from the 1990s, on.

The rise of the dominant wing of the bourgeoisie occurred within the context of this orientation of the new bourgeois republic. The fact that this was not only secularism, but a forcible civilizational shift, was very significant in the formation of its material connections and its ideology. This wing of the bourgeoisie never travelled east, never sent its sons and daughters to study at Middle Eastern universities, looked down on Arab culture as a backward, archaic backwater, and showed off, both to itself and to the West, by looking and acting Westernized, even at times plus royaliste que le roi. Westernization was only sociocultural, legal, educational, and ideological in nature in the interwar period. But in the aftermath of World War II, Turkey set out on a wholesale *institutional* integration with the West, becoming a member of the Council of Europe, of NATO, of the Organization for Economic Cooperation and Development (OECD—the poor cousin in the rich countries' club!), a process culminating in the saga of Turkey's long-drawn out, and still not completed, accession process to the EU. Turkey's foreign policy became almost wholly attuned to US policy, although there was serious discord and tension at different moments, and economically speaking Turkey was almost integrated, over time, into Europe in terms of trade, capital flows, and regulation. This reinforced the earlier bias of the dominant Westernized-secular wing of the bourgeoisie even further, since the earlier cultural-ideological bent was now buttressed by narrow economic interest. It has to be emphasized that a kind of horror lives on in the ranks of this class fraction regarding the Muslim world, in particular the detested Middle East, this being both cause and consequence of Turkey's wholesale Westernization.

Islam Strikes Back: An Overview of the Period since 1945

It is commonplace to assert that what Kemalism did was to relegate religion to the private sphere, to personal life. This is certainly true when informed by a secular outlook on life. However, from the point of view of the devout, the question may seem somewhat different. The difference may be expressed as one of the definition of public versus private. Is education, the dress code, or practicing one's religion in a dervish lodge to be considered private or public? To the large masses of devout Muslims, especially those gathered in religious (Sufi) orders (*tarikat*) or communities (*cemaat*), the secular reforms first of the Young Turks and later of Kemalism looked like direct, even brutal, infringement of their rights to religious practice. The networks of Islam formed over centuries found themselves cornered under the rule of the bourgeois revolutionaries of the first half of the twentieth century.

So when considered as a network of movements, Islam was totally on the defensive between 1908 and 1945. With the banning of religious orders and the closing down of dervish lodges, Islamic networks went underground. They tried to survive as best they could, extending their influence and enlisting the younger generations by organizing Koran courses. Those orders whose rituals did not require chanting and dancing carried on by gathering their congregations in people's homes. But overall this was a long passing through the desert for Islamic movements. Yet had it not been for this organized kernel of Islamic believers, it would have been almost impossible for Islamist politics to revive even after the thaw that began in the wake of World War II.

The quarter of a century that spanned the years between 1945 and 1970 was a period during which the first signs of revival were witnessed, as Islamic movements resurfaced through the cracks thanks to the new political situation. Having lived under a single-party system in the interwar years, Turkey had to reorient itself in the aftermath of World War II under the impact of both domestic and foreign dynamics and to create a multiparty system. The single-party period had seen the introduction of an extensive industrialization through state hands, which was financed, in addition to some foreign loans, through the utilization of the agricultural surplus, leaving the peasantry almost in the same miserable conditions in which the young republic had found it.[12] There was great discontent in the countryside, symbolized by the peasant's hatred of the tax collector and the gendarme. The provincial agrarian and commercial bourgeoisie, which was for the first time moving to take things directly into its own hands, exploited this discontent against the bureaucratic cadres of the CHP (Atatürk himself had passed away in 1938) by harping on the question of religion, so sensitive for the masses of the poor peasantry. The CHP joined in the competition. Thus was born a new period in which the major parties curried the favors of the masses through what has been termed "concessions" to religion, as seen from the eyes of the secular establishment. The details of the process need not detain us here. However, we should remember that despite important changes, even today some of the fundamental pillars of the Kemalist system remain in effect. If one is the thriving Diyanet, another is the continued prohibition of religious orders.[13]

Receiving "concessions" was, of course, music to the ears of organized Islam after so many decades spent out in the cold. At another level, though, early attempts in the immediate postwar period to form a political party that would aim for governmental power were short-lived. It was only in 1970 that a feasible project was attempted, the National Order Party (Milli Nizam Partisi, MNP) of Necmettin Erbakan. Although this was shut down by the military during the latter's intervention in political life between 1971 and 1973, a new party, the National Salvation Party (Milli Selamet Partisi, MSP), was established in its place in late 1972. This ushered in a new period for Islamism in Turkey. Owing to the strong showing it had at the ballot box in the elections of 1973, the MSP spent the better part of the 1970s in government as a junior coalition member, first, very ironically, with the CHP, the erstwhile Kemalist party claiming to have freshly become social democratic under Bülent Ecevit, and then with the center-right True Path Party (Doğru Yol Partisi, DYP) of strongman Süleyman Demirel. There was a third partner in this latter right-wing coalition, the Nationalist Action Party (Milliyetçi Hareket Partisi, MHP) of Alpaslan Türkeş, the historic leader of Turkey's homebred fascist movement, whose specially trained storm troopers were busy murdering socialist militants and unionists when they did not engage in spectacular assassinations of left-wing intellectuals and journalists. That the Islamist movement could easily stomach this kind of behavior on the part of its coalition partner says a lot about it. This was the kind of movement out of which the AKP, to be adulated by some left-wingers as the bearer of democracy in Turkey, would emerge. The 1970s and 1980s may be considered the period of apprenticeship for the Islamist movement in Turkey, when, as a party of government and later of the opposition, it gained legitimacy in the eyes of the populace at large but also, if only partially, in those of the government establishment.[14] It also promoted its organic intellectuals as higher-echelon cadres in many a ministry, including that of education.

This period of the 1960s and 1970s was interrupted by an interregnum as a result of the military dictatorship of 1980, when the armed forces took over the government and shut down not only the MSP, but all existing parties. Out of the ashes of the MSP was born the Welfare Party (Refah Partisi, RP). This was not a very easy process, but we need not dwell on the difficulties of this rebirth. By 1987, Erbakan was at the head of the party and running in elections.

The period between 1991 and the present may be considered, from one point of view, as a period of sustained ascendancy for the Islamist movement. Erbakan reentered parliament in 1991 at the head of an alliance of extreme right-wing parties, an astute tactical move given the 10 percent threshold imposed by the new constitution, barring the entry of smaller parties into parliament. From then on the new Welfare Party achieved resounding victories, first at the local elections of 1994, gaining the Istanbul and Ankara metropolitan municipalities for the first time, and the general elections of 1995, when it became the party with the highest number of votes. This was the period when Erbakan was fighting for power, that is, for premiership, for the first time—and attained it at the head of a coalition government in mid-1996.

This government, however, would be short-lived, since it was brought down by another military intervention in 1997. So, from another point of view, the period 1991 to the present, although one of sustained ascendancy for the Islamist movement, is really divided into two subperiods: 1991–97 and 2001–present, with another interregnum of confusion, disorientation, and dissension in between.

It was out of this dissension that the AKP of Tayyip Erdoğan was born. Having been abandoned by his former aides (Abdullah Gül, the current president of the republic, and Bülent Arınç, the current vice premier, as well as Erdoğan himself), the historic leader Erbakan had his loyalists establish two more successive parties, which remained extremely small when compared to the success of his own Welfare Party in the 1990s or to that of the AKP in the 2000s. (Erbakan himself died in 2011, but his last party, the Party of Bliss, is still alive.)

The AKP, as everybody is aware, has run from victory to victory at the polls since 2002, winning parliamentary elections with an ever-rising share of the vote in 2002, 2007, and 2011, local elections in 2004 and 2009 (albeit with a declining overall share in this latter year), and the constitutional referendum of 2010 in a landslide (close to 58 percent). I will be looking at the dynamics and the worldview of both the Welfare Party of Erbakan in the 1990s and the AKP of Erdoğan in the 2000s in the coming sections, but before finishing this overview, several points should be underlined.

One is obvious even to those who are not familiar with the Turkish political scene. From the most radical secular reforms of the first quarter of the twentieth century, Turkey has moved to a two-decade ascendancy of Islamist movements at the end of the twentieth and the beginning of the twenty-first centuries. The distance covered, and the contrast between the two periods, is simply breathtaking. No wonder, then, that Turkey has lately been the scene of fiery debates and dirty maneuvers.

The Islamic movement, which remained on the defensive in the first half of the twentieth century, slowly reared its head and finally, starting in the 1970s, went on the offensive. What distinguishes the period after 1970 is that Islamism has found expression in the party form, an organizational form that stands for fighting for power. Ever since that watershed year, political parties have been at the forefront of Islamism's struggle for supremacy (however this may be defined, a question we will return to when we discuss the changing horizon and program of Islamism in the following sections). This does not mean, however, that political parties have totally eliminated the importance of the earlier organizational form, that is, religious orders and communities. One should, on the contrary, regard the birth of political parties out of the organizational form that is the religious order as one of *aufhebung*, that is, the dialectical process of supersession, but equally of conservation. The relevance of the religious order as a form of organization peculiar to Islamism has continued or even been enhanced, as the sprawling empire of the so-called Gülen community, named after the imam Fethullah Gülen, attests to. We will have occasion to come back to the importance of this community for the future of Islamism in Turkey.

The next few sections will look at the social forces behind the Islamist movement, the reasons for its almost uninterrupted rise for at least the last two decades, and the contradictions that have beset the movement at the different stages of its development. As the worldview and program of the Welfare Party of Erbakan and the

AKP of Erdoğan differ on certain vital points, the two parties will be considered separately.

The Forces and the Dynamics behind the Rise of Islamism

The class nature of most phenomena is clear for all to see at the original moment of birth, but subsequently gets shrouded in the mystification of its ideological idiom. The Islamist movement in Turkey is starkly a case in point. So obvious are the motives that led to the birth of the MNP, the first party of Erbakan, that not one single commentator, whatever their personal persuasion, can avoid citing intraclass conflict as the main driving force.

Erbakan, Özal, and Demirel, three outstanding leaders of Turkish right-wing politics, were all educated as engineers at the same college, Istanbul Technical University, at around the same time. They remained friends later and their paths crossed one another's at different junctures. They were all involved in looking for solutions to the quandaries of right-wing politics after the coup d'état of 1960. Why was it, then, that Erbakan took a road that was different from the other two? Why was it that he opted for the formation of a party that would vie for power in the name of Islam, while the other two, themselves devout Muslims, would only promote the interests of the Islamic community through broadly secularist parties that made only partial reference to questions of religion?

The reason is that Erbakan, at a certain stage of his political career, allied himself with the small- and medium-scale capitalists of the provinces and fought the unchecked sway of the cosmopolitan capital of big cities over economic life, with respect to the allocation of credits, the granting of tenders and import quotas (the latter no longer applicable, but important once), the sharing of the spoils of privatization after a certain stage, and so forth. It was with their support that he became in 1968 the president of the Union of Chambers and Commodity Exchanges of Turkey, the umbrella professional organization of the Turkish bourgeoisie, only to be removed from office forcibly by the police under the express orders of Demirel, then prime minister. It was with the support of the capitalists of Konya, the archconservative central Anatolian town with a fledgling industrial base in the late 1960s, that he was elected an independent member of parliament for the first time in 1969, after, significantly, his attempt to declare his candidacy on the list of Demirel's own party had been vetoed by the latter. (One wonders what course history might have taken had Demirel not done this, but instead adopted him as a lieutenant, thus absorbing his energies into the secularist movement.) It was on the basis of this victory that he formed the MNP in 1970, enlisting, in the process, two members of parliament (MPs) of Demirel's party in his new party.

It is true that the MNP was almost the brainchild of Mehmed Zaid Kotku, the leader ("sheikh") of a religious order, the Nakşibendi, the most important order politically(Çakır 2004: 545; Çalmuk 2004: 561–63; Yalçın 2012). So one may tend to attribute a certain autonomy to religious movements vis-à-vis social classes. But we should remember, first, that religious orders are themselves dense webs of interest that cater not only to the spiritual needs of their members, but equally to their material well-being. It is only through a detailed study of religious orders that one can assert with certitude that they are really spiritual networks within which the worldly interests of sections of the ruling classes are also served. However, all existing evidence points in that direction. The best-documented evidence for this comes from the business network that the community of Fethullah Gülen has constructed, one that functions as a rallying force for the politics of the group (Çetinkaya 2010; Şener 2010; Senem 2011). Second, it is of great relevance to remind ourselves that Erbakan was able to win the 1969 elections on an independent slate not because (or not only because) of his political skills, but equally as a result of the financial and political support he received from a certain section of the capitalist class of Konya. Now, it is an established fact that this support was procured through the intermediation of the Nakşibendi order (Yavuz 2004: 591). This shows how bourgeois the order itself was in nature. So it was the marriage of a religious movement that survived the winter of repression and the material interests of a certain section of the provincial capitalist class that led to the creation of the MNP. The Nakşibendi order had been around for almost two centuries, but only now, after the crystallization of a fledgling fraction of the industrial bourgeoisie in the smaller cities, was it able to establish a party that would fight for a share of governmental power.

The SMEs of Anatolian cities were the owners, so to speak, of the MNP and later of the MSP that replaced it. The clientele, or the electorate that they were able to rally, was made up in its majority of the poorer sections of the population of small towns and villages, starting with the Kurdish region, which, at that time, had hardly been awoken to capitalist relations. However, it is important to note that, despite the pleasant surprise of the 1973 elections (11.3 percent and 48 MPs out of 450, quite respectable for a very young party), the MSP stalled for the rest of the 1970s. The reason should be sought, in addition to certain specifically political factors peculiar to the heady 1970s, in the fact that the small and weak bourgeoisie of the Anatolian hinterland was not able to support, financially and politically, a stronger movement. It was only in the 1990s, when the nature of the Islamist bourgeoisie changed, that Erbakan's movement was able to muster greater support from the electorate.

The reasons for the much greater success of the Welfare Party of the 1990s may be attributed to several factors, and these are important to understand. There was first the fact that the ground had been prepared for the Islamist movement by the strategic line of the military regime of the early 1980s. Having taken power in the midst of rampant civil strife, the real objective of the military, with the indisputable backing of even the most sophisticated capitalist groups, was clearly to put down the very radicalized workers' movement, to reset the rules of the game in industrial relations, to destroy the exceptionally strong series of left-wing revolutionary movements, and to prevent the youth from being won over in the future by left-wing ideas. The military was extremely successful in this endeavor. Hence, by inflicting a serious defeat on the left, the military inadvertently made it possible for the Islamist movement to rally all discontent among the poorer strata of society.

More important still is the fact that although the MSP of Erbakan had been shown as one of the culprits paving the way for the coup, the military regime chose to infuse Islamic ideas into sociocultural life under the carefully selected appellation of the Turkish-Islamic synthesis, so as to lull both young workers and students into quiescence.[15] One move made by the military is worth mentioning for its deep symbolism: religion courses were made compulsory for school children for the first time in the history of the republic. A decade of these policies prepared the ground for the emergence of a much stronger Islamist movement than before the coup. Here we see in action the tendency of the entire bourgeoisie, irrespective of their stance on secularism versus Islamism, to abandon all earlier principles and utilize religion to anesthetize a very combative working class. And this contribution of the military to the strengthening of the Islamist movement, unintended though it surely was, proves that the firm belief of some Kemalists in the unshakeable secularism of the military is at bottom an illusion. It is not the influence of Islam that the military is unwilling to permit; it is the Islamist movement, which, they worry, might break Turkey away from the Western alliance.

The major social force behind the Welfare Party of Erbakan, in other words, the Islamist fraction of capital, had become much stronger in the 1990s relative to its state in the 1970s. One reason was the favorable treatment given in the 1980s to (non-interest-paying) Islamic finance from the Gulf countries for the first time ever. Under Prime Minister Turgut Özal, who was a centrist, so to speak, on matters of Islamism, large financial companies from Saudi Arabia, Kuwait, and other Gulf principalities operating in Turkey both provided much-needed funding to modest-sized, Islamist-oriented capitalists, thus strengthening this fraction of capital, and acted as greenhouses where mid-level and senior cadres were trained for the soon-to-rise conglomerates of Islamist political persuasion. In general, the repressive policies of the period, by keeping wages down and workers' rights limited, helped small- and medium-scale capitalists even more than they did large conglomerates. And growing export markets in the Middle East, in particular those of Iraq and Iran, at each other's throats during the 1980s, formed lucrative outlets for the capitalists of some provincial cities in the southeast of the country, in particular Gaziantep and Kahramanmaraş. All in all, the 1980s were a period of transition for some units of Islamist capital from the status of SMEs to large holding companies. It was this much stronger fraction of the capitalist class that was now ready to settle accounts with the older dominant fraction for domination over the accumulation of capital and for governmental power.

Once Erbakan's National Vision movement gained momentum and made a breakthrough in the local elections of 1994, this caused a snowball effect, increasing its strength in several ways (Yavuz 2004: 596–98). The tenders and other business relations of metropolitan and local municipalities became ever-greater sources of new wealth for the rising fraction of the bourgeoisie. New arrangements under the neoliberal regime implied that the partially privatized municipal companies did not even have to organize tenders, which led to privileged treatment of certain capitalist groups on an ever-greater scale. The rewards were returned in the form of graft, nothing peculiar to either the Islamist municipalities or to Turkey for that matter. This made the party richer and better prepared to fight future elections. Municipal administration also proved to be another greenhouse for the Islamist movement, where future government notables and state administrators received their apprenticeship. Erdoğan himself served as mayor of greater Istanbul from 1994 on until he was removed from office by the central government. Overall, his term as mayor famously displays all of the characteristics enumerated above.

The party organization of the Islamist movement has always been exemplary. The use of state-of-the-art technology, combined with self-sacrificing and disciplined work carried out by the rank and file, contributed greatly to the success of the movement. It is perhaps here that religious devotion played a very important part. These were quasi-Leninist organizations of the right, so to speak, geared, of course, toward not revolution but electoral politics (Yavuz 2004: 599 cites breathtaking if somewhat dubious figures for the membership and the activists).

The Islamic networks represented by the religious orders proved very valuable in the development of Islamism in the political sphere. It has already been mentioned that the National Vision movement of Erbakan was conceived, so to speak, in the womb of the Nakşibendi order. But other, smaller orders and communities were behind the National Vision movement as well. The *iftar* (fast-breaking) dinner offered by Erbakan to *tarikat* and *cemaat* leaders during the month of Ramadan while he was prime minister, a move that caused immense uproar in the secular establishment, was in effect an act of recognition of debt on the part of the political wing of the movement toward the social wing.

New types of organizations also arose in the course of the development of the movement. Most noteworthy are the organizations formed by employers of an Islamist persuasion. It is interesting to note that Türkiye Sanayici ve İşadamları Derneği (Turkish Industrialists' and Businessmen's Association, TÜSİAD), the organization of the crème de la crème of the Westernized-secular wing of the Turkish bourgeoisie, was founded in 1971, precisely on the eve of the rise of the new dominant fraction of capital, the sprawling conglomerate in the form of the holding company. On the other hand, Müstakil Sanayici ve İşadamları Derneği (Independent Industrialists' and Businessmen's Association, MÜSİAD), its nemesis, was set up in 1990, this time on the eve of the meteoric rise of Islamist capital to the same status.

There is also no doubt that the triumph of the Iranian mullahs under the leadership of Khomeini, first over the shah in 1979 and then over the working-class movement and the left in 1981, and the victory obtained by the mujahideen in Afghanistan in the 1980s boosted the morale of Islamist movements all around the world, including in Turkey. This is true despite the fact that the Iranian mullahs are representatives of the Shia, while 80 percent of the Muslim world, and the majority of Muslims in Turkey, are Sunni.

To sum up, Islamism was an idea whose time had come in the 1990s. It is certainly true that the existence of dense webs of organizing in the form of the religious orders and ideology in general had their impact. But it is instructive to remember that the first attempts to form Islamist parties go back to 1945, all of which proved to be abortive. The National Vision movement of the 1970s did attain a first plateau in the 1973 elections, with around 10 percent of the electorate supporting it. But then the movement stagnated and even slid back under the impact of the coup d'état of 1980. It was only in the 1990s, when a new fraction of capital had started to equal the strength of the dominant Westernizing wing, that the Islamist movement was finally fit for a struggle for power.

The Coherence of the National Vision Movement and Its Demise

It is extremely important to understand the specific difference between the worldviews and programs represented by the National Vision movement of Erbakan and the AKP of Erdoğan. Only thus can we come to an understanding of, first, the significance of the AKP for Turkish society and for the region at large and, second, the reasons for the resilience of the AKP in the face of all the attacks on it, whereas the Welfare Party was not able to maintain power for longer than a year.

The National Vision movement of Erbakan was truly a homegrown product. It represented the combination of the world outlook of a certain section of the ruling class that was at once imperial and parochial. Its imperial aspect derived from nostalgia for the grandeur of the Ottoman state, at once an earthly empire that spread across three continents and a spiritual leader of the Islamic world in the person of the sultan, who was also the Islamic caliph. So whatever the concrete boundaries of the worldly empire, the whole *umma* of Mohammad looked to the sultan, for he represented their unity. These two concepts, the *umma* and the caliphate, are of key importance for any authentic Islamist movement. But in the Turkish case, because until Kemalism abolished the caliphate it was the Turks that carried the honor of representing the Islamic *umma*, it also stands for national pride and grandeur, over and above its spiritual significance.[16] This is why unity among Islamic countries in opposition to the Western world was so important for the National Vision movement. Erbakan counterposed his own view of the world, the National Vision, to that of what he termed the "imitators," all the other establishment parties that, in his account, took over lock, stock, and barrel the ways of the West. He was clearly against Turkey's accession to the "Western club," that is, the EU (or the Common Market, as it was called when he started to criticize it—though his famous quip, "What they have in common is to exploit our market," was really an imitation of the left). He was not as outspoken on NATO, probably because he knew that harping on security questions would strike a raw nerve in his main opponents, the armed forces. However, it should not be forgotten that in his blueprint for Islamic unity, he included not only an Islamic common market, but an Islamic common defense establishment as well (for other elements of the Islamic unity project, cf. Çakır 2004: 566).

The parochial aspect was, ironically, consistent with the imperial one, although it really sprung from the needs of the small- and medium-scale businesses of provincial towns. In order to wrest Turkey from the yoke of Western interests, which also happened to be immediate allies of the dominant wing of the bourgeoisie, one needed a "heavy industry thrust." Having been trained as a mechanical engineer, Erbakan made abundant use of his specialization and experience in engines to harp forever on the importance of all kinds of vehicles and motors. This concurred with the imperial aspect of his worldview, since it was supposed to counter the weight of the West, but also fit in nicely with the parochial horizon of Anatolian small- and medium-scale businesses, which certainly at the early stage when the National Vision movement was formed had no interests extending beyond the domestic market of Turkey. What the idea of a "heavy industry thrust" implied for his economic views is interesting in itself. Erbakan was very clear on his preference for private property and enterprise and he explicitly counterposed his views to communism. (This, by the way, is one reason why it is totally absurd to pretend that, before the advent of the AKP, the adherents of the National Vision movement posed any "challenge" whatsoever to capitalism.) However, once he admitted the priority of private property, Erbakan then, in a subsidiary manner, insisted on the importance of heavy state involvement for the purposes of achieving the "heavy industry thrust." This special-purpose *étatisme* would prove to be an obstacle in his way in subsequent stages of the movement.

The coherence of the National Vision movement was open to debate when it came to Erbakan's relations with the Arab world, in particular with Saudi Arabia. There were close ties between his movement and this most reactionary Arab kingdom, an indomitable ally of the United States, the leader of the "Western club" of which Erbakan was so critical. This was difficult for Erbakan to explain. While he never had direct ties to the United States, the relationship with Saudi Arabia was indicative of a weak spot in his overall vision.

Nevertheless, even admitting a lacuna here, one must grant that a certain coherence existed in Erbakan's outlook on the world. After all, even if it was a close ally of the United States, Saudi Arabia was an Islamic country and home to Mecca and Medina, and thus a very precious part of the *umma*. The unity of the *umma* was entirely consistent with the rejection of the "Western club." However, of the two halves that went into the making of this (at least partially) coherent worldview, one underwent a transformation that made the outlook incongruous with the new situation. The imperial aspect was of course not open to negotiation. But the parochial aspect became more and more obsolete as the economic nature of the bourgeois fraction that supported the National Vision movement was transfigured. The rise of the Islamic conglomerates heavily involved in the world market came increasingly into contradiction with certain aspects of the National Vision movement. For one thing, the stress on a voluntaristic orientation toward "heavy industry" and the *étatisme* that was to be instrumental in attaining that goal sounded like Kemalist antics in the atmosphere of an orgy-like adulation of the free market, a legacy firmly established by Özal. So Erbakan gently laid his pet idea of "heavy industry" to its death-bed. And right before the 1995 elections he fine-tuned his economic policy to fit the requirements of neoliberalism, with privatization and the rest figuring clearly on his platform. But even more damning was the change in his position on the EU. His fall from grace in the aftermath of the military intervention in 1997 coincided with Turkey's striving to get the EU to agree to its candidacy for accession, which was refused in 1997 but ratified in 1999. And because the most decisive elements of Erbakan's constituency within the bourgeoisie were heavily exporting to the EU in the wake of the Customs Union of 1995–96, Erbakan had to soften his stance on that issue as well. Probably all this was too late and too little. The National Vision movement had been useful for the Islamist bourgeoisie at a certain stage of its development, but had outgrown this usefulness. How prepared Erbakan was to overhaul it completely was an open question. But the real blow came from within the ranks of his party, from the so-called reformers. Let us now turn to this episode in order to understand how the AKP differed from Erbakan's National Vision movement.

A New Globalist and Neoliberal Islam

In order to understand the specific ways in which the AKP differs from the earlier National Vision movement, we need to understand the lineup of political forces during the military intervention of 1997. This episode has been clownishly characterized as the "postmodern coup," an appellation that really aims to conceal more than it reveals. It was a cunning operation organized by the general staff of the armed forces in order to bring the Erbakan government down in a context in which Turkey was waiting at the door of the EU. Everyone knew that the latter would have to shut the door for a while, even if it did not wish to, were a full-scale coup to turn the government of the country over to the armed forces. So a subterfuge was tried instead: a front composed of civilian forces, one that became widely known as the "unarmed forces," was put together and pushed to the forefront, with the general staff pulling the strings from behind curtains, a familiar game in a country where *Karagöz*, the shadow play, had traditionally been the most popular pastime of the population. In addition, on 28 February 1997, a pronunciamiento was delivered to the government by the armed forces in the guise of a resolution to be adopted by the National Security Council, a body that routinely brings together the government with the top brass. Moreover, successive "briefings" provided to different bodies by representatives of the armed forces regularly involved thinly disguised threats to the government. To understand the lineup of forces in this game will be instructive when looking into subsequent developments.

The major *actors* that were behind the operation to bring down the Erbakan government were three: the United States, the TÜSİAD bourgeoisie, that is, the core of the Westernized-secular wing of the bourgeoisie, and the Turkish armed forces. The grievances were various. For one thing, Erbakan in power was following a foreign policy that accorded clear priority to Islamic countries: he visited Iran and Libya, the two black sheep at that time of the Western world, and, even more importantly, launched with great pomp the so-called D8, a group of the economically most advanced Islamic countries, in explicit opposition to the G8 ("D" stood for "developing"). There were still other problems that worried the United States. It should be remembered, though, that both the Westernized-secular wing of the Turkish bourgeoisie and the armed forces are intransigent regarding the priority of Turkey's alliance with the Western system, so Erbakan's foreign policy was no less disturbing to these two forces.

The other aspect of the grievances related directly to the advantages enjoyed by the *parvenu* businesses of an Islamic persuasion, dubbed "green capital." This was the most annoying aspect for the members of the TÜSİAD community. As for the armed forces, they protested most vehemently against the fact that in many spheres of social life there was an increasing encroachment of Islamic practices at the expense of secularism. I believe, however, that they were in fact more worried about Turkey's relations with NATO and the EU.

The "unarmed forces" were *instrumentalized* for the fight against the Erbakan government. Three different forces should be singled out here due to their importance. First, there was the media, heavily controlled by large capitalist conglomerates. The majority of the media outlets, both television and print journalism, loyally acted out the script written by the general staff. Second, there was what later came to be called the "band of five," consisting of two employers' organizations (but not TÜSİAD, which, having learned the lesson of *Karagöz*, discretely waited in the shadows), the artisans' and small traders' confederation, and, lo and behold, two labor union federations, one of which had been shut down by the previous military regime for eleven years. Third, there was an array of institutions that made up part of the civilian apparatus of the state that constituted the elements of a system of protection, formed over time, of the status quo. Chief among these were the judiciary, with the Constitutional Court playing a salient role by closing down unwanted political parties, including the Welfare Party, and the public universities, first and foremost the notorious Council of Higher Education, a legacy of the military regime of the early 1980s. We need not linger here on the details of the unfolding of the intervention. Suffice it to recall that Erbakan had to resign in mid-1997, another government was soon formed, and the Welfare Party was shut down by the Constitutional Court (and Erbakan himself banned from politics for five years) some months later.

Born of the factional struggle between the "traditionalists," loyal to Erbakan, and the "renovators," the partisans of Erdoğan, Gül, and Arınç,[17] the AKP is the product of two convergent requirements: on the one hand, an aggiornamento of the program in line with the changing needs of the patrons of the movement, that is, the Islamist wing of the bourgeoisie, and, on the other hand, an operation aiming at dividing the front of forces that brought down the Erbakan government so as to weather a new crisis, should the AKP come to power and should a crisis somewhat inevitably arise.

Each precept of Erbakan's economic platform that had become problematic in the environment of the Washington Consensus was entirely discarded. *Étatisme* was obliterated and privatization embraced wholesale. No wonder, then, that the AKP government has presided over close to 80 percent of all the privatization carried out in the last three decades, that is, the neoliberal era. Free-market policies rejecting any voluntarism (of the "heavy industry thrust" type) on the part of the state were adopted. Foreign direct investment, surely a sign of the domination of the "Western club" over Turkey, was not only accepted as a fact of life, but was actively encouraged with the setting up of a special agency (ISPAT) reporting directly to the prime minister and the annual convening of discreet consultation meetings between Erdoğan, sitting together with his experts, and the CEOs of top multinational companies with a stake in Turkey or the prospect of one. Leaving aside all qualms regarding interest-paying finance, Istanbul was projected as a regional, and subsequently world-scale, financial hub. In short, the AKP's economic program became neoliberal tout court.

Parallel to the overhaul of the party's economic precepts, the AKP, once in power, also threw itself zealously at clearing the way for Turkey's accession to the EU. It was as a result of this show of active support on the part of the AKP government that the EU resolved to open negotiations at the December 2004 summit and did open them in October 2005. (The subsequent procrastination in the negotiation process does not really relate specifically to the AKP, but can be understood as yet another period of crisis in the half-century-long relations between the EU and Turkey.)

Finally, the AKP's attitude to the United States changed drastically as well. Erbakan was not invited to the White House a single time, but Erdoğan has been a frequent visitor, the first time being even before he was an elected member of parliament.[18]

This change in the economic and foreign policies of the Islamist movement also immediately implied that the AKP had divided the front formed in 1997. We ought to remember that the driving forces behind that intervention were the United States, the TÜSİAD bourgeoisie, and the Turkish armed forces. With the United States (and the EU) out, Erdoğan and company also moved to partially neutralize the Westernized-secular wing of the bourgeoisie. This was a much thornier target and was never completely achieved; far from it. However, it should be noted that two points led to at least a thaw between the AKP and TÜSİAD. One was obviously the change in the economic program of the AKP, making it attuned to the needs of the whole bourgeoisie. The other derived from the fact that the AKP was the first single-party government serving after a spell of coalition governments that lasted for longer than a decade. This meant it could attack the working class much more consistently and implement unpopular policies much more easily. These two traits made the AKP government attractive for all fractions of the bourgeoisie across the board.

This metamorphosis of the Islamist movement as it was embodied in the AKP implied that the front that had been put together against Erbakan was reduced to the *instruments* rather than the major *actors* of the Westernizing project of the Turkish bourgeoisie, except for the armed forces, which were, of course, the most formidable foe. But the variegated forces of the media, of the "band of five," and the civilian bureaucracy could all be manipulated or conquered through divide-and-rule policies. This took time, but was achieved through a well-thought-out strategy.

Explaining the Enigma

The AKP has now been in power for over a decade, having won, as we have already noted, all the contests at the ballot box through the years. This would have been remarkable even if it were a regular establishment party like those of Menderes, Demirel, Ecevit, or even Özal. It is all the more noteworthy when one remembers that it is the first government with Islamist roots in Turkey that has even been able to establish a stable government. And even more significantly, perhaps, it has been able to weather all the different storms caused by the plans of the armed forces and supported, to different degrees, by other secular forces within the country. What is more, before the onset of the popular revolt that erupted in June 2013, many would have wagered that Erdoğan and the AKP would remain in power for another decade. So the question of why is worth trying to answer.

The list of reasons is long. Let me start out by noting that Erdoğan is not alone in having remained in power for longer than a decade in the recent period. Some other names immediately suggest themselves: Putin, of course, but the Kirchners and Chávez in his time as well. It is notable, to take just one example, that Mrs. Fernández de Kirchner scored even higher in the last presidential elections, pulverizing the establishment opposition movement in the process, than Erdoğan's spectacular showing in 2011. Despite the many differences between these political figures, whose victorious march forth each needs to be studied in depth, there is one point in common. This is the fact that these are all governments that brought stability and some semblance of order and prosperity to their countries in the wake of a traumatic crisis. In the case of Venezuela, this was the *Caracazo* of 1989, when bread riots were quelled with extreme brutality, shooting people inside their homes by police fire through their windows, ending in a massacre that counted hundreds of poor working people. In Russia, it was not only the most shocking economic disruption that the country faced in a country where economic stability and security had been for decades the mainstay of social life, but also a political and cultural crisis of such proportions that the soul-searching reached the level of a civilizational trauma, the whole thing reaching its apex in the moratorium of 1998, all presided over by a drunkard named Boris Yeltsin. In Argentina, it was an economic crisis of immense proportions, creating extreme poverty and misery in a country that had been among the most advanced in the world only half a century before, coupled with a political crisis that brought down four presidents in the space of less than a month. In Turkey, Erdoğan rode to power in the aftermath of the deepest economic crisis of the modern history of the country; the economy came to the brink of an even worse depression in the summer of 2001 but was luckily spared. I would call such cases "posttraumatic government." If the government can ride the storm, master the contradictions of the traumatic crisis the country has experienced, and provide even a modicum of order, stability, and prosperity, chances are it will remain in power until totally new contradictions mature.

Moving to reasons specific to Turkey, I should first mention a somewhat structural factor. This relates to the Turkish exceptionalism discussed earlier. This has resulted in a situation in which a system of class oppression and exploitation also appears to the laboring masses as a system of cultural divorce between the haves and have-nots. It is against this background that the new Islamist fraction of the bourgeoisie emerged. The political leadership of the Islamist bourgeoisie, with its "oriental" culture and conservative ways, has a head start against the representatives of the Western-secular wing since they seem to be so much closer to the have-nots. Erdoğan, himself a self-made capitalist with plebeian roots, seems to the multitude of the urban and rural poor as "one of their own." This structural divide in Turkish society has been thoroughly used and abused by Erdoğan throughout his decade in power. He has kept alive a policy of social polarization between what he calls the "bureaucratic oligarchy" together with the "interest rate lobby"(these are names that denote, respectively, the armed forces and the secular wing of the bourgeoisie) on the one hand, and the authentically Turkish and Muslim people of the country on the other hand. This is a problem that is difficult to cope with in the short run and can only be overcome if the left—to a great extent an offshoot of the secular, Kemalist tradition of bourgeois progressive movements—can heal the cultural divide with the laboring classes.

Another factor is the specific context of the elections of November 2002 that brought the AKP to power. Turkey, as has already been noted, had gone through longer than a decade of inept coalition governments and suffered successively in 1994, 1999, and 2001 the three deepest economic crises of the republican period, each worse than the previous one (Balkan and Yeldan 2002: esp. 41, table 1). This was a country ripe for the taking for a new political force that projected an image of competence and reliability. Erdoğan's record as mayor of Istanbul provided precisely that. The old parties had been totally discredited.[19] It was in this context that the AKP received one-third of the popular vote, which was beyond anything that the parties belonging to the National Vision tradition had ever attained. (Erdoğan himself had become mayor of Istanbul in 1994 on the basis of a mere one-fifth of the popular vote only because the other parties were so fragmented.) And thanks to the 10 percent threshold, the party picked two-thirds of the seats in parliament on the basis of this one-third of the votes. (One party was stuck at 9.5 percent, another at 8, still another at 7, and still another at 6.) This firm majority, which contrasts starkly with the coalition government that Erbakan had to manage in the 1990s, gave immense leverage to Erdoğan in future political conflicts with the secular camp.

Still another factor was the final demise of the center-right in Turkish politics, at least for the foreseeable future. At bottom, despite all the complications that arose as a result of party closures and the blossoming of certain other political currents, Turkey had a firmly established two-party system in the first three decades of its multi-party experiment from, roughly, 1950 to the military coup of 1980, one center-right and the other center-left. However, having banned from politics the outstanding leaders of the two traditions, Demirel for the center-right and Ecevit for the center-left, the military regime of the early 1980s created the unintended consequence of enduring fissures within both camps. How the problem was overcome on the center-left does not concern us in this context, but the center-right fared very badly as a result. Two overpowering figures, Özal and Demirel, were at each other's throats until the former died in 1993, and the legacy of this division led to the demise of both currents, at the hands of particularly inept subsequent leaders, one should add. This was a long-drawn-out process in which the two parties of the center-right, which had traditionally garnered, between the two of them, close to 65 percent of the popular vote as late as 1991, saw, in election after election, their share gradually and painfully fall to slightly above 10 percent combined in 2002. This almost incredible bleeding was, it must be emphasized, only partially related to the rise of the Islamist movement (were it not so, our proposition would have been tautological). Witness the fact that in 1999, the last elections before the fateful 2002 elections, the share of the center-right continued to decline even though the Islamist party of the day, the Virtue Party, saw its share fall as well. Thus, the collapse of the center-right left the AKP alone on the right wing of the political spectrum, save for a fascist party that was afflicted in this period with a distinctly unprepossessing, even positively repulsive leader.

The constant rise in the AKP's vote over successive elections has somewhat baffled commentators, but the secret lies in the electoral system. The 10 percent threshold, unparalleled in the world, to my knowledge, by making it totally useless to vote for smaller parties, incontrovertibly acts in favor of the big parties that are closer ideologically or politically to those inevitable losers. In election after election, the AKP has nibbled into the vote of all the small right-wing parties, starting with the center-right ones, bringing them to naught. In the last elections, the AKP even reduced the remnants of the National Vision movement, which seemed to be the most resilient due to ideological reasons.[20] No wonder Erdoğan adamantly refuses to bring down the 10 percent threshold, hiding behind the smokescreen of political stability.

Apart from these intricacies of the Turkish political system, which have, in amazing serendipity, contributed to the success of the AKP, other, less technically political factors need mentioning as well. A very important, almost decisive, factor is the economy. After three profound crises in the space of seven years, the Turkish economy enjoyed six straight years of high growth until the Lehman Brothers collapse. Following a hitch in the form of a recession in 2009, it then recovered rapidly to reach impressive growth rates, second only to China among the G20 countries, in 2010 and 2011. However, a caveat must immediately be added. This positive balance sheet was not of Erdoğan's making. It is really the result of the traumatic experience of 2001–2, when the whole Turkish business and political establishment was so scared that it got its act together to establish sound bases for the economy. Given the extremely positive environment of the world economy, this was bound to deliver its results in the aftermath of the 2001 crisis. It is true that the condition of the world economy has become drastically adverse since the Lehman Brothers collapse, but the Turkish economy had already gone through its own banking crisis a decade ago and taken draconian measures to rule out a repetition of such a crisis. That is why, exceptionally among the OECD countries together with Canada, the Turkish banking sector did not suffer at all from the credit crunch, since the prudential indicators of Turkish banks were already above the levels required by Basel III. One should add to this the buoyancy of the international capital markets up until 2007–8, which brought a large amount of capital inflow into Turkey, and the favored treatment that Erdoğan gets from the finance-rich Gulf countries. Whatever the causes of this globally positive macroeconomic record, it brought in a lot of support to the government from the poorer strata of the Turkish electorate, this despite the worsening distribution of income and loss of rights for the working class, on which, partially at least, this whole record relied in the first place. It is instructive to point out that the only elections in which the share of the AKP declined (by eight percentage points) were the local elections of spring 2009, when the Turkish economy was in a brief but very deep recession (running at that point at 6 percent on an annual basis). In addition to the macroeconomic record, social assistance schemes and charity work conducted by Islamic charitable organizations also feed into the AKP's popularity in the poorer strata of society.

The dismantlement of the bloc that prepared the downfall of Erbakan in 1997 was, of course, a major condition for the resilience of the AKP government. The armed forces and its allies were no less actively trying, at least up until 2007, to erode the support for and finally bring down the AKP government. However, this time around Western powers, in particular the United States, did not lend a helping hand, despite having their own accounts to settle with the AKP. In addition, the TÜSİAD bourgeoisie was more ambivalent in its relations with the AKP than in its straightforward hostility to Erbakan's movement, because this was the first single-party government in a decade ready to push through unpopular reforms in favor of the capitalist class. So to the Westernised-secular bourgeoisie, this was a Janus-faced government that both served its class interests well, but also acted against its interests in its intraclass struggle with the new rising fraction of Islamist capital.

We have to be very clear on one thing: the resilience of the AKP government owes more to the division of the earlier rival front than its repeated victories at the ballot box. In other words, had the United States and the EU supported the Turkish armed forces in its quest to bring down the AKP government and had the TÜSİAD bourgeoisie taken up an icy attitude toward Erdoğan, as it had vis-à-vis Erbakan, the success at the election booth may not have saved Erdoğan. Of course, it did make an immense difference that the AKP had an overwhelming majority in parliament, as opposed to Erbakan's Welfare Party, which never enjoyed more than a plurality. But, given the traditions of Turkish political life, the array of forces that had brought down Erbakan could possibly have ousted Erdoğan, if only they had been able or willing to come together.[21]

It is not possible to go into the details of all the coup plots allegedly prepared in the years 2003–4 and the failed pronunciamento of 2007, the first military ultimatum in world history in virtual form, since it was transmitted to the country through the website of the general staff. The government struck back boldly in response to the pronunciamento of 2007. Some days later Erdoğan himself cornered the chief of the general staff at a tête-à-tête meeting, called the "Dolmabahçe meeting," after the name of the palace where the Istanbul office of the prime minister is located. This meeting, in defiance of all customary practices, has so far remained confidential between the two men; not a single word has been leaked, and, as far as the public is aware, it has no written record or minutes. This turned out to be the turning point, and as a result, the AKP government seems to have brought to heel, even if temporarily, the armed forces. It was in all probability the content of this meeting that paved the way for the notorious trials dubbed Ergenekon (allegedly a secret counterinsurgency organization after the name of a mythical home of the Turks in Central Asia) and Balyoz (Sledgehammer), in which many members of the top brass, retired or on active duty, were arrested, kept in prison for years on end awaiting trial, were convicted to terms that reach up to aggravated life imprisonment, but have now been released after the crisis of late 2013, which we will touch upon below. There were notorious criminals among the defendants as well as hundreds of others, including one party leader and many intellectuals, journalists, university professors, so forth, whose involvement in coup plotting is dubious, to say the least.

This puts social scientists in a difficult situation. Despite all the other factors that I have been analyzing here that contribute to the strength and resilience of the AKP, one factor, the new state of relations between the government and the armed forces, cannot really be analyzed, because nothing, absolutely nothing, is known of the content of the "Dolmabahçe meeting." And that may be the decisive factor in the shift in the balance of forces between the armed forces and the AKP government. Future historians, it is to be hoped, will be more fortunate than we are, as we are trying to grope our way in some kind of darkness in this aspect.

Another feature that distinguishes the situation of the AKP government from that of the National Vision government of the 1990s is the support it has received from two different quarters. The first is by far the more important one. The Gülen community, under the leadership of Fethullah Gülen, lent the AKP its political support. As I have already had occasion to point out, this is a religious community that has a sprawling empire of schools in the remotest corners of the world, so it acts as a relay for the newly acquired expansionist urge of the Turkish capitalist class and the neo-Ottomanist political strategy of the Erdoğan government. But the significance of its support is certainly not limited to that. The community, as well as being a spiritual universe, is a dense web of economic interests and is, therefore, rich in resources, making it a powerful propagandist for the government.[22] This is the first time Fethullah Gülen is supporting an Islamist government. He firmly supported the military coup of 1980 and sided even with the military intervention of 1997, criticizing Erbakan for his rashness and ineptitude. The reason for his change of mind when it comes to the AKP lies in his well-thought-out strategic orientation. Gülen apparently decided early on that the revival of the grandeur of Islamic Turkey (an aim shared by all Islamists alike) was to be achieved not against the West and in particular the United States, but in alliance with it. This was a view that was radically different from, even diametrically opposed to, the National Vision movement. It was only with the conversion that the AKP represented in the Islamist political movement that Gülen moved to support it. We will see, though, that this support has been subject to rapid erosion lately.[23]

The other kind of support came from a quarter that, at first sight, was more surprising: the liberal intelligentsia of Turkey, with heavy roots in the left-wing movements of the 1960s and 1970s, supported the AKP wholeheartedly, until the AKP abandoned it recently. Superficially, this seems incomprehensible, given the cosmopolitan culture, the viscerally secular outlook, and the libertarian lifestyle of this segment of the intelligentsia. However, after the 1980 coup Turkish liberals decided that Turkey was congenitally unable to attain a democratic regime through its own forces and that EU membership (and more generally globalization) was the panacea. So any force in Turkish politics that looked toward the EU was to be supported, even if it was the successor to Erbakan, who had always been viewed with suspicion by the whole gamut of secular intellectuals in Turkey. Liberalism is not a politically strong current in Turkey, but since every bourgeois pretends hypocritically to be liberal, the liberal intelligentsia has a considerable weight in intellectual life.[24] So from their columns in mainstream newspapers and at interminable talk shows on television, liberal intellectuals pontificated on the democratic character of the AKP. This surprising propaganda made serious inroads in the ranks of the secular urbane electorate. The 58 percent of the vote that was cast in favor of the constitutional referendum in 2010, the highest tally Erdoğan ever reached, no doubt included many with their hearts to the left of the political spectrum but dreaming of a new dawn for Turkish democracy under the AKP, courtesy of the disquisitions of the liberal intelligentsia.

The 2000s did not only contrast with the 1990s with regard to the economy or coalition governments versus a stable single-party government. The major reason behind the economic and political instability of the 1990s, perhaps the root cause of all hardships in Turkey in recent decades, was the war that raged between the guerrilla forces of the PKK, fighting since 1984 against the protracted assimilation of the Kurds of Turkey, and the forces of the government, adamant in denying the rightful demands of this oppressed people. The war gobbled up hundreds of billions of dollars, left close to forty thousand dead (on official count), ravaged the Kurdish cities and countryside, and led to forced migration for millions of Kurds, resulting in deteriorated conditions of existence not only for them, but also for the urban poor of the metropolises of Turkey living already miserable lives, since it led to increased competition for scarce resources. No government would be able to survive the shocks unleashed by this war, let alone the weak coalition governments torn asunder by the disagreements between the parties in power, and no government was able to put an end to the war. The 2000s contrasted sharply with this scene. The war subsided for a reason that was not, again, the making of the AKP government. Abdullah Öcalan, the all-powerful leader of the PKK, was hunted down by the United States' Central Intelligence Agency (CIA) in his hideout in Kenya and turned over to the Turkish government in 1999. This changed the whole situation. Not that it automatically implied a defeat for the PKK, but it did bring about a change in the aims of the movement and its course of action. So the

2000s were a period of relative calm, and this fed into the resilience of the AKP government. (I will briefly touch upon the current situation regarding the Kurdish question later in this chapter.)

So it was a combination of renunciation of the historic program of the movement, astute tactical maneuvering, and plain luck that contributed to the decade-long success of the AKP. There is no doubt that Erdoğan has a certain charismatic charm for a large section of the population. He was highly popular even before the electoral victory of the AKP (Aydın and Dalmış 2008: 201–3) and after a decade in power is now a very strong man with a real spell over his hard-core followers. However, to explain the decade-long success of the AKP on this basis alone would simply amount to a personality cult of the worst kind.

What seems like a long stretch of successes when viewed from afar was nonetheless a process filled with conflict, tension, and bitterness. The Turkish establishment fought hard against this newcomer in the political system. This was viewed by many as a defense of republican values or lifestyles or secularism. There may be a point in each of these. But all that was on the surface. Beneath that surface lay the cold calculation of interest on the part of two fractions of the same class, the bourgeoisie.

Epilogue: The Rebellion

On the night of 31 May, as the calendar turned from Friday to Saturday and from May to June, precisely around midnight, the whole of Turkey rose in rebellion. Struggles had been going on for some days over Gezi Park in Taksim Square at the center of Istanbul, and the brutality of the methods the police used against demonstrators had been disturbing many people, but that was only the triggering factor. The eruption on that night was historic by its sociological and geographic sweep. People who had not even once gone out to protest anything in their lives were now at least banging pots and pans (the Latin *cacerolazo*) on their balconies, and hundreds of thousands, if not millions, had left their homes to demonstrate at three o'clock in the morning. This went on for almost the whole month of June. Then aggressive policing finally pushed the mass movement back, but even for the whole of July, in the bigger cities at least, big crowds gathered in neighborhood parks to discuss in the most democratic fashion conceivable methods of future action. After a brief flare in September the movement ebbed and has not recovered since.

This is not the place to analyze this gigantic and variegated movement even in bare outline. I have tried to do this in several shorter pieces written during the revolt (see Savran 2013a, 2013b, 2013c, 2013d). Here we will simply take up the question of what this rebellion means for the future of Erdoğan, of the AKP, and of Islamism in Turkey. It should first be made clear that the popular revolt was a direct result of the very widespread reaction to the AKP's policies at different levels. The rebellion was so multifaceted that it is impossible to enumerate all the different grievances that people were voicing. Just to mention a few of these, the demonstrators at Gezi Park were certainly protesting the crass commercialization of the very rare green areas left in the city; the Alevis revolted against the bald denial of their rights as a minority religious group; youth refused the intervention of a conservative prime minister in every aspect of life, including how many children people should have and how much alcohol they should consume; women protested the planned ban on abortion and the bald refusal by the prime minister of the equality of the genders; gay, lesbian, bisexual, and transgender (GLBT) people rose up in rage against the conservative environment that made them easy prey for hate crimes; the people of Hatay, the province neighboring Syria, which saw the highest level of street fighting, were enraged because of the criminal sectarian war the government instigated in that country. And so on and so forth.

But the red thread that connected all this was the arrogant violation by the government and by Erdoğan of democratic rights. In a certain sense, the eruption of the popular revolt in response to the police brutality exercised against the ecologists of Gezi Park was also a delayed response to all the other instances of groups protesting against the infringement of their rights, because everyone who has recently tried to voice grievances has been put down with tear gas and water cannon and batons. Kemalists and other nationalists revolted because they had been charged by the police for committing the crime of trying to celebrate the anniversary of the republic in Ankara on 29 October 2012. Politically advanced workers and socialists revolted because they had been gassed and clubbed only one month before as they were trying to reach Taksim Square to celebrate May Day. Everyone, in short, had had enough of the repressive policies of the government. The government's response to the revolt reproduced the same pattern all over again, and in the process at least five demonstrators were dead and dozens lost an eye to plastic bullets. So the problem that has given rise to the rebellion has really been reproduced on an extended scale.

Finally, in the background to all this, not yet voiced aloud, lies the discontent experienced by large sections of the working population as a result of the policies of privatization, flexibilization, deunionization, and precarization that have been the hallmark of the AKP's economic policy. The working class has not yet stepped in with demands and methods of its own, and if and when it does, the revolt is likely to reach proportions unmanageable for the government.

I should also note that the revolt came as thunder in a blue sky to many observers and commentators. This is simply a result of an erroneous assessment of the strengths and weaknesses of the AKP government. Many of the sources of strength of the government had already begun to turn sour before the eruption of the rebellion at the end of May.

On the economic front, growth was already down to around 2 percent in 2012. The vulnerabilities of the Turkish economy are now making themselves felt, especially the structural problem of the current account deficit and the very high and still rising indebtedness of the private sector in foreign currency. The recent change of mind at the United States' Federal Reserve, bringing on the agenda a phasing out of quantitative easing, has led to serious volatility in Turkish financial markets, much more so than in many other countries. The catchword for dynamism of the Turkish economy was economic and political "stability," in a region where this is the rarest bird. That trump card is now spent. Turkey is once again becoming one of the weak links of the world economy.

The foreign policy of the government has received successive blows. The "zero problems with neighbors" policy of Foreign Minister Ahmet Davutoğlu is in shambles. Turkey is pursuing a policy of hostility with at least three of its eastern and southern neighbors—Syria first and foremost, but Iran and Iraq as well. In the case of Syria, the expectation of the Erdoğan government of a quick downfall of the Assad regime in Syria has proved to be a fatal mistake, with serious consequences for Turkey. The killing of at least fifty-three people in Reyhanlı, a small town near the Syrian border, as a result of a pair of bomb explosions and the fact that Erdoğan was put down during his visit to Washington DC by Obama over his excessive zeal in dealing militarily with Syria, both in the month of May 2013, caused a significant loss of prestige for the government. Lately, the war between the military forces of the autonomous Kurdish region of Syria (called Rojava or "the West" in Kurdish) and the fundamentalists of the Jabhat al Nusra on the Turkish-Syrian border has added insult to injury. The war is now moving across frontiers into Turkey's territory.

Disputes with Fethullah Gülen have also been on the rise since 2010, when the imam disowned the flotilla led by the ship *Mavi Marmara*, standing with Israel, to the shock of many rank-and-file Islamists. Other issues have set the two powerful figures on contradictory courses. Despite his Islamism, Fethullah Gülen is distinguished by an extremely pragmatic and flexible political style and could, during the several electoral occasions of 2014, establish an alliance with more secular political forces.

Erdoğan has also lost the support of the liberals, who had been instrumental in making him seem acceptable to wide swathes of urbane voter groups. His brutal repression of all show of dissent and his arrogance in dismissing all criticism have become too much to stomach even for those who are (or were, since many have been fired) on the payroll of pro-government newspapers or television channels. Together with this rift between Erdoğan and the liberals goes down the drain the whole theory that it was the center in Ottoman and republican Turkey that was the source of all authoritarianism and the periphery (or civil society) that was the mother of all democracy. Liberals now find themselves abruptly awoken from a dream.

What remains for Erdoğan as sources of strength are his popularity with the more conservative sections of the population—an almost structural advantage—and his policy of a peaceful resolution of the Kurdish question. Although that policy is shrouded in such mystery that one suspects it may collapse at any moment, for the moment at least it is this policy that has given him breathing space during the rebellion, as the Kurdish movement has kept to the sidelines for fear of upsetting the fragile "peace process."

This subterranean shifting of the ground under Erdoğan's feet was probably one of the preconditions that made it possible for the popular revolt to mature. The revolt itself has of course dealt a very serious blow to his power. He is now at loggerheads with his patrons in the West, who consistently rebuked him for his strong-arm tactics during the rebellion. He has seen the resurgence of conflict with the Westernized-secular wing of the Turkish bourgeoisie, whereas lately certain sections of this bourgeoisie, out of conviction or interest, had taken some steps toward Erdoğan. In a development that is entirely novel, he has even come up against rifts within his own ruling AKP. Abdullah Gül, the current president of the republic, and Bülent Arınç, the current vice premier, numbers two and three in the AKP hierarchy, respectively, took a different road during the rebellion, one that laid the onus of resolution much more on negotiations than on repression. In this, Kemal Kılıçdaroğlu, the leader of the main opposition party, the CHP, was their prominent ally. Abdullah Gül seems to be a serious contender for the next presidential elections, supported visibly by the CHP. If, as is likely, the Gülen community also turns its favors on Gül, Erdoğan, who wishes to run for president, will be facing the first serious electoral challenge since his rise to power. Whether Erdoğan wins the elections for president of the republic or not will be decisive for his political future. But one thing is certain: he will almost certainly not be able to realize his dream of creating a presidential system in the image of the American one, on the basis of which he was hoping to rule Turkey single-handedly for two successive terms until 2024, past the centenary of the foundation of the republic in 2023. He may even have become a burden on his erstwhile supporters and may be duly discarded for the good of the party.

But it is not only a question of a loss of electoral strength. Should the revolt continue further and perhaps even flare up again, Erdoğan will be hard-pressed to remain in power even before the elections. Behind the façade of the unmovable and unshakeable strong man of Turkey, one senses the erosion of power and prestige as a result of the mighty struggle of the masses. It is not that the AKP is condemned to fall. Erdoğan's fate as well as that of the people depends on the future of this extraordinary movement. Two powerful forces have still not joined in the fray. If the working class of Turkey and the Kurdish movement decide to take their part in the popular revolt, then a new future will come on the agenda, not for Turkey alone, but for the whole region.

Postscript: Civil War within the Civil War of the Bourgeoisie

This chapter was completed in the late summer of 2013. Since the plan for this volume was conceived even earlier, the people's revolt of the summer of 2013, widely known under the appellation of the Gezi Park protests, was taken up separately in the epilogue above. The editing process of every book naturally takes some time. Together with the people's revolt, Turkey has entered such a period of convulsions that between the writing of the epilogue and the final preparations for publication, another severe irruption appeared on the political scene, this time the profound political crisis that set against each other the two wings of the Islamist coalition that has been ruling Turkey for the last eleven years. As the whole world is aware, on 17 December

2013 an early dawn raid by the police resulted in the revelation, on the basis of irrefutable evidence, of a deep network of graft and corruption in the government, involving four ministers (with the sons of three of these also implicated directly), who subsequently had to resign from their posts. There is not a shred of doubt that this was the result of the conflict that had been brewing for the last three years between the two partners of the thinly disguised coalition that the AKP government has always been, a coalition between two forces dominated so far by two undisputed leaders: Tayyip Erdoğan, the prime minister, and Fethullah Gülen, the spiritual and political guide of the religious community of which quite a lot has already been said in the main body of this chapter. The latter wields a very well-established network in the police force and the judiciary, painstakingly built over years and decades. It was this network that started the series of investigations into the messy financial practices of the government after 17 December.

What ensued thereafter cannot even be summarized in a postscript. Suffice it to say that at the time of writing, Turkey is not only still in the throes of a deep political crisis, but is also being threatened by an economic crisis of daunting proportions, symbolized by the headlong plunge of the Turkish lira at the end of January 2014, momentarily arrested by the doubling of the policy rate by the central bank. And this is not all. What we see unfolding is a veritable *crisis of the state*, since the state apparatus is being torn asunder as a result of the contrary actions of the two sides, which have both built a hold on different levers and posts within that apparatus. The judiciary and the police force are now paralyzed. The intelligence agency (Milli İstihbarat Teşkilatı, MİT) has found itself in confrontational situations with prosecutors, the police force, and even the gendarmerie, which is a law-and-order arm of the military. There are even photos that show gendarmes taking aim with their rifles at MİT agents. What we have all along been calling a bloodless civil war has, it would seem, come to the brink of turning into a bloody one. (This is not without precedent, however: there were at least two similar episodes during the earlier phase of the civil war of the bourgeoisie, when it was the Westernizing camp and the Islamist one as a whole fighting each other.)

So even in a country whose history seems to be made up of a sheer concatenation of crises, this is a crisis of extraordinary proportions. It creates potentials that could beget the most radical upheavals and transformations one could hardly dare to imagine in normal times. It would be a wanton exercise to try to speculate on the outcome. In times of such profound crisis, it is the living human forces of groups and individuals, starting with classes, that will have the last say on the order of things to come. So everything is possible. One thing is clear, though: whichever side of the Islamist camp wins this war, it will be a Pyrrhic victory. The two sides have become so enmeshed throughout these years of inebriating successes against their erstwhile common enemies and are so well-informed about the illicit methods used in achieving control of so many institutions that this is bound to become a struggle unto death. This is precisely the reason why Turkish politics has now become a war of spooks, so to speak, with confidential video shootings and voice recordings revealing nauseating details about political mischief or private lives. All in all, this infighting may be heralding an eclipse, if not the durable decline, of Islamism on Turkish soil.

The only thing to do, in the very midst of the crisis, is to try to learn from this crisis, in particular concerning the grave mistakes that were made by large sections of the intelligentsia concerning the nature of the AKP.

The first point to be made is that the root cause of this crisis lies in the fragility of the ground upon which the seemingly invincible alliance between the two forces had been built. Between the partners of this alliance there was a difference of *strategic* orientation. Tayyip Erdoğan and the bulk of the AKP come from the National Vision tradition. And although Erdoğan, as explained above, diverged at a certain point from the orientation of his historic leader and compromised with the United States and the EU, he is the leader of a movement that is not organically nor inseparably linked to these powers. Fethullah Gülen, on the other hand, made his whole career dependent on good relations with the United States and Israel. Though united in their struggle against their common enemies (the Westernist-secular wing of the bourgeoisie and the armed forces), they fell out once that enemy seemed vanquished. But since the strategic penetration of the Gülen community into the state apparatus had advanced beyond imagination during the years of alliance, it was not possible to extirpate its cadres from their posts without a war. Hence the crisis of the state.

So behind this schism there was a structural rift between the two allies. This rift first came out into the open in 2010 during the *Mavi Marmara* incident with Israel, when Gülen sided with the latter, opposing an overwhelming majority of the country, let alone of Islamists. So the rift has been there for more than three years. Why is it, then, that it has broken into the open so explosively only now?

This, in my opinion, is directly a consequence of the people's revolt of the summer of 2013. This tremor led to the diminution of Erdoğan's stature in the eyes of all of his supporters and allies. He was no longer to be trusted as a leader who would be able to establish political and economic stability in Turkey. Stability in a region torn by war, civil war, armed conflict, and political disunion was what made Turkey so special in the decade of Erdoğan's rule. This lost, all his supporters and allies started to abandon the sinking ship one by one. This is what brought into the open the simmering conflict between the two allies that had jointly shored up the strength of the AKP government.

What kind of light does this picture shed on past conceptions of the rise of the AKP? Most immediately, it is an indictment against the self-imposed deception of the liberal and left-liberal circles of the intelligentsia, who had deluded themselves into thinking that the AKP and Erdoğan as its supreme leader were the bearers of the dynamics of democratization in Turkey. The whole argument put forth by Erdoğan himself regarding the "parallel state" established by the Gülenists is a clear admission that, far from suppressing once and for all, as the liberals had assumed, the "deep state" that had characterized the earlier period of postwar Turkish political history, the Islamist government had consciously and astutely formed a "deep state" of its own. This has now turned against Erdoğan, who finds himself in the unenviable position of the sorcerer's apprentice, who, having let the genie out of the bottle, can no longer cope with its deeds.

Another delusion that has been revealed for its eminently false nature is the assertion, made time and again by the self-same liberals with unwavering confidence: that the AKP and democracy had triumphed *irreversibly*, Turkey thus having grown out of a definite stage of its history. The sight of Erdoğan and the AKP coming to the edge of the precipice and even currying the favor of the cadres of the "deep state" of yesteryear in order to avoid disaster should be instructive against such rash conclusions.

There is a mirror image of this kind of mistake in other circles of the left intelligentsia and politics. Some confidently asserted that a "second republic" had been established by the AKP, thus laying the first, or Kemalist, republic to its death bed, which the defenders of this idea deplored even if in studiedly ambivalent terms. The alliance now emerging between the former "deep state" of the "first republic" and the rulers of the "second republic," an alliance certainly riddled with contradictions but nonetheless real, throws devastating light on this unwarranted periodization of modern Turkish history.

To conclude, Turkey is in the throes of a deep convulsion. It is going through a crisis that is so profound as to leave an imprint on the future for some time to come, not only of the country itself, but also of the entire Middle East. Those social forces that can weather the crisis and command the immense energy set free by this explosion will master this future.

Notes

The author is indebted to the readers of Berghahn Books for the extremely careful reading they have made of this chapter and for their perspicacious comments and wise recommendations.

1. For the reader who does not feel s/he has a command of the overall evolution of Turkish politics in the modern era, and in particular the periodically recurring military coups of the second half of the century, see an overview sketched some time ago in Savran (2002).
2. The classical text here is Mardin (1973). So many books and articles have been produced in Turkish expounding this theory that to quote any single one for the international reader would be impractical. A good, sophisticated overview and critique in English may be found in Yalman (2002). For a book-length discussion of the same topic, see Yalman (2009).
3. This literature is full of verbatim reports of confidential meetings between US and Turkish statesmen. This is done without ever explaining how the author had access to the substance of these meetings. Then others come along, quote the earlier author, who himself has not cited any sources, and in this way an authoritative version (!) of events is formed. This is the way history is written!
4. For a debate on this book, see Morton (2011) and Tuğal (2011).
5. This is why at least two of the articles in this volume (Tanyılmaz and Öztürk) are so significant in the way they analyze Islamist capital. See also, in Turkish, Buğra and Savaşkan (2010).
6. We have here a perfect example of a conspiracy theory that isolates a certain aspect of concrete reality to make it the basis of an outlandish "grand theory." In this case, because the United States has pursued an accomodationist policy vis-à-vis moderate Islam, not only in the case of the AKP but, after the Arab revolutions, in other countries such as Egypt and Tunisia as well, it has been deduced from this fact that the United States is "redesigning" the Middle East and North Africa particularly along Islamist lines so as to destroy the Turkish republic or republicanism in general. But many of the commentators who advance this "grand theory" do admit that whatever support the United States extends to moderate Islam is really meant to avert the rise of a more radical fundamentalism, which should immediately make it clear that the United States is "redesigning" nothing but instead responding to a difficult situation and, more importantly, that it is trying to protect its client states from falling under the sway of Islamic regimes and, hence, is protecting republicanism, that is, pro-Western regimes, under difficult circumstances.
7. For a discussion of the contradictions this creates in the AKP, see Yılmaz (2004).
8. The classic account of this process of secular onslaught against the domination of religion can be found in Lewis (2002) and Berkes (1998), both sources marred, in my opinion, by their theoretical premises informed by modernization theory.

9. For the extremely controversial issue of bourgeois revolution in Turkey, I cannot but refer the reader to my own work in Turkish (Savran 2011b), where I lay out not only my own view, but the major contending schools of thought as well. For a summary of my views in English, see my article written under a pseudonym during the military dictatorship in the early 1980s (Taylan 1984). For a somewhat different viewpoint, one should consult the classic source in English on Turkish development in the modern era (Keyder 1987).

10. The figure in Turkish lira is over five billion (Koşar2013). With the recent slide in the Turkish lira, this is now equivalent to around two and a half billion US dollars.

11. Hence, to see "cultural explanations that regard political Islam as a protest movement against Western colonial domination [as] inappropriate in the Turkish case" because "Turkey was never subjected to colonial domination" (Eligür 2010: 7) implies a flight into a half truth. The Turkish bourgeoisie did avert colonization in the aftermath of World War I, but at the expense of a quite peculiar process that one may call, for lack of a better term, "self-colonization," that is, the new state treating its own people and its own culture like those of a colony. Thus, Eligür's further remark that "[t]he Turkish Revolution… was a successful struggle to forestall Western imperialism and domination" (2010: 7) is true in its first aspect, "imperialism," but not in its second, "domination." All this is important because Eligür represents an outlook, informed by Kemalist mythology, that prevents one from seeing the extent of the reaction to this radical "self-colonization" within the ranks of the common people.

12. The young republic had abolished the precapitalist tithe (*ashar*) in 1925, but new taxes were imposed on the peasantry soon after the fallout from the Great Depression reached Turkey in 1929 (Gürel 2008: 87).

13. If out of a multitude of different aspects of this I choose these two, that is because these are organizational forms that bring believers together. Hence, they are forms of power seeking. It is true that many religious orders and communities, starting with that of Fethullah Gülen (of whom more later), have gained immense de facto strength in recent decades, but I do not think that the legal prohibition is without its importance. Witness the fact that the leader of the strongest of these religious groups, the self-same Gülen, has been forced to live in exile in the United States since 1999.

14. Sarıbay (2004: 584) points out that one of the major motives for the participation of the MSP in various coalition governments in the 1990s was a quest for legitimacy.

15. Eligür (2010) quite correctly emphasizes this point.

16. The concept M. Hakan Yavuz employs to indicate this aspect of the National Vision movement is "green Kemalism" (2004: 600).

17. A fourth founding personality, Abdüllatif Şener, later fell out with the rest of the leadership and abandoned the AKP in 2007 to form his own party in 2009, which, however, has remained a marginal force.

18. Erbakan's only visit to the United States in 1994, upon the invitation of US Muslims, was a failure regarding his talks with mid-level US officials (Çakır 2004: 570).

19. It is significant that the other parties that did well were also either new or had no responsibility in the making of the crisis in a certain sense. A makeshift party that was hastily put together, out of self-interest, by a young and handsome capitalist (called the Young Party) received more than 7 percent of the vote. And of the two parties on the center left, while the one in power, that led by Ecevit, received 1 percent of the vote, as opposed to 21 percent in the previous elections, it was the other, which had failed to get any members of parliament elected in the previous elections, that was able to get in, simply because in the eyes of the electorate it bore no responsibility in bringing about the crisis.

20. I have shown this with mathematical precision in Savran (2011a).

21. I analyzed the differences in the new situation relative to what had happened in the 1990s very early on in an article that characterized the impending struggle as the "civil war of the bourgeoisie" (Savran 2003).

22. With customary exaggeration, M. Hakan Yavuz cites clearly inflated figures to emphasize the strength of the Gülen movement (2004: 11). It is interesting to note that his source is a newspaper column by another adept of the Gülen community.
23. For a detailed study of the thinking of Fethullah Gülen, strictly partisan but informed, see Ergil (2010).
24. For an article that explores at greater length this group of intellectuals, written before the AKP came to power, see Erdoğan and Üstüner (2002).

References

Aydın, Ertan, and İbrahim Dalmış. 2008, "The Social Bases of the Justice and Development Party." In *Secular and Islamic Politics in Turkey*, ed. Ümit Cizre, 201–22. New York: Routledge.
Balkan, Erol, and Erinç Yeldan. 2002. "Peripheral Development under Financial Liberalization: The Turkish Experience." In *The Ravages of Neo-Liberalism*, ed. Neşecan Balkan and Sungur Savran, 39–54. New York: Nova Science Publishers.
Berkes, Niyazi. 1998. *The Development of Secularism in Turkey*. New York: Routledge.
Bila, Fikret. 2007. *Sivil Darbe Girişimi ve Ankara'da Irak Savaşları* [Attempted civilian coup and Iraq wars in Ankara]. Istanbul: Güncel Yayıncılık.
Buğra, Ayşe, and Osman Savaşkan. 2010. "Yerel Sanayi ve Bugünün Türkiyesi'nde İş Dünyası" [Local industry and the business world in present-day Turkey]. *Toplum ve Bilim*, no. 118: 92–123.
Çakır, Ruşen. 2004. "Milli Görüş Hareketi" [The National Vision movement]. In *Modern Türkiye'de Siyasî Düşünce* [Political thought in modern Turkey], vol. 6, *İslamcılık* [Islamism], ed. Yasin Aktay, Murat Gültekingil, and Tanıl Bora, 544–75. Istanbul: İletişim.
Çalmuk, Fehmi. 2004. "Necmettin Erbakan." In Aktay, Gültekingil, and Bora, *İslamcılık*, 550–67.
Çetinkaya, Hikmet. 2010. *Fethullah Gülen'in 40 Yıllık Serüveni* [The 40-year adventure of Fethullah Gülen]. Istanbul: Cumhuriyet Kitapları.
Eligür, Banu. 2010. *The Mobilization of Political Islam in Turkey*. Cambridge: Cambridge University Press.
Erdoğan, Necmi, and Fahriye Üstüner. 2002. "Quest for Hegemony: Discourses on Democracy." In *The Politics of Permanent Crisis*, ed. Neşecan Balkan and Sungur Savran, 195–213. New York: Nova Science Publishers.
Ergil, Doğu. 2010. *100 Soruda Fethullah Gülen ve Hareketi* [Fethullah Gülen and his movement in 100 questions]. Istanbul: Timaş.
Gürel, Burak. 2008. "Türkiye'de Kırda Sınıf Mücadelelerinin Tarihsel Gelişimi" [Historical development of class struggles in rural Turkey]. *Devrimci Marksizm*, nos. 6–7 (Spring/Summer): 71–104.
Keyder, Çağlar. 1987. *State and Class in Turkey: A Study in Capitalist Development*. London: Verso.
Koşar, Arif. 2013. "8 bakanlık bir Diyanet etmedi." [Diyanet's budget larger than eight ministries combined] *Evrensel*, 11 June. Accessed 23 June 2013. http://www.evrensel.net/haber/71458/8-bakanlik-bir-diyanet-etmedi.html.
Lewis, Bernard. 2002. *The Emergence of Modern Turkey*. Oxford: Oxford University Press.
Mardin, Şerif. 1973. "Center-Periphery Relations: A Key to Turkish Politics?" *Daedalus* 102, no. 1: 169–90.

Morton, Adam David. 2011. "Sosyolojik Marksizmin Sınırları?" [The limits of sociological Marxism?]. *Praksis*, no. 27: 9–40.

Öcal, Mustafa. 1986. "İlahiyat Fakültelerinin Tarihçesi" [The history of schools of theology]. *Uludağ Üniversitesi İlahiyat Fakültesi* 1, no. 1: 73–102.

Rabasa, Angel, and Stephen Larrabee. 2008. *The Rise of Political Islam in Turkey*. Santa Monica, CA: Rand Corporation.

Sarıbay, Ali Yaşar. 2004. "Milli Nizam Partisi'nin Kuruluşu ve Programının İçeriği" [The foundation of the National Order Party and the content of its program]. In Aktay, Gültekingil, and Bora, *İslamcılık*, 576–90.

Savran, Sungur. 2002. "The Legacy of the Twentieth Century." In Balkan and Savran, *The Politics of Permanent Crisis*, 1–20.

_____. 2003. "29 Şubat" [29 February]. *İşçi Mücadelesi*, old series, no. 7 (June–July): 9–19.

_____. 2011a. "Barajlar Sultanı" [Sultan of the Thresholds]. *Gerçek*, 18 June. Accessed 17 August 2013. http://gercekgazetesi.net/secim-2011/barajlar-sultani.

_____. 2011b. *Türkiye'de Sınıf Mücadeleleri* [Class struggles in Turkey]. 3rd ed. Istanbul: Yordam Kitap.

_____. 2013a. "C'est une révolte, pas (encore) une révolution." *The Bullet*, no. 834 (5 June). Accessed 17 August 2013. http://www.socialistproject.ca/bullet/834.php.

_____. 2013b. "The Future of the Revolt and the Fate of Turkey's Strong Man." *New Left Project*, 27 June. Accessed 17 August 2013. http://www.newleftproject.org/index.php/site/article_comments/the_future_of_the_revolt_and_the_fate_of_turkeys_strong_man.

_____. 2013c. "Gezi Park Evacuated, Istanbul and Turkey Explode." *The Bullet*, no. 837 (16 June). Accessed 17 August 2013. http://www.socialistproject.ca/bullet/837.php.

_____. 2013d. "A Taste of Tahrir at Taksim." *The Bullet*, no. 831 (1 June). Accessed 17 August 2013. http://www.socialistproject.ca/bullet/831.php.

Senem, Nusret. 2011. *Emniyet'in Işık Evleri Raporu* [The "Işık Evleri" report of the police administration]. Istanbul: Kaynak Yayınları.

Şener, Nedim. 2010. *Ergenekon Belgelerinde Fethullah Gülen ve Cemaat* [Fethullah Gülen and the community in the Ergenekon documents]. Istanbul: Destek Yayınları.

Taylan, Turgut. 1984. "Capital and the State in Contemporary Turkey." *Khamsin*, no. 11: 5–46.

Tuğal, Cihan. 2009. *Passive Revolution: Absorbing the Islamic Challenge to Capitalism*. Palo Alto, CA: Stanford University Press.

_____. 2011. "Pasif Devrimlerde Toplum, Siyaset ve Bloklar" [Society, politics, and blocs in passive revolutions]. *Praksis*, no. 27: 41–54.

Yalçın, Soner. 2012. *Erbakan*. 2nd ed. Istanbul: Kırmızı Kedi.

Yalman, Galip. 2002. "The Turkish State and Bourgeoisie in Historical Perspective: A Relativist Paradigm or a Panoply of Hegemonic Strategies?" In Balkan and Savran, *The Politics of Permanent Crisis*, 21–54.

_____. 2009. *Transition to Neoliberalism: The Case of Turkey in the 1980s*. Istanbul: Istanbul Bilgi University Press.

Yanardağ, Merdan. 2007. *Operasyon Partisi* [An operation party]. Istanbul: Destek Yayınevi.

Yavuz, M. Hakan. 2004. "Milli Görüş Hareketi: Muhalif ve Modernist Gelenek" [The National Vision movement: A dissident and modernist tradition]. In Aktay, Gültekingil, and Bora, *İslamcılık*, 591–603.

Yılmaz, Nuh. 2004. "İslâmcılık, AKP, Siyaset" [Islamism, AKP, Politics]. In Aktay, Gültekingil, and Bora, *İslamcılık*, 604–619.

Zürcher, E.J., and H. van der Linden. 2004. "Searching for the Fault-Line." In Netherlands Scientific Council for Government Policy, *The European Union, Turkey, and Islam*, 83–173. Amsterdam: Amsterdam University Press.

– Chapter 3 –

THE DEEP FRACTURE IN
THE BIG BOURGEOISIE OF TURKEY

Kurtar Tanyılmaz

Introduction

In 2010, one of the leading newspapers in the United States, the *Wall Street Journal*, published a story about the political conditions in Turkey and the arrests that had taken place in the country that year. Defining Turkey as a "Muslim country on Europe's periphery," the article characterized the struggle between secularists and the Islamist-leaning government as a "bloodless civil war" and urged the two sides to reach a peaceful compromise, claiming that "the police, gendarme and even the intelligence services are fighting amongst each other" (quoted in Yıldırımkaya, 2010). In the same year, seventy companies representing two different fractions of Islamist capital, Müstakil Sanayici ve İşadamları Derneği (Independent Industrialists' and Businessmen's Association, MÜSİAD) and Turkish Confederation of Businessmen and Industrialists (Türkiye İşadamları ve Sanayicileri Konfederasyonu, TUSKON), were ranked among a list compiled by the Istanbul Chamber of Industry (İstanbul Sanayi Odası, İSO) of the five hundred largest industrial companies in Turkey. The domestic press reported this development as indicating a "conservative ascendency." Taken together with the long-running debates about the changing orientation of Turkish foreign policy from Western countries to countries of the Middle East region, the constitutional referendum, and related matters, we can see evidence of an increasing polarization taking place in Turkish society. The public tension between the Erdoğan administration and Türkiye Sanayici ve İşadamları Derneği (Turkish Industrialists' and Businessmen's Association, TÜSİAD) during the constitutional referendum process represented a new milestone in this conflict. In response to TÜSİAD's ambiguous stance on the referendum Erdoğan threatened that "those who don't take a side will be eliminated" (2010a). Targeting what he called "Istanbul capital," Erdoğan made explicit the fissure among the Turkish bourgeoisie, claiming that "from the beginning, Istanbul capital worked with us when it came to making money, but for some reason we couldn't reach an agreement when it came to politics. They excluded Anatolian capital... But whether they like it or not, Turkish capital is changing hands in a serious way... For us, this is a very important source of confidence" (2010b).

The question of whether or not a certain segment of the small- and medium-scale enterprises in Anatolia have assumed the character-istics of monopoly capital in an Islamist guise since the 1980s and have increasingly proven to be a formidable economic force vis-à-vis the previously dominant Western-secular-oriented capital frac-tion underlines the terms of the "civil war" among the Turkish ruling classes. If, as it is argued, owing to their relative strength and size, the "Anatolian Tigers" represent "local" and "democratic" forces in con-trast to the "monopolistic" and "statist" bourgeoisie, then this newly rising capital fraction will ultimately become subsumed under the hegemonic capital bloc, albeit sometimes through conflictual means, and, other times through cooperative means. If this is the case, then the tensions between the Adalet ve Kalkınma Partisi (Justice and Development Party, AKP) government, the army, and the state bu-reaucracy have much more to do with political rather than economic differences. If, on the other hand, this new fraction reflects a type of Islamist capital that has already achieved monopoly status, and if the AKP is understood as the political representative of this newly em-powered economic class, then we should expect the AKP to engage in political struggles not on behalf of the Turkish bourgeoisie as a whole, but on behalf of this particular segment.

Demonstrating that what lies behind the struggle between the army and the AKP is not simply a "superstructural" problem of the republican regime or republican cultural values, but rather a struggle over the economic interests of particular class fractions, is of critical importance in developing an independent working-class politics in the face of changing labor-capital relations in Turkey. The aim of this chapter is to show that the objective bases of the polarization within the bourgeoisie and the contemporary contradictions in Turkish capi-talism, often portrayed in the language of "us and them," are not simply superstructural but are rooted in a qualitative transformation in the structure of the capitalist class in Turkey.

To this end, I will first provide an overview of the various conflicts taking place among the two capitalist fractions and the ways in which these processes have been analyzed. In the third section, I will show that the class basis of this differentiation is rooted in the separation of political and economic interests (markets, incentives, technology transfers, etc., and the political means by which changes in these domains are realized). In the fourth section, I compare the economic strength and effects of the Western-secular bourgeoisie (as represented by TÜSİAD) and the Islamist bourgeoisie (as represented by MÜSİAD, TUSKON and Anadolu Sanayicileri Konfederasyonu, Association of Anatolian Businessmen, ASKON), in order to ascertain whether or not a monopolist, Islamist capital is the economic force behind the political ascendancy of the AKP. To conclude I will summarize some of the main findings of this chapter.

At the outset it will be useful to provide some conceptual clarification. The different parties involved in this conflict between the capitalist classes are referred to by a variety of names. Terms such as "Anatolian Tigers," "entrepreneurial middle class," and "authentic bourgeoisie," vis-à-vis the "Kemalist bourgeoisie," "Istanbul capital," and "Bosphorus bourgeoisie" are generally employed by liberal and left-liberal groups. In contrast, nationalist left-wing groups prefer terms such as "sectarian capital," "green capital," and "partisan capital" versus "secular capital," and "national capital." I believe that such terms are not accurate. These definitions, while abetting ideological, cultural, and political divisions, ultimately serve to conceal a rupture within the ruling class over the (political) conditions under which capital accumulation should be pursued. Accordingly, throughout this chapter I utilize the terms "Western-secular bourgeoisie" and "Islamist bourgeoisie" since they more accurately reflect the material division under consideration.

A Concrete View of the Deep Schism at the Heart of the Turkish Bourgeoisie: The "Us and Them" Distinction

I indicated earlier that the conflict among different capitalist segments in the last ten years has taken place not only at the political level, but also at the economic level. I shall try to illustrate how this conflict has been experienced by way of a few notable examples.

The first example comes from the clashes experienced in the institutionalization of the export-oriented sector. TÜSİAD demanded that
the Turkish Exporters' Assembly (Türkiye İhracatçılar Meclisi, TİM)
be dissolved, since it is essentially an organization in which competitors of TÜSİAD are most active. A journalist provided the following
account of the background of this conflict (Özkan 2010):

> There had been complaints and people who had recounted personal
> experiences in informal conversations but the "war of capital" was first made
> explicit in a meeting attended by the Russian leader [Dmitry] Medvedev.
> Turkey and Russia set a goal of increasing bilateral trade to one hundred billion
> dollars in five years and there were talks of a nuclear power station, a very
> historic moment for Turkey. Behind the curtain there was an organizational
> battle taking place. Up until very recently Foreign Economic Relations Board
> (Dış Ekonomik İlişkiler Kurulu, DEİK) had played a leading role in hosting
> foreign economic delegations. As is evident by its name, DEİK is the primary
> organization in bilateral economic relations. In the meeting attended by
> Medvedev there were three names displayed on the wall behind the speaker's
> podium: TOBB, TİM, and TUSKON. TOBB, the Union of Chambers and
> Commodity Exchanges of Turkey, is an organization that every member of
> the business world is required to join. DEİK is more or less a subsidiary of
> TOBB. TİM is the Assembly of Exporters. And TUSKON is, as the saying goes,
> the organization established by "the man in Pennsylvania" [Fetullah Gülen].
> Like TÜSİAD and MÜSİAD, membership in TUSKON is voluntary and it is an
> organization that looks after its members' interests. How is it that TUSKON,
> by the directive of the undersecretary for foreign trade, is elevated to the status
> of partner with the organizing members of the conference attended by the
> Russian leader Medvedev? Moreover, how is it that DEİK's logo is prevented
> from being displayed in the meeting room? Apparently DEİK's logo was
> added at the last minute after a series of frantic phone calls right before the
> leaders entered the room. It's also said that the undersecretary of foreign
> trade doesn't make independent decisions. In the final analysis, it's the policy
> of Zafer Çağlayan, the minister of foreign trade. A former president of the
> Ankara Chamber of Industry, Zafer Çağlayan keeps his distance from DEİK
> and TOBB. It's rumored that this distance is actually the result of his adverse
> relationship with TOBB president Rıfat Hisarcıklıoğlu. And of course, at the
> government level, a favorable environment has been created for TUSKON
> that enables it to act freely. Government officials are rumored to say, "Up
> until now, DEİK was the only game in town, it should share its authority from
> now on." And the TUSKON circles like to emphasize that they are "strong,"
> and demand the "right to speak" in countries where they are active. We've
> heard a lot of grumbling along the lines of, "I can't get a municipal contract
> because I'm not close to the AKP" or, "Their partisans win all the contracts."

The second example is the well publicized stand-off between
Prime Minister Erdoğan and the Doğan Group, one of the prominent

monopoly capitals in Turkey. This stand-off has resulted in the airing of dirty laundry on both sides. A journalist explains the conflict of interest that is at the root of this fight as follows:

As you know, Aydın Doğan's Petrol Ofisi (Petroleum Office, Corp.) has a foreign partner. It's an Austrian petrol company called OMV. Aydın Doğan bought a 50 per cent stake in Petrol Ofisi from İş Bankası (İş Bank) for five hundred million dollars and then sold a 34 per cent stake to this Austrian company for one billion euros. OMV and Aydın Doğan have been partners for about three years now and are looking for joint investment opportunities in Turkey together. Among these investments is an oil refinery in the city of Ceyhan. However, Petrol Ofisi has been unable to secure the necessary license to build the refinery. They've tried for years. The Çalık Group[1] was granted a license, but Aydın Doğan's Petrol Ofisi was not. Aydın Doğan has given up hope of obtaining this license, in spite of whatever position his media conglomerate takes toward the government, be it moderately critical or supportive. Knowing the government's weakness vis-à-vis foreign capital, OMV intervened. Their CEO, Wolfgang Ruttenstorfer came to Turkey and met with Prime Minister Erdoğan. He told the prime minister that they "had planned on making a multi-billion dollar investment in Turkey but that they were unable to secure a license for the refinery and had gotten stymied by the bureaucracy." He added that "this was a big loss for Turkey." Erdoğan answered the Austrian CEO curtly. He told him: "You're working with the wrong people in Turkey. As long as you work with Doğan, you'll never be granted permission for any type of investment. Don't even dream about getting the license for the refinery." He went as far as to suggest that the CEO of OMV forge a new partnership with the Çalık Group, since they already received a license for the refinery. Ruttenstorfer was shocked by what he had heard. He came back to Istanbul and recounted the details of his meeting to Aydın Doğan and told him: "Forget about new investments in Turkey with this administration. In fact, you should forget about doing business in Turkey altogether. I saw the look in the prime minister's eyes when he was talking about you. I wouldn't even recommend that you live in Turkey when this government is in charge.[2]

The third example is a fight that took place during the election process of the two largest capitalist organizations that direct the Turkish economy. In 2009 both the Istanbul Chamber of Industry (İSO) and the Istanbul Chamber of Commerce (İstanbul Ticaret Odası, İTO) held elections that resulted in a shuffling of their board of directors with no change in their respective presidencies. Whereas MÜSİAD's influence grew within the İTO, members of TÜSİAD gained a stronger position in the İSO (*Milliyet* 2009). The board of directors of the İTO added six MÜSİAD members, one TUSKON and one TUMSİAD (Association for All Industrialists and Businessmen) member, and three ASKON members. A newspaper article preceding the election suggested that members of MÜSİAD, TUSKON and

ASKON had formed a "triple alliance against the leadership of the İSO" and indicated support for MÜSİAD member Hasan Büyükdede against the current chamber leadership.

> It is important to highlight the tension that these disputes created among the traditional (big) bourgeoisie. Ayça Dinçkök, a member of the board of directors of Akkök Holding, who served on TÜSİAD's board of directors for five years expressed her frustration with the government's approach to TÜSİAD in an interview with the business magazine *Capital* as follows: "Sometimes there are meetings where TÜSİAD is not invited. Why are they excluded when other associations and civil society organizations aren't? How is such discrimination possible? As a businesswoman this situation makes me uncomfortable. They've created a division between "us" and "them." How do you separate them from us? (*Milliyet* 2010b)

Journalist Serpil Yılmaz recounts the friction experienced during a closed-door meeting of the High Advisory Council of TÜSİAD in 2009 as follows:

> Arzuhan Doğan Yalçındağ, the president of TÜSİAD's board of directors, spoke first. Yalçındağ, who is also a shareholder and chairwoman of the Doğan Group, said, "As you know, I do not dwell on the unjust tax penalties imposed upon the Doğan Group in my speeches as the president of TÜSİAD because this is a private issue related to my business. But you are all overly cautious about this matter. You should acknowledge that this is a problem for all of Turkey. You give the impression that 'we are all silent together'." After her speech, Ali Koç, a member of the board of directors of Koç Holding, took the podium. His words implied that the dispute could harden: "Arzuhan is right. We've been too quiet on this [tax] matter. We should have lent our support. We're losing our influence as TÜSİAD. We need to bang our fist on the table when it's necessary to do so. I don't approve of the way things have been managed by TÜSİAD. We're starting to be perceived as even weaker than MÜSİAD. They are being taken much more seriously than we are." (Yılmaz 2009)

There is no need to dwell on these examples, which are important to the extent that they highlight the scope of the ongoing struggle. The real question is whether or not these tensions should be understood in terms of tactical maneuverings and political differences between the AKP government and the big bourgeoisie, as represented by TÜSİAD or if the AKP represents one side in the underlying material and economic struggle. To put it more explicitly: what is the material foundation of the division of the Turkish bourgeoisie into two competing camps? Before we answer this question, let us first review a few different approaches to this "conservative ascendency."

The Embourgeoisement of the Islamists and the Islamization of the Bourgeoisie: A Dispute over Lifestyle?

Among liberal and left-leaning liberal circles, these developments (the ascendancy of a new capital fraction and its confrontation with the dominant capital fraction) are usually read as the rise of a non-monopolistic, entrepreneurial middle class. It is argued that the ascendancy of a more competitive, more democratic, non-monopolistic, export-oriented "new middle class" that is independent of the state reflects the march of the previously excluded from the periphery to the center. The notion that the AKP, as the political representative of this ascendancy, has had a positive effect on the democratization process is widely accepted.

In his assessment of the first AKP victory in the elections of 3 November, 2002, Professor Erol Katırcıoğlu (*Radikal*, 2002) asks:

> Does the 3 November election indicate that the historical consensus between the private sector and the state, which grew out of the need to create a "domestic national bourgeoisie", has ended? What I'm referring to is, in fact, a story about a world of SMEs[3] that were hitherto excluded from the prime minister's foreign junkets, that were prosecuted as "green capital," that were forced to stand in line in front of the big banks in large cities in order to procure a measly amount of credit, whose offers to collaborate in joint ventures with TÜSİAD were rejected time and time again by a MONOPOLIST and STATIST capital, for whom the doors of government were always open, who hobnobbed with the prime minister on his private plane, and who easily got whatever laws they needed passed. And this conflict is now being resolved in favor of the SMEs.

Professor Ahmet Insel (2010) provides a similar analysis:

> The development of Turkey, the strengthening of capital, and the emergence of newcomers is a very natural occurrence in the process of societal change. Of course we've seen the ascendancy of Anatolian capital over the last twenty to thirty years. When we look at this from the perspective of national development, the expansion of capital outside of what is held by the classic bourgeoisie in the large cities is a necessary development. Otherwise it demonstrates that we are nostalgic for a monopolistic capital. It's also very clear that Anatolian capital has emerged from a conservative cultural milieu. Those who speak about how capital is changing hands believe in a market economy and accept the fact that capitalism is a superior economic system. They should know that in a market system, capital is not static. It doesn't remain with the same people. If they accept competition, they need to accept this fact, too.

The journalist Oral Çalışlar (2010) suggests that the "Anatolian bourgeoisie" is not very powerful, and that the conflict in question is really between the big bourgeoisie and the implementation of AKP policy:

> We can identify the foundation of this conflict as the "breakdown of the relationship between the traditional government and the big bourgeoisie". The Istanbul bourgeoisie used to win the lion's share of government contracts and projects. They were unrivaled in this regard. Each successive administration saw itself as responsible for granting them these privileges. The fact that the AKP has taken a different attitude toward this matter has generated a lot of discomfort and discontent among the Istanbul bourgeoisie. Whatever might be said about the AKP's policies, it is not very difficult to see that there has been a tremendous shift in the balance of the Turkish bourgeoisie (and in the distribution of state resources). That the Istanbul bourgeoisie has managed to continue to grow steadily over the last eight years is another aspect of the issue.

Among the nationalist left, these developments are understood as the result of a politics of "Islamization" pursued by an "authoritarian" AKP government, which coincides with the imperialist "moderate Islam" project spearheaded by the United States. To put it differently, the conflict is read as occurring not between an Anatolian and an Istanbul bourgeoisie, but as a struggle between "religious reactionism" and secularism, whose primary fault lines are political. At the root of the conflict are questions over nepotistic political appointments and debates over whether the administration is dragging the country towards authoritarian rule. Professor Emre Kongar (2005) provides a good example of this point of view:

> Turkey, a country that has more or less completed the process of class stratification, is now feeling the effects of a system of religious education and urban plunder that has been in place since the transition to a multi-party democracy. These effects include the electoral victory of a party that "takes religion as its reference." Utilizing the organs of the state (or more precisely, the organs of government and local administration), this party is now trying to "Islamize" the capitalist class that was fostered by the state during the republican period. Despite its paeans to "free competition", it has pursued every kind of "unfair competition" by extending loans, contracts, credits, subsidies and other forms of government support to those with "Islamic" characteristics. This has led to the embourgeoisement of the "Islamists" and the "Islamization" of the bourgeoisie. The embourgeoisement of the Islamists is not necessarily a bad thing, but if the bourgeoisie is becoming "Islamized" then this is clearly a direct "threat to the regime."

Mustafa Sönmez, who has written about these matters for a long time from the nationalist left perspective, cautions against exaggerating the power of Islamist capital and argues that the conflict is conjectural (2008b):

> The thesis that the AKP has been able to create its own organic capitalists who are allied to the project of creating an Islamic society and that this group has rapidly gained economic power vis-à-vis the "others", particularly TÜSİAD, is an overstatement and grants the "AKP bourgeoisie" much more power than they actually have. The power still belongs to big capital, to TÜSİAD. The AKP did not come to power in spite of TÜSİAD. It won the 2003 elections with the support of those who had been negatively affected by the 2001 economic crisis and who wanted to "try the untried." In 2007 they benefited from the positive conjuncture in the world economy and by putting the winds of TÜSİAD in their sails. But when the AKP played their "nationalist movement"[4] hand, racketed up the tension, and began faltering in the economy, the "holy alliance" was shattered and will swiftly unravel as the crisis deepens.

In short, the fraction that is termed "Anatolian capital" and is understood as the foundation of the AKP's power is an exaggeration, a myth. The presumed conflict between this fraction and TÜSİAD is an overstatement. The two sides are by no means evenly matched.

Where these two perspectives (the liberal/liberal left and the nationalist left) diverge is over the question of whether or not Islamist capital has had a positive or negative effect on free competition and democratization. They both agree that the tensions and conflicts experienced between the AKP and big capital is driven by political and/or cultural-ideological factors and can be explained as a "lifestyle" matter. The problem is framed as a question of how compatible the city-bound rural "entrepreneurial middle class" will be with the republican project of modernization. In order to assess the perspectives that address the internal clash among the bourgeoisie, I will now turn to the material foundations of the rise of Islamist capital and the ensuing polarization.

When the Dream of Becoming a "Regional Power" Backfired on the Turkish Bourgeoisie

At this point let us pose two questions:

1. Is there a difference in perspective, a divergence among the two capital fractions about the conditions under which capital accumulation and

exploitation should take place and the appropriate policies required to achieve these goals?

2. As a result of the aforementioned developments, has Islamist capital assumed a magnitude that could appropriately be termed "finance capital" vis-à-vis the Western-oriented, secular capital that favors integration into the world economy?

Both questions are of critical importance if we wish to understand why the AKP is experiencing tension with a segment of Turkish capital while simultaneously pursuing policies that favor big capital. If the answer to both questions is "no," then we can assume that the strain between the AKP government, TÜSİAD, Turkish Armed Forces (TSK) and the bureaucracy is largely the result of political and ideological factors. In light of certain historical developments, however, I believe that the answer to both questions is "yes." In what follows I will attempt to provide some evidence for this claim.

Schengen or Şamgen?

> If Turgut Özal hadn't deliberately promoted the "organized industrial zones," if currency convertibility and membership in the Customs Union hadn't occurred, could Calvin himself been able to create the "Anatolian Tigers?"
> —Mehmet Barlas, "Olayın Sırrı Calvin'de mi Gizli?"[5]

The first question has to do with whether there are deep-rooted differences between the two capital fractions over the conditions under which capital accumulation should take place and how integration with global capitalism should be pursued. This question can only be answered by considering the internal struggles in the development of Turkish capitalism and the historical dynamics involved in the formation of the Turkish bourgeoisie.

Since its foundation, the Turkish republic has been strategically oriented toward integration with Western imperialism. The Western orientation of the dominant fraction of the big bourgeoisie, as represented by TÜSİAD and its circles, is a product of the need to articulate the interests of international capital and Western imperialism. From the 1950s onward the new capital fraction that emerged predominantly in Anatolia but also in Istanbul kept their distance from the West and provided the economic and social base for political Islam. In the period following the military coup of 12 September 1980, this fraction saw an opportunity to conglomerate and evolve as a part of finance capital. The political and economic conflicts between the late-comers, the Anatolian bourgeoisie, and the big bourgeoisie, as symbolized by TÜSİAD, quickly assumed the dimensions of a political civil war.[6]

The factors that led to the strengthening of Islamist capital after 12 September 1980 can be summarized as follows:

- Imperialist policies aimed at wiping out leftist and working-class movements by lending support to anti-revolutionary organizations in what was termed a "Green Belt" strategy in the 1980s.
- The increasing importance granted to the Middle East and Central Asia in the imperialist sphere of influence following the collapse of the bureaucratic workers' states in the 1990s ("The Greater Middle East Initiative").
- The political alignment of the ruling class, which, following the military coup in 1980, cleared the path for, turned a blind eye toward, or protected religious-based political movements as a counterweight to the revival of working-class movements in what was referred to as the "Turkish-Islamic synthesis."
- An export-oriented strategy of capital accumulation pursued by the ruling class and an increase in trade and investment with Eurasian and Middle Eastern countries in an effort to enhance Turkey's strategic interests and position it as a "regional power."
- Efforts to attract capital from both conservative Turks living abroad and from the Arab and Gulf states, which began during the Özal administration (particularly through the activities of Islamic financial enterprises under the rubric of interest-free banking, which helped foster the aforementioned finance capital fraction, played a critical role in attracting Arab capital and in the development of religious and sectarian enterprises).
- The implementation of neo-liberal policies aimed at disciplining the working class (such as the adoption of "flexible production" methods in SMEs located in the organized industrial zones of large Anatolian cities such as Konya and Kayseri, in which religious or cultural values and bonds were harnessed for the purposes of capital accumulation and the exploitation of labor).
- The opening of municipal services to segments of Islamist capital during the process of privatization of local administrative activities.

These processes benefited not simply Islamist capital, but the big bourgeoisie of Turkey as well. However, attempts to unite the Western-secular bourgeoisie with the Islamist capital that was widespread in Anatolia and under the control and domination of the former during the Özal-ANAP (Anavatan Partisi, Motherland Party) period threatened the TÜSİAD bourgeoisie, the hegemonic capital fraction in Turkey. The following factors played an important role in the ascendency of Islamist capital and in shaping the threat it posed to the Western-secular bourgeoisie (Doğan 2006):

- The creation of new financial opportunities for Islamist circles through activities pursued by religious associations and foundations such as the construction of new mosques and the establishment of new schools, private universities, tutoring centers and dormitories combined with what could be considered traditional socio-cultural practices such as giving alms to the poor.
- The rapid growth in membership in Islamist capital organizations, notably MÜSİAD, but also TUSKON, Business Life Cooperation Association (İşhayatı Dayanışma Derneği, İŞHAD), ASKON, etc. and the development of socio-cultural networks and a certain manner of conducting business that provide the foundation of the Islamic sub-economy – not simply domestically, but internationally through groups connected to Fethullah Gülen that operate in the Middle East, Africa, and even Australia – and have created new centers for capital.[7] The Islamic sub-economy, which operates outside of the traditional credit/loan system of the classic money-market has grown and fostered the creation of large companies, groups and holdings.[8]
- Periodic statements by Islamist capital about the developmental model allegedly employed by countries in the Far East like South Korea and Malaysia, which display a dismissive attitude toward the relationships developed by the big capitalists of Turkey with US and EU capital, and suggest that Turkey should face East rather than West in its future developmental trajectory.
- The discontent felt among dominant capital circles by the capital accumulation methods employed by certain constituents of Islamist capital (holdings such as Kombassan, Yimpaş, and İttifak), and the growth of these Islamist holdings to the point where they are able to claim a slice of the privatization pie (as seen with Kombassan Holding's winning of the PETLAS[9] contract).[10]

In sum, the strategy pursued by capital to renew itself in response to the crisis experienced by the Turkish ruling class in the 1970s has resulted in a qualitative transformation in the internal structure of the capitalist class, while serving as an obstacle to its own development because of the contradictions at the heart of this developmental strategy. The AKP government did not initiate this process of "crony capitalism," but it has been able to benefit from the contradictions of this process as the representative of a growing capital fraction.

With reference to the historical factors that have played a role in the ascendancy of Islamist capital or the ways in which it has become a threat to the Western-secular bourgeoisie, we can determine that the division between the Western-secular wing and the Islamist wing of the Turkish bourgeoisie has occurred along three dimensions:

1. An economic struggle over who can obtain a greater share of the total surplus value generated.

2. A political struggle over what place the bourgeoisie will have in the new world order and a struggle over *priorities* in its relations with the imperialist West and the Islamic world during the process of economic integration.
3. An ideological struggle over lifestyle questions and secular, Western, or Islamic values.

Taking these factors seriously shows us that the struggle cannot be explained solely in cultural or ideological terms. The division is principally about economic interests and political preferences. To elaborate, in contemporary capitalism, the role of the state in the economy has both decreased in some areas and increased in others according to the requirements of capital accumulation. The principal means through which the state facilitates the transfer of wealth or the transfer of existing public sector resources to the private sector in order to integrate national/local capital with the global market and create the conditions for profitable investment are as follows: (1) large-scale bids for public services opened at the national level; (2) bids at the local administrative level (municipal services, infrastructural investments, Housing Development Administration of Turkey, Toplu Konut İdaresi Başkanlığı, TOKİ,[11] etc.); (3) credits issued through public banks; (4) privatization; and (5) public facilities transferred to the private sector for management. When we add to this list the creation of market opportunities, supplying cheap inputs, and public/private joint ventures, all of which are critical for international competitiveness, we can see why there is a cut-throat struggle between the two capital fractions over who can claim a larger share of the surplus value generated by the state's distribution channels.

Certain barriers exist for Islamic capital to enter the world market and develop relations with the West, in short, to integrate with the imperialist world. Particularly in light of the strategic advantages and priorities accorded to the Western-secular bourgeoisie in its relations with the West during its historical development, the ability to gain access to state resources and to shape economic and political policy according to its own capital accumulation requirements is of critical importance for the capital fraction that is coming up from behind. The former president of MÜSİAD, Ömer Bolat, gave the following response to the question "Why are your economic views different than TÜSİAD's?":

> The policies implemented by the IMF-backed program and the winds of globalization tend to serve the financial circles. There is a divergence between TÜSİAD and us here. The financial sector is quite prominent among the members of TÜSİAD. Moreover, companies with large capital holdings who are technologically developed benefit substantially from this program.[12]

The strategic perspective of the capital fraction represented principally by MÜSİAD is to form a bloc comprised primarily of states from the Islamic world, the Turkic republics and East Asia. Their primary objective is to create a private sector trade association "from Gebze to Gaza," similar to the "Medina Market,"[13] the "Cotton Association,"[14] and the D-8,[15] in lieu of a "just economic order." Based on former MÜSİAD president Ömer Bolat's assertion that "the D-8 must be advanced and deepened" (8bülten.com 2007), we may surmise that the Islamist fraction seeks to integrate with global capitalism primarily through such regional formations. An extension of this perspective is the suggestion that given the prominence granted to Asia, Africa, the Middle East, and the Far East in the multipolar new world order, the countries of the D-8, led by its founding member, Turkey, should determine a new expansionary politics, add ten new members, and "design" the D-18 as a global organization (*Milli Gazete* 2009).

Of course, we should not overlook the fact that the Islamist fraction is an important extension of Turkish capital's attempt to gain influence in the "Ottoman" region as a whole. It is too early to tell whether any significant advances have been made in this direction. The main point of divergence or strategic difference is whether or not the bid for "regional leadership" will take place under the guidance and supervision of the United States.

Table 3.1. Distribution of Turkish Exports by Region (%)

	2006	2008	2012
European Union Countries	56	48	38.8
Free Zones of Turkey	3.5	2.3	1.5
Other Countries	40.5	49.7	59.7
Europe	9.3	11.9	9.4
Africa	5.3	6.9	8.8
The Americas	7.4	4.9	6.3
Asia and the Middle East	17.8	24.6	34.8

Source: Turkish Statistical Institute (TÜİK) data set, 2012

Setting aside the effects of the global economic crisis of 2009, when we look at the distribution of exports by region during the period 2006-8 (table 3.1), we see that the total share of exports to EU countries have decreased and that exports to North Africa, the Near East, and the Middle East have increased significantly (Soybilgen

2013). As Prime Minister Erdoğan pointed out in one of his speeches, trade with neighboring countries increased three-fold in the last nine years, while in the past seven years, trade with fifty-three African countries grew by 500 per cent trade with countries in the Near and Middle East grew by 458 per cent and trade with the Turkic republics increased by 448 per cent (*Yeni Şafak* 2010).

If we examine the regional distribution of the international investments made by Turkish capitalists we see a similar trend (table 3.2). Investments made in Near and Far Eastern countries have increased notably between 2002 and 2010. Based on these figures, it is important to point out that while the Western-secular bourgeoisie has maintained a large share of capital exports to former Ottoman territories, the Islamist bourgeoisie, led by holdings such as Ülker, Çalık, Sanko, and Boydak have made significant inroads and important investments (according to their strategic orientation).

Table 3.2. Distribution of Turkish Foreign Investment by Country (per million dollars)

	2009	2010	2002-10
Europe	**636**	**573**	**7.390**
EFTA Countries	13	11	439
Other European Countries	9	91	697
Africa	**12**	**20**	**377**
North African Countries	11	20	377
Other African Countries	1	0	38
Americas	**13**	**27**	**936**
North American Countries	10	26	913
Central American Countries	2	1	19
South American Countries	1	0	4
Asia	**105**	**253**	**3.341**
Near and Middle Eastern Countries	94	225	3.017
(a)Gulf Countries	10	124	282
(b)Other Near and Middle Eastern Countries	84	191	2.590
Other Asian Countries	11	28	324
Oceania	**0**	**0**	**30**
Unclassified Countries	**0**	**0**	**13**
Total	**766**	**873**	**12.087**

Source: Central Bank of the Republic of Turkey, 2011

Thus, the evidence presented here demonstrates why the answer to the first question I posed above is "yes."

Islamist Bourgeoisie: From "Myth" to Reality

Now I shall try to answer the second question. Let's put aside Erol Katırcıoğlu, Ahmet Insel, and a number of other left liberals – including liberals like the journalists Taha Akyol and Cengiz Çandar – who have repeated ad nauseam the same stories about the "entrepreneurial middle class" (that the "Anatolian Tigers" have somehow developed independently of the state, that they are not monopolists, that they defend free competition and want a more democratic economic order, etc.) and consider some more substantive arguments.

One of these is a thesis advanced by both Oral Çalışlar and Mustafa Sönmez that Islamist capital is not very large and its progress should not be exaggerated. Oral Çalışlar defends this position by pointing out that "there are less than 10 people" who could be considered close to the AKP on a list of "The 100 Richest Turks" published by *Forbes* in 2010 (Çalışlar 2010):

> It appears as though the bourgeoisie that are believed to support the AKP (and referred to from time to time as the Anatolian bourgeoisie) are not in a position to compete with Istanbul. It seems more realistic to speak about a "medium-sized" capital accumulation taking place around the AKP and the concomitant emergence of a new "middle class."

Mustafa Sönmez (2008b) puts forth a similar argument:

> The notion that the organic capitalists created by the AKP who have submitted to the "project of an Islamic community" are gaining rapid economic power and pose a threat first and foremost to TÜSİAD and "the others" is highly exaggerated.

Is the strengthening of the Islamist bourgeoisie, which some have described as a "conservative ascendance" an exaggeration or a myth? Let's look at the facts to test this view. Table 3.3 outlines the relative distribution of the Western big bourgeoisie represented by TÜSİAD and TÜRKONFED[16] and the Islamist bourgeoisie represented by MÜSİAD, TUSKON, and ASKON within the Turkish capitalist order.

When MÜSİAD was formed in 1990, it had 12 members. By 2000 it had 1,387 members, and grew to 2,136 in 2004. By 2012, its membership had increased to more than 6,500. The number of firms attached to MÜSİAD stands at around 15,000. The employment capacity of firms affiliated with MÜSİAD in 1998 was 600,000, their export volume was

Table 3.3. A Comparison of the Various Business Organizations in Turkey by Size

	TÜSİAD	TÜRKONFED	MÜSİAD	TUSKON	ASKON
Number of Businessmen Members	600	>11.000	>6.500	43.000 (2012)	2.300
Number of Firms	3.500	n/a	15.000	100.000	n/a
Employment	626.000	>1.000.000	>1.200.000	n/a	125.000
Share of National Income (%)	40	n/a	15	n/a	n/a
Share of Total Exports (%)	45 (2010)	n/a	15-20 (2010)	n/a	n/a
Export Volume (in billions of $)	45	>65	22.5	n/a	n/a
Business Volume (in billions of $)	62.7	208	n/a	n/a	n/a
Share of Total Value Added	50 (2012)	n/a	n/a	n/a	n/a

Sources: Compiled from the websites of TÜSİAD, MÜSİAD, TUSKON, ASKON and from Sönmez 2010b

6 billion dollars and their share of national income was 10 percent. These developments show that Islamist capital has developed quite rapidly over the past 20 years.

As shown in the data above, the capital segments and organizations that have formed as competitors to TÜSİAD comprise about one-third of the capital power (in terms of their share of the national income, exports, and business volume). The enormous growth that they have achieved due to their close, organic relationship with the AKP government is a source of anxiety for the Western-secular bourgeoisie as represented by TÜSİAD. However, it would be premature to suggest that Islamist capital has become a wing of the big bourgeoisie based on this data alone. What this chapter has emphasized is that Islamist capital, led by members of MÜSİAD, has advanced beyond the stage of the "Anatolian Tigers" or domestic SMEs by organizing along the lines of large capital holdings. Moving forward, it will be useful to examine other indices such as where the headquarters of these capital fractions are located, the net wealth of the founding investors of the companies, their position among the top five hundred industrial enterprises in Turkey, their relationships with financial corporations, and their propensity to conglomerate.

Sixty-eight percent of the headquarters of TÜSİAD members are based in Istanbul, whereas only 28 percent of MÜSİAD member firms have their headquarters in Istanbul (Taşkın 2009). 23 percent of TÜSİAD member firms were created between 1980 and 1989 while 75 percent of MÜSİAD firms were formed between 1989 and 1995. Members of MÜSİAD and ASKON are well represented in industrial centers like Kocaeli and Gebze, which can be considered extensions of Istanbul (Buğra/Savaşkan 2010). These observations show that Islamist capital came into being after the 1980s and grew rapidly from the 1990s onward, and that it has moved beyond a simple Istanbul-Anatolia capital division by concentrating its headquarters in the Western part of Turkey.

Between 2006 and 2010 there were approximately fifteen to twenty families from the Islamist bourgeoisie who were ranked either for

Table 3.4. Families Connected to Islamist Capital among the "100 Richest Families in Turkey"

The Ülker Family (Ülker Holding)
The Boydak Family (Boydak Holding)
Ahmet Keleşoğlu (Selçuk Ecza Group)
The Cevahir Family (Cevahir Holding)
The Konukoğlu Family (Sanko Holding)
The Çalık Family (Çalık Holding)
Nuri Özaltın (Özaltın Holding)
Aziz Torun (Torunlar Holding)
Cihan Kamer (Altınsay Kuyumculuk)
The Topbaş Family (BIM)
Yahya Kiğılı (Hayat Holding)
İbrahim Çeçen (Cengiz Holding)
The Küçük Family (Taha Holding)
The Zapsu Family (Azizler Holding)
İhsan Kalkavan (Kalkavan Denizcilik)
The Kiler Family (Kiler Holding)
The Kazancı Family (Aksa Enerji)

Source: "The 100 Richest Families in Turkey," Ekonomist, 2006–10 the first time or continuously on a list of the "100 Richest Families in Turkey" (table 3.4).

TUSKON administrators have indicated that 130 member firms of TUSKON were ranked in the İSO's top five hundred industrial enterprises list of 2008 - albeit without naming the firms directly (Altıntop 2009). It is not possible to determine how accurate this information is. On the other hand, MÜSİAD had 26 member firms in the İSO top five hundred industrial enterprises list of 2008, and 30 member firms

Table 3.5. The Number of Firms Connected to Islamist Capital in the İSO 500 (2009)

	2003	2004	2006	2007	2008	2009
MÜSİAD	4	8	20	23	26	31
TUSKON	n/a	n/a	n/a	n/a	n/a	45
ASKON	n/a	n/a	n/a	n/a	n/a	2

Source: Milliyet (2010a)

ranked among the İSO second tier five hundred enterprises in the same year (Buğra and Savaşkan 2010: 106). In the 2009 İSO top five hundred industrial enterprises list, MÜSİAD, TUSKON, and ASKON had 31, 45 and 2 member firms respectively (table 3.5).

However, when the firms that were members of both MÜSİAD and TUSKON were disaggregated, the number of member firms in 2009 that were solely affiliates of MÜSİAD was twelve, of TUSKON twenty-nine, and of both MÜSİAD and TUSKON, sixteen. This shows that (in light of the data presented by *Milliyet* [2010a], the real number of firms connected to Islamist capital in the İSO 500 (in 2009) was fifty-seven. According to my own estimates, this number exceeded eighty when the other affiliate firms were taken into account. In addition by 2010, I estimate that eighty-five to ninety-five firms connected to Islamist capital were ranked among the *Capital* 500 and ninety to ninety-five were ranked within the *Fortune* 500. Among the top one thousand exporting firms ranked by TİM in 2009, firms connected to Islamist capital numbered between sixty and seventy.

Islamic banking, which has played a critical role in the development of Islamist capital and continues to function as a source of finance, has grown rapidly in the banking sector since the 1980s. This growth was particularly visible in terms of the funds generated after their entry into the private finance initiative (PFI) market, their business volume, number of branches and project capacity (Ergüneş 2009). In chronological order, Al Baraka Turk Finance was established in 1985, Family Finance in 1985, Faisal Finance in 1985, Kuwait-Turk

Table 3.6. Private Finance Corporations in Turkey

Arab-Turkish Bank (1977, established as a subsidiary of *İş Bank* with Arab capital)
Turkish-Saudi Investment Holding (1988, established as a partnership between Sümer Holding and the Development Bank of Turkey)
Al Baraka Turk Finance (1985, established as a partnership of Topbaş/BİM and Yıldız Holding/Ülker; connected to the Nakşibendi order)
Faisal Finance (1985, established first as a partnership with Kombassan, then with Yıldız Holding), → **Family Finance** (2001) merged with **Anadolu Finance** (1991, established by the HES Group and MÜSİAD members and acquired by Boydak Holding) to become Anadolu Family Finance (co-owned by Yıldız and Boydak Holding)
Kuwait Turk Evkaf Finance (1989, established as a partnership with BIM; connected to the Nakşibendi order)
İhlas Finance (1995, established by İhlas Holding; shut down in 2001)
Asya Finance → **Bank Asya** (1996, established as a partnership between Faruk Berksan/Kar Group, Abdülkadir Konukoğlu / Sanko, Ahmet Çalık, Aydın Group, and İhsan Kalkavan; connected to the Fethullah Gülen community)

Evkaf Finance in 1989, Anadolu Finance in 1991, İhlas Finance in 1995, and Asya Finance in 1996 all entered the PFI market. Three of these are financed by foreign capital, while the rest were established solely with domestic capital (table 3.6).

Islamic financial practices in Turkey are implemented by designated banks[17] within the larger banking order. These "participation banks" comprise a small minority of the banking sector, their shares have been steadily increasing. Within the last nine years, there has been rapid growth among participation banks. Between 2003 and 2012, the total assets of participation banks increased by thirteen times, the total funds collected increased by eleven times, and the funds spent by these banks increased by sixteen times. Since 2012 there are four participation banks alongside forty-four conventional banks in Turkey. The number of branches of participation banks has increased from 128 in 2003 to 828 in 2012 (www.tkbb.org.tr, *Milliyet* 2013).

In 2012, these banks controlled 5 percent of the total assets of the banking system, 5.1 percent of its share of deposits, and 5.8 percent of its credits. The share of interest-free banking in the overall banking system is roughly 5 percent. It is believed that this sector aims to increase its market share to 10 percent within the next 10 years.

Table 3.7. TUSKON and MÜSİAD Member Holdings Ranked in the İSO 500 (2009)

TUSKON Member	Number of Firms within the İSO 500 (2009)	MÜSİAD Member	Number of Firms within the İSO 500 (2009)
Hayat Holding	2	Tosyalı Holding	2
Taha Holding	1	İpek-Koza Holding	2
Eroğlu Holding	1	Yıldız Holding	13
Naksan Holding	2	Boydak Holding	7
İhlas Holding	1	Çalık Holding	1
Kipaş Holding	4	Ekinciler Holding	1
Aydınlı Holding	1	Yimpaş Holding	1

Source: author's own calculations from İSO 2010

Another indication that Islamist capital has become an important wing of the big bourgeoisie is the substantial size of the holdings under its control. The data presented in table 3.7 illustrate the number of firms connected to Islamist capital and ranked among the İSO 500 in 2009 that are incorporated in or are a subsidiary of a particular holding.

Table 3.8. The Geographical Distribution of the Top One Thousand Exporting Firms in Turkey by City

	2003	2009	2010	2011
İstanbul	523	492	484	475
İzmir	89	67	66	66
Bursa	68	52	55	48
Ankara	39	52	55	48
Kocaeli	31	41	44	62
Adana	16	15	17	17
Manisa	18	20	20	14
Mersin	15	17	14	10
Kayseri	14	11	12	10
Gaziantep	24	49	52	63
Denizli	31	22	27	23
Konya	2	6	6	4
Kahramanmaraş	6	8	6	8

Source: TİM, Survey of the Top One Thousand Exporting Firms of Turkey, 2011 and 2012

Another development is the growing tendency to conglomerate in Anatolia. According to a report published in *Capital* magazine (Aksakal 2010), the number of Anatolian holdings increased from 144 in 2002 to 204 in 2009, representing a growth of more than 40 percent. However, the report points out that the most rapid growth took place during the "wave of entrepreneurship" and incorporation of the 1990s, reflected in the 477 holdings that came into being by 1995. The "Anatolian entrepreneurs" entered the market in the 2000s and the number of holdings grew to over 500, reaching 628 in 2002 and 993 in 2009. The new centers of these holdings are cities like Gaziantep, Denizli, Kayseri, Konya, Bursa and İzmir. If we set aside the cities of Bursa and İzmir, the geographical dispersion of the top one thousand exporting firms (table 3.8) in Turkey highlights the growing importance of Anatolian centers of capital in recent years.

It is estimated that the large gains in Anatolia will continue apace and that the number of holdings will reach 250 in the coming years. The same publication (Aksakal 2010) also reports that the firms Anadolu Birlik in Konya and Naksan and Gülsan in Gaziantep (which are both connected to Islamist capital) are amongst the recently rising holdings in Anatolia.

Let us also examine the firms that grew most rapidly in recent years. Of the fastest growing thirty companies in a study conducted by *Capital* several (which have grown at a rate of more than ten times the national average) are connected to MÜSİAD and/or TUSKON. For example, Has Kablo, which grew 360 percent, is ranked as the twelfth fastest growing firm in the country. Hasan Basri Bozkurt's thirty-year-old company Hidromek, which produces heavy machinery, has grown 318 percent in the past five years, with an annual average growth rate of forty-three percent. Despite having entered the export market only ten years ago, they currently sell their products to fifty countries on five continents.

Kastamonu Entegre has grown by 330 percent in the past five years, with an average annual growth rate of 44 percent. Alongside Hayat Kimya, it constitutes one of the two most important companies of Hayat Holding. As the leading firm in the industrial sector, Sarkuysan has grown by 449 percent over the past five years and is currently exporting to nearly fifty countries in five continents. Finally, Nursan Çelik, the eleventh fastest-growing company in Turkey and the fastest growing company in the steel sector grew by 368 percent between 2003 and 2007.

As far as I have been able to discern, there are six companies tied to Islamist capital among the list of the fifty fastest growing companies between 1997 and 2003 published in *Capital 500*. There are seventy such firms in the *Fortune 500*'s "top Turkish companies" list, and sixty such firms are ranked in the 2009 *Capital 500* survey. In a study conducted by *CNBC-e Business* magazine (2009) which looked at the ten year (1998-2008) performance of 3,500 companies and identified the top 100 firms out of 547 with a net-value of 100 million US dollars or above, at least twenty of the 100 firms have direct or indirect links to Islamist capital.

It was determined in the same study that the fastest growing sectors in the economy are metal casting (thirty-one companies), food (fifteen), information technology (eleven), automotive (eight), chemicals (five), and petroleum (five). The leading capital groups of the Islamist bourgeoisie appear to invest more heavily in textiles, food, metal casting, iron and steel, construction, and more recently, real estate and energy. Since these sectors are also invested in heavily by the Western-secular bourgeoisie, there is a spirit of fierce competition rather than a complementary relationship between the two camps. The primary sectors within which Western-secular and Islamist capital have been competing domestically are clothing and textiles (Tema-Taha, Aydınlı, Kiğılı, Eroğlu, Çalık), retail (Adese, BIM, Kiler), media (ATV, Sabah, Bugün, Kanaltürk, Star, Kanal 24, TGRT), energy (Çalık, Aksa, Sanko), and food (Marsan, Ülker).

In light of all these developments, it is clear that the Islamist bourgeoisie has undergone a qualitative transformation as a product of the internal struggles among the Turkish bourgeoisie and has grown to the point where it would be accurate to describe it as finance capital.

Mustafa Sönmez, who had previously defended the "exaggeration and myth" thesis as outlined above, has come around to a position that is more in line with my analysis (Sönmez 2009):

> There is a "class war" in Turkey today. Nice things come to mind when we speak of class wars. But the working class is not an actor in this war, it is being decimated. The conservative-Anatolian capital fraction is fighting against Istanbul capital in an attempt to widen its arena. The liberals insist that "this is a revolution." They view this as a democratic revolution of the petite bourgeoisie and the middle class. But the fraction that is growing and becoming more powerful is not fighting against the remnants of feudalism, it is a reactionist fraction vying for hegemony. Islamist capital wants a bigger share of the pie. But this capital fraction is not monolithic. While there are large capitalists like Ülker, Sinpaş, etc. among them, there are also small to medium-sized capitalist groups. And in the final analysis, their interests are in conflict with one another. Let's be clear: "big capital" has not been eliminated, it is only changing hands. In the lists of the "largest Turkish companies" published by *Forbes* magazine in recent years, we see growing

numbers of firms connected to Islamist capital. And the Anatolian / small to medium-sized capital is trying to increase its share of the surplus wealth. All of these fights are taking place through the AKP. It should not be forgotten that the capitalist order will not be shaken no matter who wins this struggle for power.

Mustafa Sönmez (2010a) adds the following:

> This historical break is really a struggle over the transfer of power that has deepened among the hegemonic class blocs that have directed Turkish societal formation. On the one side is the political representative of the conservative-Islamist capital fraction, as embodied in the AKP-Fethullah Gülen coalition. The capital fraction that this wing depends upon is in part comprised of big capital and in part of SMEs, which are incorporated into the formal associations of TOBB and the "civil" organizations of MÜSİAD and TUSKON. Simply calling them "Anatolian Tigers" is insufficient. They are well represented in the industrial, trade and service sectors in Istanbul. On the other side is secular capital, organized again under TOBB and the "civil" organization of TÜSİAD, and the medium-sized capitalists who are members of TÜRKONFED. The other allies in the bloc dominated by the traditional (secular) bourgeoisie are drawn from the higher ranks of the civil-military bureaucracy. With its triumph in these battles, the AKP found the courage to take more aggressive steps in its projects of conservative social transformation. It undertook efforts to weaken the civil-military bureaucracy, an important pillar of the opposition bloc, through the Ergenekon trials and other attempts to discredit it. While on the one hand it sought to discredit the TSK [Turkish Armed Forces], subordinate the judiciary to the executive branch, and neutralize TÜSİAD, it simultaneously pursued policies that would strengthen TÜSİAD and TUSKON. The tax operations undertaken to weaken the media and economic power of the Doğan Group sufficed to silence the rest of TÜSİAD. TÜSİAD members who were unable to protect or support Doğan feared that they could be subject to similar forms of harassment, and were nervous about being blacklisted in the bidding for private contracts in sectors like energy and real estate.

I believe that the above findings show that Islamist capital is not a myth and that a new capital fraction has taken its place on the stage of Turkish capitalism. In order to avoid any misunderstandings, let me put it this way: I am not suggesting that Islamist capital has become larger, stronger, or carries greater weight in the economy vis-à-vis Western-secular capital. Rather, I maintain that a new monopolistic capitalist class has emerged that has a different perspective regarding the conditions under which capital accumulation and exploitation should take place, and that this class has a greater voice in the political process.

Conclusion

"He's paid a lot of taxes. This is not an easy task, my friend. See if you can employ three workers. Have you ever lost sleep at night thinking 'how am I going to pay the check tomorrow?' No, because you earn a salary. The perspective is different when you're looking from Ankara or from Istanbul. We look from Istanbul."

Kemal Unakıtan, "Efendim Enflasyon İnmiyor, Evet İnmeyecek"[18]

"A good worker is one who obeys his employer."

Former MÜSİAD president Erol Yarar

The findings and analysis that I have presented above lead me to this conclusion: with the aid of their strong financial resources and the capital they have accumulated, Islamist capital groups have become important players in the Turkish economy. What we see today is a new capital fraction with its own monopolists, financial capital, and perspective on foreign trade. The AKP is first and foremost the political representative of this capital fraction.

The present-day conflict within the ruling class cannot be explained solely by political or cultural-ideological terms. Behind this conflict is a struggle over financial resources and over who will take the lion's share of capital accumulation in Turkey. This is the class and material basis of the internal conflict among the bourgeoisie. The new Islamist bourgeoisie, which had gained strength after the military coup of 12 September 1980 (creating its own cadres under the patronage of Turgut Özal and getting rich thanks to the support of Gulf capital and Islamic banking), and moved beyond the status of "Anatolian capital" to become a monopolistic capital fraction, is now locked in a struggle for hegemony with the traditional, Western big bourgeoisie over different strategic and tactical priorities.

However, it should certainly not be inferred from my findings that an *irreconcilable* difference exists between these two camps. Ultimately, the pressure exerted by imperialist capital, the world economic crisis and the changing equilibrium of domestic class struggle will help determine both the boundaries of this conflict and its solution. Yet whether this means a continuation of a "bloodless civil war" or a resolution through "historical compromise" will largely depend on the course of the class struggle between capital and labor in Turkey, whether or not the exploitation of the working class is intensified, and the external pressures applied by the imperialist powers in the strategies they pursue in the face of a deepening of the crisis of world capitalism.

114 | *Kurtar Tanyılmaz*

Notes

This chapter was translated from the Turkish by Osman Balkan. The editors thank him for his various other contributions as well.

1. Çalık Holding is an Islamist capital group that is close to the AKP government.
2. See http:/Superonline.com/haber/2008/06/18/2696.html.
3. Small and Medium-scale Enterprises (SMEs).
4. The Nationalist Vision movement (Milli Görüş) is a religio-nationalist political project, with references to the Ottoman past, within a developmentalist discourse of new economic and social order based on "national" as opposed to Western principles. Its wellknown leader was Necmettin Erbakan.
5. Turgut Özal, who is praised by the journalist Mehmet Barlas, is a politician and statesman who served as the prime minister and president of Turkey after the military coup of 12 September 1980. During his reign he implemented neoliberal policies in line with Reagan and Thatcher. Organized industrial zones refer to regional production facilities whose purpose is to develop SMEs in underdeveloped countries.
6. For a more detailed account of the events summarized here, see Savran 2004, 2011.
7. Ahmet Küçükbay, chairman of the board of Küçükbay Yağ ve Deterjan Sanayi, one of the largest vegetable oil manufacturers in Turkey and a member of TUSKON, says that the number of countries they export to has reached eighty thanks to the help of Turkish schools (*Zaman*, 2010). Küçükbay says: "There are 120 Turkish schools around the world. Those who established schools have a good reputation with the local population and are well respected. Our exports benefit from these schools." Küçükbay, who says that these schools are an important inroad for Turkish businessmen, claims that "the suppliers from these countries now prefer Turkey. For example, a company who buys oil from me also wants pasta, tomato paste, and I introduce them to another Turkish company."
8. According to a report prepared by the Western Study Group (Batı Çalışma Grubu) in 1997 in conjunction with the military general staff during the 28 February process, as the pronunciamento of 28 February 1997 and consequent resignation of the government is called, the 385 companies that control a capital sum of around 500 trillion Turkish lira are split along the following lines: Fethullah Gülenists [Fetullahçı] (208 companies), Nakşibendi (56 companies), National Vision movement [Milli Görüş] (47 companies), Süleymanists [Süleymancı] (29 companies), radical Islamists (31 companies), New Asia Group [Yeni Asya Grubu] (6 companies), New Generation Group [Yeni Nesil Grubu] (6 companies), and Kadirists [Kadiriler] (7 companies). The same report indicates that companies that belong to an additional twenty sects and community circles, companies that belong to İŞHAD, which is close to MÜSİAD and Fetullah Gülen are excluded from the list. When larger and smaller companies are added, the real number would be closer to 4.000. (http://kacmazmetin.blogcu.com/1924-cemaat-tarikat-ekonomisi-2006-holdinglesen-islam-ekonomisi/2206523, accessed 21 August 2007).
9. PETLAS, one of the leading tire manufacturers in Turkey, was privatized in 2005.
10. The investigative commission set up by the Grand National Assembly of Turkey (Türkiye Büyük Millet Meclisi, TBMM) with regard to Islamist holdings listened to the testimony of Doğan Cansızlar, the president of the Capital Markets Board (Sermaye Piyasası Kurulu, SPK) in its meeting on 21 June 2005. The SPK president submitted a four-hundred page report to the commission that contained the names of seventy-eight firms, including holdings like İttifak, Jetpa, Kombassan, and Yimpaş,which he claimed "took money from the people illegally." According to statements made by TBMM commission members Bihlun Tamaylıgil and Nezir Büyükcengiz, these

companies had collected nearly four billion euros from about three hundred thousand people (*Radikal*, 2005).

11. Housing Development Administration of Turkey, TOKİ.
12. See www.spothaber.com, accessed 25 August 2005.
13. An international trade fair organized by Muslim businessmen under the leadership of MÜSİAD in order to improve trade relations, particularly with African and European countries.
14. An alternative common market initiative established in the 1990s under the guidance of MÜSİAD in a geographical area that extends from East Asia to the Balkans among the cotton- manufacturing countries with prominent textile and clothing sectors.
15. An economic cooperation organization, that consists of Turkey, Iran, Pakistan, Bangladesh, Malaysia, Indonesia, Egypt and Nigeria.
16. Turkish Enterprise and Business Confederation.
17. Participation banking is an interest-free banking model that collects funds on the basis of profits and losses, and provides credits through trade, partnerships and financial leasing.
18. Kemal Unakıtan is the former AKP minister of finance. This quote was originally from a speech given at a ceremony in which successful taxpayers were presented with awards.

References

Aksakal, Ayşe Tarcan. 2010. "Anadolu'nun Yükselen Holdingleri" [The rising holdings of Anatolia]. *Capital*, February.

Altıntop, Muhsin. 2009. "TUSKON'un Hedefi Uzak Diyarlar" [TUSKON's goal is faraway lands]. *Infomag*, no. 10: 94.

Barlas, Mehmet. 2006. "Olayın Sırrı Calvin'de mi Gizli?" [Does the secret lie in Calvin?]. *Sabah*, 28 January.

Buğra, Ayşe, and Osman Savaşkan. 2010. "Yerel Sanayi ve Bugünün Türkiyesi'nde İş Dünyası" [Local industry and business life in today's Turkey]. *Toplum ve Bilim* 118: 92–123.

Çalışlar, Oral. 2010. "Türkiye Burjuvazisi ve AK Parti" [Turkish bourgeoisie and the AKP]. *Radikal*, 28 February.

CNBC-e Business. 2009. "En İstikrarlı 100" [The most stable 100]. October.

D8Bulten.com. 2007. "Ömer Bolat: D8 Geliştirilmeli ve Derinleştirilmeli" [D8 must be developed and enhanced]. 2 July.

Doğan, A. Ekber. 2006. "Siyasal Yansımalarıyla İslamcı Sermayenin Gelişme Dinamikleri ve 28 Şubat Süreci" [The developmental dynamics of Islamist capital, its political effects and the 28 February process]. *Mülkiye Dergisi* 30, no. 252: 60–63.

Ekonomist. 2006–10. The Richest Turkish Families, special issues.

Erdoğan, Recep Tayyip. 2010a. "Bitaraf Olan Bertaraf olur" [The neutrals will be eliminated]. *Milliyet*, 18 August.

_____. 2010b. "Sermaye El Değiştiriyor" [Capital is changing hands]. *Cumhuriyet*, 10 September.

Ergüneş, Nuray. 2009. "Banka Sermayesi Üzerinden Sınıf-İçi Çatışmaları Anlamak" [Understanding interclass conflicts through banking capital]. *Praksis*, no. 12: 133–56.

İnsel, Ahmet. 2010. "Belli ki TÜSİAD'da Statükocu Çevrenin Gücü Kırılmış" [It looks like those for status quo are getting weaker in TÜSİAD]. *Sabah*, 28 February.

İSO, 2010. "Türkiye'nin 500 Büyük Sanayi Kuruluşu-2009" [Top five hundred industrial enterprises- 2009]. İstanbul Sanayi Odası (www.iso.org.tr).

Katırcıoğlu, Erol. 2002. "Bir Dönemin Sonu (mu?)" [Is this the end of a period?]. *Radikal*, 16 November.

Kongar, Emre. 2005. "Burjuvazi İslamcılaştırılırken" [As the bourgeoisie is being Islami-cized]. *Cumhuriyet*, 5 September.

Milli Gazete. 2009. "Türkiye D-8'i D-18 Yapmalıdır" [Turkey must turn D8 to D18]. 23 June.

Milliyet. 2009. "Müstakil İstanbul Ticaret Odası" [The independent Istanbul Chamber of Commerce]. 1 March.

_____. 2010a. "Muhafazakâr Yükseliş" [The rise of conservatism]. 28 July.

_____. 2010b. "Siz-Biz diye Ayrım Yaptılar" [They discriminated as "you" and "us"]. 2 March.

_____. 2013. "Katılım Bankalarının 2012 kârı açıklandı" [Profits of the participation banks are announced]. 7 March.

Özkan, Funda. 2010. "Kamplaşma Sermayede de Başladı" [The bourgeoisie is getting po-larized as well]. *Radikal*, 14 May.

Radikal. 2005. "78 'Yeşil' Şirketi 300 Bin Kişi Besledi" [78 "green" companies were main-tained by 300 thousand people]. 22 June.

Savran, Sungur. 2004. "20. Yüzyılın Politik Mirası" [The political heritage of the 20th cen-tury]. In *Sürekli Kriz Politikaları, Türkiye'de Sınıf, İdeoloji ve Devlet*, ed. Neşecan Balkan and Sungur Savran, 13–43. Istanbul: Metis Yayınları.

_____. 2011. *Türkiye'de Sınıf Mücadeleleri, Cilt 1: 1908–1980* [Class struggles in Turkey, vol. 1, 1908–1980]. 3rd ed. Istanbul: Yordam Yayıncılık.

Sönmez, Mustafa. 2008a. "Anadolu Kaplanları Efsane, AKP İstanbul'u ve TÜSİAD'ı isti-yor" [Anatolian tigers want myths, AKP wants TÜSİAD and Istanbul]. 19 September. www.bianet.org.

_____. 2008b. "Kahraman'a Cevap: Emek, Sermaye ve AKP Üzerine" [Reponse to Kahra-man: On Labor, Capital and the AKP]. 27 September. www.bianet.org.

_____. 2009. "Denge Bozulmaya Çalışılıyor" [They are trying to destabilize]. *Birgün*, 28 July.

_____. 2010a. "AKP-IMF ve cemaat kapitalizmi" [AKP-IMF and capitalism of religious community]. *Cumhuriyet*, 19 March.

_____. 2010b. *Türkiye'de İş Dünyası'nın Örgütleri ve Yönelimleri* [Business organizations in Turkey and their orientations]. İstanbul: Friedrich Ebert Stiftung.

Soybilgen, Barış. 2013. "2012'de İhracatı Altın Sırtladı" [In 2012 gold shouldered exports]. *Betam Araştırma Notu*, 13, no. 145.

Taşkın, Yüksel. 2009. "Türkiye'de Sınıfsal Yeniden Yapılanma, AKP ve Muhafazakar Popül-izm" [Class restructuring in Turkey, the AKP and conservative populism]. In *AKP Yeni Merkez Sağ mı?*, ed. Ümit Kurt, 157–80. Ankara: Dipnot Yayınları.

Unakıtan, Kemal. 2008. "Efendim Enflasyon İnmiyor, Evet İnmeyecek" [Inflation is not go-ing down; no, it will not]. *Milliyet*, 10 May.

Yeni Şafak. 2010. "Anadolu Kaplanını MÜSİAD yetiştirdi" [MÜSİAD bred the Anatolian tiger]. 4 April.

Yıldırımkaya, Gülin. 2010. "Türkiye 'Kansız Bir' İç Savaş'ın İçinde mi?" [Is Turkey in a "bloodless" war?]. *Habertürk*, 6 May.

Yılmaz, Serpil. 2009. "TÜSİAD Üyeleri de Açılım İstiyor" [TÜSİAD members want expan-sion as well]. *Milliyet*, 2 October.

Zaman. 2010. "Türk Okulları Sayesinde 80 Ülkeye İhracat yapıyoruz" [We are exporting to 80 countries thanks to Turkish schools]. 29 June.

– Chapter 4 –

THE ISLAMIST BIG BOURGEOISIE IN TURKEY
Özgür Öztürk

Introduction

The Islamist bourgeoisie is an important social class section and a transformative force in present-day Turkey. There are many indicators that point to the growing influence of Islamic capital in the last decade—the era of conservative-neoliberal Adalet ve Kalkınma Partisi (Justice and Development Party, AKP) rule. For example, the number of MÜSİAD and TUSKON members in the five hundred largest industrial enterprises of Turkey list is increasing.[1] When MÜSİAD was established in 1990, it had only eight members among the five hundred; this figure increased to twenty-three in 2007 and thirty-one in 2009. The list included more than seventy "conservative" businessmen in 2009 (*Milliyet* 2010).

Although figures are not available for the years after 2009, it is pretty clear that Islamic capital is on the rise. Yet one more point has to be mentioned: there are important inequalities within the list of the five hundred largest enterprises, and the most powerful enterprises are not Islamic companies but TÜSİAD members, the main organization of Turkish big business for the last forty years.[2] Indeed, the combined share of the sales of MÜSİAD and TUSKON members in the 2009 list was 7.48 percent.[3] This was less than the share of a single company, Turkish Petroleum Refineries Corporation (TÜPRAŞ), the largest enterprise which commanded a share of 7.56 percent. The Koç Group, one of the prominent members of TÜSİAD, controlled five of the first ten largest corporations, including TÜPRAŞ, and just these five companies had a combined share of 15.8 percent.[4] Hence, the rise of Islamic capital is not as spectacular as it may seem at first.

Many scholars and journalists suggest an increasing polarization within the Turkish bourgeoisie. On one side, we have the Western-oriented and presumably secular big bourgeoisie organized in TÜSİAD; on the other, there are the pro-East and predominantly small- or medium-scale Islamists of MÜSİAD and TUSKON.[5] While the former group is concentrated around Istanbul, the latter is located primarily in the newly industrializing cities of Anatolia. An analysis of this polarization is obviously crucial for an explanation of the political conflicts and transformations going on in present-day Turkey. However, the issue is usually interpreted within a liberal framework that has certain shortcomings. According to this line of thought, which is shared by many conservatives, conflicts between the secularists and the Islamists can be conceived as the outcome of a deeper tension between the oligarchic big business of Istanbul and the grassroots Anatolian bourgeoisie. The old and "static" big business has a monopolistic character and an illiberal/undemocratic attitude because of its close relations with the Turkish state; but the dynamic and competitive new entrepreneurs of Anatolia do not depend on such links, hence, they are essentially liberal/democratic in outlook (Demir et al. 2004; Ülsever 2005; Kahraman 2008).

This thesis has the merit of placing shallow conflicts within a socioeconomic perspective. However, it has some problems, since in the liberal literature a series of simply erroneous qualities are attributed to both sides of the conflict. Basing its analysis on the duality of state and civil society, the liberal view conceives big business as an integral part of the state apparatus, and at the same time suggests that Islamic capital is a part of civil society. Hence, all the negative qualities associated with the state in the liberal account are projected onto the big bourgeoisie, while the other side is conceived solely in terms of its virtues. In reality, the *basic* difference between the assumed sides is *primarily* about scale. Islamic capital has proved its ability to use business-state linkages for capital accumulation, especially in the last two decades. Unless one accepts the idea that small is beautiful, it is hard to find any more virtue in Islamists than the presumably secular big bourgeoisie.

Second, the identification of "Anatolian" and "Islamic" capital is misleading. In fact, many small- and medium-scale enterprises (SMEs), that is, over ten thousand firms, are organized in TÜRKONFED,[6] a confederation of business associations supported by TÜSİAD. This organization was established in 2005, but its origins go back to the 1990s. The business ties (subcontractor, supplier, vendor relations) between the large firms and the SMEs create a need on the part of the big bourgeoisie to control and direct smaller capitals. Indeed, there is competition between TÜSİAD and MÜSİAD over the control of local accumulation processes (Gündoğdu 2009).

Third, and more crucially, the sides of the conflict are not as clear as asserted. Typical participants of Islamist business associations are indeed SMEs, while TÜSİAD is *the* club of big business. Yet if the sides are defined as secular big bourgeoisie and small Islamic capital, a weighty category becomes invisible, the category of Islamic/conservative big business groups. These groups (e.g., Ülker, Boydak, Topbaş, Kale, Çalık, Sanko, Albayrak, Sancak, Toprak) have characteristics that allow them to be classified in either side, as big business *or* Islamic/conservative capital, depending on the aims of the observer. Moreover, they provide many links between the assumed sides, which may not be as divergent as they seem at first.[7]

In short, ideas shared by liberals and conservatives are questionable on various grounds. This chapter aims to contribute to such questioning by presenting the formation of Islamic big business—a topic usually neglected in discussions about Islamic capital in Turkey. Though Turkish finance capital had a conservative component from the start, the main growth of Islamic/conservative big business occurred after 1980.[8] This came as a by-product of neoliberalism and the gradual Islamization of society that accompanied it. The results were the rise of the AKP, conflicts within the ruling class because of the inclusion of Islamic big business, and a simultaneous transformation of Islamism—which, altogether, led to a reconfiguration of political power relations and the state.[9] This chapter will not discuss all of these processes in detail, however, and will instead focus on the formation and development of Islamic big business.

Problems of Classification

Clearly, there are no exact criteria for determining whether a specific company is Islamic or not. Classification of capitals according to their political or ideological characteristics is a theoretical problem that still waits to be solved. For the Turkish case, there is an ad hoc solution to this problem in the literature: the political or ideological position of any capital(ist) is predicted by his/her membership in various business associations. In practice, MÜSİAD and TUSKON are usually accepted as Islamist organizations, while TÜSİAD members are assumed to be secular. Such distinctions obviously cannot cover real-life complexities. But despite the growing interest in Islamism and related issues, the absence of in-depth empirical studies about business networks and their political linkages is striking. For example, the topic of interlocking directorships within Islamic capital or between Islamic capital and other firms has not been studied yet. The lack of concrete data forces one to adopt a more cautious approach.

To be sure, what is called "Islamic capital" (or the "Islamist bourgeoisie") does not constitute a homogenous mass. Indeed, there are various Islamic capitals with different scales and scopes (Doğan 2006; Hoşgör 2011). In this regard, first, we have the complex and wide networks of religious orders (*tarikat*), which are collections of small- or medium-scale capitals. Each religious order commands a significant sum, and the diversified firms are usually organized under a "holding" company, such as Server Holding of the İskenderpaşa order (a branch of the Nakşibendi community). These holding companies are structurally similar to the big conglomerates of Turkey, but are probably smaller. Due to data collection problems, there is not much information about this type of enterprise. What we know comes mostly from journalistic writings (e.g., Can 1997; Bulut 1997, 1999).

Second, one can speak of "individual" Islamic firms that do not belong to a religious order. These are mostly of the SME type, usually engaged in textiles, construction, or services. The labor-intensive nature of these sectors sharpens their sensitivity to labor relations and results in more repressive and paternalistic attitudes on the part of bosses. Concentrated in new industrial centers such as Kayseri, Gaziantep, Denizli, and Konya, some of these firms are successful exporters. Their growth has accelerated in the last thirty years, and hence heterogeneity is increasing within this group (Doğan 2006). Yet this category is still best described as small Anatolian/Islamic capital. Koyuncu (2002: 360–61) claims that the politicization of Islamic SMEs is a result of "globalization"; but as we will see below, this process began much earlier.

Third, we have the "Anatolian holding companies," as defined by Özcan and Çokgezen (2003)—business groups with large numbers of shareholders and highly diversified business portfolios. This model became popular during the 1980s and 1990s. Kombassan, Jetpa, Yimpaş, İttifak, and Endüstri Holding are examples of this category, which depends on religious affiliations to raise capital. Most of these groups came under pressure during the "postmodern coup" performed by the Turkish armed forces in 1997 (known as the "28 February process") and failed as a result (Adaş 2009). Because some went through scandalous bankruptcies, they attracted public (and academic) attention, more than other forms of Islamic capital.

Finally, there are big business groups that are more professional and less religious than others. Some of these conglomerates (e.g., Ül- ker, Kale) were definitely part of Turkish big business before 1980; others (e.g., Çalık, Albayrak, Boydak) typically grew after that date. They usually have connections with religious communities and other types of Islamic capital, as well as with the secular bourgeoisie of TÜSİAD. But compared with the Anatolian holding companies, this section of Islamic capital depends less on religious affiliations. Thus, classifying them as "Islamic" is more problematic. For lack of a better term, I will call them "conservative finance capital," implying some dose of Islamism.

To give an example, Ülker is the oldest and largest of these groups. The classification of Ülker as "Islamic" is justified on the grounds that the Ülker family has participated in the establishment of many Islamic foundations (Mollaveisoğlu 2008: 112–15) and has formed partnerships with numerous local and international Islamist entre- preneurs, some connected to the Saudi Binladen Group (Özdemir 2002). However, the family usually rejects such claims and insists on the "just business" nature of their affiliations. The head of the group, Murat Ülker, says he knows only the US dollar as "green money" (a metaphor for Islamic capital), meaning that there is no religious crite- rion in their business dealings (*Radikal* 2006). During the 28 February process Ülker was at pains to prove that it is not an Islamic company, and donated huge sums of money to secular organizations. Yet its reputation as "Islamic capital" continues even today.

The topic of this chapter will be the two variants of Islamic big business: Anatolian holding companies and conservative finance capital. Although some "hybrid" entities (such as İhlas Holding) can also be observed, these two types have constituted the basic forms of Islamic *big* business in Turkey up until today.

Industrial Concentration and the Formation of Finance Capital

The emergence of Islamic capital was, from the beginning, a part of the monopolization and conglomeration processes in Turkey. These, in turn, were a result of the development of capitalist relations of production. As is typical for a late industrializer, capitalist industrial production took off in Turkey around the mid-1950s. Before that date, there were only minor investments in industry since the Ottoman period. Production depended on agriculture, and merchants—mostly

Ottoman minorities—exported primary goods to and imported industrial goods from the capitalist world. At the beginning of the twentieth century, in the course of the collapse of the empire and the foundation of the new republic, harsh attacks on minorities transferred this intermediary role of merchants to Turkish Muslims. Commercial accumulation continued, now performed by new actors, but with no fundamental change in the structure of relations of production (Keyder 1987: 81).

It must be noted that, though the commercial intermediary position of Ottoman minorities was transferred to Turkish Muslims during the establishment of the republic, Islamist currents were repressed and were usually on the defensive in the first half of the twentieth century. The new republic banned religious social and educational institutions such as dervish lodges (*tekke* and *zaviye*) and madrassas, unified the then messy education system under a secular ministry, and abolished the caliphate, a symbolic but effective measure, since the caliph was supposedly the commander of the Islamic world. At the same time, the Directorate of Religious Affairs was founded to control religious practices throughout the country. These attacks against religion were not accidental, since, prior to the fall of the Ottoman Empire, the bourgeoisie had already discussed and dismissed Islamism and Ottomanism as feasible political options. The republic tried to contain Islam within a nation-state project by restricting it to the private sphere, and indeed succeeded in this for some time (Yavuz 2003: 49–50; Eligür 2010: 39–48).

Through reforms in many areas of social life, the republic accelerated the development of capitalist relations in Turkey. Moreover, especially during the Great Depression of the 1930s, the Turkish state undertook import-substituting industrialization efforts, since international prices in primary goods had decreased sharply (Boratav 1974). World War II interrupted these efforts considerably, and the Korean War (1950–53), by causing an increase in the world prices of primary products, gave a fresh impetus to the commercial accumulation that had been going on for decades. Industrialization in Turkey gained momentum again only after the Korean War, around the mid-1950s. In this period, "certain sections of merchant capital ... underwent a transformation into industrial capital in direct and indirect co-operation (i.e. through joint ventures and license agreements) with foreign capital" in Turkey. An import substitution industrialization (ISI) process began, in "a typical pattern where technology, capital goods and inputs were imported and the final product was domestically produced ... this gained clarity in the 1960s" (Gülalp 1985: 337).

Late industrialization made its mark on the political economy of Turkey, and private industrial monopolies emerged within a decade. In the context of late development, first-mover advantages meant that an industrial producer would face limited competition, since entrepreneurs with enough money capital would prefer not to invest in those already occupied sectors but instead in new fields. Moreover, in industrial sectors with more than one big producer (such as ceramic production, where a clear duopoly could be observed), there were cartel-type agreements between industrialists in order to ensure domination for each one of them in at least one branch. Thus, monopoly capitalism established its rule in a very short time. An early study of industrial concentration reports that in 1969 more than half of the total production belonged to at the most three enterprises in 236 of the 251 mass consumption goods (Silier 1977: 31). As can be expected, under ISI with protected national markets, these monopoly positions proved to be permanent.

There were two basic outcomes of industrial monopolization. First, almost within a decade, industrial monopolies turned into diversified business groups, and these quickly adopted the "holding" form of capital organization. The basic reason behind this transformation was the extra profits earned in most of the industrial sectors, thanks to the protection measures related to the ISI model. Industrialists usually preferred to invest these extra profits in new fields, since the limited size of the national market made it meaningless to invest in the same sector in order to increase scale. For example, at the end of 1970, and according to the four-digit ISIC (International Standard Industrial Classification) measurement, the Koç Group had activities in *at least* forty-three (mostly unrelated) sectors, while others such as the Sabancı Group had activities in thirty-one, Çukurova in fifteen, and OYAK of the Turkish army in fourteen (Öztürk 2010: 466). Thus, diversified business groups were formed with new investments in various fields of economic activity. Following the example of Koç Holding, established in 1963, other business groups also began adopting the "holding" model at the end of the 1960s. This model allowed them to manage their widely diversified investments from a single center. Moreover, by creating an "internal capital market" within a business group, the holding model provided the ability to use capital effectively, since capital could be easily shifted from one group company to another with the use of methods such as transfer pricing in intragroup trade, reciprocal shareholdings, and commercial credits between group companies.

Second, a conflict between the monopolistic big business groups and smaller capitals became increasingly visible at the end of the 1960s. As industrial monopolies internalized various economic activities (commerce, production, and finance) within their "holdings," they effectively blocked the growing potential of smaller capitalists, unless this latter group accepted a junior partnership in the commercial hierarchy (as commercial distributers, vendors, subcontractors, etc.). However, relatively smaller capitals and sections of the commercial bourgeoisie managed to find some channels to pursue their own interests at the expense of monopolistic big business, especially within the semiofficial chambers of trade and industry (Bianchi 1984: 252–53). In this context, the "Erbakan event" that took place in 1969 was a symptomatic phenomenon.

The Erbakan Event

Until the 1970s, the main business organizations for Turkish capitalists were the chambers of trade and industry. Enacted in 1925, the first law (no. 655) related to the chambers during the republican period prevented the establishment of separate chambers for industrialists and forced them to be organized together with merchants within the chambers of trade and industry. This signified the power of the commercial bourgeoisie at the time, but an updated law (no. 5590) in 1950 allowed the formation of separate industrial chambers, acknowledging the rise of the industrial bourgeoisie (Koraltürk 1999).

As semiofficial institutions, the chambers provided facilities for capitalists to express and achieve their demands. However, there was an institutional hierarchy, with Türkiye Odalar ve Borsalar Birliği (Union of Chambers and Commodity Exchanges of Turkey, TOBB) at the top, and TOBB continued to favor commercial capitalists throughout the 1950s. During the 1960s, the influence of the industrial bourgeoisie within TOBB increased, resulting in an open conflict between industrialists and merchants (Tuna 2009). The major points of dispute included the distribution of import quotas and allocations of foreign exchange. TOBB had the authority to deal with these issues at that time, and usually gave priority to the demands of the commercial bourgeoisie (Alkan 1998: 113). The representation mechanism within TOBB allowed the commercial bourgeoisie and smaller capitalists to maintain power (Öncü 1983), hence the failure of big business to control TOBB through chambers of industry (Gülfidan 1993).

Divergences grew between merchants and industrialists and between small capitalists and big business. The result was a separatist movement on the part of (especially bigger) chambers of industry. At the end of the 1960s, several chambers of industry attempted to part with TOBB and formed the Sanayi Odaları Birliği (Union of Industrial Chambers), an organization with no official recognition. Yet smaller capitalists were not entirely happy with TOBB either. Smaller chambers in Anatolia revolted in 1969 under the leadership of Necmettin Erbakan, a mechanical engineering professor and the representative of religious currents within the then ruling Adalet Partisi (Justice Party, AP).

As Erbakan gained the support of Anatolian chambers, he ran for the presidency of TOBB, an attack that also signaled a schism within the AP (Alkan 1998: 193–94). The AP government declared that the executive board of TOBB would continue for one more year. Yet Erbakan managed to organize a coup in the general assembly of TOBB, and won the controversial election for the executive board (*Milliyet* 1969). This fait accompli led to a legal as well as a political struggle between the government and Erbakan. In the end, Erbakan was forced to leave the presidency under police control (Genç 1969). He then left the AP and established the Milli Nizam Partisi (National Order Party, MNP), the first important Islamist political party in Turkey.

As we have seen, Islamism was on the defensive in the first half of the twentieth century. Later, especially when the Demokrat Parti (Democratic Party, DP) government came into power in 1950, religious currents gained strength at the social and political levels again. There were some attempts on the part of Islamists to politically mobilize, and several political parties were established before Erbakan's MNP. Between 1945 and 1950, "twenty-four political parties were founded, and at least eight had explicit references in their party programs to Islamic themes" (Eligür 2010: 52). However, these efforts did not bring any considerable success at the time. Hence, it was more practical for the Islamist currents to form interest-based links with ruling parties, rather than organizing independently. In particular, the Nakşibendi and the Nurcu communities, two of the most effective religious groups in Turkey, supported the DP in the 1950s and the AP (as the successor of the DP) after 1960 (Bulut 1997: 256–57). Under the Cold War conditions, Islamists integrated with the ruling center-right parties and came on the scene "as a front against communism and the Left in Turkey" (Yavuz 2003: 62).

With the establishment of Erbakan's MNP, political Islam emerged as a separate entity (Eligür 2010: 66). The party, however, was shut down by the Constitutional Court after the military coup of 12 March 1971. But a successor party was established, the Milli Selamet Partisi (National Salvation Party, MSP). The movement would be known as the "National Vision movement" from that point on.[10] During the 1970s, the religious and developmentalist rhetoric of Erbakan influenced some segments of the Anatolian bourgeoisie, and the MSP took part in several coalition governments.[11] Moreover, religious communities and business practices proliferated across the country, as well as in Europe (especially in Germany), where more than two million Turkish citizens lived as workers at that time.

The results of the Erbakan event were manifold. As well as initiating the mobilization of political Islam, this event also displayed the power of small chambers, and hence accelerated the formation of a separate business organization to defend the interests of big business. Less than two years later and just three weeks after the 12 March 1971 military coup, big business groups of Istanbul and İzmir established TÜSİAD, the core business organization for Turkish finance capital since that time. For the big bourgeoisie, it was clear that the composition of TOBB would not allow the representation of their interests effectively.[12] On the other hand, for the SMEs, their dominance in TOBB did not bring serious advantages, since some of the powers of TOBB (e.g., the distribution of import quotas) were revoked after the military coup (Alkan 1998: 197–201).

The Emergence of Conservative Finance Capital

As hinted at above, one of the basic reasons behind the religious aspirations of smaller capitalists was the rise of big business, which had constrained their growth potentials. But it would be wrong to propose a simple causality in this context, since "Islamists" comprised just a fraction of the small-scale entrepreneurs and, moreover, there were "conservative" currents within the big bourgeoisie also. The combination of Islam and capitalist market practices came in various configurations, and the formation of Islamic big business was an important aspect of this synthesis. Indeed, a group of "conservative" businessmen had managed to expand their activities during the ISI period of 1960–80, not in opposition to, but alongside, the "secular" business groups.

For example, it is significant that, when the Anadolu Group[13] started to produce beer at the end of the 1960s, the bosses of the group were worried about the reactions of "conservative business people," since alcoholic beverages are forbidden in Islam. However, a proposal from the Ülker and Topbaş groups, two famous conservative families, to build a joint industrial plant gave them some relief (Yazıcı 2007: 103). After an aluminum factory was put into operation in 1973, the collaboration of Ülker and the Anadolu Group continued in new joint ventures. Thus, there was cooperation between the secular and Islamist big bourgeoisie, at a time when the divide between big business and SMEs was growing.

As a food monopoly, Ülker started its activities in 1944 in a small workshop, producing biscuits. The first factory went into operation four years later, and during the 1950s Ülker became a monopolist in the biscuit market thanks to its large distribution network covering the whole of Turkey. With the establishment of a rival company (Eti) in 1962, the market took the shape of a duopoly, but Ülker continued to dominate it with a more than 50 percent share. This duopoly structure proved stable for about fifty years. A similar situation can be observed in the ceramic sector, where a "gentlemen's agreement" between the "conservative" Kale Group and the secular Eczacıbaşı Group signed at the end of the 1950s has led to a similar result (Öztürk 2010: 399–400).

The "conservative" faction of Turkish finance capital emerged in collaboration with the "secular" one. Moreover, there was no visible difference between the two in terms of organization and business characteristics (such as diversification). In the case of Ülker, the group started to produce chocolate during the 1970s and became a monopoly in this field also. In time it diversified into new sectors, but these were still "related" branches such as packaging and the production of raw materials such as flour, sugar, and fats. Hence, the group integrated vertically in food products by internalizing all the production stages. When this kind of vertical integration was completed, Ülker started a horizontal integration during the mid-1990s and diversified widely into new subsectors such as dairy products, instant coffee, baby food, cakes, convenience foods, soft drinks, and so forth. At the beginning of the twenty-first century, Ülker had a clear monopoly position in most of these branches (Öztürk 2010: 300–10). In 2008 it had 53 factories (of which nine were established abroad) and was producing some 2,700 articles under 160 brands (Ülker Bisküvi 2009: 6).

While Ülker and other conservative groups were definitely a part of Turkish finance capital from the beginning, Islamist big bourgeoisie as a whole was not very effective during the ISI period. Apart from Ülker, Topbaş (which was organically linked to Ülker), and Kale, what I call "conservative finance capital" grew typically after 1980 in the context of a neoliberal economy, as shown by the emergence and development of newer conglomerates such as Çalık, Sanko, Boydak, Toprak, and Albayrak.

Conservative Finance Capital under Neoliberalism

In the second half of the 1970s, the ISI process that had been going on for the previous two decades faced a great crisis in Turkey. With increasing worker militancy on the one hand and the permanent foreign exchange problems associated with ISI on the other, Turkish capitalism had reached a critical conjuncture. Apparently, there were two alternatives for the bourgeoisie at the time: either the ISI process would continue expanding or the economy would be liberalized with an outward-oriented model. At the end of the 1970s, Turkish big business clearly tended toward the second option, which was in line with the demands of the International Monetary Fund (IMF), the World Bank and other institutions of world capitalism. In 1978, TÜSİAD was demanding structural transformation of the economy, while the Koç Group was campaigning for the abandonment of the "inward-oriented development model" (Öztürk 2010: 125). An ambitious liberalization project took off in 1980, backed by the most violent military coup in the history of Turkey.[14]

The year 1980 was a clear turning point for Turkish capitalism. Inward-oriented development ended and a new, outward-oriented and liberal model was established. To be sure, this was not an easy task, and it took decades to gradually create an "open economy." Two interrelated processes accompanied this transformation. On the one hand, there was systematic repression of the working class during the "liberalization" of the economy. Real wages went down consistently throughout the next thirty years, except for brief periods. On the other hand, the military junta promoted Islamism as an antidote to socialist currents, and a Turkish-Islamic synthesis came to represent the official ideology of the state (Şen 2010). According to M. Hakan Yavuz, since 1980, Turkey has experienced the gradual Islamization of society, the market, and the state, coinciding with the construction of a new official Turkish-Islamic state ideology. The official policy of promoting a "Turkish-Islamic synthesis" was meant to co-opt socially powerful Islamic movements ... and to use them against what in hindsight was a much-exaggerated leftist "threat." (2003: 38)

Gradual Islamization, pro-business governments, and contralabor policies characterize the post-1980 period of Turkey. In a general sense, the military coup and the ensuing government of Turgut Özal's Anavatan Partisi (Motherland Party, ANAP) signified an alliance of all the business factions against labor. The alliance of liberals and conservatives was personified in Özal himself, displaying the conservative proclivities of neoliberalism (Doğan 2006).[15]

In 1983, following the reign of the military junta, one of the first decrees of the first elected government (Turgut Özal's ANAP) was about the formation of new financial bodies, so-called special finance institutions (SFIs). These institutions would perform banking activities in accordance with religious rules, that is, *without* interest revenues. At the time of a petro dollar glut, there was an obvious intent on the part of the government to establish close links with international Islamic financial capital. Korkut Özal, the brother of the prime minister, was a key figure in this relationship (Bulut 1997).

SFIs (later called "participation banks") became important channels for the integration of Turkish and Arabic capital.[16] But they could not break the oligopoly power of a small group of private banks. As of 2010, after twenty-five years of operation, there are four SFIs in Turkey, three of them owned by foreign capital, and their total assets are less than 5 percent of the Turkish banking system (TKBB 2010). Only a few banks continue to dominate the banking sector, thanks to the "holding banking" practice that signifies the controlling of banks by big business groups. In a country with a bank-based financial system, this means that business groups managed to control the main sources of money capital, which resulted in the exclusion of the SMEs from the credit system. In this regard, SFIs were important but not very effective institutions. Islamic capital had to find some new ways to overcome money capital scarcity.

The answer came in the form of Anatolian holding companies (Özcan and Çokgezen 2003, 2006; Adaş 2009). These were multishareholder enterprises, usually established by collecting the idle capital resources of religious community members. Ideal participants for such undertakings were the Turkish workers in Europe, with high amounts of savings and Islamic sensibilities. Anatolian holding companies operated in accordance with Islamic finance rules, issuing shares and bonds to share their profits and losses. Around two hundred holding companies were established in the conservative cities of Anatolia (especially Konya) in this way. But their operations were in fact largely illegal; to avoid legal limitations they were not registered in the Capital Markets Board.

The golden age of the Anatolian holding companies was the 1990s, especially the brief ruling period of Erbakan's Welfare Party (June 1996–June 1997). This was the first instance of an openly Islamist prime minister in Turkey. Increasing its influence and winning the two most important municipalities (Istanbul and Ankara) in the 1994 local elections, political Islam came to power in 1996 as a major coalition partner. Not surprisingly, the rise of Islamic capital accompanied the rise of political Islam. The municipalities turned into channels for capital accumulation, and fast growth opportunities emerged for the Islamist bourgeoisie. At the time, companies such as Kombassan, Jet-Pa, and Yimpaş had thousands of shareholders.

For example, Kombassan was established in 1988, and over time had collected money from more than thirty thousand small investors. With a diversified business portfolio spread across ten different sectors, it owned 56 factories with 27,500 workers and an overseas retail chain (Hit or Miss) in the United States (Dinçel 1998). However, the 28 February process signified the end of the good times for Kombassan and the other Anatolian holding companies. Many of them were liquidated, and almost all of them were investigated by state agencies in this period (Özcan and Çokgezen 2003).

Anatolian holding companies attracted the savings of religious people by promising Islamic economic development and large-scale industrial investments. As can be expected, potential shareholders were not enthusiastic to share the losses of an enterprise, so the investments of these companies were typically concentrated in quick-return commercial sectors. In an almost totally unregulated environment, swindlers also emerged, some of them with huge collections of assets but no real investments. When the Welfare Party was closed down by the Constitutional Court, their political support disappeared. The bankruptcies of Jet-Pa and İhlas Finance, huge enterprises with thousands of investors, triggered the failure of many others by ending the money capital inflow. The system collapsed, leading to a disaster in which several hundred thousand small investors lost money (Adaş 2009).

The case of İhlas is interesting because it represents a hybrid form, partly an Anatolian holding company and partly conservative finance capital. The group belongs to the Işıkçılar branch of the Nakşibendi community and started publishing a daily newspaper (*Türkiye*) in 1970. During the 1980s, the group started a home appliances business that included production and marketing, thanks to the advertisement and distribution facilities provided by the newspaper. Close personal links with the Özal government brought fast growth, and İhlas soon diversified into new sectors such as construction, which led to further ventures including tourism, private hospitals, thermal spring hotels, and so forth. In the 1990s, İhlas diversified even further and started businesses in mining, textiles, soft drinks, energy, production of bicycles and motorcycles, and radio/TV broadcasting. Moreover, İhlas made a spectacular entry into the financial sector, establishing an insurance company, an SFI for Islamic banking, and partnerships with two commercial banks. Hence, İhlas was collecting money deposits from religious customers and community fellows via İhlas Finance, and from "secular" customers via other banks. However, soon after establishing these operations İhlas fell into trouble. At the turn of the millennium, İhlas Finance collapsed, with total deposits of 1.2 billion dollars in 270,000 accounts. This failure affected all the group companies, and in the 2000s İhlas sold many of its assets, downsizing in order to survive (Bulut 1999: 88–100, 300–2; Öztürk 2010: 439–45).

In retrospect, Anatolian holding companies can be regarded as passing forms of finance capital that cannot survive under "globalized" accumulation. The illegal nature of their deposit collection methods was in fact the secret of their success, and their eventual downfall. Yet they were not blocked by the state for about a decade (Adaş 2009). In a sense, they functioned as "vanishing mediators" that enlarged the capital base of the financial system by collecting otherwise idle money resources, and when they grew enough, the state and big business launched a campaign against "Islamic capital": these holdings were violating the rules of the competition game, just like the Welfare Party backing them.

Apart from the Anatolian holding companies and "hybrid" examples such as İhlas, a much more important development was the growth of conservative finance capital under neoliberalism. New business groups such as Çalık, Sanko, Toprak, Sancak, Boydak, Albayrak, and so forth grew in this era, usually starting from a strong export base focused on textile production and then diversifying into new sectors. For example, the Çalık Group was active in the textiles business for decades. Ahmet Çalık, the son of the founder of the group, established his first factories during the 1980s and then started a construction business. During the 1990s, he formed close personal links with the president of the newly independent Turkmenistan. In 1995, he was appointed vice minister of the Textiles Ministry of Turkmenistan. New textile factories and construction projects in Turkmenistan followed. This growth directed Çalık to new sectors in Turkey, such as energy, oil, banking, cellular network operations, and even the media. The group diversified geographically as well, with banking and telecommunications companies in Albania, construction projects in the Middle East and the Balkans region, and so on. These moves were backed by the AKP government. Indeed, Çalık was perhaps the most favored business group by the AKP. It increased its assets fourfold, from 1 billion to 4.4 billion dollars between 2002 and 2008 (Öztürk 2010: 418–25). But similar trajectories for other conservative groups can also be observed.

As seen clearly in Çalık's case, the fall of the Soviet Union provided new activity areas for Turkish business groups.[17] Although not as successful as the Western imperialist countries, Turkey also seized the opportunity, and Turkish firms tried to invest in the former Soviet republics (Jung and Piccoli 2001: 184–86). The Caucasian and Central Asian countries emerged as especially suitable areas for capital exports by Turkish business groups of all kinds. Surely not a significant and independent power on its own, Turkish capitalism started expanding into neighboring regions in the last twenty years in collaboration with Western powers. The rise of the AKP cannot be understood without taking into account this international expansion. As Islamist currents became much more "globalist" and business-friendly in their outlook, a synthesis between Islam and neoliberal capitalism embodied in the pragmatist approach of the AKP emerged. At the same time, "liberal" capitalists became much more sympathetic toward religious practices. Although this looked like a fragile and contingent alliance at first, it turned out to be necessary for both sides.

The Rise of the AKP

In parallel with the liberalization and "opening" of the Turkish economy, conservative and religious currents gained strength in Turkey. This process brought two basic advantages for the Turkish bourgeoisie as a whole. First, the working class clearly lost its militancy and became much less combative in the meantime. In this regard, trade unions such as the nonmilitant TÜRK-İŞ (Türkiye

İşçi Sendikalari Konfederasyonu, Confederation of Turkish Trade Unions) and the Islamist HAK-İŞ (Türkiye Hak İşçi Sendikaları, Confederation of Turkish Real Trade Unions) were supported by the government at a time when the revolutionary DİSK (Türkiye Devrimci İşçi Sendikaları Konfederasyonu, Confederation of Progressive Trade Unions of Turkey) was banned. Yet, on the whole, trade union membership declined significantly since the 1980s (Çelik and Lordoğlu 2006: 27–28). This created a basic "competitive advantage" for Turkish companies in the global market. Specifically in the Islamic firms, a paternalistic and informal model of labor relations developed along with increasing export capacity. The flexible and export-oriented nature of production in these firms means that they are "crucial nodes within a new international division of labour" (Hoşgör 2011: 350). The growth of Islamic capital is not surprising, since it fits well into the new configurations of capitalist relations of production.

Second, religious discourses helped the Turkish bourgeoisie overcome the limitations of its earlier nationalistic outlook. Islamic identity functioned as the key for investments in many countries, especially in the Middle East and Central Asia. For example, the Gülen movement, a branch of the Nurcu community, is famous for its transnational Islamist network that includes schools, hostels, and other "educational" institutions. With hundreds of missionary schools in about one hundred countries, the Gülen movement is tightly organized around the world, creating a space for various economic activities at the same time (Hendrick 2009: 358). TUSKON, the business branch of the movement founded in 2005, has twelve thousand members and is focused on building commercial relations with Africa, the Middle East, and Asia (TUSKON 2011), taking advantage of the personal links formed via the Gülen schools.

The fusion of Islam and capitalism is not a new phenomenon in Turkey. But the capitalist outlook of Erbakan and other Islamist currents were not globalistic and liberal enough for the new era. Hence, as the integration of the Turkish economy with the world capitalist system intensified, Erbakan's policies became increasingly outmoded. This was seen clearly during his brief appointment as prime minister in 1996 when all the big business groups and the armed forces revolted against the government after only one year of his term.

As can be expected, Islamist business associations did not take part in this opposition to the government. At the time, these were new kinds of business organizations, with MÜSİAD as the pioneer.

Established in 1990, MÜSİAD was demanding an increase in the share of the SMEs within the Turkish economy, and became very effective especially during the rule of Erbakan (Alkan 1998: 167). Similar associations emerged at around the same time, such as İş Hayatı Dayanışma Derneği (Business Life Cooperation Association, İŞHAD) of the Gülen community in 1993 and Anadolu Aslanları İşadamları Derneği (Association of Anatolian Businessmen, ASKON). The latter was established in 1998 as a splinter group from MÜSİAD (Çemrek 2002: 150).

MÜSİAD members were (and still are) usually small- or medium-scale firms with less than fifty workers, most of them founded after 1980 and focused on textiles, construction, food, and services. Its membership increased regularly until 1998, when it reached three thousand, but then started to decrease (for a short time) because of the fall of the Welfare Party government and the Asian crisis (Çemrek 2002: 166–68). Indeed, the Asian crisis affected MÜSİAD negatively, since the association was proposing the "Asian tigers" model that would supposedly favor the SMEs as opposed to big business.

Islamist business associations created platforms for Islamic capital clusters of various sizes, including conservative finance capital, Anatolian holding companies, SMEs, and companies of religious orders. These organizations formed the most dynamic elements behind political Islam, at a time when Turkish capitalism was becoming increasingly integrated with the world capitalist system. In this process, not only the big business segments but also the SMEs of the newly industrializing cities of Anatolia expanded into the global markets. On the other hand, the same developments also accelerated differentiation within Islamic capital. Some of the SMEs acquired remarkable dimensions, typically diversified into new sectors, and established "holding" companies (Aksakal 2010). They started to question the existing distribution of economic power.

However, the 28 February process and the failure of the Anatolian holding companies created disillusionment on the part of the new Islamist bourgeoisie. Coupled with the Asian crisis and the Turkish crises of 2000–1, these events forced MÜSİAD to reduce its earlier radical emphases considerably. Hence, at the turn of the millennium, the Islamist bourgeoisie tended to adopt a more "moderate" position in Turkey (Doğan 2006; Demiralp 2009). When the AKP emerged in 2001 as a splinter party from the Fazilet Partisi (Virtue Party, FP) of the National Vision movement, and as a political party in line with the requirements of globalized capitalism, MÜSİAD and other conservative business organizations more than opted for this new party. "For instance, about ten MÜSİAD members were also founding members of the AKP, and about 20 MÜSİAD members became AKP deputies in the 2002 elections" (Şen 2010: 71). There were organic links between the AKP and conservative finance capital. Even Prime Minister Tayyip Erdoğan was operating distributor companies for the Ülker Group. Not surprisingly, Ülker grew very fast during AKP rule, but other groups grew also, with a tempo perhaps not matched throughout their history (Öztürk 2010: 185, 302).

When in power, the AKP pursued neoliberal policies uncompromisingly, thus giving a new impetus to neoliberalism as a project, which had slowed down in the second half of the 1990s (Doğan 2010). The policies included an aggressive privatization program, concessions to foreign capital in various fields, commodification of health and education services, plundering of natural resources to increase the profitability of capital, a new labor law that legalized flexible work and other demands of business groups, and various "social aid" programs for the management of poverty. Moreover, especially during its first term between 2002 and 2007, the AKP made a great effort to advance Turkey's membership in the European Union (EU). These neoliberal and pro-EU policies provided the government continuous support from TÜSİAD.

The AKP represents the class interests of the conservative bourgeoisie, and especially the big business segment of this group. It can be claimed that, with the advantage of political power, conservative finance capital has placed itself as a subject that has to be taken into account within the power structure of Turkey. This has produced some tensions and struggles (if not a "civil war") within the big bourgeoisie (Tanyılmaz 2011). Analysis of the political conflicts going on between the various factions of the bourgeoisie in Turkey is beyond the scope of this chapter. However, despite its opposition to some of the AKP government's policies, TÜSİAD still supports the AKP. Moreover, international support from the United States and the EU also continues. This suggests that, behind the apparent conflicts in the political scene, there is a strong cooperation. Indeed, the implementation of neoliberal policies requires conservative or repressive administrative practices, and the AKP is preferable for Turkish big business, at least for the moment, not in spite of its conservatism, but exactly because of it.[18]

Conclusion

As a late industrializer, Turkey has witnessed the rise of big business in a very short time. Monopolistic capitalism was well established at the end of the 1960s, and this created some contradictions between finance capital and smaller capitalists, symbolized by the Erbakan event in 1969. At the same time, a conservative finance capital faction emerged not in opposition to, but in cooperation with, the "secular" business groups. Yet the main growth of conservative finance capital came after 1980, when the Turkish economy was restructured along a neoliberal line. In this new period, gradual Islamization of society went hand in hand with neoliberalism. The basic and interrelated consequences of increasing conservatism were the decline of working-class militancy and new opportunities for the international expansion of Turkish capital, especially after the fall of the Soviet Union.

The rise of Islamism also meant resistance *against* monopolistic capitalism. The Anatolian holding companies of the 1990s held such a stance. By drawing on the capital resources of religious people, these enterprises assumed the size of big business for a brief time period. However, the 28 February process was a turning point in their fate, and most of them were liquidated at the turn of the millennium.

Conservative business associations emerged in the 1990s as another objection to the rule of big business. MÜSİAD and the others following it demanded economic policies favoring SMEs, with a vision based on the success of the "Asian tigers." However, the Asian crisis and the 28 February process destroyed that vision as well and created disillusionment on the part of the Islamist bourgeoisie.

As Turkish capitalism became integrated with the world economy, smaller capitalists of Anatolia formed close links with international capital. With the help of lower labor costs, many SMEs in the newly industrializing cities such as Konya, Gaziantep, Denizli, and Kayseri became exporters or subcontractors for foreign producers. A transformation in their worldview gradually took place, making the National Vision of Erbakan increasingly obsolete. Hence, a new and "globalist" approach was necessary for Islamists, and the AKP emerged as the candidate to realize such a synthesis between Islam and neoliberal capitalism. Islamist entrepreneurs, and especially conservative finance capital, preferred the AKP and rapidly left the National Vision movement. This new synthesis was also preferable for the secular segments of the big bourgeoisie, and the AKP clearly succeeded in satisfying their demands.

Islamist *big* bourgeoisie was a part of Turkish finance capital from the beginning. This faction displayed a low-profile existence during the ISI period, but became more visible in the neoliberal epoch, especially after the 1990s. While the Anatolian holding companies virtually disappeared during the 2000s, conservative finance capital found the opportunity for fast growth, but this was true for the secular faction of the big bourgeoisie also. Even if blurred by many complex relations, this is basically a class issue. In order to understand the rise of Islamism in Turkey, or other places, an analysis of class relations is essential. Only then can one see that beneath the surface there is a solidarity of the various factions of capital against labor.

Notes

I would like to thank the editors for their continuous support in the writing of this chapter.

1. These are the two most effective Islamist business associations in Turkey. MÜSİAD is the acronym for Müstakil Sanayici ve İşadamları Derneği (Independent Industrialists' and Businessmen's Association), and TUSKON stands for Türkiye İşadamları ve Sanayiciler Konfederasyonu (Turkish Confederation of Businessmen and Industrialists). The "MÜ" of MÜSİAD, from "Müstakil" ("independent" in Turkish), simultaneously suggests "Muslim." While MÜSİAD does not belong to a single religious community (*cemaat*), TUSKON is usually accepted as the business branch of the Fethullah Gülen community (also known as the Gülen movement).
2. TÜSİAD is the acronym for Türk Sanayicileri ve İşadamları Derneği (Turkish Industrialists' and Businessmen's Association).
3. Incidentally, seventeen companies were members of both associations.
4. Calculated from ISO (2010).
5. As of 2008, MÜSİAD members (around 3,000) produced between 6 and 8 percent of the gross national product (GNP) and realized 11.5 percent of Turkey's exports. For TÜSİAD (with 576 members), these figures were 38 and 45 percent, respectively, in 2007 (Toprak 2009).
6. Türk Girişim ve İş Dünyası Konfederasyonu (Turkish Enterprise and Business Confederation).
7. For example, conservative groups such as Çalık and Boydak are TÜSİAD members (see the list of members in TÜSİAD [2013: 83–91]). The food monopoly Ülker Group, the ceramic monopoly Kale Group, and the conglomerate İhlas Holding have (or had) memberships in both TÜSİAD and MÜSİAD (Can 1997; Bozkurt 2006). Some members of TÜSİAD (e.g., Cüneyd Zapsu) have (or had) close business ties with well-known Islamic capitalists (Dündar 2006). Even the founding president of MÜSİAD, Erol Yarar, is the son of a wealthy industrialist and TÜSİAD member (Özgentürk 2009).
8. I am using the concept of "finance capital" here in a sense close to the original, as developed by the Austrian Marxist Rudolf Hilferding one century ago (Hilferding 1981). It is the combination of bank capital, industrial capital, and commercial capital

fused in a typically monopolistic manner. Turkish business groups (or "family holdings") clearly have the characteristics of finance capital. For more information on Turkish business groups, see Öztürk (2010) and Gültekin-Karakaş (2008).

9. See Tanyılmaz (2011), who places a much stronger emphasis than this chapter on the internal divisions and conflicts within Turkish finance capital.

10. The political parties founded by the National Vision movement (and closed by the courts) were the MNP (1970–71), MSP (1972–80), Refah Partisi (Welfare Party, RP, 1983–98), and Fazilet Partisi (Virtue Party, FP, 1997–2001). The Saadet Partisi (Felicity Party, SP), founded in 2001, is the latest party of this political line.

11. Throughout the ISI period two center parties, AP on the right and Cumhuriyet Halk Partisi (Republican People's Party, CHP), supposedly on the left, dominated the majority of votes, while the remaining minority was shared by the nationalist Milliyetçi Hareket Partisi (Nationalist Action Party, MHP), the Islamist MSP, and the socialist Türkiye İşçi Partisi (Workers' Party of Turkey, TİP). This political configuration changed after the 1980 military coup, and Islamist currents gained strength at a time when the socialist left was literally smashed by the military junta.

12. However, there were additional factors in the establishment of TÜSİAD. First, the worker insurgency of 15–16 June 1970 had caused a real fear among big capitalists, and they had decided to pursue their interests more actively by shaping public opinion through various channels. Moreover, they needed an organization in order to pressure for integration with Europe (Gülfidan 1993).

13. This group should not be confused with "Anadolu Finance" referred to in note 16 below.

14. Yalman (2009) provides a good analysis of this "transition to neoliberalism."

15. Interestingly, Özal was a parliamentary candidate of Erbakan's MSP before 1980. Yet his appointment as the minister of economy by the military junta was fully supported by TÜSİAD.

16. During the 1980s three SFIs were established by Arabic capital, namely, Albaraka Türk, Faisal Finance, and Kuveyt Türk, followed by three more in the 1990s, this time by Turkish capital: Anadolu Finance, İhlas Finance, and Asya Finance (Bank Asya). İhlas Finance went bankrupt in 2001. Anadolu Finance was acquired by the Boydak Group in 1999, and Faisal Finance was acquired by the Ülker Group in 2001. These two SFIs merged in 2005 under the name Türkiye Finance, to be sold to the Saudi Arabian National Commercial Bank in 2008.

17. "By the end of the 1990s, 2500 Turkish companies were operating in a wide range of investment projects in the Central Asian republics, with their investment reaching $8.4 billion and involving $4 billion in construction services. Trade volume climbed from a meager $145 million in 1992 to over $5.6 billion in 1999. Moreover, Turkey extended bank credits amounting to $1.5 billion, with official agencies such as the Turkish Eximbank playing an instrumental role. Significant investments undertaken by Turkey in telecommunications played an important role in linking the republics to international markets" (Öniş 2001: 68).

18. In this regard, contrary to the claims of Gümüşçü and Sert (2009), the unclear nature of the AKP's conservatism and its ambiguous relationship with political Islam do not seem to be a weakness on the part of the AKP. First, there is no clear border between Islamism and conservatism in Turkey, and transitions from one to the other are always possible within the context of the Turkish-Islamic synthesis. Second, in order to cover a wide electoral base, a certain dose of vagueness in political-ideological issues is an ability that a mass party like the AKP makes use of.

References

Adaş, Emin Baki. 2009. "Production of Trust and Distrust: Transnational Networks, Islamic Holding Companies and the State in Turkey." *Middle Eastern Studies* 45, no. 4: 625–36.
Aksakal, Ayşe Tarcan. 2010. "Anadolu'nun Yükselen Holdingleri" [The rising holdings of Anatolia]. *Capital*, February.
Alkan, Haluk. 1998. "Türkiye'de Baskı Grupları: Siyaset ve İşadamı Örgütlenmeleri (Odalar–TÜSİAD–MÜSİAD)" [Pressure groups in Turkey: Politics and organization of businessmen (The Chambers–TÜSİAD–MÜSİAD)]. PhD dissertation, Marmara University.
Bianchi, Robert. 1984. *Interest Groups and Political Development in Turkey*. Princeton, NJ: Princeton University Press.
Boratav, Korkut. 1974. *100 Soruda Türkiye'de Devletçilik* [Statism in Turkey in 100 questions]. Istanbul: Gerçek.
Bozkurt, Turhan. 2006. "Murat Ülker: Hem TÜSİAD'a Hem MÜSİAD'a Hem Fener'e Üyeyim" [Murat Ülker: I'm a member of TÜSİAD, MÜSİAD and Fener]. *Zaman*, 22 December.
Bulut, Faik. 1997. *Tarikat Sermayesinin Yükselişi* [The rise of religious orders' capital]. Ankara: Doruk.
_____. 1999. *Tarikat Sermayesi: II—İslamcı Şirketler Nereye?* [Religious orders' capital: II— whither the Islamist companies?]. Istanbul: Su.
Can, Kemal. 1997. "Tekkeden Holdinge Yeşil Sermaye" [Green money from the dervish lodge to the holding]. *Milliyet*, 11–18 March, in eight parts.
Çelik, Aziz, and Kuvvet Lordoğlu. 2006. "Türkiye'de Resmi Sendikalaşma İstatistiklerinin Sorunları Üstüne" [On the problems of official unionization statistics in Turkey]. *Çalışma ve Toplum*, no. 2: 11–29.
Çemrek, Murat. 2002. *Formation and Representation of Interests in Turkish Political Economy: The Case of MÜSİAD (Independent Industrialists' and Businessmen's Association)*. PhD dissertation, Bilkent University.
Demir, Ömer, Mustafa Acar, and Metin Toprak. 2004. "Anatolian Tigers or Islamic Capital: Prospects and Challenges." *Middle Eastern Studies* 40, no. 6: 166–88.
Demiralp, Seda. 2009. "The Rise of Islamic Capital and the Decline of Islamic Radicalism in Turkey." *Comparative Politics* 41, no. 3: 315–35.
Dinçel, Gülay. 1999. "Konya'nın Kombassan'ı ve Haşim Bayram'ın Yükselişi" [Kombassan of Konya and the rise of Haşim Bayram]. In *75 Yılda Çarkları Döndürenler* [Those who turned the wheels in 75 years], ed. Oya Baydar and Gülay Dinçel, 151–65. Istanbul: Tarih Vakfı.
Doğan, Ali Ekber. 2006. "Siyasal Yansımalarıyla İslamcı Sermayenin Gelişme Dinamikleri ve 28 Şubat Süreci" [The development dynamics of Islamic capital with its political reflections and the February 28 process]. *Mülkiye* 30, no. 252: 47–68.
_____. 2010. "AKP'li Hegemonya Projesi ve Neoliberalizmin Yeniden Dirilişi" [The hegemony project carried by the AKP and the resurgence of neoliberalism]. *Praksis*, no. 23: 85–109.
Dündar, Can. 2006. "Zapsu, Erdoğan ile Yasin El Kadı'yı Evinde Tanıştırdı" [Zapsu introduced Erdoğan to Yasin El Kadı at his home]. *Milliyet*, 17 July.
Eligür, Banu. 2010. *The Mobilization of Political Islam in Turkey*. New York: Cambridge University Press.
Genç, Rafet. 1969. "Batur'u 'Koltuk'a Polis Oturttu" [Batur came to power with the help of the police]. *Milliyet*, 9 August.
Gülalp, Haldun. 1985. "Patterns of Capital Accumulation and State-Society Relations in Turkey." *Journal of Contemporary Asia* 15, no. 3: 329–48.

Gülfidan, Şebnem. 1993. *Big Business and the State in Turkey: The Case of TÜSİAD.* İstanbul: Boğaziçi University Press.

Gültekin-Karakaş, Derya. 2008. *Global Integration of Turkish Finance Capital: State, Capital and Banking Reform in Turkey.* Saarbrücken: Vdm Verlag Dr. Müller.

Gümüşcü, Şebnem, and Deniz Sert. 2009. "The Power of the Devout Bourgeoisie: The Case of the Justice and Development Party in Turkey." *Middle Eastern Studies* 45, no. 6: 953–68.

Gündoğdu, İbrahim. 2009. "Sermayenin Bölgesel Kalkınma Eğilim(ler)i: Kalkınma Ajansları Yasası Üzerine Tarihsel-Coğrafi Materyalist Bir İnceleme" [Capital's tendencies in regional development: A historical-geographical materialist investigation on the law of regional development agencies]." *Praksis*, no. 19: 267–302.

Hendrick, Joshua D. 2009. "Globalization, Islamic Activism, and Passive Revolution in Turkey: The Case of Fethullah Gülen." *Journal of Power* 2, no. 3: 343–68.

Hilferding, Rudolf. 1981. *Finance Capital: A Study of the Latest Phase of Capitalist Development.* London: Routledge & Kegan Paul.

Hoşgör, Evren. 2011. "Islamic Capital/Anatolian Tigers: Past and Present." *Middle Eastern Studies* 47, no. 2: 343–60.

ISO (Istanbul Chamber of Industry). 2010. "Türkiye'nin 500 Büyük Sanayi Kuruluşu—2009" [500 Largest Industrial Enterprises of Turkey—2009]. Accessed July 2010. http://www.iso.org.tr.

Jung, Dietrich, and Wolfango Piccoli. 2001. *Turkey at the Crossroads.* London and New York: Zed Books.

Kahraman, Hasan Bülent. 2008. "Anadolu-İstanbul Meydan Muharebesi" [The Anatolia-Istanbul battle]. *Sabah*, 15 September.

Keyder, Çağlar. 1987. *State and Class in Turkey: A Study in Capitalist Development.* London and New York: Verso.

Koraltürk, Murat. 1999. "İmparatorluktan Cumhuriyet'e Türkiye'de Sanayi Sermayesinin Örgütlenmesi" [The organization of industrial capital in Turkey from the empire to the republic]. In Baydar and Dinçel, *75 Yılda Çarkları Döndürenler*, 291–98.

Koyuncu, Berrin. 2002. "Küreselleşme ve MÜSİAD: Eklemlenme mi, Çatışma mı?" [Globalization and MÜSİAD: Articulation or conflict?]. In *Liberalizm, Devlet, Hegemonya* [Liberalism, state, hegemony], ed. E. Fuat Keyman, 358–76. İstanbul: Everest.

Milliyet. 1969. "Prof. Erbakan Odalar Birliği Başkanı Oldu" [Prof. Erbakan elected president to the Chambers]. 26 May.

———. 2010. "Muhafazakâr Yükseliş" [The rise of conservatism]. 28 July.

Mollaveisoğlu, Tuncay. 2008. *Görünmez Holding: Bir Yolsuzluk Belgeseli* [The invisible holding: A documentary of fraud]. İstanbul: Siyah Beyaz.

Öncü, Ayşe. 1983. "Cumhuriyet Döneminde Odalar" [The Chambers during the republican period]. In *Cumhuriyet Dönemi Türkiye Ansiklopedisi* [The encyclopedia of the republican period of turkey], ed. Murat Belge, Seyfettin Gürsel, Mete Tunçay and Bülent Özükan, vol. 6, 1566–76. İstanbul: İletişim.

Öniş, Ziya. 2001. "Turkey and Post-Soviet States: Potential and Limits of Regional Power Influence." *Middle East Review of International Affairs* 5, no. 2: 66–74.

Özcan, Gül Berna, and Murat Çokgezen. 2003. "Limits to Alternative Forms of Capitalization: The Case of Anatolian Holding Companies." *World Development* 31, no. 12: 2061–84.

———. 2006. "Trusted Markets: The Exchanges of Islamic Companies." *Comparative Economic Studies*, no. 48: 132–55.

Özdemir, Sadi. 2002. "Ülker, Kadı ile Saraç'ı Gönderdi" [Ülker sent away Kadı and Saraç]. *Hürriyet*, 21 April.

Özgentürk, Jale. 2009. "Solcu, TÜSİAD'çı Babanın Muhafazakar MÜSİAD'çı Oğlu" [The conservative, MÜSİAD member son of the leftist, TÜSİAD member]. *Referans*, 15 August.

Öztürk, Özgür. 2010. *Türkiye'de Büyük Sermaye Grupları: Finans Kapitalin Oluşumu ve Gelişimi* [Big business groups in Turkey: The formation and development of finance capital]. Istanbul: Sosyal Araştırmalar Vakfı.

Radikal. 2006. "Murat Ülker: Tayyip Beye Ülker'i Bırak Demiştim" [Murat Ülker: I had told Tayyip Bey to leave Ülker]. 22 December.

Şen, Mustafa. 2010. "Transformation of Turkish Islamism and the Rise of the Justice and Development Party." *Turkish Studies* 11, no. 1: 59–84.

Silier, Orhan. 1977. "Genel Olarak ve Türkiye Sanayiinde Yoğunlaşma, Toplulaşma, Tekelleşme" [Concentration, agglomeration, monopolization in general and in the Turkish industry]. In *1976 Sanayi Kongresi*, 1–42. Ankara: MMO.

Tanyılmaz, Kurtar. 2011. "Burjuvazinin İç Çatışmasının Sınıfsal Temelleri" [Class bases of the internal struggle of the bourgeoisie]. *Devrimci Marksizm*, no. 12: 66–95.

TKBB (Participation Banks Association of Turkey). 2010. "Türk Finans Sisteminde Katılım Bankaları" [Participation banks in the Turkish financial system]. Accessed July 2010. www.tkbb.org.tr.

Toprak, Levent. 2009. "'İslamcı' Sermaye ve Fethullah Gülen Cemaati/1" ["Islamic" capital and Fethullah Gülen community/1]. *Marksist Tutum*, no. 52. Accessed July 2010. www.marksisttutum.org/islamci_sermaye_ve_fethullah_gulen_cemaati_1.htm.

Tuna, Ş. Gürçağ. 2009. "Birikim Sürecinde TOBB'un Tarihsel Gelişim Uğrakları" [The historical development of TOBB in the accumulation process]. *Praksis*, no. 19: 303–36.

TÜSİAD (Turkish Industrialists' and Businessmen's Association). 2013. "2012 Çalışma Raporu" [2012 activity report]. Accessed May 2013. http://www.tusiad.org.tr.

TUSKON (Turkish Confederation of Businessmen and Industrialists). 2011. "Presentation." Accessed May 2013. http://www.tuskon.org/uploaded/pdf/bro_en.pdf.

Ülker Bisküvi. 2009. "Ülker Bisküvi Sanayi A.Ş. 2008 Faaliyet Raporu" [Ülker Bisküvi Sanayi A.Ş. 2008 company report]. Accessed July 2010. http://www.ulkerbiskuvi.com.tr.

Ülsever, Cüneyt. 2005. "Türkiye'nin Yeni Dinamiği Muhafazakar Girişimciler" [Turkey's new dynamic: The conservative enterpreneurs]. *Çerçeve*, no. 35 (March): 26–28.

Yalman, Galip L. 2009. *Transition to Neoliberalism: The Case of Turkey in the 1980s*. Istanbul: Istanbul Bilgi University Press.

Yavuz, M. Hakan. 2003. *Islamic Political Identity in Turkey*. New York: Oxford University Press.

Yazıcı, Kamil. 2007. *Ortak Akıl* [Common intellect]. Istanbul: Anadolu Grubu.

– Chapter 5 –

ISLAMIC CAPITAL

Evren Hoşgör

❧

Introduction

The emergence of a specific business group in Turkey, Islamic capital (also known as "green" capital or the Anatolian Tigers), has been an interesting topic for many researchers. Some explain their rise in terms of individual efforts or "entrepreneurial spirit" (Özdemir 2004).[1] Others either rely strongly on the religious/conservative discourse of such businessmen (Koyuncu 2002; Özdemir 2006), or concentrate on their specific consumption patterns and lifestyle as the main indicator of class formation (Sandıkçı and Ger 2001; Demir et al. 2004). Moreover, since contradictions among different business groups (capital fractions) are generally reduced to distributional conflicts, the rivalry between the Istanbul-based business circles and the Anatolian Tigers are equated to size- and region-related conflicts (Öniş and Türem 2001). This also leads to a general misconception that Islamic capital is mostly composed of small- and medium-scale enterprises (SMEs) and that its economic domain is reducible to an enclave or subeconomy. However, there has been a significant change in its size, scope, and regional orientation; hence, it is not fair to label all SMEs as Islamic, or all Islamic capital as SMEs. Despite the growing literature, researchers still have difficulties in distinguishing between the two, however (Can 1997).

This chapter discusses the development of Islamic capital from a rather different perspective. It argues that such research does not provide a criterion with which Islamic capital as such can be identified as a separate capital fraction that pursues a *distinct* and *collective* agenda. Indeed, a group of individual capitalists arising out of some incidental concurrence of interest do not constitute a separate fraction. For fractions are "portions of capital, distinguished from one another by some structural characters referring to distinct positions in the process of capital (re)production and circulation" (Overbeek 1988: 22). These assertions do not deny the explanatory capacity of the term "Islamic capital," but instead underline the necessity of an alternative framework that can explain this peculiar mode of capital accumulation in relation to Islamic motifs. This means that we need to understand the ways in which Islam is formulated as a regulatory force. However, such an analysis should also refrain from reducing religion to a "tool" for economic success (cf. Buğra 1998, 1999; Özcan and Çokgezen 2006).

The chapter first identifies different stages of capital accumulation in the Anatolian region. It interprets the development and success of Anatolian capitalists as the product of multiple determinants that only became possible as a result of the neoliberal transformation from 1980s onward, and the export-orientation strategy and its specific forms of promoting SMEs (including subcontracting activities and informal economies). Such an endeavor aims to break the myth that these companies established themselves as significant market players *merely* as a result of their own individual or joint efforts. It also establishes the unique features of this process of capital accumulation by discussing the symbiotic relationship among Islamic business groups, interest-free banks (IFBs or special financial houses), and communal linkages. Second, the chapter elaborates on the institutional, political and moral dimensions of the class project Islamic capital has pursued since the 1990s. As this mode of accumulation is mediated through various forms of networking via religious organizations, business associations and political parties, the implications of this project on economics, state and civil society are elaborated. Third, it demonstrates the limits of communal, religious, and other nonmarket networks in pursuing further economic development, and the possible solutions these capitals have pursued to resolve their dilemmas. As a final remark, the chapter discusses the future prospects with particular reference to the internationalization of capital accumulation and emerging multiple power relationships among different capital fractions. By doing so, it attempts to go beyond simplistic analyses that differentiate capital groups merely in terms of their location (Islamic/Anatolian versus Istanbul-based capitals) or the size of enterprises (large enterprises versus SMEs). This method would seem better for empirically recognizing the possible multiplication of fractions and the differentiations in their strategies as an approach closer to the complex and concrete analyses of internationalization of accumulation.

Two "Waves" of Industrialization in the Anatolian Region

Different industrialization waves can be identified in the Anatolian region of Turkey. In the initial stage, the then governments channeled the savings of Turkish immigrants in Europe into village cooperatives in the mid-1960s and later initiated a regional industrialization program based on small- and medium-scale production in the 1970s. During this initial stage, around three hundred worker-owned companies were established under state initiatives, mainly in priority development regions and sectors determined by the State Planning Organization (Özcan and Çokgezen 2003: 2068). Therefore, neither the idea of supporting SMEs for industrial diffusion nor using family savings and workers' remittances for capital accumulation were unique to the Islamic movement. It was originally a project of Cumhuriyet Halk Partisi (People's Republican Party, CHP) that emerged under the slogan of "People's Sector." However, these firms failed to raise capital through remittances due to the absence of a stock market and no experience with financial transactions; only a few survived. Concomitant to CHP's failure to remain in power and the economic crisis of the 1970s, the objectives of policy makers diverged from such projects. Disillusioned with previous experiences, savings also either remained dormant or moved away from productive investments toward speculative investments (real estate and gold). However, various developments in the 1980s created opportunities for a second wave of industrialization in Anatolia, albeit with significant differences from the initial project, for they were strongly connected to market deregulation and financial liberalization policies.

The initial export boom that followed the neoliberal prescriptions (and the export-oriented accumulation strategy) of the early 1980s did not continue as expected. The major "winners" of this strategy were large conglomerates. Despite their export departments, these were mainly inward-oriented industrial companies. But there was also a group of SMEs that benefited from such policies. Operating in the rising sectors (textiles, construction, and service), these firms were located in the new industrial growth centers in inner Anatolia, but they had strong direct (and indirect) transnational connections. They were concentrated strongly in labor-intensive sectors, mainly working as the subcontracted manufacturers of domestic and foreign capitals. They had wholesale and retail chains both in Turkey and abroad, and their share in exported manufactures had increased significantly in the 1990s (Adaş 2003: 42). The proliferation of these enterprises was not coincidental, but was closely linked to active government support through public bank credits, preferential treatment in public contracts, and/or construction of organized industrial districts. Furthermore, public investments of the 1980s concentrated less on manufacturing and more on infrastructural investments (transportation, energy, communication, and urban renewal projects), while liberalization of the trade regime provided opportunities for importing necessary inputs without high tariffs and other import surcharges and exporting the final products directly. A significant number of these firms were concentrated in sectors that took off with the export-orientation strategy (e.g., textiles) and other sectors, such as construction and service, that realized a growth potential because of developments in the domestic market (ESI 2005). Indeed, the concept of SMEs was first introduced during this era. More than five hundred thousand firms were established between 1983 and 2000, and in 1990 SMEs accounted for almost 90 percent of all manufacturing firms in Turkey, employing more than one-third of all workers in the manufacturing sector (Adaş 2003: 71–72). With reference to either their geographic location or their desire to replicate the strategies of the export-oriented SMEs in East Asian newly industrializing countries (EANICs), they were usually called "Anatolian capital" or "Anatolian Tigers."

Two more factors particularly facilitated the revival of the Anatolian industries. The first was the growth of the Middle Eastern economies and the concomitant injection of Saudi capital into the Turkish economy, taking advantage of opportunities that arose during the economic (especially in the financial sphere) liberalization of the 1980s. The introduction of IFBs facilitated the revival of the Anatolian SMEs in two interrelated ways. First, on the one hand, they facilitated the initial mobilization and concentration of small sums of capital into larger amounts as a basis for investment; on the other hand, they provided a constant flow of capital for these growing or new companies, thereby encouraging their further expansion. Second, the savings of Turkish guest workers in Europe were directed through unofficial channels, that is, informal linkages based on trust relations and facilitated through kinship, friendship, and other networking forms. Although savings were initially collected to finance religious and cultural services for migrant communities in Europe, they were later directed to investments in Turkey when market deregulation and export orientation created new opportunities.

IFBs were introduced as part of a policy to diversify financial institutions operating in the domestic market. The 1983 special legislation on IFBs was to encourage Middle Eastern capital to invest in Turkey, hence granting them advantages in comparison with conventional banks (Kuran 1995; Adaş 2003). Turkish IFBs operate like their foreign counterparts: they offer profit-loss sharing (PLS) accounts in accordance with Islamic principles.[2] The first IFBs were Turkish-Saudi joint ventures: the Al Baraka Finance House and Faisal Finance were established in 1985, followed by another Arab-Turkish investment, the Kuwait Turkish Finance House, in 1989. In the 1990s, Arabic capital's share decreased, and Turkish private investors established Anadolu Finance, İhlas Finance House, and Asya Finance House in 1991, 1995, and 1996, respectively. They were owned by holdings operating in divergent sectors of industry and media: Anadolu Finance was owned by the İstikbal Group, a leading furniture manufacturer, while Faisal Finance was sold first to Kombassan Holding in 1998 and then to the Ülker Group, a leading food producer, in 2001.

The market share of IFBs rose from 1.59 percent in 1991 to 2.56 percent in 1993, and stayed around that level until 2001; the number of branches increased from 25 in 1991 to 120 in 1997 (Bulut 1999b: 4, 7). Although IFBs outperformed conventional banks in a few cases, their performance was generally below the latter; and they did not become very popular among Turkish depositors, unlike in some other Muslim-dominated countries. IFBs aimed to attract not only domestic savings but also the remittances from migrant workers in Europe and the Gulf countries. The latter indeed constituted a significant source of capital for the second wave of industrialization, and the most powerful Anatolian-based holdings were founded primarily with these savings (Adaş 2003; Demir et al. 2004). An estimated figure is that over three million migrants from Europe sent five billion US dollars to Turkey during the late 1990s (Yeşilada 2002: 78).

IFBs had two functions in the process of capital accumulation. First, they targeted savings that were not channeled to the conventional banking system ("the money under the pillow," as expressed by a local idiom). However, their conformity with Islamic norms and values was not the only reason for attracting these savings. First, the 1982 banker's scandal had seriously eroded investors' confidence in the conventional banking system.[3] Indeed, when IFBs were introduced, an estimated fifty billion US dollars of savings was being kept out of the system (Adaş 2003: 80). Second, they provided funds to capital groups that lacked sufficient capital and/or faced certain barriers in obtaining financial credit from public and private commercial banks. This form of capital accumulation, however, affected the sectorial preferences of firms: instead of sectors that necessitate long-term, risky, skilled labor, and high-tech investments, the majority of the firms channeled investment toward areas where cash flow is fast and secure, such as consumer durables, hajj[4] organizations, and construction. Some of the largest and widespread super/hypermarket chains were owned by these groups (Özcan and Çokgezen 2003).

Religious orders (or sects) have also played a significant role in increasing the speed of capital accumulation, especially in its initial phase. Through personal charisma and revelations, "missionary merchants" became key agents in conveying the holy message and converting individuals to the idea of Islamic "economic rejuvenation." The founders of two leading Islamic holdings, Kombassan and YİMPAŞ, are oft-cited examples of such "entrepreneurial preachers" who were not originally businessmen and had no accumulated capital when they started (Özcan and Çokgezen 2003; Demir et al. 2004). With the money collected from their members in the form of charities, these sects provided religious and educational services by building mosques and providing Koranic courses, schools, and dormitories. However, the role of sects went beyond the limits of intracommunity support; they provided capital and a customer base (Bulut 1999a, 1999b).

Religious networks had four functions in establishing business deals and reaching capital and markets in and beyond the national economy. First, sect members undertook joint investments, obtained loans from each other, and/or established mutual assistance networks to purchase inputs (raw materials, intermediary goods, and machinery) so as to reduce their transportation and transaction costs. Therefore, an important feature of Islamic capital is their ownership structure (Adaş 2003: 42–49). In contrast with big conglomerates in Turkey, which are generally family-owned firms, ownership in Islamic firms is spread around to many shareholders, including transnational investors. For example, Kombassan had nearly thirty thousand shareholders and owned companies in Turkey, Germany, and the United States. Another distinct feature was the legal character of firms' assets: investors had no legal entitlements to the assets, since their shares had no legal basis, yet they received a share of the profit (a fixed return) from their investments. These companies were mostly not registered with the state and their shares were not quoted on the Istanbul Stock Exchange (ISE).

Second, religious networks helped these firms distribute their products and capture a niche market by creating a "religiously sensitive" consumer base. For example, Ülker products were distributed by the Nurcu sect[5] in Anatolia and Central Asian republics (Yavuz 1997). Investments in mass media, newspapers, magazines, and television and radio channels played a crucial role in organizing these sects and constructing a distinct religious identity among their members. The purchase of their goods was promoted as a religious duty; commercials explicitly acknowledged their conformity with Islamic principles; firms adopted Islamic titles for company names/ brands. It is notable that prior to this period there was nothing called "a typical Islamic dress." This shift brought a new dress code (turban) for the pious and led to the growth of an Islamic fashion industry. Consequently, recent decades have witnessed the rise of consumers/ believers who dress in Islamic fashions, shop at Islamic supermarket chains, stay in Islamic five-star hotels, watch Islamic TV channels, read Islamic newspapers and magazines, and entertain themselves with Islamic pop/arabesque, stand-up comedians, and films.

Third, sect-affiliated private schools, universities, courses, and dormitories not only enabled these firms to maintain their organizational base, but also provided them with an "observant" labor force. This created a body of devoted cadres from all segments of the working population, including the professional, urban middle class.

Fourth, religious networks played a significant role in providing legitimacy for their operations. Community leaders, religious teachers, and preachers encouraged their members to provide resources for these firms with the help of Islamic ethics in relation to the common good: Muslims should support business activities, since "more business means more jobs, more bread for all." Put differently, a synthesis of industrialization, development, and Islam evolved in order to provide the core motivation for investing in these companies and supporting their commercial activities.

The Islamification process not only divided the market and everyday life along "Islamic" and "non-Islamic" norms, but also among different sects. Although some holdings were sect coalitions (Kombassan), market competition and insufficient capital led to a war between sect-affiliated firms. In case of a bankruptcy or severe competition in a specific sector, sect leaders called on their followers to boycott the other products and/or secure their firms by pooling private resources (Bulut 1999b: 45). Also, fatwas were used to legitimize activities that fall outside Islamic principles: when İhlas Holding wanted to enter the ISE, it set up an advisory board constituting top Islamic scholars to gain Islamic credibility and avert criticism (Bulut 1999a: 256). The decision to join the ISE was crucial for accumulating the necessary capital for groups that wanted to enter privatization bids and/or for those planning to expand into sectors that necessitated huge investments. Indeed, some Islamic firms accepted that they were working under an interest-bearing system and openly declared that this should not be considered haram.[6] Similar boards were founded and fatwas were issued by other sects in the mid-1990s when they joined the race (Bulut 1999a: 256–59, 267). Eventually, this widened the gap between holdings and SMEs and ultimately created a division not only between capital "haves" and "have-nots," but also between fatwa "haves" and "have-nots."

Islam, Accumulation, and Regulation

The founding of Müstakil Sanayici ve İşadamları Derneği (Independent Industrialists' and Businessmen's Association, MÜSİAD) was the real breakthrough for Islamic capital. However, the important point here is not its members' individual commitment to Islamic ethics or principles (Koyuncu 2002; Özdemir 2006), but rather the organization's specific formulation of Islam as a regulatory force. MÜSİAD helped them to go beyond their mere "economic-corporate interests."

MÜSİAD was founded by five businessmen in 1990, but its membership grew fast, reaching twenty-seven hundred in 1997, which amounted to ten thousand affiliated firms. Unlike Türkiye Sanayici ve İşadamları Derneği (Turkish Industrialists' and Businessmen's Association, TÜSİAD), which was founded by the largest conglomerates of Turkey in 1971, a majority of MÜSİAD firms were founded after the 1980s. Only a few date back to the pre-1960s. While TÜSİAD members come from large firms geographically concentrated in Istanbul and the adjacent industrial districts of the Marmara region, MÜSİAD is mainly comprised of Anatolian SMEs employing fewer than fifty workers (Öniş and Türem 2001). Nevertheless, MÜSİAD firms operate in various sectors that are well integrated into the capitalist core and are both national and transnational. They are mainly concentrated in the booming sectors of the post-1980s noted above, and other sectors such as chemicals and mining, food, furniture, forestry, machinery and spare parts, automotive auxiliary and accessory products, and electronic and consumer products (Adaş 2003: 42–43). In close connection with their ownership structure, they are involved in partnerships with each other; hence their investments are diversified in different activities and sectors, which protect them against risks that occur due to market contraction and other uncertainties.

MÜSİAD functions both at the national and international level (Adaş 2003: 50). First, it aims to strengthen solidarity and cooperation among its members through input supply, outsourcing, subcontracting, and retailing relationships. Given the limited capital available to SMEs, this intermediation is significant because it reduces uncertainty, prevents the breaching of contracts, and minimizes the cost of information gathering and monitoring (Buğra 2002). As expressed by its then president, MÜSİAD was established to allow the rather inward-looking small businessman "to step out [of] his shell and get into relationships with the general sector of industry, [enable] him to overcome the difficulties he encounters in such relations, and [obtain] adequately rich knowledge and information concerning technology and markets" (Özdemir 2006: 171).

Second, MÜSİAD encourages nationals living abroad to invest in their projects, and hence promotes a "global Muslim business network" that enables mutual assistance and joint venture investments. It organizes international business fairs, conferences, and trips abroad and establishes contacts with businessmen, government officials, and managers from other public/private organizations. Although Muslim countries and countries with Muslim-dominated communities were initially prioritized (the Middle East, Central Asia, and other Asia-Pacific countries), it currently encourages operations in Europe, Latin America, and the United States. Therefore, MÜSİAD notes that its international orientation differentiates it from other local solidarity associations, since those cannot facilitate international expansion.[7]

MÜSİAD publishes bulletins, journals, and reports and holds meetings with politicians, academics, journalists, and religious scholars where domestic and foreign investment opportunities and public policies are discussed. Therefore, like TÜSİAD, MÜSİAD, too, goes beyond simple interest-group representation that merely organizes individual capitalists into a collective group or builds networks among its members. It is important because of its ability to establish contacts with local and central governments to influence economic policies and to mobilize resources for its affiliated members. MÜSİAD is also worth studying because it formulates an alternative societal project that ensures the consolidation of its members and their survival as a class. Although this project draws legitimacy primarily from religion, it also addresses the diversified needs, demands, and interests of the broad social formation. The project of building *Homo Islamicus* should be understood in this context.

In 1994, MÜSİAD published a report called *The Muslim Person in Working Life: Organizational Behavior in Firms Governed by Islamic Principles* (MÜSİAD 1994). The notion of *Homo Islamicus* attunes Muslim identity with the present-day understanding of modern capitalist economy and also offers an alternative model to *Homo economicus*. While the latter was criticized for being self-centered/individualistic, "Islamic businessmen" would base their acts on social morality. The "Westernist modernization project" of early republican generations is rejected because it failed to reach the Western levels of economic and technological development, and because it created socioeconomic inequalities, dependency, and an identity crisis. Yet this model criticizes not only the Western capitalists and/or Turkish secular/big business (considered a pale copy of *Homo economicus*), but also "traditional businessmen" (*esnaf*). This "man of small needs and means" owns a workshop, relies on household labor or few laborers, is strongly pious, and is devoid of the entrepreneurial spirit to motivate him to accumulate capital. In contrast, *Homo Islamicus* could and should acquire wealth and earn profit freely as long as it is derived from productive activities (not from speculation, gambling, hoarding, or destructive competition) and is not used solely for individual consumption or hedonistic purposes (Kuran 1995). Therefore, the newly rich whose lifestyle is based on conspicuous consumption are heavily criticized. Interestingly, despite their anti-Western discourse, these businessmen aspire to the Protestant ethic and call themselves "Islamic Calvinists." The rise of Anatolian capitalists has been linked to their Protestant work ethic (ESI 2005: 24): it is argued that unlike the traditional (precapitalist) businessman, *Homo Islamicus* is a self-maximizing, rational, calculating, competitive, innovative, and utilitarian person, but someone who also considers the well-being of society at large. To sum up, the notion promotes "moral capitalism."

Homo Islamicus goes beyond the simple terms of Islamic management and hence also defines the relationship between capital and labor, which helps political representatives to gain the consent of the working masses. It argues that loyalty to Islamic ideals of justice and brotherhood assures peace and productive industrial relations (Adaş 2003: 162): "While workers have religious obligations to work hard, avoid idleness, respect their employers and must show utmost care not to harm the means of production, the employers, in turn, must be just and fair toward their employees and should give their due rights before their sweat is dried." Hence, workers' religiosity becomes an important criterion for their employment. Islamic companies promote this by weekly religious training courses (instead of vocational training) and/or by organizing working hours according to daily prayer times (Bulut 1999b). According to this logic, since mutual trust and social responsibility ensures harmony between capital and labor, there is no need for any formal labor codes and/or trade unions to mediate this relationship. Labor strikes are also harshly criticized for disrupting harmony and productivity, for it renders laborers lazy and idle. This adherence to a paternalistic model, where workers' rights and responsibilities are determined by informal relations, as opposed to redistributive principles of modern capitalist industries is a shared feature of many SMEs. It is also prevalent within the growing informal sector of the region, characterized by unskilled and unorganized elements of the labor force (children and women), low payment, no job security or social security, and long and irregular work hours. Export orientation then strategically fits Anatolian SMEs into a flexible production system and relocates them as crucial nodes within a new international division of labor (Köse and Öncü 1998; Eraydın 2000). Since this general characteristic of small-scale production can also be seen in other developing countries, it is argued that "the rise of Anatolian Tigers can be seen as part of a larger process of restructuring production into a global core–periphery model" (Cizre-Sakallıoğlu and Yeldan 2000).

Moreover, trade unions are seen to be by-products of the Western model, which divides society into classes. It is argued that classes would not emerge in a system where personal wealth is not used to oppress other people: "people who make their fortune along the true path of Islam would not constitute a class," argues the chairman of the Konya Chamber of Commerce (quoted in Buğra 1998: 533). Yarar, the then president of MÜSİAD, asserts that although they own capital they are not capitalists, for "no one can accuse someone who spends his wealth for the well-being of humanity" (Koyuncu 2002: 366; my translation). This vision of a classless society was not only preached by Islamic businessmen and intellectuals, but also shared by the Kemalist cadre of the etatist period. Nevertheless, in the present context it can be seen as part of a larger process of fragmentation and depoliticization of the labor force since the 1980s, demonstrating continuity in the bourgeois parlance rather than a rupture.

Despite this self-affirmation of non-class identity, some adherents of the Islamic model support the idea of voluntarily appointed worker representation or different models of social movement unionism to displace radical unionism (Buğra 2002). Under the model of the "productivist trade unions," "workers would share the risk and responsibility with the employers in quantity and quality of the products produced, rather than an understanding of conflict and contradiction between them" (Adaş 2003: 162). Moreover, in the course of the 1980s, the Islamic trade union, Türkiye Hak İşçi Sendikaları (Confederation of Turkish Real Trade Unions, HAK-İŞ), has established itself as a national force and captured members from all segments of the labor movement, including workers who were formerly affiliated with Türkiye Devrimci İşçi Sendikaları Konfederasyonu (Confederation of Progressive Trade Unions of Turkey, DİSK). Although the representatives of capital and labor, MÜSİAD and HAK-İŞ, agree on the critique of the statist model of the previous era and the social project designed around religious themes, class conflict has revealed itself in various sectors and over different periods. As put by one commentator, the "Islam of capital" and the "Islam of labor" are not one and the same (Adaş 2003: 164).

What we can infer from the above arguments is the existence of a strategic similarity between Islam and the neoliberal ideology. Necmettin Erbakan, the leader of the Islamic National Vision (Milli Görüş) movement and Refah Partisi (Welfare Party, RP), clearly stated that the "just economic order" did not perceive any contradictions between Islamic principles and free-market logic (Erbakan 1991, 1993). As repeated by many Islamic intellectuals, the first Islamic society established during the Prophet's era relied on a "free-market economy." This system (the "Medina model") was celebrated not only for its noninterventionist, nonmonopolistic, and tax-free environment, but also because of its redistribution system (*zakat*), which is promoted as an unmatched method for the reduction of inequality (Çınar 2005). *Zakat* refers to spending a fixed portion of one's wealth on the poor and the needy when one's annual wealth exceeds a minimum level (*nisab*). Although there were attempts to institutionalize these payments through state-run *zakat* systems in Pakistan, Saudi Arabia, Malaysia, and Sudan, or to extend the obligation to firms, in most cases it is levied on individuals and is subject to their will. So the Islamic alternative attempts to fill the vacuum created by social spending cutbacks (in especially health and education) via community work: charities, schools, clinics, and cooperatives. Indeed, municipal governments run by Islamic political parties have played a crucial role in channeling resources into housing and basic necessities for low-income families, including the sale of bread, meat, fruit, and vegetables at bargain prices, the distribution of free food during Ramadan and fuel in winter, as well as providing support during family celebrations and crises, such as arranging weddings, funerals, circumcision for children of the needy, and hospital beds for the sick. Moreover, communal efforts are also channeled into creating employment opportunities for those seeking jobs; many sect followers and Islamic party members are employed in municipal governments and state bureaucracy as well as companies, schools, hospitals, and law firms established by Islamic networks and capital. Therefore, this grassroots approach not only targets the marginalized and the excluded but also includes the professional urban middle classes, who have in turn created a body of devoted cadres coming from all walks of life for the Islamic alternative.

The "just economic order" model was not only limited to domestic policies; it also provided important elements to augment international competitiveness. This was reflected in its foreign policy formulations. It aimed to forge a closer union with the Islamic world, including Middle Eastern countries, the emerging states of post-Soviet Central Asia, and second-generation EANICs with predominantly Islamic populations (Malaysia and Indonesia). Both MÜSİAD and Islamic politicians referred particularly to the East Asian model as the most viable strategy for achieving technological and economic development for the SMEs with a "lean and mean" welfare mechanism, as opposed to the large-scale capital-intensive industries of the Western model with a highly interventionist state (Buğra 2002: 116). The success of Association of Southeast Asian Nations (ASEAN) SMEs is attributed primarily to a state that provides guidelines for macro- and microeconomic plans/projects and engages only in establishing and coordinating the rules of the market, and secondly to their ability to incorporate/harmonize cultural identity, traditional values, and institutions. MÜSİAD's self-description as the voice of the "Anatolian Tigers" who have adopted the principle of "high morality and advanced technology" reflects an admiration of the Confucian ethic. The ASEAN success was not only emphasized by Turkish Islamic entrepreneurs, intellectuals, and politicians, but also embraced by Western policy makers and academics, since it assumed a model that minimizes fiscal dependency on the welfare state and compensates for this with communal/family bonds and solidarity networks. Yet these success stories do not take into consideration the positive impact of interventionist strategies and active industrial policies. Ironically, along with a strong antistatist discourse that advocates deregulation, liberalization, and privatization, MÜSİAD has also promoted incentives for SMEs and privileges for domestic firms in the face of international competition.

The model was also extremely critical of any future union with Europe: instead of the Customs Union, it supported the establishment of an Islamic common market. This had been on the agenda of many other Muslim countries, since various regional organizations—the North American Free Trade Agreement (NAFTA), the European Union (EU), the ASEAN—stimulated the idea of economic integration and cooperation in Muslim countries as well. The Cotton Association, which later developed into a more sophisticated project, the D8 (the "developing" 8), aimed to build an intra-*umma*[8] cooperation among Turkey, Pakistan, Bangladesh, Egypt, Indonesia, Iran, Malaysia, and Nigeria. The project also included the establishment of a United Nations of Muslims to resolve potential problems among Islamic countries, and a Muslim Defense Alliance to protect them against the non-Muslim world; the introduction of the dinar as the common Muslim currency to ease commercial transactions; and the foundation of other cultural institutions to form a unified entity. Yet, not only did this project receive only halfhearted support from other Islamic countries, but there were also opposing views within Islamic circles in Turkey: some Islamic firms (İhlas Holding) opted for a less ambitious project, and other sects adopted a less controversial strategy vis-à-vis the West (Dinç 2006).

Limits to Islamic Capital Accumulation

The 28 February process seriously limited the organizational and financial resources of Islamic capital.[9] A wide range of methods and strategies, including criminalization of the capital accumulation process through legal actions, police and financial investigations, systematic public display of unlawful acts by Islamic companies, and boycotts and campaigns supported via the media were implemented. The Capital Markets Board (CMB) put these companies under close scrutiny and issued warnings, asking for the disclosure of company activities and more information on the nature of their bonds. CMB later froze the assets of some Islamic holdings due to their illegal money collection and capital generation activities in Turkey and abroad. Legal action was taken against some companies, including Kombassan, YİMPAŞ, Kaldera, Kübra Endüstri, Şule Besicilik, Jet-Pa,

Trakya, and Kimpaş. MÜSİAD was charged with antisecular views, its then president was put on trial, and some members were arrested on money laundering charges. Although these charges were later dropped, its membership dropped from twenty-nine hundred to twenty-three hundred. Nevertheless, the spokesman of the association attributed this decline to the impact of the economic crisis and stricter requirements by the organization for admitting new members and maintaining existing ones (Öniş 2001).

These businesses were also excluded from military contracts. Official discrimination was coupled with citizen calls for a boycott of the products of Islamic firms. Their names and products were listed by the mainstream media, which also uncovered bribery scandals involving Islamic companies. All this cast a shadow over their businesses. A ban was introduced to prevent the donations of animal skins to religious networks and nongovernmental organizations. Hence, a *secularly sensitive* consumer base was created. Some Islamic companies directed their efforts to transnational markets in the Far East, Europe, and the United States to compensate for their losses in the domestic market. In order to cut their transnational financial links, CMB then published several ads in Turkish newspapers (to be distributed in Europe) warning immigrants not to lend their savings to these companies. This blocked their main sources of capital and credit, and following the economic crises in the 2000s, Islamic holdings experienced an increasing number of bankruptcies and corporate collapses. Jet-Pa, İhlas, Kombassan, and several others sold some of their investments, while the surviving companies preferred to maintain a low profile.

IFBs were also banned from opening new branches and their privileges were abolished. Following the investigations, IFBs could not increase their assets (Jang 2003: 5–6). Despite a recovery in 1999, their loans, deposits, the funds in their current accounts, and their profits declined, and several companies realized negative growth rates. Faisal Finance was sold a year after the intervention. A new banking law (no. 4389) became effective in 1999 to annul the 1983 special legislation on IFBs. Although the new law integrated them into the official banking system, they still did not have a state guarantee on deposits and were not included in the deposit insurance fund. However, another banking law (no. 4491) enacted in May 2001 provided them with a more secure position and guaranteed the legal arrangements they demanded. Both laws were implemented under the supervision of the International Monetary Fund (IMF) to reform the Turkish financial system. The financial crisis of 2001 was ascribed mainly to the collapse of İhlas Finance, which possessed about 40 percent of IFBs' total assets in February of the same year. After the collapse, the financial activities of all other IFBs were stopped for a short period, resulting in losses of hundreds of millions of dollars.

The 28 February process forced Islamic capital to modify its strategies and policies on a number of important issues. MÜSİAD put more emphasis on region- and size-related differences in expressing economic concerns, and asked its members to avoid using religious/ sacred symbols in their commercials and promotional activities (Adaş 2003: 172). Some fraud-stricken companies (Jet-Pa and GAP Holding) were expelled and others (such as Endüstri Holding) were forced to resign. Moreover, some businessmen claimed that they had been put on the blacklist by mistake. To clear their names, they ran advertisements and interviews in newspapers declaring their loyalty to the secular regime and stressing that they are not as "different" as they are usually portrayed. Some even denied that there is such a thing as Islamic capital (Bulut 1999a: 167).

Moreover, the Islamic party of the post-1997 period, Fazilet Partisi (Virtue Party, FP), distanced itself from its predecessors by adopting a moderate posture in terms of its programmatic commitments via de-Islamizing its discourse. It omitted all references to leaving the North Atlantic Treaty Organization (NATO), modification of the financial system along Islamic principles, and a multiple legal order that aimed to enact secular and Islamic legal principles at the same time. This represented a quest for a new consensus rather than a mere pragmatic political turn. Indeed, the famous "Abant workshops" brought together several intellectuals and politicians from various backgrounds across the Islamic movement.[10] Also in 1998, the Fethullah Gülen sect[11] declared that they do not favor an Islamic state (Bulut 1999b: 81).

Perhaps the most striking difference was the change in the strong anti-European ethos. FP not only stopped defining the EU as a "Christian club," but also supported Turkey's future accession to the EU. Nevertheless, these modifications should be analyzed in a broader context to include the impact of the Customs Union and the 1997–98 Asian crisis on domestic actors. While the former allowed Islamic SMEs to reach a larger market, enjoy partnership opportunities with Western companies, and thus bypass structurally inscribed "strategic selectivities" of the Turkish state[12] that favor large conglomerates in the domestic market, the Asian crisis seriously undermined the viability of the East Asian development model, hence reorienting these economic actors toward the EU market (Öniş and Türem

2001; Keyder 2004). Therefore, it is better to approach this topic as a competition between alternative models of development and societal projects, that is, the East Asian model and *Homo Islamicus*.

Future Prospects

Despite their persisting disadvantages vis-à-vis large conglomerates, the religiously conservative Anatolian businesses found great opportunities under the rule of Adalet ve Kalkınma Partisi (Justice and Development Party, AKP), which came to power in 2002. It has been widely noted that the wealth of Islamic capitalists has been flourishing in proportion to the AKP's growth (Tekin 2004). Thanks to the public administration reform that limited the authority of central government in favor of local governments, there has been a rise in the number of public contracts awarded to conservative businessmen through AKP-run municipalities (Gülen 2006: 154–55). The government's decision to provide scholarships and grants to students of the lower middle classes and the poor mainly benefited the private schools established by religious sects/networks. Islamic capital also extended its share in the media. Media companies put under the control of the Savings Deposit and Insurance Fund (the *Sabah* newspaper and the television channel ATV) were not only transferred to AKP-affiliated companies, but the prime minister himself "stepped in to force the withdrawal of all competing bidders, and also removed state bank governors who'd objected to financing the sale because of the proposed loan's breach of their bylaws" (Rubin 2008). IFBs were allowed to set up a parallel Islamic deposit insurance scheme that invests the deposit insurance pool according to Islamic investment principles, and they doubled their market share in 2003 (Parker 2004).

MÜSİAD's support for the AKP is also undeniable. The "Urgent Action Plan" of the AKP prepared before the 2002 elections noted that "[a]rrangements shall be made to protect the rights and interests of the shareholders of those companies with many small shareholders" (AKP 2002). The AKP's antimonopoly references were indeed instrumental in securing the organization's support. It is an established fact that the government has been channeling resources to them through public banks, privatization bids, and local governments (Tekin 2004: 224). It is also noted that excessive borrowing has accompanied the "green money" influx. Saudi businessmen have shifted an important part of their finances from tightly regulated US bank accounts into Turkey since 11 September 2001. Between 2002 and 2005 approximately two hundred companies were established in Turkey by Saudi capital, and their share in the economy increased by 50 percent in the first six months of 2004 alone (Rubin 2005). It has even been argued that "if it were not for the Green Money influx Turkey might soon face another devaluation of the scale of the 2001 currency crisis" (Rubin 2007: 3).

In order to distinguish the analyses in this chapter on the present condition of Islamic capital from other readings, it is necessary to highlight a couple of points argued above. First, this article does not perceive the current rivalry merely as a typical distributional conflict between Istanbul-based companies and Anatolian-based Islamic firms, or between holdings and SMEs. Hence, it is at odds with studies that equate this rivalry to size- and region-related conflicts or explain the fundamental difference between the two fractions as a matter of identity. Although this chapter does not underestimate differences related to size, region, and identity, it argues that such explanations are misguided because they reduce the economic domain of Islamic capital to an enclave or subeconomy. On the contrary, there has been a significant change in the size, scope, and regional orientation of these companies (Doğan 2006). Not only have they secured an important position in the domestic market that goes beyond a niche (e.g., the Ülker Group), but some have become large transnational players with investments in Europe, Central Asia, and the United States. YİMPAŞ, for example, owns over twenty-four companies, employs ten thousand workers, and has investments in Germany, Bulgaria, and Turkmenistan, while Kombassan has forty companies, employs eight thousand workers, and is active in Kazakhstan and Germany (Özcan and Çokgezen 2006).

Moreover, studies reveal that in terms of the regional concentration of IFBs, "İstanbul is the most concentrated region possessing fifty nine branches out of 159 as the total branch numbers of all the Islamic banks in spring of 2002," which makes it harder to differentiate them as Anatolian capital (Jang 2003: 12). Indeed, in 1995, under the supervision of İhlas Holding and some prominent Islamic intellectuals, an exclusive organization, the Istanbul Club, was founded to provide certain privileges to the Islamic elite (Bulut 1999b: 154). Therefore, it is better not to be misguided by the heavily SME-based discourse of these firms and (dis)regard them as backward-looking small businesses who have been threatened by rapid industrialization and the opening of the economy. This discourse underestimates the concentration and centralization tendencies among Islamic capital.

Moreover, the dependency on religious legitimacy tends to decline as their capital and power increase.

Second, this chapter does not confine the contradictions merely to a struggle between outward-oriented commercial capital and inward-oriented productive capital, but rather explains it in relation to the process of internationalization of productive capital (Ercan 2004). By organizing itself at different levels and through assuming different functions in the circuit of capital, Islamic capital devised strategies to overcome the contradictions arising from its nature. To begin with, Islamic SMEs engaged in import/export and subcontracting activities with other Turkish firms and multinational companies. Hence, they assumed the role of commercial capital in directing those products to different markets. For example, while Aydınlı, an Islamic textile firm, was working as a subcontractor to Pierre Cardin and supplying material to some three hundred firms from all over the world, other companies were authorized to import products from Far Eastern electronic and automotive industries. Therefore, as outlined in a MÜSİAD report, they opted for a mixed implementation of import substitution and export orientation (Koyuncu 2002). Also, neither the holding structure nor the affiliation between banks and industry are limited to the Istanbul holdings. Not only did many Anatolian companies (İhlas Holding, Kombassan, Sanko, Kar Şirketler Grubu, YİMPAŞ, Çetinkaya, Jet-Pa, Ülker, Kalebodur) establish their own IFBs, but their financial activities were also well integrated with interest-bearing banks (Peköz 2006). These variations in activities are linked to the broader process of internationalization of capital, which led different accumulation strategies to be implemented simultaneously and at the same geographical location, yet not without leading to a contradiction between the balance of forces, albeit a contradiction different from previous periods.

In this regard, instead of drawing a simple conclusion and arguing that Islamic capital is currently yielding large profits thanks to the distribution of key positions in the state bureaucracy to personnel closely linked with AKP governments, it is necessary to look for a more complex answer that explains the multiple power relationships (in terms of both strategies and struggles) among different capital fractions in Turkey.[13] It is necessary to illustrate and explain in the first place how the internationalization of capital accumulation creates a whole series of contradictions between capital fractions that have a strategy of international expansion and those with a strategy of limited expansion within the national economy, and secondly how fractions may pursue multiple strategies to benefit from different state policies in relation to their strengths and weaknesses in the international markets.

When the articulation between national and international contexts is considered, three main capital fractions can be identified with conflicting demands on the state: big internationalized capital groups having a partial control over the global market; newly growing medium-sized capital groups trying to internationalize and integrate with the global market; and capital groups, mostly composed of SMEs but not exclusively, still operating in the national market.[14] Such an analysis can therefore tell us more about how fractions can establish different alliances depending on their specific concerns: under what circumstances internationalized big "domestic" capitals tend to ally with global capital (against domestic SMEs) in order to benefit from the advantages of internationalization, while at the same time allying with other domestic capitals, such as the newly growing and internationalizing medium-sized domestic capitals, against "foreign" capitals to preserve their privileged positions in the domestic economy. This "contradictory process" not only explains the fractional alliance(s) behind the AKP, especially in its early period in government, but also helps us understand why certain regulatory reforms/laws could be implemented without a major conflict whereas others created serious confrontations among the government, business circles, upper echelons of the bureaucracy, and external actors.

Therefore, the neoliberal restructuring process in Turkey not only referred to the concentration and centralization of domestic capital in a few hands in the national context, but also to the constant tendency among "domestic" players to expand their accumulation base and further integrate with the world market (Ercan 2005). While financialization enhanced their power to attract overaccumulated global capitals (mainly in the form of money capital), structural changes allowed them to cooperate with global productive and money capitals to use local opportunities in large-scale privatization bids and other investments. Internationalization also resulted in multiple power relationships: first, it led to a series of contradictory and unequal power relationships; second, it allowed for cooperation among capitals of different size and sectorial orientation against a "common enemy." In sum, in the present situation, divisions within capital into blocs clustering around rival political and economic agendas may not be captured through crude distinctions based on differences in geographic origin, overall firm size, or sectorial preferences. To understand the true metamorphic changes that

Islamic enterprises undergo, we need to analyze the process of internationalization of capital as well as recent transformations in the functions of the nation-state.

Notes

1. The same author also argues that Islamic capital can be perceived as the real "domestic/national capital" that has been sought since the 1900s in Turkey (Özdemir 2004: 838).
2. It is worth noting that there is an ongoing debate as to whether the interest-free returns made through IFBs essentially correspond to the interest-based returns of Western banks. It is often said that IFBs have been refraining from providing capital for risky and long-term investments, instead directing their funds toward secure, short-term projects mainly in nonproductive sectors such as commerce, distribution, and services. Even in the productive sector investments are generally limited to consumer goods.
3. The interest rate competition among and within the banks and bankers skyrocketed the interest rates. Some two hundred and fifty listed bankers and another one thousand institutions bankrupted when thousands of depositors lost their confidence in the system and rushed to collect their savings. Note that high interest rates were intended to encourage savings and (re)direct them into productive investments.
4. Muslims from all over the world gather annually at the holy sites in and near Mecca to perform a series of rituals based on those conducted by the prophet Muhammad during his last visit to the city. Hajj is considered a religious duty for Muslims who are physically and financially able.
5. "Nurcu" is the name given to groups that claim to be the followers of the Sunni Muslim theologian "Bediüzzaman" Said Nursi, who wrote a tafsir (Islamic exegesis) on the Koran, the *Risale-i Nur Collection*.
6. "Haram" refers to any act that is forbidden by Islamic law.
7. MÜSİAD is not the only representative of such business interests. Alongside various chambers of industry and commerce, many other business organizations were established in the 1990s: ÇUSİAD (Çukurova Sanayicileri ve İşadamları Derneği, Çukurova Industrialists' and Businessmen's Association) and İŞHAD (İş Hayatı Dayanışma Derneği, Business Life Cooperation Association), founded by Alevi businessmen and the Fethullah Gülen sect, respectively, are examples.
8. *Umma* is the Arabic word for "nation" or "community." The term "intra-*umma*" refers to relations among Muslim communities in various Muslim countries.
9. At the National Security Council meeting held on 28 February 1997, the military members expressed their concern about the growing religious reactionism and handed over a list of policy "recommendations" to the Erbakan-led coalition government to curtail the tide of radical Islam in Turkey. Thus, a string of "pro-secular" measures were introduced to weaken the organizational strength of the Islamic movement. The 28 February process is often referred to as a "soft coup," "postmodern coup," "covert coup," or "civil coup." These terms point to two peculiar characteristics of the military intervention: (1) the cooperation among the armed and "unarmed or civil" forces; and (2) the *atypical* or *unusual* character of the intervention, that is, the absence of a governmental takeover.

10. Launched in 1998 under the leadership of an Islamic nongovernmental organization, Gazeteciler ve Yazarlar Vakfı (Foundation of Journalists and Writers), the Abant workshops or Abant platform is a discussion forum known for dealing with contemporary political issues. The 1998 meeting was titled "Islam and Secularism." Other critical meetings such as "The New Constitution" and "Turkey: A Bridge between Civilizations" were held in 2007. The seventeenth and eighteenth meetings took place under the title of "The Kurdish Problem: Peace and Seeking the Future Together."

11. An Islamic religious community (*cemaat* in Turkish) led by Fethullah Gülen, who preaches the teachings of Said Nursi.

12. Strategic selectivity refers to "the specific configuration of state branches, apparatuses and institutions, their specific powers and prerogatives of action, their specific relative autonomies and institutional unities, and their specific patterns of domination and subordination. ... This means that the state is not equally accessible to all social forces, cannot be controlled or resisted to the same extent by all strategies, and is not equally available for all purposes" (Jessop and Sum 2006: 98).

13. Although municipalities and certain bureaucracies have been manned by Islamists throughout the 1990s, the AKP not only perfected this process, but also focused on those areas that had been ignored and/or could not be penetrated beforehand, and long-term Islamic activists were appointed to significant posts of important ministries and state corporations. Key positions in state-owned banks and financial institutions were occupied by Islamic bankers. The AKP also tried, though failed, to replace the head of the Central Bank with a (loosely) affiliated figure. In order to encourage early retirement and vacate positions, secular midlevel bureaucrats were either pushed out of their posts and transferred to rural areas or were forced to undertake meaningless tasks. There are multiple examples of these attempts.

14. See Ercan and Oğuz's (2006) research on the new public procurement law that sets the legal framework for governmental purchases of goods and services from the private sector. The article not only gives good examples of these multiple power relationships but also provides the main theoretical framework for the arguments presented here. The authors also note that because contradictions among these fractions are already internationalized, state intervention in favor of a certain fraction amounts to an indirect intervention in favor of a certain fraction/section of the global capital

References

Adaş, Emin B. 2003. "Profit and the Prophet: Culture and Politics of Islamic Entrepreneurs in Turkey." PhD dissertation, University of Illinois.

AKP. 2002. "Urgent Action Plan." Accessed 23 September 2003. http://www.akparti.org.tr.

Buğra, Ayşe. 1998. "Class, Culture and State: An Analysis of Interest Representation by Two Turkish Business Associations." *International Journal of Middle East Studies* 30, no. 4 (November): 521–39.

———. 1999. *Islam in Economic Organizations*. Istanbul: TESEV Yayınları.

———. 2002. "Labor, Capital, and Religion: Harmony and Conflict among the Constituency of Political Islam in Turkey." *Middle Eastern Studies* 38, no. 2 (April): 187–204.

Bulut, Faik. 1999a. *Tarikat Sermayesi I: İslam Ekonomisinin Eleştirisi* [Islamic capital I: The critique of Islamic economy]. Istanbul: Su Yayınları.

_____. 1999b. *Tarikat Sermayesi II: İslamcı Şirketler Nereye?* [Islamic capital II: Where do Islamic firms go from here?]. Istanbul: Su Yayınları.

Can, Kemal. 1997. "Yeşil Sermaye Laik Sisteme Ne Yaptı?" [What did green capital do to the secular system?]. *Birikim* 99 (July): 59–65.

Çınar, Menderes. 2005. *Siyasal Bir Sorun Olarak İslamcılık* [Islamism as a political problem]. Ankara: Dipnot Yayınları.

Cizre-Sakallıoğlu, Ümit, and Erinç Yeldan. 2000. "Politics, Society and Financial Liberalization: Turkey in the 1990s." *Development and Change* 31 (January): 481–508.

Demir, Ömer, Mustafa Acar, and Metin Toprak. 2004. "Anatolian Tigers or Islamic Capital: Prospects and Challenges." *Middle Eastern Studies* 40, no. 6 (November): 166–88.

Dinç, Cengiz. 2006. "The Welfare Party, Turkish Nationalism and Its Vision of a New World Order." *Alternatives: Turkish Journal of International Relations* 5, no. 3 (Fall).

Doğan, Ekber A. 2006. "Siyasal Yansımaları ile İslamcı Sermayenin Gelişme Dinamikleri ve 28 Subat Süreci" [The effects of the growth dynamics of Islamic capital on the polity and the 28 February process]. *Mülkiye Dergisi* 30, no. 252 (Fall): 47–68.

Eraydın, Ayda. 2000. "Dış Pazarlara Eklemlenmeye Çalışan Konfeksiyon Sanayiinde Üretimin Örgütlenmesi ve Emek Süreçleri" [The organization of production and labor processes in the export-oriented textile industry]. *ODTÜ Gelişme Dergisi* 27, nos. 1–2: 91–117.

Erbakan, Necmettin. 1991. *Adil Ekonomik Düzen* [The just economic order]. Ankara: Refah Partisi.

_____. 1993. *Adil Düzen* [The just order]. Ankara: Refah Partisi.

Ercan, Fuat. 2004. "The Contradictory Continuity of the Turkish Capital Accumulation." In *The Ravages of Neo-Liberalism: Economy, Society and State in Turkey*, ed. Neşecan Balkan and Sungur Savran, 21–39. New York: Nova.

_____. 2005. "Alternatif Bakışları Sorgulamak: Türkiye'de Sermaye Gruplarının Küresel Kapitalizmle Bütünleşmelerindeki Rolleri" [Questioning alternative perspectives: The role of capital groups in Turkey in the articulation with global capitalism]. International Conference on Acts of Resistance from the South against Globalisation, Ankara, 5–7 September.

Ercan, Fuat, and Şebnem Oğuz. 2006. "Rescaling as a Class Relationship and Process: The Case of Public Procurement Law in Turkey." *Political Geography* 25 (August): 641–56.

ESI (European Stability Initiative). 2005. *Islamic Calvinists: Change and Conservatism in Central Anatolia*. Berlin and Istanbul: European Stability Initiative.

Gülen, Fikret. 2006. "AKP'nin İktidarda Olduğu Dönemde Kabul Edilen Yasalar Hakkında Değerlendirme" [An analysis of laws passed during AKP governments]. *Mülkiye Dergisi* 30, no. 252: 154–55.

Jang, Ji-Hyang. 2003. "The Politics of Islamic Banks in Turkey: Taming Political Islamists by Islamic Capital." 2003 Annual Meeting of the Midwest Political Science Association (MPSA). Chicago, IL.

Jessop, Bob, and Ngai-Ling Sum. 2006. *Beyond the Regulation Approach: Putting Capitalist Economies in their Place*. Cheltenham, UK: Edward Elgar.

Keyder, Çağlar. 2004. "The Turkish Bell Jar." *New Left Review* 28 (July–August): 65–84.

Köse, Ahmet, and Ahmet Öncü. 1998. "Dünya ve Türkiye Ekonomisinde Anadolu İmalat Sanayii: Zenginleşmenin mi Yoksa Yoksullaşmanın mı Eşiğindeyiz?" [Anatolian manufacturing industry in the world and Turkish economy: Are we at the threshold of prosperity or poverty?]. *Toplum ve Bilim* 77 (Summer): 135–58.

Koyuncu, Berrin. 2002. "Küreselleşme ve MÜSİAD: Eklemlenme mi, Çatışma mı?" [Globalization and MÜSİAD: Articulation or conflict?]. In *Liberalizm, Devlet, Hegemonya* [Liberalism, state, and hegemony), ed. Fuat Keyman, 358–76. Istanbul: Everest.

Kuran, Timur. 1995. "Islamic Economics and the Islamic Subeconomy." *The Journal of Economic Perspectives* 9, no. 4 (Fall): 155–73.

MÜSİAD, 1994. *İş Hayatında İslam İnsanı* [The Muslim person in working life]. Istanbul: MÜSİAD Yayınları.

Öniş, Ziya. 2001. "Political Islam at the Crossroads: from Hegemony to Co-existence." *Contemporary Politics* 7, no. 4: 281–98.

Öniş, Ziya, and Umut Türem. 2001. "Business, Globalization and Democracy: A Comparative Analysis of Turkish Business Associations." *Turkish Studies* 2, no. 2: 94–120.

Overbeek, Henk W. 1988. "Global Capitalism and Britain's Decline." PhD dissertation, University of Amsterdam.

Özcan, Gül B., and Murat Çokgezen. 2003. "Limits to Alternative Forms of Capitalization: The Case of Anatolian Holding Companies." *World Development* 31, no. 12: 2061–84.

———. 2006. "Trusted Markets: The Exchanges of Islamic Companies." *Comparative Economic Studies* 48, no. 1: 132–55.

Özdemir, Şennur. 2004. "MÜSİAD ve HAK-İŞ'i Birlikte Anlamak" [To understand MÜSİAD and HAK-İŞ together]. In *Modern Türkiye'de Siyasi Düşünce* [Political thought in modern Turkey], vol. 6, *İslamcılık* [Islamism], ed. Yasin Aktay, 837–44. Istanbul: İletişim Yayınları.

———. 2006. *Anadolu Sermayesinin Dönüşümü ve Türk Modernleşmesinin Derinleşmesi* [The transformation of Anatolian capital and the growth of Turkish modernization]. Ankara: Vadi Yayınları.

Parker, Musthak. 2004. "Islamic Banking Sector in Turkey Emerges Much Stronger." *Arab News*, 29 March. Accessed 10 June 2008. http://arabnews.com/node/246763.

Peköz, Mustafa. 2006. "İslami Sermayenin Ekonomik Gelişme Düzeyi" [The development of Islamic capital]. *Sendika*. Accessed 19 March 2008. http://www.sendika.org.

Rubin, Barry. 2005. "Green Money, Islamist Politics in Turkey." *Middle East Quarterly* 12, no. 1 (Winter): 13–23. Accessed 10 July 2008. http://www.meforum.org/article/684.

———. 2007. "Will Turkey Have an Islamist President?"' *AEI Middle Eastern Outlook*, 2 February. Accessed 28 May 2007. http://www.meforum.org/article/1637.

———. 2008. "The Case Against Turkey's Ruling Party." *The American*, 20 June. Accessed 10 July 2008. http://www.meforum.org/article/1924.

Sandıkçı, Özlem, and Güliz Ger. 2001. "Fundamental Fashions: The Cultural Politics of the Turban and the Levi's." *Advances in Consumer Research* 28: 146–50.

Tekin, Üzeyir. 2004. *AK Partinin Muhafazakar Demokrat Kimliği* [The conservative-democrat identity of the AK Party]. Istanbul: Orient Yayınları.

Yavuz, Hakan Y. 1997. "Political Islam and the Welfare (Refah) Party in Turkey." *Comparative Politics* 30, no. 1 (October): 63–82.

Yeşilada, Birol A. 2002. "The Virtue Party." *Turkish Studies* 3, no. 1 (Spring): 62–81.

– Chapter 6 –

REPRODUCTION OF THE ISLAMIC MIDDLE CLASS IN TURKEY

Erol Balkan and Ahmet Öncü

e~ͻ

Introduction

In a well-known passage in *The Communist Manifesto*, Marx and Engels claim that the bourgeoisie "creates a world after its own image." Inspired by this observation, we argue that in its struggle to attain hegemony, the rising Islamic bourgeoisie in Turkey is attempting to fashion a "world in its own image," and we present some of the results of a comprehensive survey with selected middle-class families of both the "laic" and "Islamic" communities in Istanbul. The Islamic and laic bourgeoisies are two separate capitalist classes that emerged in two different social sectors during the twentieth-century evolution of modern Turkey. The Islamic bourgeoisie has overtaken the laic bourgeoisie as we enter the twenty-first century. The constitutionally backed political power and role of the army, which was at the top echelons of the social hierarchy during the reign of the laic bourgeoisie, has been eroding, and political parties and organizations of civil society have been ascending; the importance of Ankara, the capital of the republic, has been diminishing, while Istanbul and several Anatolian cities have been gaining more prominent positions. These developments and many others that are analyzed in the contributions to this volume support the idea that these two ruling classes can be conceptualized as two distinct capitalist classes with two different types of orientation to hegemony building.

We suggest that one of the underlying reasons behind this radical social change is the transition from national developmentalism (i.e., a version of the embedded liberalism on the periphery) to neoliberalism, and the concomitant inability of the laic bourgeoisie, due to its ideology being shaped in the era of national developmentalism, to fulfill its ruling class position in the neoliberal era, which operates in accordance with the requirements of capital accumulation on the world scale as well as "accumulation by dispossession" (Harvey 2005). In this sense, we maintain that the rise of the Islamic bourgeoisie as a new hegemonic class in Turkey parallels the rise of neoliberalism around the globe. Various aspects of this development that contribute to the main argument of this volume are discussed in detail in other chapters. In this chapter, we focus on the middle class to help better understand the peculiarities of contemporary Turkish society. This is the middle class that has been assigned by the laic and Islamic bourgeoisie the duty of organizing relations with lower classes as they (the bourgeoisie) aim to "create a world in their own image."

In what follows, we first introduce the premises of the theoretical framework that guides us throughout this chapter. We argue that the dynamics of any capitalist society can be analyzed from a class-theoretical approach insofar as class as a theoretical concept can provide a departure point for examining three interrelated processes. These are: (1) the underlying material bases of ideological formations, competitions, and conflicts; (2) the structural roots of social inequality and social mobility; and (3) the economic factors involved in the emergence and prevalence of a set of social practices at work in processes of social reproduction. Next, by drawing on our class-theoretical framework, we provide a brief historical account of the bifurcation of Turkish society into laic and Islamic social sectors, and the ramifications of this process for state formation and class dynamics in different eras of capital accumulation, namely, national developmentalism (1923–80) and neoliberalism (1980–present). Then, we turn to the question of the middle class in order to provide an account of an ongoing social formation driven by the emergence of an Islamic bourgeoisie in the neoliberal era. Here, we first take up the theoretical puzzle concerning the difficulties involved in conceptualizing the middle class, and provide a short version of our position on this debate by drawing on the work of Pierre Bourdieu. Following this, we present some of the major findings of our survey of middle-class households in Istanbul in a comparative manner to specify differences and similarities among the "new" laic and Islamic middle-class factions that have benefited economically, socially, and culturally from the neoliberal regime. Based on our analysis of the findings of the survey, we suggest that in each faction a new middle class reflecting neoliberal values and lifestyles emerged and separated itself from the rest. Thus, although they have had different ideological and cultural pasts and orientations, both the laic and Islamic factions of the new middle class converged into a new status group as the "winners" of the neoliberal landscape.

Class-Theoretical Analysis of Capitalist Society

The abstract analytic approach to class and class formation, represented by both Karl Marx in the middle of the nineteenth century and Max Weber at the turn of the nineteenth century, grappled with the question of what made modern society "modern." These authors theorized connections between technological change, the rise of industrial capitalism, and the concomitant changes in political and social institutions at a particular "moment" of what would prove to be a "total" social transformation. Marx and Weber continue to be valuable touchstones for class analysis because of their contrasting views of the foundations of an industrial social hierarchy. Marx, focusing primarily on social relations within the capitalist mode of production, emphasized sharp divisions forming between capital and labor based on differences in the distribution and ownership of property and the exploitation of labor by capital. These conditions, he theorized, would result in the formation of antagonistic relations between the two dominant classes in the emergent class structure of nineteenth-century industrial capitalism and result in class conflict as the engine for further social transformation. Weber, looking at the same historical moment of industrialization (but a few decades later and from a different physical location), focused primarily on the rise of a new kind of political authority that would transform the old relations of patronage and personal power of the state into a new form of efficient and impersonal legal and bureaucratic-administrative organization. Rather than emphasizing "class," Weber emphasized social "status" hierarchies that would take into account moral, legal, and cultural distinctions as well as economic ones in shaping modern society. In the ensuing literature, Marx and Weber came to stand for different trajectories in the more general study of social stratification within the emergent discipline of sociology. The Marxist approach elaborated on and refined the study of stable and enduring class boundaries buttressed by an objective social consciousness or "ideology." In contrast, the Weberian approach elaborated on and refined social mobility patterns institutionalized in the form of shifting status groups anchored by their subjective awareness or understanding of various "distinctions" arrayed in hierarchies of "prestige" or some other criterion of social and cultural distinction.

Class matters to persons as members of socially meaningful collectivities because it stands for advantages and disadvantages that shape life chances by constraining opportunities (Rutz and Balkan 2010). At its root, class analysis is concerned with issues of social justice. More than a taxonomic classification of social hierarchy, the analytic importance of the concept of "class" derives from the ability of researchers to focus on and analyze the *dynamics* of structured inequality in a system that distributes wealth, knowledge, and power unevenly among different groups. In this sense, to study class is to study the very structure of society. We emphasize the word "dynamics" because we are interested not in class structure per se but in class *formation*. The concept of "class" acquires meaning from at least three sources. It is an analytic concept used by social scientists to understand inequality, a social construction of reality for people living in capitalist societies, and a set of definite practices under material conditions of existence of a particular kind.

Scholars differ in their approach to analyzing social classes, not to mention their views on the relevance of class analysis, but there is general agreement on four characteristics. The first is that classes are formed dialectically in a system of conflict and accommodation. Most class analysts adopt some variant of dialectical materialism in which classes are understood to be mutually dependent but simultaneously opposed in their interests, which results in contradictions in their social relations. The degree to which classes compete or conflict with each other remains contingent upon historically particular conditions, including the degree of class consciousness as an objective condition of the social construction of reality. Dialectical materialism is grounded in a belief that material conditions of existence exert considerable influence over the way people think and act, and that the social construction of reality is constantly being transformed along with changes in material conditions. The dialectic of structured competition and potential conflict between classes extends to competition among factions within a particular class. In this chapter, for example, we are primarily concerned with the competition and conflict between the laic and Islamic factions of the Turkish bourgeoisie and their extensions within middle-class formation and reproduction in the era of neoliberal globalization.

The second area of agreement is a need for a historicist perspective on the development of capitalism and its relation to social classes. In other words, the origin of the class system is to be found in the capitalist mode of production. Problems of class formation are conceptualized as social transformations linked to various rounds or "phases" of capital accumulation. Capital denotes any materials, knowledge, or ideas used to produce, transport, create, or alter commodities, which by definition are produced for exchange. Marketable intangibles, such as credit, promises, good will, copyrights, brand names, trademarks, patents, stocks, bonds, and franchises are among the items included as capital. Capital goods provide income for present wants without depletion of the stock or savings for future wants or reinvestments. The class system refers to a more comprehensive system that denotes a political community oriented toward the goal of material accumulation and the protection of profit through private ownership of the means of production. As a historical phenomenon, modern capitalism represents the displacement of merchant and agrarian capital by industrial capital as the hegemonic form of accumulation. The rise of an industrial bourgeoisie was accompanied by the emergence of a class of wage earners, creating the modern class system in which capital was inextricably joined with labor yet opposed to it in its fundamental interests. Neoliberalism refers in part to a displacement of the primacy of capital accumulation through industrial activities by finance capital that increasingly focuses on accumulation by financial speculation and dispossession.

Modern capitalism is buttressed by moral ideas about how the market is fair and therefore how the given social hierarchy is a form of social justice. The well-honed ideology of class culture in capitalist societies embraces the logic of a rational economic person, a social morality of possessive individualism, and a spirit of political liberty reduced to its lowest common denominator in the form of economic freedom or free enterprise. Thus, the third characteristic of class analysis on which there is general agreement is the relationship between class and the capitalist economy and the relationship between a capitalist class system and the social formation in which it is embedded. The term "social formation" denotes political, social, and cultural institutions and ideas that lend meaning, regulation, and justification to a class system that owes its derivation to the capitalist mode of production. State and family are among the most important institutions that help regulate the capitalist economy and shape the class system. By "state," we mean the regulation and standardization of the system itself and its institutionalization in enforcement, judicial, and legal institutions and their attendant bureaucracies. Although capitalist ideology emphasizes enterprise free from state interference, in reality the state has always played a major role in shaping the evolution of capitalism and vice versa. Understanding the relations between market and state are critical to an understanding of class formation. Their mutual dependence and contradictions are part of the dialectic of every capitalist social formation. These, along with the context of historically contingent conditions, must be taken into account in an analysis of class formation. Historical state, market, and family relationships in Turkey are an important part of our analysis of bifurcation within the Istanbul middle class during the most recent period of Turkey's integration into the neoliberal global economy. To this triumvirate of agencies we would add education as central to our understanding of class dynamics in the Turkish middle class.

This brings us to the fourth characteristic of class analysis, namely, the recognition that, while these nested systems of social class, capitalist economy, and nation-state have some coherence and stability, their historical development is also characterized by conflict, contradiction, ambiguity, and change. These dynamics were best described by Karl Marx, who observed that capitalism is fundamentally a system of "creative destruction." Class systems have a structure, but that structure is always in flux. At rare moments in history, there is a conjuncture of forces that fundamentally alters the existing social formation. For such rare moments, social theorists adopt the use of labels such as "Industrial Revolution" or, to return us to the present, "Information Revolution." At the beginning of the twenty-first century, readers are well aware that we are living in one of those infrequent world-historical conjunctures in which the foundations of a previous form of capital accumulation is being replaced and creative destruction is all around us. But we have no more glimpse of its shape and direction than did those who lived at the end of the eighteenth century, when observers who could describe upheaval only had an inkling of understanding about its true significance.

A Brief Macro-historical Background of the Class System of Turkish Capitalism

The transition to capitalism in Turkey, particularly in the period after the foundation of the republic in 1923, resulted in the division of society into two large social groupings, in addition to smaller sectors of minorities such as Alevis, Kurds, and non-Muslims. One of these groupings is represented by those who have adhered to the secular institutions introduced and imposed from above by the founders of the state. These individuals have adapted almost entirely to the new social habits of thought and action aspired to by the founding fathers. In contrast to this group of mostly urbanites, there exists another large social formation of people of mostly rural background scattered across the Anatolian heartland. This second group includes people who have in various manners opposed the secular institutions and remained faithful to their age-old traditional religious doctrines, practices, and networks ingrained in their prevalent social habits. Using the notions of Turkish daily vernacular, the first group can be referred to as the "laic sector" (*laik kesim*), while the second one can be called "conservatives" (*muhafazakarlar*) or the "Islamic sector" (*İslami kesim*). In what follows, we provide a brief account of the division of society along the laic-Islamic axis and its ramifications for the processes of state formation and the dynamics of class reproduction in the modern Turkish social formation.

As one would expect, there have been many subsectors, groups, and classes within both the laic and Islamic social sectors, creating both social hierarchies internal to each sector and a hierarchy between the sectors. Leaving aside for now the hierarchies internal to the sectors, until the end of the twentieth century, the laic sector was on the top of the hierarchy of society as a whole. As will become clear, this was mainly because of the supremacy of the laic bourgeoisie in the capital accumulation process under the social and political conditions of national developmentalism in the aftermath of the establishment of the Turkish nation-state. In the emergence of the latter, the role and function of Islam in the Ottoman Empire played a decisive role. During the long reign of the Ottomans, both official orthodox and heterodox Islam prevalent in civil society hindered the development of capitalism internally (İnalcık 1969). This came about for the most part by precluding capital accumulation on the part of merchants involved in long-distance trade by confiscating their wealth, a practice that was more or less institutionalized by the Ottoman state. Thus, the Ottoman state elite constituted the only social sector with wealth accumulation comparable to the capitalists in Western Europe. All of this together acted as a brake on the emergence of capitalism à la Western Europe from within.

The leadership of the revolution that had waged the national liberation war in the beginning of the 1920s and effectively secured political power with the establishment of the Republic of Turkey saw the deterrence of capitalism from within as one of the chief reasons for Turkey's socioeconomic backwardness. They proclaimed the dual objectives of political and economic independence as the raison d'être of their revolution. On the economic front the leading coalition of the new state, by convening a national conference in İzmir on the economy of the country in the months preceding the foundation of the republic, forged an interclass political consensus among the delegates representing the interests of landlords and commercial and industrial bourgeoisies together with the representatives of labor. The political consensus manufactured was geared toward a socioeconomic development path based on the private enterprise system, which gave the political revolution its bourgeois character. In line with an economic policy favoring the interests of the bourgeoisie, the founders of the state aimed to enhance the social and political status of the nascent capitalist class by regulating the role of Islam within both the state and civil society. A committee formed in the Faculty of Divinity at the Istanbul University in 1928, for example, along with the banishment of tarikat (religious fraternities), explicitly aimed to help create personal-based religious practices in tune with the requirements of capitalist social relations by reforming and modernizing Islam (Gürbey 2009: 375). According to the committee, Islam would have to be rendered a "rational" and "scientific" faith in order to make "religious life" harmonious with "economic life." Islamism, as both a political and an intellectual current, emerged as a reaction to the "secularization" of Islam in order to retain a positive public impression of traditional Islamic practices and disseminate counterarguments against the unquestioned appropriation of Western values and structures (Aydın 2006). In the late 1940s, with the onset of multiparty politics, Islamism gained further ground in civil society and empowered many people to assert and declare their collective Islamic identity publicly. In the 1950s, it was obvious that capitalist development in Turkey had divided the society into two sectors: those who were supportive of the secular national development model of the founding fathers of the republic, that is, "the laic sector," and those who were against it, that is, "the Islamic sector."

There was another twist to this picture. Back in the 1920s, when the republican developmental project under the leadership of the pro-bourgeois leadership was given a start, the economy was still wide open to foreign capital inflows and flow of foreign goods and services because of the international treaties inherited from the Ottoman past. Given the absence of internationally competitive large-scale private industrial enterprises, industrialization efforts based on private sector initiatives were unsuccessful. With the onset of the Great Depression both foreign capital inflows as well as foreign trade plummeted considerably, leaving the leaders of the state with only the option of a radical change in the direction of industrialization. From the failure of industrialization led by the private sector, there emerged a successful model of state-led industrialization in the 1930s, later to be coined "etatism" in the Turkish political economy literature. The etatist model was one of the earliest models of national developmentalism in the world. Lasting until the end of World War II, it helped built the foundations of large-scale mechanized industry owned and managed by the state. Of all the new enterprises of this period—most of them public—those in the sectors of textiles, metallurgy, energy, and processed food had not only put the economy back on track but also set in motion an irreversible process of industrialization. The latter, to be sure, would fundamentally transform the class relations and formations in the country.

The 1950s witnessed another major advance in the industrialization process. This time, alongside the public enterprises, private commercial and industrial concerns gradually came to occupy and control the manufacturing sectors of the economy. The private sector was more often than not tied to foreign corporations via various business links due to the liberal foreign capital regime. Thus, the relatively independent industrialization model of the 1930s came to a sudden end, and another cycle of dependent accumulation started, this time on a higher and larger scale.

Throughout the 1950s the Demokrat Parti (Democratic Party, DP) ruled the country. Known as "the Menderes years" after the head of the party, Adnan Menderes, this decade saw the entrance of Islamism into mainstream political life. Some of the leading *tarikat* immediately supported the DP government because of its lenient approach to unofficial versions of Islam, while others avoided politics altogether (Mardin 1971, 1993).

This was the age of Keynesian "embedded liberalism" that came to dominate a larger part of human life on a world scale under US industrial hegemony (Arrighi 1994). The main beneficiary of this era in Turkey was the laic bourgeoisie, which moved upward and toward industrial investments. The state helped this industrial capitalist class by providing low-cost credits and the required organizational and legal environment. Despite the backing of the state, the laic bourgeoisie, located largely in Istanbul, failed to establish a stronghold of political representation in the parliament. Supporting and supported by the DP governments, the laic bourgeoisie remained politically dependent on landlords and small commercial capitalists of Anatolia—the two propertied classes within the Islamic sector (Savran 1992; Ahmad 1977). As the DP government did not have the luxury to lose the backing of the latter group, given the disproportionately large size of the electoral vote concentrated in Anatolia, the laic bourgeoisie began to move away from the DP in search of independent political representation in the second half of the 1950s. This political stalemate gave way to a political crisis that was dissolved by a military intervention. With the new political regime that emerged after the 27 May 1960 coup d'état, the hand of the laic bourgeoisie was strengthened. The new regime not only introduced a more democratic constitution based on the separation of powers but also gave impetus to the further development of an industrial base, grounded in five-year development plans and economic policies that provided protection for Turkish industry. As a result, the laic sector came to occupy the top of the social hierarchy of Turkey.

With the acceleration of industrial capital accumulation at the beginning of the 1970s, a modern proletariat emerged with concomitant political and economic organizations. However, another political crisis arose in the 1970s (Ahmad 1977). Because governments were split between the laic bourgeoisie and the conservative Anatolian propertied classes, they represented two conflicting and disparate mandates (Schick and Tonak 1987). They faced increased demands from the laic bourgeoisie, which had economically become the dominant class, and the ocean of small capital scattered throughout the rest of the country. In tandem, the growing opposition of the working class through strikes and civil unrest threatened capital accumulation, thereby further destabilizing the economic foundation of the laic bourgeoisie's claim to rule (Öncü 2003). Inevitably, the latter conflict led to the restriction of democratic rights, whose effective use required strong governments controlled by the laic bourgeoisie (Savran 1992). However, the division of the propertied classes on the laic Istanbul–Islamic Anatolia axis prohibited this political condition from being materialized. With the coup d'état on 12 September 1980, the legislature came momentarily under the control of the laic bourgeoisie in a context completely under the surveillance of the army (Ahmad 1981; Savran 1992).

In recent years, the supremacy of the laic bourgeoisie in the ruling coalition has been seriously challenged by the rise of a capitalist class from within the Islamic sector. Particularly after the election of the Adalet ve Kalkınma Partisi (Justice and Development Party, AKP) under the leadership of Recep Tayyip Erdoğan, this class has pursued an aggressive strategy of conquering the commanding heights of the economy. This surprising shift in the social hierarchy of Turkey has been very much an unforeseen consequence of the transition from national developmentalism (i.e., the peripheral form of Keynesian embedded liberalism) to neoliberalism as the dominant mode of capital accumulation in the aftermath of the 1980 coup d'état.

The main substantive achievement of neoliberalism in Turkey, beginning with the Anavatan Partisi (Motherland Party, ANAP) governments of Turgut Özal in the 1980s and deepening in the 2000s with the AKP governments of Erdoğan, has been to redistribute, rather than to generate, wealth and income. This has been done through what David Harvey (2005) calls "accumulation by dispossession." Accumulation by dispossession has four main features: privatization and commodification, financialization, manipulation of crises, and state redistribution. Let us briefly recall how all of this has happened with the transition to neoliberalism in Turkey.

Privatization and commodification. The privatization of public assets has been an important feature of Turkish neoliberalism, as elsewhere. Public utilities of all kinds (water, telecommunications, transportation), social welfare provision (social housing, education, health care, pensions), and public institutions (universities) have all been privatized to some degree throughout Turkey. Starting during the mid-1980s, the government privatized most state enterprises (steel, cement, textiles, etc.), transportation, major state banks, telecommunications, petroleum and other energy companies, and real estate (large holdings of land and real estate formerly owned by the treasury were also privatized). The appearance of several gated community projects along the hills of the Bosphorus (previously forest land) and other locations in Istanbul were developed for upper-middle-class residences. Similarly, many office buildings sprung up, where mostly the service sector (financial, advertising, accounting, etc.) was housed. The commodification of culture and history in the form of "cultural goods" of all types, such as jewelry of Hürrem Sultan (the wife of Süleyman the Magnificent) and a gated community called Venice in Istanbul was also a main feature of neoliberalism during this period. The period also witnessed a concentration of media and media-related services. New television channels, Internet services, and hundreds of new and specialized magazines (from fashion to real estate) flourished. All of these processes amount to the transfer of assets from the public to the private and class-privileged domains. The Turkish state sold off its assets at incredibly devalued prices.

Financialization. Deregulation allowed the financial system to become one of the main centers of redistributive activity through speculation. During the period of neoliberalism new financial institutions emerged. The establishment of the Istanbul Stock Exchange, along with many mutual funds and investment banks, usually with foreign partners, helped to launch a financial market in which domestic and foreign investors began to invest in the Turkish financial markets.

Manipulation of crises. During the period of neoliberalization the Turkish economy underwent a series of structural adjustment programs resulting in fiscal discipline, the reordering of public expenditure priorities (through reductions in public spending on education, health care, and social security), tax reform in favor of capital (both domestic and foreign), trade liberalization, liberalization of interest rates, privatization, and deregulation of property rights. With pressure from the International Monetary Fund (IMF), the Turkish state reduced public spending on services such as education and health care, resulting in their deterioration. The end result was the collapse of the old middle class, which relied heavily on these social expenditures in order to protect its class positions in Turkish society. Once the best public schools became heavily burdened by reduced expenditures, large class sizes, and the decline in the quality of education, middle-class families were forced to shift toward the flourishing private school network at all levels of education. This was indeed a new schism happening within the middle class as a whole with respect to their capability to access high-quality education.

State redistribution. Once neoliberalized, the state became the primary agent of redistributive policies. It achieved this in the first instance through privatization schemes and cutbacks in state social expenditures such as education, health care, and social services. The neoliberal state also redistributed wealth and income through revisions in the tax code to benefit returns on investment for owners of capital.

In sum, Turkey's integration into the global neoliberal capitalist system has been achieved through a series of policies aimed at liberalizing its financial system, privatizing public enterprises and state-owned land, and deregulating the economy. With the transition to neoliberalism, the Turkish state apparatus was completely transformed in order to facilitate the mobility of global capital. Especially during the AKP's reign in the first decade of the twenty-first century, the opening up of entrepreneurial opportunities as well as new structures in trade relations have allowed substantially new processes of class formations to emerge. Although the capitalist class as a whole gained from the AKP's successful implementation of neoliberal policies, the government acted as the political arm of the rising Islamic bourgeoisie, who succeeded in accumulating billions of dollars of extra capital in less than a decade by means of the advantages and favoritism provided in privatization initiatives and public tenders.

The Middle Class and Its Reproduction

The French sociologist Pierre Bourdieu, following in the steps of Antonio Gramsci a generation before, set out in the 1960s to explain how noneconomic forms of domination are linked to "the reproduction of social stratification and interact with one another and the economic" (Fine 2002: 3). What, then, are the "noneconomic" practices that reproduce the middle class? Against the trend of "economics imperialism" over the social sciences in recent decades, Bourdieu argued that the social world in which capitalism is embedded is the proper field for "the constitution of a general science of the economy of practices" (1997: 47). Theoretically, Bourdieu's "multiple capitals" approach holds the prospect that class, status, and mobility can be subsumed under a single framework of analysis. Such a "science" would lead to an understanding of capital and profit *in all its forms* by providing principles whereby the types of capital—economic, social, and cultural—are convertible into each other. However, as Bourdieu states, "the principles that structure the functioning of the social world are not reducible to the calculus of an economic science that would reduce the universe of exchanges to mercantile exchange" (1997: 46). Reconciling these apparently contradictory statements exposes problematic aspects of multiple capitals theory, but also reveals some of its strengths.

In the remainder of the chapter, we move on to the discussion of those social and cultural dimensions that are most closely connected with the material bases of middle-class formation and reproduction in the neoliberal era of Turkish capitalism. As we have mentioned in the previous section, with the transition to neoliberalism, the material conditions of the reproduction of classes radically changed. This was especially true in the case of the most industrialized metropolis of Turkey, Istanbul, which became a "global city" by the beginning of the 2000s. As a result, the class structure in Istanbul changed considerably, reflecting the substantial rise in the share of non-manual classes working in the service sector and a large marginal underclass of low-skilled, low-paid, or unemployed workers. Two decades ago, the working class, employed in both public and private industrial enterprises, along with an ocean of small shopkeepers representing the traditional petty bourgeoisie, was the dominant class structure both numerically and culturally. Today "the middle class" of the service sector in general appears to dominate the social and cultural life of Istanbul, which is very much under the sway of the neoliberal economic processes of privatization, commodification, and gentrification. Under these new material conditions, the general commodification of education and culture has placed a high premium on the accumulation of social and cultural capital among middle-class families (Bourdieu 1997: 46–48). Here we identify the problem of the middle class as within-class competition among families for quality education and the accumulation of cultural and social capital in general. This is a problem of competition and increasing differentiation between a faction that can be safely called the "new middle class" of professionals and managers because of their advantageous position within neoliberalism and the older core middle class of industrial and public administrative employees mostly inherited from the period of national developmentalism.

While there would appear to be a global trend in economic, social, and cultural differentiation within the middle class along these lines, accompanied by a crisis of access to and affordability of quality education, the dynamics of middle-class formation cannot be understood fully without taking into account the peculiarities of the Turkish local context in which the contingencies of economic, social, and cultural history come into play. Our foregoing macro-historical account of class formations, for example, has already drawn attention to a potential dynamic of an extra within-class differentiation among Turkish middle-class families in addition to the distinctions between new and old factions that could be found elsewhere. Thus, to be sure, our own theoretical approach to middle-class formation was largely influenced by field research in Istanbul as much as by the class-theoretical analysis of Turkish capitalist modernity presented above. Early on in our research we made a decision to focus on laic and Islamic Istanbul middle-class households and families as the agents of middle-class reproduction and transformation to understand the emergent neoliberal landscape. At first, we focused on the meaning and content of changing household consumption habits because, we reasoned, these formed a nexus of activity at the intersection of economy and society, a meeting of our respective professional fields of inquiry. The result was a survey in 2009 of 434 middle-class families that (a) helped us to sharpen our understanding of both the laic and the Islamic middle classes, (b) gave us a picture of changing tastes and preferences in middle-class culture in general and in each of these particular sectors of the middle class, and (c) provided us with a clear view of families that comprised a new Islamic middle-class faction that had benefited economically, socially, and culturally from the neoliberal regime.

The common way to think generally about the middle class in a capitalist society is to think about it as the class in between the capitalist class and the laboring class. Anchoring classes in their capitalist relations of production also reflects the way most people think about themselves and their class location, namely, by their occupations and the material rewards they receive for their work. This leads to triadic tiers of occupations with such labels as "owners," "managers," and "workers" corresponding to tiers of material rewards labeled "profits," "salaries," and "wages." These classificatory schemes presume the power and influence of large corporations and bureaucratic organizations in modern working lives. Indeed, the view that the industrial middle class is composed of professional, managerial, and technical elites who sell their services to owners of capital and who rely primarily on their expert knowledge and formal educational credentials for their power and privilege will suffice as our point of departure for conceptualizing the middle class. Moreover, these distinctions pertain to class structures in all industrialized or late industrializing societies. Each class has an interest in protecting and maintaining the primary resource that constitutes its reproduction—capital, education, or labor.

Classes can be differentiated by their possession of a preponderance of one resource over another. Both upper and lower classes have in common a preponderance of economic resources, albeit upper-class families derive their economic resources primarily from possession of wealth and its direct social transmission, while lower-class families derive their economic resources from possession of wages and therefore ultimately through the biological reproduction of labor. In both cases, the *transmission* is direct and relatively uncomplicated. Middle-class social reproduction is neither as direct nor as uncomplicated as that of the capitalist or wage-laboring classes. From the perspective of the middle class, the solution to the problem of class reproduction can be posed in terms of a preponderance of cultural resources owned.

As we have mentioned earlier, the theorist who has done the most to bridge gaps between theory and empirical inquiry in the field of middle-class reproduction is Bourdieu. His guiding belief was that lived experience is constitutive of class and "cannot be directly 'deduced' from an objectivist map of the class structure" (Wacquant 1991: 52). He distinguishes among three forms of capital for purposes of analysis. The first he labels *economic capital*, "which is immediately and directly convertible into money and may be institutionalized in the form of property rights." The second is *cultural capital*, "which is convertible, on certain conditions, into economic capital and may be institutionalized in the form of educational qualifications." The third is *social capital*, defined as "the aggregate of the actual or potential resources which are linked to possession of a durable network of more or less institutionalized relationships of mutual acquaintance and recognition [that] provides each of its members with the backing of collectively-owned capital as actual and potential credit" (Bourdieu 1997: 51). With regard to Bourdieu's institutionalization of the forms of capital, economic capital is institutionalized as "property rights," cultural capital is institutionalized as "educational qualifications," and social capital is institutionalized as "durable networks."

Bourdieu also identifies *symbolic capital* as a type of capital, one that is derived from representations of the other types of capital. Symbolic capital is capital in whatever form—cultural, social, economic—that is apprehended symbolically, that is, as meaningful in a form of communication viewed as dialogic. The function of symbolic capital in Bourdieu's economy of practices is in the realm of rhetorical value. This much is clear when he states that

> because the social conditions of the transmission and acquisition of cultural capital are more disguised than those of economic capital, it is predisposed to function as symbolic capital, i.e. to be unrecognized as capital and recognized as legitimate competence in all markets in which economic capital is not fully recognized. (1997: 49)

The value of symbolic capital gained from any given cultural competence is derived from its scarcity in the distribution of cultural capital and, according to Bourdieu,

> yields profits of distinction for its owner. The share in profits which scarce cultural capital secures in class-divided societies is based, in the last analysis, on the fact that all agents do not have the economic and cultural means for prolonging their children's education beyond the minimum necessary for the reproduction of the labor-power least valorized at a given moment. (1997: 49)

In Turkey, for instance, the state-induced scarcity of cultural capital in the form of state-controlled and state-regulated national examinations ensures that cultural capital will receive disproportionate weight in middle-class family strategies for social and economic reproduction.

The apprehension of one form of capital as another form, e.g., cultural capital as symbolic capital, is here treated as an act of *conversion*. If this claim seems to stretch the limits of the meaning of exchange value, it nevertheless fits Gayatri Spivak's view that in capitalism "money corrupts what is natural and turns it, *in its natural form*, into a mere visible sign for the social relation of exchange" (1987: 34) Moreover, "money conceals the *heterogeneity* of social relations irretrievably by substituting the category of substitution for an exchange which is necessarily asymmetrical" (Spivak 1987: 35; emphasis added). It follows that convertibility is a process whereby "two things can be pronounced equal, identical, or substitutable by first, making equal different things, next, a forgetting of that move, and finally, a metalyptically created memory that conceals this genealogy" (Spivak 1987: 35).

For Bourdieu, cultural capital appears in three forms: *embodied*, *objectified*, and *institutionalized*. In its embodied state, it appears in the form of "long-lasting dispositions of the mind and body." In its objectified state, it appears in the form of cultural goods such as books or paintings that are the "traces" of the ideas, theories, interpretations, critiques, puzzles, or problematics that inform our knowledge about them. In its institutionalized state, it appears as "a form of objectification which must be set apart because it confers entirely original properties on the cultural capital which it is presumed to guarantee" (Bourdieu 1997: 47). His example is educational qualifications such as certification and credentialing, which are central to the analysis below.

Middle-class families' preponderance of cultural capital, especially in its embodied form, and considering its less tangible and fungible characteristics, poses special problems of transmission from one generation to the next. This problem is especially true in its institutionalized form of educational qualifications, certification, and credentialing, which are impossible to transmit directly to the next generation. The objectification of cultural capital in the form of education credentials is one way to overcome the embodiment of cultural capital that limits its convertibility, at least for the individual. Bourdieu points out that

> with the academic qualification, a certificate of cultural competence which confers on its holder a conventional, constant, legally guaranteed value with respect to culture, social alchemy produces a form of cultural capital which

has a relative autonomy vis-à-vis its bearer and even vis-à-vis the cultural capital he effectively possesses at a given moment in time. (1997: 51)

One effect of the state monopoly on high school and university entrance exams is strong state control over the institutionalization of cultural capital in Turkish society.

Bourdieu stipulates *social capital* as "made up of social obligations ('connections'), which are convertible, in certain conditions, into economic capital and may be institutionalized in the form of a title" (1997: 47). The convertibility of cultural and social capital into economic capital is neither immediate nor direct. We might add that it also is neither necessary nor inevitable (Granovetter 1985). A durable network may consist of personal relationships among individuals, but the more significant (and valuable) relationships become socially instituted and augmented through more or less continual exchanges that include the deployment of economic and cultural capital. It follows that the volume of social capital possessed by a given agent depends on the size of the durable network that can be effectively mobilized and the volume of actual capitals that can be appropriated.

Bourdieu reminds us that generalized cultural capital, enacted in the form of language habits, manners, and rhetorical competence, come into play as performative practices of social capital that also are part of symbolic capital. To the extent that "prestige," "status," and other aspects of social hierarchy are communicated and performed, the enactment of a durable network is at one and the same time the reproduction of social class (Bourdieu 1997: 57). Bourdieu states that "social capital is so totally governed by the logic of knowledge and acknowledgement that it always functions as symbolic capital" (1997: 57). Among upper-middle-class families in Istanbul this logic includes code switching among Turkish, English, French, German, and other mostly European languages in ordinary speech habits, allusion to the objectified forms of cultural capital in the form of elevated Turkish, and the presumption of intellectual enlightenment in and predispositions toward European habits of public dress, music, social intercourse, dining, and entertainment enmeshed with Turkish forms of cultural objectification.

The importance of durable social networks to middle-class families cannot be understated in the practices of everyday life in Istanbul. This statement holds for all classes albeit with different form and content. The extension and content of durable family networks varies considerably even among families with comparable economic and cultural capital, conferring unequal profits from near equal capitals. Bourdieu might as well be talking about Istanbul when he states that

> the social effects are particularly visible in all cases in which different individuals obtain very unequal profits from virtually equivalent (economic or cultural) capital, depending on the extent to which they can mobilize by proxy the capital of a group (a family, the alumni of an elite school, a select club, the aristocracy, etc.) that is more or less constituted as such and more or less rich in capital. (1997: 56)

The deployment of durable networks is integral to the long preparation leading up to the national Selective Middle School Examinations and emblematic of the form that competition takes in Istanbul middle-class life in general.

This brings us to the question, "What makes the middle class a *social* class?" The concept of social capital that we propose is a form of accumulation that is grounded in history. Its efficacy remains an empirical question, not a general proposition about its value as a positive force in that history. As we already mentioned, we opted early on in our research to view the family as the generative agent of the reproduction of class. If family is the main agent of middle-class formation in Turkey, it also is the basis of class solidarity. But on what foundation does solidarity rest? For Bourdieu, social solidarity is both foundational principle and effect of the economy of practices, which includes the durable networks that lead to the accumulation of social capital. Nothing captures the importance Istanbul middle-class families give to the durable network and its pervasiveness in their daily lives as much as the amount of time, effort, and economic and cultural capital they expend on its maintenance and extension. As Bourdieu argues, "The existence of a network of connections is not a natural given, or even a social given ... it is the product of an endless effort at institution, of which institution rites ... mark the essential moments and which is necessary in order to produce and reproduce lasting, useful relationships that can secure material or symbolic profits" (1997: 56). It is no exaggeration to claim that Istanbul families and their members invest as much time and effort in their social networks as they invest in their families. Notwithstanding this empirically grounded claim, social capital is no substitute for economic and cultural capital in the scheme of capitalist development (Fine 2001). On the contrary, the extent to which the capitals are convertible into one another is quite independent from any reductionist claim that one is in principle reducible to the others.

We argue that to a remarkable degree families in Istanbul have not lost control over the authority of their members and the social exchanges that can lead to lasting relationships. Whether through marriage, friendship, business partnership, club membership, school, and so forth, the self-interested market logic of transactions gives way to the symbolically sanctioned logic of social capital reinforced by cultural capital under the guise of symbolic capital in the form of continual favors, gifts, and other expressions of goodwill and generosity. Sociability, the general form of reciprocity in which continual exchanges, and therefore recognition, is endlessly confirmed and reaffirmed, is among the biggest investments of cultural and symbolic capital. But this is not to say that social capital is without imposition, conflict, or cost. The family invests in its own hierarchy of relationships, as Bourdieu himself made clear in essays on power relations in the constitution of a "family" and kinship as a particular form of domination (Bourdieu 1990, 1996). The accumulation of social capital by socially embedded members of the Istanbul middle class is high maintenance and therefore time intensive, the opposite of the principle of maximizing labor productivity in capitalist transactions. Ben Fine makes the point succinctly when he states that "economists can bring in the social to complement the individual because the social has been omitted in the first instance, not least with capital understood as a resource rather than as a relationship" (2002: 10).

The irreducible ambiguity of cultural capital, when combined with the problematic nature of convertibility of different capitals, can provide insight into the often-repeated claim that the middle class is structurally ambiguous in relation to both the capitalist and the working classes, at least from the standpoint of the social energy that goes into the reproduction of class. From the standpoint of capitalists who own the means of production but do not own the expert knowledge needed to design machines, organize labor, and manage, account for, and allocate resources, not to mention the many other services performed by the middle class for the capitalist class, the latter must find ways to appropriate the embodiment of cultural capital or the services of the holders of this capital. Bourdieu finds that "[t]his is no doubt the basis of the ambiguous status of executives and engineers. If they do not own the means of production, and they only derive profit from their own cultural capital, then they will be classified among the upper class, or at least associated with the owners of the means" (1997: 50). The holders of the dominant economic capital, however, set the holders of cultural capital in competition with one another. From the standpoint of the working class, the holders of cultural capital share with them a market in which they compete for the sale of their labor.

In a capitalist society, economic capital is dominant. Economistic logic dominates as a cultural ideology because the tendency is toward the conversion of all forms of value into that of the market, symbolized by money, a commodity that stands for the value of all other commodities but that has no use value of its own. Bourdieu acknowledges the domination of economic capital in a capitalist society when he states that social and cultural capitals function as "disguised" forms of economic capital. But he goes on to say that cultural and social capitals are "never entirely reducible" to economic capital (1997: 54). The reason he gives is that social and cultural capitals have their own respective "efficacies." We would add that they have their own socially bounded spheres of valuation, rules of exchange and communication, and institutionalization. It remains an empirical question whether these capitals perform the function of hiding economic capital, presumably because of the dangers associated with revealing class relations of inequality.

The social world is indeed a world of accumulated history. In the context of middle-class formation in Istanbul, to be or to become an upper-middle-class family not only requires material wealth but also social and cultural capital. Cultural capital in its objectified and embodied form of education and certification of individuals requires long-term *collective* planning and execution. It begins at birth with a plan for an education path that leads to a top university. From the standpoint of the multi-capitalized family and its middle-class norms, employment follows education, marriage follows employment, and family follows all three in the life course. The sequence is enacted through many conversions of the forms of capital. The long march of family members, or embodied capital, from primary school to university is the sine qua non of a process of accumulation that is meant to ensure not only the reproduction of the family but also the reproduction of its social class fragment. Person, family, and class are mutually constituted through capital conversions and the practices associated with them.

The Reproduction of the New Islamic Middle Class in the Neoliberal Landscape of Istanbul

The social hierarchy of Turkish social formation during the era of national developmentalism was two tiered. At the lower tier was universal literacy and, for some, public primary education in the name of national unity. Far above that, public education at higher levels would create an elite cadre that could lead national development while promoting national unity on behalf of their fellow countrymen and women. The ideology of national developmentalism, in which the state would lead the country into a form of regulated market capitalism, reigned until the end of the 1970s and, as we have seen above, resulted in the supremacy of the laic bourgeoisie in the social hierarchy. After the military coup of 1980, the state became more of an instrument of capital; its function was to integrate Turkey's national markets into the emerging markets of global finance and trade. Since then, a new middle class has come into being, which has been the locus of the spirit of "free enterprise" in the global market and in education. Successive governments abandoned their strong resistance to private education as being contrary to the republican spirit of a unified nation and began to respond to the increasing demand for private education at all levels of the educational system. This political tendency gained further momentum under the Islamist AKP governments, which generously promoted the rising Islamic bourgeoisie and thereby the new Islamic middle class tied to this class within the durable networks it established in history. Thus, there emerged two factions of the new middle class, the laic and the Islamic, in the neoliberal landscape of Istanbul where we conducted our survey research in 2009.

In our sample there were 434 households, of which 278 were from the Islamic middle class and 156 were from the laic middle class. The respondents were the household heads, that is, the husbands, according to Turkish customs. The average age of the household heads was forty-five, while the average age of the spouse was thirty-five. The majority of the household heads and spouses were raised, educated, and built their careers during the neoliberal era. In this sense our sample is highly representative of the new middle class rather than the old one. In this section, in order to emphasize the centrality of cultural capital in the reproduction of the new middle class, we focus only on a small section of our survey, directing attention only to the educational qualifications of the households, that is, their cultural capital.

We maintain that the type of schools can help us see how the respondents utilize their cultural capital in converting the value of their educational credentials into economic capital in market transactions performed according to the logic of economic exchange. We presume that higher education levels and degrees from prestigious universities and high schools will correlate with employment as professionals and managers in the alluring corporate sector of globalized firms. Oftentimes such people aspire to belong to the upper middle class and thereby share the values and lifestyles that have become dominant within the neoliberal landscape (we return to this point in the final section).

When we looked at the highest level of education obtained by the respondents, 70 percent of the laic household heads and 40 percent of their spouses had attained a university degree or above. These percentages were 58 percent for the Islamic household heads and 24 percent for their spouses. In Turkey university education options for high school graduates include public universities (with instruction in foreign languages), public universities (with instruction in Turkish), private universities (with the majority of instruction in English), and universities abroad (with the United States being the preferred destination). The majority (around 70 percent) of our respondents both from the laic and the Islamic households went to public universities. This reflects the fact that wider access to foreign universities became available only in the later decades of the neoliberal era, when our respondents had already graduated.

Table 6.1. Percentage of University and Above Education Attained in the Previous Generation

	Laic Households	Islamic Households
Head's Father	24%	4%
Head's Mother	7%	1%
Spouse's Father	22%	8%
Spouse's Mother	9%	1%

Table 6.1 illustrates the highest educational level obtained by the parents of the respondents. One generation ago laic middle-class families were remarkably more educated than Islamic middle-class families. In tandem with the supremacy of the laic bourgeoisie during the era of national developmentalism, the percentage of the fathers of the laic families who attained an education at the university level or above was significantly higher than those of the Islamic ones. The remarkable difference in this regard between the spouses' fathers, again in favor of the laic families, provides further support for the observation that one generation ago reaching upper-middle-class positions through higher and better educational qualifications was mostly a privilege of the laic social sector. Another interesting

observation is the very low percentage of mothers who attained an education at the university level or above in both factions of the middle class as compared to their spouses. This may show that one generation ago there was a wide gender gap between men and women in terms of access to university education regardless of one's social sector, that is, the laic and Islamic sectors, although the women of the laic sector had a better chance of pursuing a university degree relative to their counterparts in the Islamic sector.

The type of high school that an individual graduates from is an important determinant of success in the highly competitive university entrance exams in Turkey. Graduates of foreign immersion high schools are always among the top achievers. Since education in those schools are in one of the Western languages (e.g. English, German, or French), the graduates of such schools have a definite advantage in entering Turkish universities where one of those languages are used as a medium of instruction. Both public and private universities of this type are among the top universities in Turkey, and some rank within the top five hundred universities in the world. These universities require fluency in the foreign language used and monitor this via second language proficiency exams. Graduates of foreign immersion schools pass the foreign language proficiency exams without difficulty, while the students coming from regular public and vocational schools most often need to go through language preparation courses for one to two years.

Some of the public schools known as Anatolian high schools (*Anadolu Liseleri*) emulate the curriculum of the foreign immersion schools in order to provide wider access to affordable, high-quality high school education. The number of Anatolian high schools, some of which were established during the era of national developmentalism, continued to increase during the neoliberal decades. Anatolian high schools admit their students based on their performance in the nationwide high school entrance exam, which is administered to those who finish eight years of primary school. Several private schools also followed the Anatolian high school model, adopting foreign languages as the language of instruction, particularly as an alternative to American, French, and German immersion schools. There is a large range, however, among these private schools in terms of quality of education provided and success rates in the university entrance exams. The ones that are chosen by the new Islamic middle-class families are usually newly established schools and among the top achievers, equaling if not surpassing the best foreign immersion and Anatolian high schools. All other high schools in Turkey, including the regular vocational schools, are public and teach in Turkish. Foreign languages are only provided as elective courses.

Among the public schools, there is a type of vocational school called İmam Hatip schools, which were founded to train government-employed imams and muezzins (preachers). The first İmam Hatip schools were established in 1951. Following the military coup of 1960, the government threatened to shut them down. With the new constitution in 1961, graduates of these schools were required to fulfill the course requirements of regular high schools in addition to their religious curriculum to be able to continue to university programs. This stringent requirement became a hotly debated issue between the Islamic and laic sectors, as it restricted the chances of İmam Hatip graduates to enter university programs. Until 1971 the İmam Hatip schools also had junior high schools, but these were shut down after the military intervention of that year. In 1974 İmam Hatip junior high schools were allowed to reopen. After the coup of 12 September 1980, graduates of İmam Hatip high schools gained the right to enter all university departments without any restrictions. In 1985, for the first time Anatolian İmam Hatip schools started to open in order to fulfill the needs of Islamic middle-class families demanding a high-quality education within the framework of a religious curriculum. In 1997 the number of students in İmam Hatip schools in all forms reached more than five hundred thousand. Considering that there were only about forty thousand İmam Hatip students in the beginning of the 1980s, this was a massive increase in numbers. Likewise, the number of İmam Hatip high schools increased and reached a total of more than one thousand in 1997. The research shows that this increase can be attributed to commitment of Islamic families to religion and increases in the demand for religious education, admission of female students to İmam Hatip schools, and the availability of scholarships and dormitory facilities. Interestingly, half of the students of İmam Hatip schools are female, although women are not eligible to become imams or muezzins. There was a sudden decline in the popularity of İmam Hatip schools in 1997, after they were remodeled once again as vocational high schools, with the introduction of eight years of compulsory primary education before enrollment in an İmam Hatip school. Enrollment in İmam Hatip schools declined from 11 percent in 1997 to 2 percent in 2002 (when the AKP came to power) in the relevant age group of students (Finkel 2012). The 1997 figures included the students who chose to go to İmam Hatip schools after elementary school. After the separation of junior high schools from İmam Hatip schools, the students choosing to continue to high school in İmam

Hatip schools dropped to 2 percent, as reflected in the 2002 figures. The AKP government introduced a new educational reform in March 2012 that extended compulsory education to twelve years, with four-year blocks of primary school, middle school, and high school. This was seen as an overhauling operation for the İmam Hatip schools to increase their enrollment. The new regulation enables students to enter İmam Hatip schools after the fourth grade.

Table 6.2. Percentage Distribution of Graduation of Household Heads and Spouses by Type of High School

School Type	Laic Households		Islamic Households	
	Head	Spouse	Head	Spouse
Foreign Immersion and Anatolian High Schools	11%	0%	0%	0%
Private High School	9%	8%	3%	
Public High School	60%	60%	41%	28%
İmam Hatip High School			15%	13%
Nonreligious Vocational School	10%	6%	13%	8%

Table 6.2 shows the distribution of our survey respondents in terms of the type of high schools they graduated from. The laic families have higher representation in the top-achiever foreign immersion high schools, Anatolian high schools, and private high schools than the Islamic families. This is the case for both heads and spouses. Another difference between these two factions of the middle class is, as expected, the number of graduates from the İmam Hatip schools. While we do not observe any İmam Hatip graduates from the laic families, around 15 percent of heads and 13 percent of spouses of the Islamic families are graduates of these religious schools.

As mentioned previously, a foreign language that one knows is not only an *embodied* cultural capital owned by a person, but also alludes to a perception that this person possesses an *objectified* form of cultural capital. This is because in certain social contexts knowledge of a foreign language *symbolizes* one's belonging to the upper middle class. Although we surveyed all the foreign languages known, including Western (e.g., English, German, French, etc.) and non-Western (e.g., Arabic, Kurdish, etc.), we hereby only report knowledge of the English language, as it is the language of the neoliberal global environment.

Table 6.3 confirms the fact that English as a second language became widely common among both types of families when we consider their heads, that is, the current generation. This shows that both types of families follow the global trend and learn English in order to thrive in the competitive struggle for upper-middle-class positions. The low percentage of heads' fathers with knowledge of English among the laic families and the absence of this competence among heads' fathers of the Islamic families show that English was not a decisive factor in the reproduction strategies of the middle classes in the era of national developmentalism.

Table 6.3. Knowledge of the English Language by Household Heads, Spouses, and Parents

	Laic Households	Islamic Households
Head	51%	35%
Head's Spouse	37%	19%
Head's Father	5%	1%
Head's Mother	0%	0%
Spouse's Father	5%	2%
Spouse's Mother	2%	0%

Given that middle-class reproduction is neither as direct nor as uncomplicated as that of the capitalist or wage-laboring classes, it involves strategic thinking and planning on the part of the parents, especially in regard to the schooling of their children. In the competitive struggle among the middle-class families for prolonging their class privileges into the next generations, the institutionalized form of cultural capital occupies a primary concern, because this form of cultural capital promises an almost guaranteed ticket to the upper middle class by providing high-quality educational credentials. As part of our survey, we asked our respondents to rank the purposes of their savings and investments in terms of their perceived degree of importance. The answers we obtained are worthy of note. First, both types of families considered the education of their children one of the most important reasons to save and invest. Second, the percentage of the heads of Islamic families who declared the education of their children to be the most important reason exceeds the percentage of those of laic families by more than 10 percent. While 52 percent of the heads of Islamic families claim that the education of their children is the most important purpose of their savings and investments, 41 percent of the heads of laic families see their children's education as the most important purpose for their savings and investments. When compared to their parents' low educational attainment levels, this finding is indicative of the Islamic middle-class families' changing attitudes toward the role of education in attaining upper-middle-class positions. Indeed, when we consider the answers given to one of our survey questions, which asks about the level of education the respondent would minimally expect his children to obtain, we find that 95 percent of the heads of Islamic families look forward to seeing their children's completion of a university degree program. This is 96 percent among the heads of laic families. In other words, both types of families have converged and now hold a similar opinion regarding the importance of education in their class reproduction strategies.

Table 6.4. Type of Schools Household Heads Aspire to Send Their Children To

School Type		Laic Households	Islamic Households
Elementary			
	Private (Foreign Immersion and Turkish)	45%	53%
High School			
	Private (Foreign Immersion and Turkish)	41%	36%
	Anatolian High School	13%	8%
	Science High School	15%	29%
	İmam Hatip High School	0%	9%
	Public High School	6%	9%
University			
	Abroad (USA)	29%	24%
	Private University (Foreign Language)	23%	14%
	Public University (Foreign Language)	14%	26%
	Public University (Turkish)	16%	30%
Graduate Studies (Masters)			
	Abroad (USA)	60%	63%
	Private University (Foreign Language)	11%	7%

Further support for this important observation can be found in table 6.4, which provides some of the findings regarding the type of schools that the household heads aspire to send their children to at different levels of the education system in Turkey. What is remarkable is that the Islamic families' aspirations in general are higher than those of the laic families. While 45 percent of the laic families would expect their children to attend private schools at the elementary level, 53 percent of the Islamic families desire their children to attend such schools, which are the domain of a privileged few. When we reflect on their preferences for high school education, the first thing to note is the drop in the choice of the İmam Hatip schools as schools desired for the children among the Islamic families. Here we see that only 9 percent of the families anticipate seeing their children attending these religious schools. This is an interesting finding in that in the midst of alleged Islamization of Turkish society in recent years, one would have expected to observe an increase in this choice. Yet the opposite occurs, reflecting again the changing attitudes of the Islamic families toward the role of education in the competition for upper-middle-class positions. Another noteworthy finding is about the choice of science high schools. These schools are modeled after Ankara Science High School established in 1964 with a curriculum concentrated on natural sciences and mathematics. Due to the considerable success of its graduates in both professional and academic careers, the science high school model has become a popular institution and many public and private science high schools mushroomed across the country. Among the private science high schools, those allegedly opened by the Gülen movement became one of the most desired schools among the Islamic families. Our findings support this common stock of knowledge in Turkish civil society. In the table we read that 29 percent of the Islamic families expect their children to study in these schools. In tandem with this choice, almost 60 percent of the Islamic families anticipate that their children will attend one of the three types of universities where the medium of instruction is a foreign language—that is, English. In this regard, we do not observe any significant difference between the two types of families. Our final observation is perhaps the final word on this debate. The majority of the Islamic families, just like their laic counterparts, look ahead to see their children going abroad, mostly to the United States, for graduate studies, which is the trademark of the upper middle class in the global neoliberal environment.

Concluding Remarks

Notwithstanding the very important state interests in national unity, Turkish identity, and civil society, the state also has an interest in managing the middle class in the interest of a capitalist class of industrial and commercial families who own the means of production, distribution, and marketing. In the neoliberal era of the post-1980s, the knowledge and skills of the old middle class were devalued. Corporate capital was a major source of investment in new private universities, increasing the supply of new middle-class labor that was directed primarily at corporate business and related producer services. The new middle class also served to create an important symbolic buffer between the capitalist class and the middle class, creating the appearance of a middle class more in tune with the interests of a capitalist class that was in the process of becoming a transnational capitalist class. This class could claim that the middle class, by which they meant the professionals and managers employed in the corporate sector, was "rising." At the same time, the core middle class experienced deteriorating material conditions and relative devaluation of its services, which brought it closer in its class relations to the lower middle class of teachers and clerks than to the upper middle class to which it aspired. Middle-class polarization became a reality.

If the strong presence of global financial institutions is an indicator of a globalizing city, then Istanbul meets the test. By the end of the 1990s, a glass city that became the home of the fledgling Turkish stock market, investment banks, insurance carriers, and five-star international business hotels could be seen a few miles to the north of the old city center, just over the hills from the Bosphorus and minutes from the intersection of highways that brought workers over the bridge from the Asian side to merge with the traffic caused by the north-south commuters on the Western side. Maslak, as the new financial area is called, became the headquarters of some of the largest Turkish transnational corporations, most of them owned and controlled by the laic bourgeoisie. The rapid change was quite dramatic when compared to the preexisting 1930s state banks headquartered mostly in the central Anatolian capital of Ankara in order to be close to the state bureaucracy that regulated them, a pattern the early private banks followed from 1950 to 1980.

New five-star international hotels catering to businessmen, conventioneers, and groups of tourists appeared in the new financial center but also in other parts of the city. Istanbul had no modern international hotel until 1955, when the Hilton was built on Cumhuriyet Boulevard near Taksim Square, a center for foreign travelers and international tourism since the mid-nineteenth century. The following year the exclusive Divan Hotel was built a few blocks away. Two decades would pass before the Sheraton and Marmara hotels were added to the rising skyline around Taksim. In contrast, the decade after 1982 saw the construction of numerous international hotels, several of which were located near corporate headquarters in the financial district.

Nowhere was the polarization *within* the middle class more visible than in the appreciation of residential real estate and the geographical separation of new middle-class housing from the housing of other middle-class factions. The spatial separation within middle-class housing that further differentiated new and upper-middle-class housing from the rest of the middle class was carried out during the real estate booms of the 1990s and 2000s. Skyrocketing residential real estate prices on the high end of the market was the defining factor.

Upper-class families that live in Istanbul have palatial homes and compounds distinct from the pattern of exclusive housing developments, whether these are high-rise, low-rise, or villa-style. Upper-middle-class and middle-class households who were able to reap substantial material benefits from trade, finance, and investment activities in the growth sectors of the new economy during the neoliberal era have come to be the main residents of the latter. What is remarkable is that both the laic and Islamic new middle-class families share the tendency to live in such exclusive housing developments. That shows that they were able to assert neoliberal values as superior to those of the struggling middle-class factions that were shaped in the era of national developmentalism. The struggle within the middle class from 1980 to the present was all about what it meant to belong to the middle class—materially, morally, and socially. We observe this particular ideological struggle both within the laic and Islamic middle-class families. In each faction a new middle class reflecting neoliberal values and lifestyles emerged and separated itself from the rest. Thus, although they have had different ideological and cultural pasts and orientations, both the laic and Islamic factions of the new middle class converged into a new status group characterized by social differentiation by spatial separation, the added value of appreciating real estate prices, and quick access to workplaces and shopping centers via motorways and beltways and so on.

As more public projects focused on rapid transportation and public parks, more private capital flowed into the housing market to meet growing demand for "naturalized" site locations, stylish exterior and interior design, and consumer services of all kinds. Outdoor amenities such as planted miniature forests, lawns, gardens, fountains, and pathways became more common in the spaces on the edge of the city. The appearance of artificial lakes, recreation areas, and health clubs were responses to a new awareness of, and fascination with, the body. In this regard both factions of the new middle class led the way. With money came more choice, and with more choice came more self-conscious identity play with consumer lifestyles from many foreign countries. It was the actualization of the global ideology of consumer culture in the social spaces of Istanbul that turned older cosmopolitan ways into new globalizing lifestyles. The new Islamic middle class, just like its laic counterpart, could gaze at a plethora of billboards, television personalities, and slick magazine advertisements as if people were seeing themselves through a looking glass. Advertising and media set out to deliver consumers to products that were designed to satisfy the desire to gaze at others and be a part of the "scene." There was an equally strong urge to be private and exclusive. In a world of commodified culture, all things seem possible, even if they are "sinful."

There are at least two commodity aesthetics at work in producing new middle-class living arrangements in globalizing cities such as Istanbul. The first we might call "commodity cosmopolitanism," fueled by the desire to be surrounded by new upscale shopping malls and boulevards, cinema complexes, ethnic restaurants, coffee houses, art galleries, museums, and other sites for culture and leisure such as yacht harbors, health and athletic centers, bistros, and social clubs. Being surrounded by "a dense jungle" of places for pleasure and leisure is crucial to a commodity aesthetic that relies upon the conspicuous consumption of exquisite objects. The symbolic objectification of social differentiation by asserting a form of consumption from which core middle-class and lower-middle-class factions have been conspicuously excluded was an important globalizing phenomenon of the 1990s and 2000s. Excluded in large part by high prices and declining real wages, these factions also experienced exclusion from the codes governing commodity aesthetics at a historical moment when cultural capital became the calling card of the new middle class.

The second commodity aesthetic also has to do with class symbols and meanings, but in this case the content is about health related to the body and its embodiment in a reconstituted urban "nature." The body and the process of embodiment become associated with self-discipline and control over the body in ways that are analogous to neoliberal ideas about freeing the market from constraints imposed by the state. Living a healthy life in an imagined environment of planted forest, plumbed waterfalls, fountains, and human-designed lakes and ponds became emblematic of an emerging *global* upper middle class. The two commodity aesthetics, one an imagined cosmopolitanism, the other a constituted naturalism of body and environment, were in reality part of a single commodity culture associated with the self-awareness of the new middle class as a globalizing middle class. The cityscape was being remade in its image and refracted in its feeling of power, privilege, and autonomy. Most luxury housing developers tried to capture the dual commodity aesthetics in their design, promotion, marketing, and advertising, whether these were directed to the laic social sector or the Islamic one.

Social values are inscribed in site location, buildings, and amenities but are variably expressed in different designs. The commodity aesthetics of conspicuous cosmopolitanism tended more toward denser high-rise complexes whose boundaries with the surrounding neighborhoods were less controlled, more porous, and therefore more open to commercial services and the use of public facilities like beaches, parks, and nearby streets with shops. The commodity aesthetics of various forms of embodiment tended to favor less dense, low-rise, multiple free-standing units closed to their surrounding commercial environment. These broad designs, the one approximating a "city" within the city, the other encompassing commercial products and services within the gates of a closed corporate community akin to a medieval walled compound, overlapped in their variations. Yet the new middle class of both factions have continued to use their wealth for purposes of social exclusion in the guise of physical seclusion, either high up in apartments with views of the skyline or on the ground behind secure walls. The visibly different built environments belied common social values of a privileged class, including privacy, seclusion, safety, security, and an intense interest in being with people like one's own. The economy of the globalizing city became dependent on their consumption of luxury commodities of all kinds, including housing.

A neoliberal regime created the ideology and conditions for transformative change in Istanbul's new and upper-middle-class culture that trickled down to other middle-class factions. It opened up new opportunities for middle-class expression and identity in the form of the consumption of foreign goods, entertainment, and travel. Upper-middle-class households, especially among the new generation, led the way in reimagining themselves—with the aid of promotional, marketing, and advertising firms in joint ventures with foreign counterparts—as participants in an emerging global middle class. The 2000s brought new print, electronic, and social media, which opened new channels of communication. In turn, channels to international information of all kinds offered up new images and then imaginings for Istanbul middle-class households eager to shed the material symbols of an identity rooted in post–World War II national developmentalism. This making of a global middle-class *culture* into its localized variants of the laic and Islamic sorts was not something added on to the formation of the middle class in a new political economy of the world and one of its globalizing cities. It was always an integral part of the whole process implied in economic globalization and the neoliberal ideology that gave it legitimacy and meaning. In the 2000s the Islamic bourgeoisie followed in the footsteps of the laic bourgeoisie in creating a world after the image of the global neoliberal bourgeois culture. What was taking place in Istanbul was also taking place in globalizing cities from Mexico City to Mumbai, subject to national and historical specificities.

The "new rich," as they are referred to in some of the literature on neoliberalism, exerted a disproportionate effect on taste and changing habits of leisure and consumption, changing the cityscape with respect to entertainment and leisure. Their tastes and habits appeared in the cityscape as whole new consumption sites for upscale shopping centers with luxury import stores, international cuisine in new restaurants, clubs and casinos, luxury housing developments, and expensive private schools. In the midst of loud claims of the reappropriation of the Ottoman Islamic heritage, emulation, conspicuous consumption, and changing codes of commodity culture in all areas of civil society, at present, cast a different appearance and sensibility on the City of Mosques, Istanbul.

References

Ahmad, Feroz. 1977. *The Turkish Experiment in Democracy 1950–1975*. London: C. Hurst.
_____. 1981. "Military Intervention and the Crisis in Turkey." *Middle East Report* 93: 5–24.
Arrighi, Giovanni. 1994. *The Long Twentieth Century: Money, Power, and the Origins of Our Times*. New York: Verso.

Aydın, Cemil. 2006. "Between Occidentalism and the Global Left: Islamist Critiques of the West in Turkey." *Comparative Studies of South Asia, Africa and the Middle East* 26, no. 3: 446–61.

Bourdieu, Pierre. 1990. *The Logic of Practice*. Palo Alto, CA: Stanford University Press.

_____. 1996. "The Family as a Realized Category." *Theory, Culture and Society* 13, no. 3: 19–26.

_____. 1997. "The Forms of Capital." In *Education: Culture, Economy, and Society*, ed. A. H. Halsey, Hugh Lauder, Phillip Brown, and Amy Stuart Wells, 46–58. New York: Oxford University Press.

Fine, Ben. 2001. *Social Capital versus Social Theory*. London: Routledge.

_____. 2002. "It Ain't Social, It Ain't Capital and It Ain't Africa." *Studia Africana*, no. 13: 18–33.

Finkel, Andrew. 2012. "What's 4 + 4 + 4?" *New York Times*, 23 March.

Granovetter, Mark. 1985. "Economic Action and Social Structure: The Problem of Embeddedness." *American Journal of Sociology* 91, no. 3: 481–510.

Gürbey, Sinem. 2009. "Islam, Nation-State, and the Military: A Discussion of Secularism in Turkey." *Comparative Studies of South Asia, Africa and the Middle East* 29, no. 3: 371–80.

Harvey, David. 2005. *A Brief History of Neoliberalism*. Oxford and New York: Oxford.

İnalcık, Halil. 1969. "Capital Formation in the Ottoman Empire." *The Journal of Economic History* 29, no. 1: 97–140.

Mardin, Şerif. 1971. "Ideology and Religion in the Turkish Revolution." *International Journal of Middle East Studies* 2: 197–211.

_____. 1993. "The Nakshibendi Order of Turkey." In *Fundamentalism and the State: Remaking Polities, Economies and Militancy*, ed. Martin E. Marty and R. Scott. Appleby, 204–32. Chicago: University of Chicago Press.

Öncü, Ahmet. 2003. "Dictatorship Plus Hegemony: A Gramscian Analysis of the Turkish State." *Science & Society* 67, no. 3: 303–28.

Rutz, Henry, and Erol Balkan. 2009. *Reproducing Class*. New York: Berghahn Books.

Savran, Sungur. 1992. *Türkiye'de Sınıf Mücadeleleri: 1919–1980* [Class Struggles in Turkey: 1919–1980]. Istanbul: Kardelen.

Schick, C. Irvin, and Ahmet E. Tonak. 1987. "Turkish Politics and Class Struggle: 1950–1975." *Middle East Report* 84: 14–18.

Spivak, Gayatri Chakravorty. 1987. "Speculation on Reading Marx: After Reading Derrida." In *Post-structuralism and the Question of History*, ed. Derek Aldridge, Geoff Bennington, and Robert Young, 30–62. Cambridge: Cambridge University Press.

Wacquant, Loic J. D. 1991. "Making Class: The Middle Class(es) in Social Theory and Social Structure." In *Bringing Classes Back In*, ed. Scott G. McNall, Rhonda F. Levine, and Rick Fantasia, 39–64. Boulder, CO: Westview Press.

– Chapter 7 –

THE QUESTION OF AKP HEGEMONY
Consent without Consensus
Evren Hoşgör

Introduction

The political balance of forces in Turkey since the 2002 elections did
not allow another political party to counterbalance the hegemonic
project initiated under the leadership of the Adalet ve Kalkınma
Partisi (Justice and Development Party, AKP). The hegemonic crisis
of the 1990s indeed not only broke the representational ties between
center-right parties and dominant classes, but also detached masses
from their traditional parties and ideologies.[1] Despite broad media
support, the social-liberal synthesis of Cumhuriyet Halk Partisi
(Republican People's Party, CHP) could not established itself as a
national-popular program under the hegemonic leadership of large
capital groups. Conversely, the AKP's hegemonic appeal pursued
multiple strategies that rested on concessions among different social
forces: it articulated the economic demands of petty bourgeoisie to
the interests of the rising medium-sized capital, and also integrated
the political-democratic demands of certain non-class forces (Kurds,
the liberal intelligentsia) into the political-religious demands of
its conservative constituency. The AKP also distanced itself from
previous Islamic parties by adopting a moderate posture in terms of
its programmatic commitments via de-Islamizing its discourse, and
was therefore widely welcomed as a center-right party that would
facilitate the transformation sought since the 1980s through a hybrid
liberal-conservative political project, or a self-described "conservative
democracy" (Akdoğan 2004). In addition, the AKP mobilized the

aspirations of certain sections of the popular masses (particularly those from urban shantytowns) through a mix of material concessions and symbolic rewards. The European Union (EU) membership and the democratization project also provided a congenial background for the AKP to constitute a hegemonic project well suited to Turkey's structural transformation.

In its initial years in power, the AKP government committed itself to the International Monetary Fund (IMF)–initiated postcrisis recovery program, and pursued policies to reduce public spending and control public debt. It also increased the pace of privatizations; opened the economy further to foreign capital; restructured the agricultural sector; drafted the State Personnel Regime Reform and the Local Government Reform; radically transformed the social security system with the enactment of the Social Security and General Health Insurance Law and the Social Security Institution Law; passed a new labor code; enacted legislations that were geared toward the EU membership; took positive steps to solve the "Cyprus problem"; and strengthened relations with the United States. Consequently, the AKP government(s) secured further IMF loans, sustained investor confidence, obtained a date from the EU for accession talks, and won the trust of big business, liberal intellectuals, and the mainstream media, who had kept their distance in the beginning. Most analysts indeed noted that initial misgivings about the AKP on the question of the IMF, the EU, and secularism were "exaggerated and lacked a serious basis" (Heper 2005; Öniş 2006b). So, despite persistent rivalries and conflicts, the prospects of political stability and economic growth resulted in a temporary truce within the Turkish capitalist class, while the discursive emphasis on social justice, income equality, and democratization helped this new power bloc to disorganize subordinate classes, obstructing the formation of a united front against neoliberal reforms. The twin promises of "justice and development" then distinguished the AKP from other center-right parties and helped it to win support from the business community, international circles, the liberal intelligentsia, and the broader public. A general wave of optimism permeated the society: Turkey was recovering from the deep economic crisis of 2000–1, transcending highly unstable patterns of development, achieving a democratic political structure, and moving toward political and economic stability.

The initial optimism over political stability later started to deteriorate as fierce debates occurred between the party and the upper echelons of the (civil and military) bureaucracy on several issues regarding the *form of the regime*, whereas the social impact of a slowdown began to reinforce concerns over the government's promise on economic stability and development. Turkey indeed faced the global turbulence with declining growth rates, increasing inflation and unemployment levels, deteriorating financial discipline, and a growing current account deficit. Furthermore, while the AKP's preferential treatment of certain bourgeois sections (Islamic capital) significantly altered the distribution of total surplus value, its controversial bias toward its religious constituency, setbacks in the democratization and Europeanization agenda, together with its attempts to change the state's institutional materiality to switch the relays and circuits of power to suit its own constituency's interests, led to a whole series of hegemonic dislocations within the power bloc.

This chapter critically assesses the key features of the AKP's "hegemonic" appeal over the last ten years. It, however, does not focus on the typical problems and themes in the bulk of the literature, which are mostly concerned with cultural habitus, ideological engagement, and/or personal attributes of actors (groups or camps) in question (Özel 2003; Tepe 2006; Yıldırım et al. 2007).[2] Instead, it offers a class-theoretical account of the power bloc and explains multiple (and contradictory) power relationships behind this hegemonic conquest.[3] Despite the general convention that *primarily* relates the AKP's hegemonic success (and possible retrenchment) to its ability to enact democratic reforms (Keyder 2004; Çınar 2006; Öniş 2006a), this account does not define the two moments (i.e., political reforms and economic development) as separate realms.[4] It argues that hegemonic projects are concerned with broader issues, which are grounded not only in economic relations but also in the field of civil society and the state. They may include military successes, social reforms, political stabilization, or moral regeneration. Relying on either explanation exhaustively would not only be unproductive for a complex societal analysis, but also either over-politicizes discussions so that they miss the interpenetration of different moments, or understands them in a simple economistic fashion that does not recognize the complexity of extra-economic mechanisms complementary to accumulation. Nor would this approach engage in a didactic discussion about which instance is the determining one in the hegemonic rise of the party. For the issue is one of relative importance and of a sequence of influences. The aim here is instead to uncover the relations/contradictions among different elements of the AKP's hegemonic project and to examine how they constitute a contradictory whole, which allows them to reach a temporary balance and interconnect coherently in a specific historical context. In short, they are studied in relational terms—each moment contingently connected with other relations.

Furthermore, the chapter argues that although the AKP's hegemonic project allows for cooperation among different social forces within a coalition against a "common enemy," it at the same time leads to a series of contradictory and unequal power relationships among the subjects of this alliance. This illuminates why certain regulatory reforms and other changes could be implemented without a major conflict, whereas some others created serious confrontations between the government and business circles, upper echelons of the bureaucracy, intellectuals, and other social forces in play. The first two parts of the text are thus devoted to different moments of the hegemony, and discuss how a relatively unified coalition behind the AKP rule has emerged as a result of constant negotiations and concessions among various contradictory interests. The third part focuses on the role of cultural hegemony and explores in what forms and by what means the AKP succeeded in establishing the mechanism of its intellectual, moral, and cultural hegemony and won the hearts and minds of people. The last part problematizes the existing difficulties in dealing with multiple power relationships, and elaborates on the *restricted* (rather than *expansive*) nature of the AKP's hegemonic appeal. It also discusses the intensification of such conflicts during the last years and resulting problems in terms of the institutional unity of the state, and explores how contradictions among different social forces create tensions between the government and certain state apparatuses (namely, the military and the judiciary) by focusing on particular strategies of the AKP rule to control strategic state capacities. The final remark is thus devoted to the transformations within the institutional architecture of the state and the wider political system in tandem with the pursuit of particular strategies and tactics in wars of position and/or maneuver.

The Making of a Hegemonic Project I: Economic Stability and Growth

The troubled state of the economy and frictions among political actors after the twin economic crises of 2000–1[5] had created a broad consensus that Turkey needed a strong and stable government—preferably a single-party majority government—at any cost.[6] Previous coalition governments were held responsible for instability, delays in deep-seated reforms, and parliamentary deadlocks, and were accused of being populist and prone to corruption (Öniş 2003; Turan 2003). In short, they were regarded as an example of bad governance. Combined with the need for external financing and foreign investments, the extent of the 2000–1 economic crises not only strengthened the hand of the IMF but also turned the EU into a more important anchor in securing capital flows. Along with the "strong government" discourse, the "stability rhetoric" thus also played a prominent role in the AKP's hegemonic appeal. It helped the government to speed up the pace of regulatory reforms and implement fiscal discipline without major opposition, and was also effective in reorganizing ideological hegemony. These discourses promoted among the public the idea that in order to achieve macroeconomic stability, structural reforms are both necessary and inevitable.[7] They together therefore portrayed the new balance as desirable, while condemning the previous one as chaotic.

The AKP, on the contrary, met the tight fiscal requirements of the IMF-sponsored stabilization program, implemented the EU-backed structural reforms, and did not indulge in "populist expansionism."[8] Inflation was lowered to single digits for the first time in three decades. Falling interest rates combined with overvalued real exchange rates created a favorable environment for economic growth. The government's ability to sustain end-of-year targets and changes in the incentive structure restored investor confidence.[9] In conjunction with rising foreign capital inflows, privatization also accelerated after 2005: long-awaited bids for state-owned enterprises such as TÜPRAŞ oil refinery and the steel and iron producer Erdemir were finalized in 2006. Thus, Turkey recorded a 7.5 percent average annual gross national product (GNP) growth during 2002–5. Some authors even argued that high growth rates could signal the end of the crisis and the beginning of a long-term sustained development, which, in the long run, could contain distributional conflicts among different sectors of the society.[10] As a result, the media, international circles, and business groups wholeheartedly celebrated the AKP government's initial performance.

The party's hegemonic conquest thus rested on its ability to reconcile the conflicting demands of diverse economic sectors: Türkiye Sanayici ve İşadamları Derneği (Turkish Industrialists' and Businessmen's Association, TÜSİAD) often repeated its satisfaction with the government's macroeconomic performance and its economically oriented vision of politics. In its periodic assessments, TÜSİAD praised the AKP's commitment to the IMF program, and credited it for its concerted efforts to deal with the problem of corruption and its bold moves to keep up with structural reforms. The banking sector regulation, for example, was received enthusiastically because it would make the financial system more resilient to possible domestic and/or external shocks. TÜSİAD particularly noted that the government should accelerate the pace of privatization and the tax and social security reforms. They were also particularly concerned with the persistence of a large current account deficit and high social security premiums. Likewise, Müstakil Sanayici ve İşadamları Derneği (Independent Industrialists' and Businessmen's Association, MÜSİAD) welcomed fiscal stability, lower levels of inflation, and overall growth. The antimonopoly references of the party program were also instrumental in securing the support of small businesses. Yet, MÜSİAD opted for a program and a development path that were less IMF-oriented. It was particularly critical of the banking/financial sector regulations and the growing power of independent regulatory agencies. It also shared TÜSİAD's concern about the large current account deficit, but unlike TÜSİAD, it explicitly preferred a more flexible implementation of the budgetary discipline, and favored controls over short-term capital inflows. This association was also highly skeptical about the import dependence of export production and regional inequality.

AKP rule was therefore considered a clean break with the previous perverse political environment and lopsided economic development. To several observers, the government appeared to have both the capacity and the willingness to finalize the long-awaited transformation of Turkish capitalism and address the chronic problems of unemployment and poverty to bring social justice to the ill-fated country (Keyder 2004; Heper 2005; Öniş 2006b). With the advantages gained by its position as a single-party government, it passed a record number of laws in the parliament, including the most controversial ones, such as the public sector and local government reforms, a new labor code, and the social security and health care reforms. Put in terms of the AKP's (neoliberal) jargon, while the public sector law claimed to increase transparency and accountability to strengthen administrative capacity and productivity, improve service quality, and maintain sustainability, the local government law was promoted under the pretext of decentralization, democratization, and deconcentration (widening of authority)—in other words, with good governance rhetoric. The content of these reforms not only satisfied individual economic-corporate interests of Turkish business groups, but also fit the logic of structural adjustment: a market open to foreign direct investment (FDI) attracting ever-increasing inward capital flows at the expense of rising competition in the domestic economy and growing poverty.[11] The IMF and other international financial circles indeed celebrated the AKP's commitment to an open but well-regulated economy.

To sum up the argument so far, the postcrisis setting not only accelerated the AKP's hegemonic conquest, but also the momentum of the neoliberal restructuring process. Confronted by popular resistance against such reforms during the 1990s, large Turkish capital groups then adopted a selective strategy that included strategic compromises with the newly growing medium-sized capitals. These compromises nonetheless went beyond being purely mechanical and tactical alliances on a limited number of issues and/or settling of accounts among economic-corporate interests. On the contrary, they sought to establish a long-term organic relation (a new power bloc) that would extend across the economic, political, and ideological fields. Since a power bloc is more than a mechanical assemblage of pragmatic alliances, broad ranges of issues were addressed, including strategies for labor relations, competition, socioeconomic policies, economic prosperity, ideological matters, social inclusiveness, democratic consolidation, civic rights, and international relations.

The Making of a Hegemonic Project II: Europeanization and "Normalization" of Turkish Democracy

Following the progress achieved in the sphere of EU relations, negative perceptions concerning the AKP had also changed to a great extent: the government not only displayed a clear determination to start accession negotiations, but also initiated reforms regarding the protection of individual rights/freedoms, the extension of cultural rights for minorities, and the improvement of the judicial system. Besides, important strides were made to alter the military-civilian balance in the political system. Therefore, most analyses tended to underline the driving role of the EU in internal political transformation, particularly with reference to the ongoing democratization agenda. From their perspective, the EU stood for a powerful "external anchor" endowed with a capacity to generate "system-transforming impacts" (Özel 2003; Keyman and Öniş 2003; Keyder 2004; Öniş 2006b).

The project of Europeanization indeed played a dominant role for the AKP in its attempt at hegemony. Instead of questioning the genuineness of the AKP's EU appeal, it would be better to analyze how this political formulation gave cohesion and cogency to the rule of particular classes/fractions through translating their idealized perspectives into a strategic orientation for the society as a whole. The "EU anchor" paradigm, however, undermines the role of institutional forms in shaping political class struggle, for it hardly acknowledges the impact of this struggle on the transformation of the state apparatus.[12] It is also rarely mentioned that the EU project not only constituted a specific "policy paradigm" that outlined the conditions of negotiation among competing interests/demands, but also assured the implementation of structural reforms negotiated with the IMF and the World Bank, and thereby guaranteed the enactment of the new labor code, the liquidation of the state-run health and social security mechanisms, the completion of the privatization process, the opening of the economy to foreign capital, the restructuring of the agricultural and financial/fiscal sectors, and the imposition of strict restrictions on public sector expenditures and public administration via the State Personnel Regime Reform and the Local Government Reform. By shaping and providing a deep-rooted agreement within the society in the name of democracy, the AKP's discursive emphasis on the "wishes of the masses" helped the ruling class to undermine the whole process of class conflict.

This nevertheless does not mean that there were no bottom-up wishes and needs for democratization (and Europeanization) projects. Nor does the above argument disregard the role of these demands in the AKP's counter hegemonic struggle with the so-called status quo (the republican establishment) and the official ideology of the state (Kemalism). Concrete hegemonic projects are more than just purely discursive matters and cannot be abstracted from the political-economic and historical context of a given social formation. Not only do they have an objective basis in material conditions, but they also emerge out of and reflect the needs and demands of different social forces, classes, and segments within a society; thus, they emerge from the clash of multiple strategies. Yet, hegemony is not only a clash of multiple strategies, but also trial-and-error experimentation. It is for this reason that the AKP's pro-reform rhetoric cannot be reduced to pure lip service or a pragmatic choice intended to meet the EU conditionalities. The appeal arose within a specific conjuncture and was rooted in the struggles of the pre-AKP period. So understanding the linkages between the past and the present is essential for "situating" the "democratization project" in time.

The role of domestic actors in shaping the political processes should therefore not be undervalued: various business associations and nongovernmental organizations (NGOs) have been pushing for an agenda of "democratization" at various intervals since the mid-1990s. The most well-known report was published by TÜSİAD in 1997 (*Perspectives on Democratization in Turkey*), which detailed the democratic deficiencies of the country and offered strategies for overcoming them. Türkiye Odalar ve Borsalar Birliği (Union of Chambers and Commodity Exchanges of Turkey, TOBB) also issued reports such as "The Eastern Question" and "The 2000 Constitution" in 1995 and 2000, respectively (Ergil 1995; TOBB 2000). Not only did such reports highlight the need to undertake wide-ranging reforms on human rights and individual and civil freedoms, but they also proposed certain amendments to the 1982 constitution, including a wide variety of topics ranging from the law on political parties and parliamentary immunity to other sensitive issues related to the freedom of expression and the extension of language and cultural rights to ethnic minorities. TÜSİAD's *Perspectives on Democratization in Turkey*, for example, proposed amendments to clarify the provisions that provided "justifications" to dissolve political parties—a vital issue for the AKP's agenda—and extend the boundaries of political representation by lowering the national threshold (from 10 percent to 5 percent), which is of great importance to the Kurdish population.

The topography of the political scene in the 1990s, however, did not allow for the establishment of a political leadership that could mobilize various segments of the society under a national-popular program to fulfill this agenda. Although most controversial issues (e.g., the Kurdish problem and the "autonomy" of the military) were handled within the context of human rights and/or linked to the EU accession procedures, not only did they face strong opposition from the state establishment, they also received criticism from conservative businessmen. Besides, growing nationalism vis-à-vis the Kurdish issue in the late 1990s was instrumental in weakening public support for both EU membership and the TÜSİAD-led democratization agenda. The opposition indeed "forced" the association to adopt a rather subdued and defensive attitude.[13]

The historical context in which the 2002 election had taken place, however, had important consequences in terms of changing the balance of power drastically. The political agenda was constructed in such a novel way that political stability, democratization, EU accession, and economic development all became the components of a grand project. With the help of the mainstream media, the material benefits of EU membership were promoted to break down resistance in domestic circles at a time when nationalistic sentiments were at their peak vis-à-vis the Kurdish issue.[14] Democratization itself became a highly important criterion in assessing governments' performances, including the AKP.[15] The party not only capitalized on this trend, but also presented itself as the primary agent of the transformative process.

The EU project thus allowed the AKP to integrate strategically significant forces as subjects with specific interests: financial crises, unemployment, and bankruptcies made the potential material benefits of EU membership more attractive. The role of intellectuals and other interest groups and their ability to shape new regulatory forms were also important in formulating pro-EU interests behind a concrete strategy. The advantages of membership were promoted through an expanded range of institutions and organizations, including the mass media, think tanks, research institutes, trade unions, political parties, and nongovernmental organizations (NGOs). It was argued that since the labor code in EU countries was more favorable to labor than current regulations at home, the EU adjustments/adaptations would bring better working conditions. It was also said that the integration of the domestic and European markets would provide job opportunities to the unemployed and wider markets to nonmonopolistic capital, and would help Turkey increase per-capita income levels, close its savings gap, enhance foreign direct investment, and benefit from regional development funds. Furthermore, the EU-led reforms provided favorable ground for the AKP to reorganize the dominant state project and the mode of political legitimation embodied in Kemalist principles. The EU pressure on democratic rights allowed the party to formulate religious freedoms within the context of pluralism and the language of rights. This not only ensured the government safeguarded the wishes and demands of its core religious constituency, but was also instrumental in helping the AKP acquire political legitimacy in the eyes of liberal democratic intelligentsia, who criticized various spheres of social life that were under the tight control of the state. According to them, although the authoritarian tendencies of the Turkish polity did not encourage full development of liberal democracy, both the 2002 election results and the prospects of EU accession had offered an excellent platform for transformation (İnsel 2003; Özel 2003; Yılmaz 2004; Çınar 2005). The EU project (with its invocation of democracy and human rights) therefore created a safe haven for certain oppositional forces that had neither the resources nor the capacity to defeat the "authoritarian state." The implementation of the Copenhagen Criteria (plus the harmonization packages) during the AKP tenure(s) was therefore welcomed as a positive development for the consolidation of democracy (Yavuz 2006), and even depicted as the end of the strong state tradition in Turkey (Keyman and Öniş 2003). In short, it was argued that the end of *dual power* would be achieved via *normalization*, and the AKP era offered such an unexpected possibility to exit from the authoritarian regime.[16] Reinforced also by the 28 February process, left-liberal intellectual circles, concerned with human rights issues (e.g., the ban on headscarves in public institutions and universities), increased their voices against the authoritarian state along with pious Muslims.[17] The appreciation of structural reforms as necessary for progressive democratization, however, limited the left to the fundamental task of deepening and expanding liberal democratic ideology. At the same time, it contributed to an intellectual paralysis vis-à-vis Erdoğan's "reformist" rhetoric, because he was particularly skillful in formulating his party as the protagonist of a broad sociopolitical transformation. In sum, this strategic alliance assisted the AKP in formulating EU membership as a national-popular project, the realization of which would advance the interests of all sectors of society and thus in return prevent any adversaries from developing an alternative to AKP hegemony.

Right-Wing Gramscism and Cultural Hegemony

The AKP not only reconciled the above-mentioned conflicting demands and interests, but also gained control through cultural and ideological leadership, colonizing the society with its rhetoric and ideas. Its electoral strength came from its ability to attract and mobilize supporters at the grassroots level, which eventually not only resulted in cultural dominance but also became the foundations of its political power. This section focuses on the role of cultural hegemony and captures various concrete historical instances in which depoliticization/repoliticization through incorporation of dissent took place.

By dedicating itself exclusively to the struggle to win cultural hegemony, the Islamic movement in Turkey aimed at winning the hearts and minds of the masses through moral prestige, cultural leadership, and ideological persuasiveness since the late 1970s. It acknowledged that if Islamic forces wanted to capture political power, they had to emerge first and foremost as a cultural force, that is, cultural hegemony must precede political and economic contest.[18] This strategy can be likened to right-wing Gramscism: "the Right applying left-wing lessons drawn from the Right drawing lessons from the Left"; yet, a version grounded on and supported by Islamic themes and connotations.[19] In this "game of mirrors," the Gramscian concept of hegemony was co-opted and harmonized with the Islamic notion of *tebliğ* (propaganda) as an effective and productive strategy for gaining influence and political power over society.[20] The Islamic "war of position" then focused on consciousness as a key ingredient, and concentrated on establishing its own organizations as the foundations of a new culture: the norms and values of a new society based on Islamic/conservative principles.[21]

Since a war of position demands enormous sacrifices by large masses of people, this was supplied by party members and various sect followers (Zubaida 1996; Yavuz 1997). Religious networks not only played an important role in constituting a capital and consumer base for Islamic capital, but also provided bloc votes for Islamic parties. The Islamic party of the 1990s, Refah Partisi (Welfare Party, RP), partly relying on such informal sect networks, was distinguished by its ability to fill the vacuum created by the decline in social spending (specifically health and education) via community work—charities, schools, clinics, and cooperatives. Since local organizations were relatively autonomous in utilizing local resources, the RP-dominated municipalities played a crucial role in channeling efforts into housing and basic necessities for low-income families by devising their own strategies. These involved the sale of bread, meat, fruit, and vegetables at bargain prices, the distribution of free food during Ramadan and fuel in winter, and the provision of support during family celebrations and crises, such as weddings, funerals, circumcision for the children of the needy, and hospital beds for the sick. Since its members regularly attended these activities and engaged in discussions with local people at coffee houses or other gathering places, these activities distinguished the RP from its political competitors, which lacked the advantages of informal networking. While the Turkish left was increasingly incapable of catering to the needs of the poor, the disadvantaged, and/or the excluded, Islamic parties were quite successful in winning the consent of the urban poor who were marginalized, living below the poverty line, and/or struggling to survive on a daily basis, working mainly in the informal sector with high job insecurity, and who had become a significant but unpredictable electorate throughout the 1990s. Besides, sect networks were helpful in creating employment opportunities in municipal governments, state bureaucracies, companies, schools, dormitories, hospitals, and/or law firms established by Islamic capital and other networks.[22] Therefore, their grassroots approach did not merely target the marginalized and excluded shantytowns, but also included professional middle classes, creating a body of devoted cadres from all walks of life.

The AKP capitalized on the inherent strengths of this Islamic networking. While the strong local government record of (ex-RP) deputies acted as a warranty for the validity of its material promises for shantytowns, its grassroots approach helped to build devoted cadres among more affluent sections of the conservative constituency. It also, at least rhetorically, prioritized people's material problems and emphasized social, cultural, and distributive justice more than its competitors. The poverty alleviation programs combined with other charity works delivered by its grassroots organizations and/or local governments helped to win support from the poor and cushion the impact of fiscal discipline imposed after the 2000–1 financial crises. Other policies targeted the urban poor as well. Like its predecessors, the AKP maintained soup kitchens, health centers, counseling offices, job training centers, and women's centers; increased grants for students and housing credits for the lower middle classes and the poor; distributed free schoolbooks; and built thousands of cheap new apartments for shantytown dwellers. Therefore, the party filled the vacuum not only by offering a strategy for economic expansion, but also by appearing under a "social democratic" guise.

Of all the institutions of daily life, Islamic media have also evolved into a highly skilled system of networks specialized in orchestrating everyday consciousness of the masses by virtue of its pervasiveness, accessibility, and symbolic capacity. The Islamification of the media allowed Islamic political figures to use strongly religious language and culturally conservative connotations to subvert the official ideology and create new spaces for maneuvering. Politicians' individual lifestyles (such as their aversion toward alcohol consumption) got great media coverage. The cultural conquest during AKP rule therefore contributed to the adoption of conservative norms and behavioral expectations by showing symbolic rewards and punishments for particular attitudes and behaviors: the AKP-run municipalities banned alcohol from local government cafés and restaurants in their districts, citing the need to protect family values. The governor of Istanbul changed the working hours of public servants to fit fasting hours during the Ramadan period. Moreover, Islamification of the education system has reached unprecedented levels since the party's ascent to power. The enrollment in İmam Hatip schools[23] and Koran courses has been on the rise, curricula in other schools have been redesigned, and textbooks have been embellished with religious/conservative connotations.

Other controversial attempts explicitly designed to test the limits of secularity have also been instrumental in maintaining the AKP's moral and cultural leadership in the eyes of its core religious constituency.[24] Because the party has been under constant strain of meeting promises to its conservative supporters, such proposals were not just arbitrary "populist" decisions. Through these attempts, the AKP proved to its radical supporters that it was not simply paying lip service to their demands. At the same time, these attempts helped the party limit and redefine the demands and expectations of its supporters. Not only did they bring greater legitimacy to religious considerations, but their symbolism gained particular importance in securing the long-term support of these groups (without real gains) in two of the most controversial issues: the headscarf issue among female university students and public servants, and the barriers imposed on İmam Hatip graduates in entering university faculties other than theology. The AKP's delayed (and relative) success in reaching compromises within the framework of the existing constitution created pressure, not only within the party but also among the newly emerging conservative middle class that it seeks to represent.[25] For unlike the pro-secular urban middle class, the fortunes of this newly emerging middle class are strongly tied to the performance of the AKP's selective policies.

In sum, all efforts to gain a dominant voice in the mass media, trade unions, associations, cultural foundations, civil society organizations, and educational institutions in order to heighten consciousness can be seen as small victories in the trenches where Islamic forces were moving back and forth across the institutions of civil society. The AKP thus aimed to surround the state apparatus with counterhegemony, created by its own mass organizations and by developing Islamic institutions and culture.

From Cultural and Moral Leadership to Political Domination

Hegemonic projects play a crucial role in maintaining cohesion among various contradictory interests in the economic sphere and civil society, and also in limiting the conflicts within and among the forces grounded in various branches of the state apparatus.[26] The AKP project, however, was not built upon or through the creation of a national-popular will. Nor did it provide a cohesive and unitary ideological and material base for the state ensemble. The reconfiguration of state power is thus achieved not through the incorporation of dissenting voices, but by their exclusion. Put differently, rather than encompassing the whole of society and the state with an *expansive hegemony*, the AKP's hegemonic project had a *restricted* character from its very initiation.[27] To a great degree this is associated with the mobilization of strategically significant conservative sectors behind its program of action, and reorganization of political support on the basis of an antagonistic division of the nation. But to no less extent it is because the AKP has increasingly excluded the "dominant but nonhegemonic groups" and the masses from the field of policy making via depoliticizing the state. However, maintaining a hegemonic appeal ultimately depends on the ability to reproduce active consent through real (albeit limited) material concessions and exercise intellectual, moral, and political leadership, while maintaining a unified power bloc.[28]

First and foremost, AKP hegemony is restricted not only in its mass basis, but also within the power bloc itself because its hegemonic appeal presupposed continued economic development. However, there were serious problems regarding the initial growth process itself, and fissures in the power bloc have become more visible after the global financial crisis.[29] The government was under fire from large business circles and investors for underestimating the global crisis and failing to disclose a comprehensive economic package to steer the country away from recession.[30] As the economic slowdown continued, not only the objective of sustained growth and distributive justice became harder to achieve, but it became also more difficult for the party to specify an economic paradigm within which conflicts over competing interests can be negotiated and accumulation can be secured. These may not necessarily create a nonhegemonic situation, but the party is less and less able to exercise hegemony over various partners of the power bloc because it lacks the material means to do so, particularly in the face of various dilemmas, risks, uncertainties, and complexities.[31] The absence of material rewards in the economic sphere, however, may not only impose certain constraints on its capacity to renew its hegemonic appeal, but also result in a systematized authoritarianism at the politico-ideological realm—both in the domestic arena and external relations. In fact, Erdoğan's authoritarian shift went beyond the rhetorical level and was accompanied by a change in the economic and diplomatic relations with Israel and Syria. With the momentum gained from these diplomatic conflicts, the AKP not only consciously exploits the extremely chauvinistic/conservative ideological climate to maintain its moral and intellectual leadership among its supporters, but also aims at a political score by a diplomatic gain despite all the defeats in the much-promised areas of economic development and social justice.

Although the AKP has compromised on secondary issues to sustain mass support,[32] it has not granted the entire population the benefits of economic recovery (Onaran 2007a). Therefore, there are other reasons to argue that the AKP's hegemonic project was *restricted* in character. This lies in the ultimately pacifying, atomizing, and disorienting effects of AKP policies on subaltern forces. Unemployment, especially among young, urban, and educated populations has increased; reduction in agricultural subsidies seriously deteriorated small producers' incomes, which led to a flow of workers from agriculture to services, manufacturing, and construction, and pushed a greater part of the working population into the informal sector.[33] As the global financial crisis expands, exploitation takes complex and disguised forms, including its specific forms of promoting subcontracting/outsourcing activities and the informal economy. In addition to reductions in real wages, working conditions have deteriorated significantly under the threat of job deficiency. Longer working hours without pay, delays in the payment of wages, offers to give holidays earlier than usual, forced retirement, and resignation followed by delays in severance pay became a common practice among employers. The lack of sufficient taxation of financial and corporate gains combined with generous tax exemptions add to these inequalities.[34] Rather than improving the welfare of the people, the AKP's economic policies depressed employment, curbed the purchasing power of the masses, and deepened poverty.[35]

Its economic program was not only weak in reproducing the active consent of the masses through real material concessions, but also aimed to pass the costs of neoliberal transformation onto the unprivileged sections of the society: both the labor code, passed in May 2003, and the 2011 "law package"[36] introduced further flexibilities into the labor market. Combined with increasing unemployment, such laws enabled capital to discipline labor and contract wages.[37] Taken as a whole with structural reforms and disinflationary policies, public debt became a key instrument in both appropriating a significant part of public revenues and also keeping unemployment and labor costs at a certain level. The growing public sector borrowing requirements, and hence the accompanying interest burden on the budget, led to qualitative and quantitative erosion in social spending, cuts in public sector investments and current expenditures (mostly in the form of personnel costs), and commodification of these services through privatization. Thus, the state's associated functions in the fields of education, social security, and health care were diminished.[38] Although depicted as purely technical matters, the content of regulatory reforms concerns above all the popular masses, because they aim to roll back those forms of state intervention that are related to the Keynesian welfare state. For example, the 2004 reforms[39] allowed both central and local governments to develop stakeholder relations with private persons, companies, and NGOs. This thereby enhanced the production and provision of public goods and services through market actors and in market conditions. This indicates the abandonment of the notion of secure employment in the public sector by altering the employment status of public servants from permanent to short-term contractual service.

The replacement of state-led welfare provisions by formal and informal safety and social assistance networks is supported with a neoconservative political discourse that valorizes the anonymous market and the individualist consumer, and promotes (Islamic) *charity* as an alternative redistribution and poverty reduction mechanism. The regulatory reforms then aim to transform the social state into a neoliberal state that draws its legitimacy primarily from religion instead of a law-based institutionalized compromise. This shift from the logic of a "social state" toward one of "charity capitalism" perfectly combines two designs that animate structural transformation in Turkey: neoliberalism and religious conservatism. As a result, social reforms do not only symbolize a process of "decommodification," but also a process of Islamification in which the countermovement (of Islamification) constitutes a response to the expansion of the market—an indispensably important mechanism for the protection of society. However, without an active, direct consensus resulting from the articulation of the interests of the popular masses, no *expansive hegemony* is possible. For such a project would have involved taking systematic account of popular interests and demands, co-opting sections of the working masses, and granting certain concessions in return for consent.

Although their relations with the organized sections of the working masses have been seriously problematic from the very beginning, the AKP governments have proved their hostility against democratic struggles of the masses. Emek Platformu (the Labor Platform), which incorporates Turkey's largest labor unions and civil servant confederations and represents over a million unionized workers, staged effective legal protests against the government's attempt to raise the retirement age and minimize employers' share in national health insurance. The government sought to discredit protests as "ideologically oriented," arguing that the platform represents only a fringe group, and enacted the above-mentioned reforms without hesitation. Since 2008, the 1 May demonstrations became important platforms that expressed the collective discontent of the working masses with AKP policies. Known as the "Tekel protests,"[40] labor resistance against neoliberal transformation was perhaps the most defining feature of this phase. A similar hostile attitude was adopted during the struggles to reclaim the commons, and other environment-oriented protests were carried out against nuclear stations. Not only did the liberal media increase its coverage of strikes and civil disobedience tactics (boycotts and factory occupations) used by recently unemployed workers, student protests over tuition fees and commodification of education, other popular struggles, and excessive police violence against protestors, but critical left-wing voices also started to appear in broadcasts.[41] Although one should not assume that the liberal media/intelligentsia would promote a left-wing alternative to the neoliberal agenda, this focus on popular struggles and demands is a self-conscious political practice as these actors appeal for support from multiple audiences in the (re)organization of hegemony in the face of internal divisions within the power bloc.

In spite of all this, the party has not faced a serious challenge at the polls so far, let alone a convincing alternative. It even confirmed its national appeal during the referendum process in 2010.[42] Yet hegemony has to do with the cohesion of the social system: hegemonic conquests rest on the ability to secure active and passive consent (or contained dissent) of diverse economic and social sectors, and mobilize diverse support behind a concrete program of action. This means that even if it holds the political power firmly in its grasp (i.e., even though it dominates), the party must continue to "lead" in order to maintain its hegemonic appeal.[43] The complex hegemonic relationships between social forces and political agents, then, cannot be reduced to mere domination or victory at the polls. Conversely, hegemonic leadership grants economic concessions and symbolic rewards to the masses and privileges to particular economic-corporate interests compatible with this program, and this means sacrifice of the short-term interests of the hegemonic group. Hegemony is therefore a question of competition between two relatively strong parts (the one in power and the one approaching it). The leading fraction is the one that has the power and ability to articulate the interests of other fraction(s) to reach a temporal unity, and the one whose specific interests at a given juncture most closely correspond with the objective state of capitalist accumulation. Yet, hegemony is also a struggle for the support of intermediate groups, that is, the conquest of supporting classes and segments of society. Indeed, while large and medium-sized capital groups from Anatolia emerged as a distinct economic force, other social categories (the military and civil bureaucracy, Kurds, and the liberal intelligentsia) were dragged into the political arena with their *pertinent effects* on the course of the political class struggle. Yet, even so, this does not constitute an effective sharing of power within the alliance between the hegemonic groups and the dominant but nonhegemonic groups and other social forces that are articulated to the power bloc. Thus, contradictions within the power bloc express themselves in the relationship between various fractions of the dominant class and dominated classes.[44] Hegemony, therefore, does not refer to a static moment. On the contrary, it defines a continuous process of articulating heterogonous struggles and demands into a bloc, through which the "unstable equilibrium of compromises" is arranged (Gramsci 1971). In effect, alternative/competing strategies would remain, each pulling toward opposite directions.

In this context, hegemony strongly depends on the party's ability to exercise intellectual, moral, and political leadership over other significant social categories that have *pertinent effects* on the course of the struggle; however, the AKP has also started to face serious criticism from "left-liberal" circles and pro-EU intellectuals as its early-reformist zeal and democratic guise began to erode (Bayramoğlu 2008). Setbacks in the EU accession process were indeed seen as backtracking in the reform process. The EU already froze accession talks on eight policy areas in December 2006 due to issues related to Cyprus. EU progress reports since 2005 cite "limited progress" with respect to democratic reforms. Although the AKP demonstrated a renewed interest in the accession talks, the severe nationalistic backlash from early 2005 onward posed a handicap not only on the EU membership and democratization front but also on the Kurdish question. Despite symbolic concessions, such as the state-run Kurdish television channel, the AKP did not properly implement democratic reforms for a long time.[45] Moreover, for many Kurdish activists and pro-Kurdish politicians, such moves are seen as a political strategy to win Kurdish votes before elections—a hoax to undermine the Kurdish movement. During the referendum period, the voters in the southeast indeed responded to the boycott call made by the Kurdish political party—Barış ve Demokrasi Partisi (Peace and Democracy

Party, BDP). The government staged a grand return to the traditional repressive approach after the 2011 general elections, jeopardizing any nonmilitary, reformist approaches to solve the Kurdish problem.⁴⁶ Despite the "Solution Process"⁴⁷ initiated by the government in 2013, there remain questions regarding the government's nontransparent approach, its attempts to monopolize the process, and Prime Minister Erdoğan's increasingly tough stance in domestic politics vis-à-vis freedom of expression and the media. Furthermore, four common demands that emerged from the two separate conferences organized by various Kurdish organizations still remain unanswered.⁴⁸ It is also difficult to speak of a constructive parliamentary engagement by opposition parties on the Kurdish question. These all cast doubts on what kind of peace will be made in the future. Last but not least, while pursuing the rhetoric on minority rights, the AKP also sided with the anti-minority campaign in the Armenian genocide debate and accomplished only few improvements concerning the rights of Christian minorities (Öniş 2007). Among unresolved issues is the AKP's relation with the Alevis.⁴⁹ The Diyanet İşleri Başkanlığı (Directorate of Religious Affairs) is still a Sunni-dominated institution, and the status of *cemevi* (Alevi places of worship) is not yet clarified.⁵⁰

As argued in the beginning of this section, the AKP also aims to restructure the state by changing its modes of representation, internal articulation, and modes of intervention in order to fit the interests of the changing balance of forces. The *real power* to fix norms and enact rules has been increasingly delegated to the executive branch and the prime minister's circulars from their respective ministries. This also corresponds to the decline of laws enacted by the parliament, because important decisions have been made through cabinet decrees (*kanun hükmünde kararname*). While political parties turned into "mere parliamentary coteries," the parliament ceased to be a place where *real power* is exercised. Respective powers of certain strategic state apparatuses are weakened during this process, as structural limits (selectivity of state structures) impose constraints on the party's capacity to pursue a successful strategy. As a result, growing contradictions within the power bloc have accentuated the state's internal contradictions and appeared as internal quarrels and divisions among state personnel and/or as personal controversies between elected deputies and bureaucrats.⁵¹

It is worth noting that conflictual relations between the government and the bureaucracy are rather related to the structure of the state apparatus and its bureaucratic mode of organization. The concentration and centralization of power at certain bureaucratic layers were a response on the part of the state to increasing internal contradictions within the dominant class throughout the 1990s. Although it was not possible to eliminate internal contradictions and disarticulations within the state once and for all, the reorganization at least aimed to control and to restrain them via shifting the nodes and focuses of *real power* toward certain strategic points. Not only did such apparatuses provide an institutional unity to the state, but they also crystallized the demands and interests of the dominant groups, thus becoming resistance centers against the demands of non-dominant groups in the power bloc. Some of the apparatuses (the Constitutional Court and the National Security Council) indeed redefined the state's political and ideological role against nonhegemonic fractions and dominated classes by virtue of their ability to present their decisions as the real embodiment of national interests.

The restructuring does not denote a one-sided weakening of the powers of the bureaucracy, but rather involves dual aspects of strengthening and weakening. The new strategy, therefore, no more includes small victories in trenches, but extends to include a frontal attack against the state.[52] In effect, the AKP has started a comprehensive operation against the state bureaucracy to control the core of its effective power and switch the relays and circuits of power to advance the long-term political interests of its constituency. These include subordination of certain state apparatuses to others, establishment of its own parallel power networks within the state bureaucracy, penetration of key apparatuses through the deployment of its own special corps, and absorption or even the decapitation of the republican bureaucratic elites. Although municipalities and certain bureaucracies had been manned by like-minded people from conservative circles throughout the 1990s, the AKP not only perfected this process, but also focused precisely on areas that had been ignored and/or could not be penetrated earlier. Long-term activists from the Islamic movement were appointed to significant posts of several important ministries.[53] Several state corporations and other institutions were filled with pro-Islamic cronies.[54] Secularly oriented midlevel bureaucrats were either pushed out of their posts and transferred to rural areas or were forced to undertake meaningless tasks to encourage early retirement and vacate positions. Universities and judicial cadres (including the High Council of Judges and Prosecutors, Hâkimler ve Savcılar Yüksek Kurulu) were put through a similar process: legislation that lowered the mandatory retirement age of technocrats enabled the government to replace almost half of the judges. Yükseköğretim Kurulu (Council of Higher Education,

YÖK) was put under the firm control of the government and several university rectors were forced to retire.[55] All appointments in higher education institutions, apart from professors and associated professors, have to be approved by the State Personnel Department and the Ministry of Finance, which are controlled by party ranks (Tekin 2004). Such examples can be multiplied.

The important point here is less the cultural/social origin or employment history of this new power elite or whether they personally profit from such positions, but rather that they became the main interlocutors of the direct expression of the (economic and political) interests of the conservative constituency via their critical positions in these power centers/networks. The AKP's counterattack against certain state structures is therefore not arbitrary, although its effects may not have been necessarily calculated and known in advance by the actors themselves. These acts were strategic to the extent that they aimed to provide an adequate institutional base for exercising political power. Hence, they targeted those branches and layers within which the central pivot of *real power* lay. The appointment of new bureaucrats/technocrats makes these power centers impenetrable to all but certain interests, thus condensing the power of the dominant fraction within the power bloc. Such arrangements allow the AKP's "alternative bureaucracies" to continue their operations without facing serious intervention from other bureaucratic layers. They also help Erdoğan's newly structured bureaucracies to retain control over strategic issues (privatizations, public procurements, and so on) not only in the immediate term but also in the long run, even when Erdoğan/the AKP may not hold an absolute majority in the parliament. Indeed, a considerable share of public revenue is now fully controlled by this new managerial team.[56]

Nevertheless, the state's institutional structure enables the opposition forces to transpose the role of dominance from certain apparatuses to others that normally have "secondary" functions, and endows them with certain "powers" or "capacities." More concretely, in the face of growing AKP control over the legislative and the executive branches, the presidency, and other state bureaucracies, decisions of the judiciary gain a crucial role in managing internal contradictions within the state and disjunctions in the political system. Since these "capacities" are activated through the agency of specific sets of politicians and state officials, contradictions within the power bloc become the state's internal contradictions, turning into internal quarrels and divisions among state personnel. Most cases appear publicly as personal controversies between elected deputies and professionals of state bureaucracy. This expansion in the decision making and administrative capacities of certain state apparatuses not only undermines the state's organizational unity, but also puts the dominant ideology in crisis since it shows that it can no longer function as the internal cement for these apparatuses and their personnel. This is reflected in the growing politicization and polarization of the bureaucracy around the two distinctive ideologies of the AKP and the republican/secularist camps. The fragmentation of state power among different groups, however, creates serious problems for the unity of the state ensemble, because it is through this organizational matrix that the state reproduces the system of political domination and secures hegemony.

These may not necessarily put AKP rule in imminent danger, but when the aspect of domination (coercion) predominates over that of leadership (hegemony as organized consent), it creates other problems for social cohesion. The party was able to represent its core constituency insofar as it exercised a balancing and arbitrating function between the interests of these groups and those of others, and was able to succeed in securing the development of these groups that it represents with the consent and assistance of allied groups. Contrariwise, the party now relies mainly on a clientelist network, which distributes state-owned resources to close allies, and a vast repressive apparatus, which tightly surrounds the media and opposing masses. Thus, it becomes harder to achieve an ethico-political conception of common interest that transcends narrower interests situated in the defensive routines of its supporters. Moreover, the "delinkage" of the AKP's leading cadre from major parts of the population has to be approached as a structural problem. In fact, as disparities widen, the AKP trades consent for coercion, *disciplining* the "less favored nation" while selectively providing new privileges and concessions for the "more favored one." The increased resorting to violence, surveillance, the withering of the law experienced during the Ergenekon[57] and Balyoz[58] trials, and the Gezi Park protests[59] during the summer of 2013 clearly demonstrate that the AKP relies predominantly on coercion in the face of opposition, instead of promoting a platform that allows for the possibility of developing a common discourse among different but unequal partners of society. In order to maintain its political and social ascendancy, the government combines greatly heightened levels of coercion with a *new attention on persuasion*, which, however, lacks the intellectual and cultural forces necessary and adequate to the task of organizing a complete and successful hegemony. In an effort to overcome the recent crisis during the Gezi Park protests, both the party and its organic intellectuals resorted to all sorts of mystification: conducting patriotic campaigns based on appeals to conservative sentiments and blaming the failure of state authority on a bunch of "looters," "extremists," and "terrorists." External pressures by Western countries also reinforce the evolving crisis of legitimacy within the single-party regime. As the institutional crisis of the Turkish state deepens, the party increasingly seeks salvation in a divine leader, as embodied by the cult of personality around Erdoğan. In the process it tries to exterminate any opposition to his leadership while simultaneously seeking mass support. The redeployment of the state's repressive apparatuses against the "less favored nation" in fact raises concerns about the state's role as the guarantor of national unity. This selective strategy further eradicates the consensual ground and intensifies the antagonistic cleavages within the state and society. After nearly a decade of strenuous negotiation and debate, the AKP governments have not been able to achieve a general formal consent to prepare a new constitution. The fragmentation experienced due to the Ergenekon trials[60] and throughout the referendum process and the Gezi Park protests illustrates how polarization becomes a culturally divisive issue within society. There is no compelling reason to demarcate crude dichotomies between consent and force—as if one would stop where the other starts. Yet as the dialectical unity of the moments of consent and coercion blurs, *consent without consensus* becomes a structural aspect of hegemony. The party then starts to dominate and not to lead, and it is increasingly less obvious that the AKP rules through relations of hegemony.

Notes

1. This period was shaped by the following crisis tendencies: the sharpening of contradictions within the power bloc and the capitalist class due to the channeling of public resources exclusively to large corporations; the growing divide between urban and rural regions owing to the state's favorable attitude toward western metropolitan areas; the politicization of the traditional and the new petty bourgeoisie from Anatolia in Islamic and nationalist parties, and the loosening of ties and traditional alliances between them and center-right parties; the intensifying ideological crisis in relation to the repressive policies toward ethnic minorities, accompanied by the growth of the Kurdish movement and the establishment of paramilitary (counterguerrilla) forces and "special warfare units" alongside the main organs of the state to maintain internal security; the declining legitimacy of public authority and the rule of law and

increasing political corruption, mafia-like relations, and organized crime; and the increasing politicization of certain state apparatuses (the military and the judiciary) in response to the political and legitimation crisis. For a detailed analysis of the 1990s, see Tünay (1993).

2. While Tepe (2006) focuses on the ideological and cultural competition among different social camps with different lifestyles and worldviews, others refer to political personality and leadership style as an explanatory factor for the AKP's victory at the polls (Özel 2003; Yıldırım et al. 2007). Given the AKP's unsuccessful attempts to provide greater freedom for its religious base, Prime Minister Erdoğan's direct personal qualities—charismatic leadership—appear to be the main explanation for the AKP's hegemonic appeal. No doubt the oft-cited attributes of Erdoğan—his discursive emphasis on "the periphery" and "the man on the street," his aggressive anti-elitism, and his overbearing manner—are of importance for hegemonic leadership. Nevertheless, it would be more productive to go beyond the question of style and focus instead on those semiotic forms, genres, and other symbols in and through which the class content of politics comes to be represented. Such discussions of language and tropes, however, should be explored elsewhere, for they necessitate a careful and detailed discourse analysis.

3. My arguments are based on the relational approach of Poulantzas (1978) as modified by Jessop's (1985, 1990, 2007) strategic relational approach. They are also inspired by two principal meanings Gramsci (1971) gave to the concept of hegemony. On the one hand, it refers to a process whereby a fraction of the dominant class exercises control over other allied fractions of the dominant class. This leading fraction has the power and ability to articulate the interest of others in a way that it serves the collective interests of capital and its own interests as a hegemonic fraction. On the other hand, it is a relationship between the dominant and dominated classes in which the former uses its political, moral, and intellectual leadership to establish its view of the world as all-inclusive and universal to shape the interests/needs of subordinate groups.

4. Çınar, for example, writes that "[t]he social current that brought AKP to power represents a broad based demand for further democratic reform" (2006: 480).

5. The crises had devastating effects on the economy: the GNP declined by 9.5 percent and the currency depreciated by 21.2 percent in real terms during the course of the crises. Both the manufacturing and the service sectors suffered huge contractions. But the crises were most severely felt in the banking sector, causing widespread bankruptcies and layoffs (Şenses 2003).

6. Characteristically, within these approaches, Kemal Derviş—a technocrat recruited from the World Bank and put in charge of initiating the "new" economic program titled "Turkey's Transition Program: Strengthening the Turkish Economy" in the immediate aftermath of the crises—is often quoted to illustrate the importance of a self-willed political actor in facilitating the implementation of the long-delayed stabilization program (Keyman and Öniş 2003). The program was backed by a series of structural reforms that had been attempted by previous governments and yet had never succeeded. It also explicitly acknowledged the role of political institutions and preceding governments in exacerbating the crisis. Derviş was deemed successful not only for his ability to resist populist demands, but also for his role in internalizing the reform package thereby. For a detailed account of the program, see Cizre-Sakallıoğlu and Yeldan (2005).

7. Several scholars acknowledge, explicitly or implicitly, the necessity and far-reaching positive effects of the IMF-led and World Bank–tailored stabilization programs and structural reforms; see, for instance, Öniş (2003).

8. The basic objective of the postcrisis program was to reach macroeconomic targets set by the IMF: fiscal and monetary discipline to achieve a primary surplus of 6.5 percent

and maintain the sustainability of public debts. For a critique of the program, see BSB (2006).

9. Some noted incentives were improvements in legal protection, the curtailment of administrative barriers to investment, and the corporate tax rate reduction.

10. The AKP's economic program, including the public sector and local government reforms, and its emphasis on distributive fairness, social justice, and multiculturalism led some studies to celebrate the emergence of a "Third Way Thinking" in Turkey (Keyman and Öniş 2003, 2007; Öniş 2006a).

11. For a detailed discussion and data, see Onaran (2007b) and Şenses and Koyuncu (2007).

12. For a critique of the "EU anchor" paradigm, see BSB (2005) and Yalman and Yıldızoğlu (2003).

13. Nevertheless, TÜSİAD published two "progress reports" on democratization in 1999 and 2001, in which it addressed the persisting problems within the framework of the 1997 report and assessed the efficacy of the political reforms that were undertaken by the coalition government (Öniş and Türem 2001).

14. Some major political reforms of the pre-AKP period—the elimination of the death penalty and certain improvements in minority rights—were passed at this critical conjuncture.

15. TÜSİAD's 2007 report, titled *Deeper Democracy, More Stable Social Structure, Stronger Economy*, stated the necessity for "deep-seated" political reforms to ensure that political instability would no longer be an obstacle in the path of economic development and Turkey's accession to the EU.

16. According to such arguments, elected political parties in Turkey are *governing but not ruling*, because the military bureaucracy and the judicial oligarchy see themselves as the "guardians of the state" and its dominant ideology, Kemalism (Jenkins 2003, 2006; Cook 2007; Kahraman 2007).

17. The "military intervention" on 28 February 1997 virtually ended the political career of the ruling Islamic party, Refah Partisi (Welfare Party, RP) and brought the Islamic movement under strict control. It is worth noting that MÜSİAD, which had close links to the RP and other Islamic organizations, also published a democratization report in 2000, titled *Constitutional Reform and the Democratization of the State*.

18. Some Islamic intellectuals often referred to Gramsci in their writings (Dilipak 1991). Zubaida (1996) also refers to some well-known Islamic intellectuals (such as Ali Bulaç and İsmet Özel) who are familiar with the Marxist discussions on fetishism and influenced by the Frankfurt School.

19. For different theoretical discussions of the concept and empirical contributions primarily on Christian right-wing forces, see Pieterse (1992).

20. The affinity of Islamic intellectuals with Gramsci's ideas is well portrayed by other researchers, who indeed discuss the attempt at ideological hegemony in related terms (Gülalp 1997; Tuğal 2009). This chapter builds on some of the ideas presented in these works, but differs to the extent that it extends the analysis beyond cultural hegemony and focuses on state power.

21. Since the 1970s Islamists had strongholds in the Ministry of Education, and their views were strongly reflected in policies, textbooks, and teacher selection (Zubaida 1996).

22. For variations in Islamic movements across the Middle East and comparisons of the socioeconomic context in which they operate, see Cook (2007) and Gümüşçü (2010).

23. Religious vocational schools that train prayer leaders and preachers.

24. These attempts include the bill involving the prohibition of alcoholic beverages in public places and the efforts to include adultery as a criminal offense in the penal code.

25. On the first issue, the government tried to overturn the headscarf ban in universities through a constitutional amendment in 2008, yet this amendment did not lift the ban in public offices. Although it was approved by the parliament, the Constitutional Court annulled the proposed amendment on the grounds that lifting the ban was against the founding principles of the constitution, thus leaving the issue unresolved. In the absence of a "final" decision, some universities allowed students to enter campuses with headscarves, while others decided to defy the amendment. As the court's decision cannot be appealed, the government took two different actions in response. The first move was to restructure the court to prevent it from challenging its decisions in the future. The second move came from the Higher Education Council. The council sent a circular stating that it was to take legal action against noncompliant institutions and lecturers. However, unless the law and the constitution are changed, the headscarf ban has still not been completely lifted.

   On the second issue, the new education system (also known as "4 + 4 + 4," four years of first-level primary education, four years of second-level primary education, and four years of secondary education), which has been implemented since 2012, permits students to enter a vocational educational stream after four years of education. The new legislation includes the reopening of İmam Hatip middle schools and also makes it possible for graduates of these vocational schools to apply to any department in universities, which was not possible under the earlier system (also known as "5 + 3 + 4"). Another outcome of the educational reform bill was to allow pupils to take a large number of elective courses, including religious studies.

26. The state, as an institutional ensemble, is divided by class-relevant (but not necessarily class-conscious) contradictions; the diverging interests of the capitalist class/fractions that constitute the power bloc are present in the material framework of the state, throughout its various apparatuses/branches and distinct networks that cut across different layers. The dominant classes then find their historical unification in the state. Because of their physical exclusion from the state, the popular masses, however, make their way into the system in a roundabout way: either divisions within the power bloc force competing fractions to include the demands of the masses into their strategic calculations, or the masses find their voices among the state personnel and intellectuals with different "class affiliations." This class affiliation, however, does not refer to their class origin; rather, it stands for their position in the social division of labor and the concentration of intellectual labor in state apparatuses and certain segments of the society (Poulantzas 1975: 163, 325; 1978: 132–33, 154–56).

27. For different types of hegemonic appeals, see Jessop et al. (1988).

28. Hegemonic crisis occurs when the leading force loses its consensus. It cannot impose its leadership on other partners of the power bloc and cannot dominate subordinate groups, but increasingly exercises coercive force. Thus, certain groups/strata find themselves alienated from their traditional parties (parliamentary representatives). But the split between different classes/fractions and their parties not only presents itself as a crisis of political representation, but also leads to an ideological crisis (or legitimation crisis). While the dominant groups can no longer live out their relation to their conditions of existence in the same way, the masses find themselves detached from their traditional ideologies, no longer believing what they used to believe. Hence, crisis begins to disintegrate the society by suspending all ordinary norms, overthrowing old habits, and breaking all accepted rules of behavior. It may be too soon to talk about a "loss of hegemony" on the part of the AKP or a "hegemonic crisis." Yet a great variety of morbid symptoms have also appeared, ringing alarming bells in this manner.

29. The sources of growth derived mainly from consumption expenditures, exports, and stock increases in the private sector instead of a structural change in the composition

of industry. FDI was mostly in the form of mergers and acquisitions and directed
to large-scale privatization, while private fixed investments remained low and production continued to specialize in labor-intensive sectors. Although export revenues
increased significantly, imports also rose rapidly due to rising demand for imported
consumer goods and the high degree of dependence of the export sector on imported
intermediate and capital goods. The import bill and resulting chronic current account
deficit has been an important source of vulnerability. Despite the availability of cheap
imported inputs, exporting industries could not compete with their East Asian counterparts and shifted their production to domestic markets. The government promoted
the construction sector via consumer credits, mass housing projects, and government
spending on big public sector projects. However, this sector later faltered following
the shift in global funds away from emerging markets since 2006 (BSB 2006). Following the 2008 global crisis, industrial output fell significantly and serious stagnations
were experienced in locomotive sectors such as construction, automotives, and textiles. The slump related to declining consumer spending not only hit small businesses
and retailers, but also led to the collapse of well-established large firms. Several firms
reduced production, closed plants, or resorted to massive layoffs (Sönmez 2010).

30. With the upside risks to inflation, political instabilities, and elections pressuring
primary spending, TÜSİAD and TOBB noted that fiscal discipline is critical. Although
the IMF standby agreement expired in May 2008, the government refused to commit
itself to austere fiscal policies that advocated further declines in public investment
and higher taxes, and did not sign a precautionary standby agreement with the IMF.
TÜSİAD not only strongly "advised" the government to continue with the IMF, but
also openly accused the government of returning to populism in its fiscal policy.
The accusations highlighted increased allocations for local administrations, the use
of privatization revenue for public investment rather than domestic debt reduction,
using the unemployment fund to cover public spending instead of transferring cash
to the unemployed, amnesty for social insurance premium payments that were in
default, attempts to change the law on public tenders, and decreasing the rate of
primary surplus from 6.5 to 3.5 percent. Yet MÜSİAD clearly noted its aversion to a
possible precautionary standby agreement with the IMF and urged the government
not to diverge from public investments and to take measures to revive the domestic
market. Moreover, the tension between the government and private banks (owned
by large conglomerates) has intensified these frictions. Small- and medium-scale
enterprises (SMEs) experienced serious problems in finding enough working capital
with which to continue day-to-day operations when the banks lowered the amount
of loans available to the private sector, increased the interest rates, and recalled loans
from firms in financial distress. The competition over public and private credits
continues and sharpens the contradictions within the power bloc.

31. As confirmed during the closure case filed against the AKP, most actors have
been unwilling to jeopardize the stability maintained by the single-party majority
government, especially in the midst of global economic recession. Instead of having
no government or a shaky coalition that would have produced an ever-deeper regime
crisis, the Turkish bourgeoisie opted for reconciliation via the legal system. The AKP
was not shut down, but a "warning" came in the form of fines. This is quite rational
on both economic and political grounds. On the one hand, the majority of voters
were willing to preserve the political balance, fearing that political instability would
increase interest rates and cause exchange rate shocks. Low interest rates enabled
cheap consumer loans and prompted a sharp boom in consumer credit during the last
few years. In addition, total loans to private sector firms and banks and the foreign
debt stock have increased immensely. The IMF and the media also nurtured this fear
during the 2007 election campaign. On the other hand, prominent EU figures warned

that Turkey could forget about membership if the trial ended in the AKP's closure. Last but not least, an anti-AKP bloc could not become hegemonic within civil society as it was in the case of the RP in the post-1997 period.

32. The AKP provided an above-inflation pension increase and set the national minimum wage above the inflation level, despite employers' strong opposition.

33. Due to the size and strength of the informal economy, the wage spreads between skilled and unskilled labor were broadened further. In addition, the celebrated high production levels were mainly due to rising labor productivity. Instead of deriving from new investments and/or technological improvements, productivity increases were made possible by increasing the surplus labor time and paying lower wages.

34. While taxes on wages and salaries have increased significantly, a growing part of tax revenues have been allocated to cover public debt/interest payments.

35. See BSB (2006, 2011) for a detailed analysis on the performance of the AKP's economic program.

36. It is called the "law package" because it contained a considerable number of laws.

37. For a detailed discussion on working time and employment mode flexibility, see Öz-demir and Yücesan-Özdemir (2006).

38. The transformation in the health care sector and the reorganization of the social secu-rity system best illustrates how commodification of public services took place under AKP rule (Erdoğdu 2006; Hamzaoğlu and Yavuz 2006).

39. The Public Sector Reform Law and the Local Authorities Law.

40. TEKEL, a state-owned alcohol and tobacco monopoly, was sold to British American Tobacco in 2008. The privatization act affected ten thousand workers. Following job losses due to factory closures and the redeployment of previous personnel (under the 4C regulation in other public sector jobs) on eleven-month temporary contracts (which also included pay cuts up to 40 percent and reduced employment rights), TEKEL workers started a protest in Ankara in December 2009. The protesting workers camped in the city center for two and a half months despite harsh winter conditions and police brutality. Thanks to the support of some NGOs and labor and civil servant confederations in Turkey, the TEKEL protests did not end up being an isolated resis-tance. Massive rallies and public demonstrations in support of the TEKEL workers were also held in Ankara, Istanbul, and İzmir.

41. The fight between Prime Minister Erdoğan and a media baron (Aydın Doğan) over corruption allegations regarding a loosely AKP-affiliated charity organization, Deniz Feneri Derneği (Lighthouse Association), can also be given as an example of the rift within the power bloc and mainstream media.

42. As the attempts of the Constitutional Commission to draft a new constitution resulted in a deadlock, the 2010 referendum aimed to enact partial amendments in the 1982 constitution. The package included a number of issues, some of which were well received by the general public, such as the right of individuals to appeal to the highest court, the establishment of the public ombudsmen, the amendments regarding positive discrimination toward women, children, and the handicapped, the right of civil servants to go on strike, the article on the protection of personal privacy, and so on. Yet some others created bitter controversy within the parliament and civil society. These included articles on the ability of civilian courts to convict members of the military, weakening the powers of the Constitutional Court to ban political parties, and changes concerning the composition of the higher judicial organs. The secularist opposition regarded these as a final assault against the secular order, yet even some liberals raised concerns regarding the expanding powers of the presidency and the executive branch over the judiciary, which problematizes the very fundamentals of the democratic system. A majority of Kurds also boycotted the referendum on the grounds that it failed to address their demands for greater political and cultural

autonomy. Yet despite these controversies, the package was agreed to by a majority of 58 percent of the votes. The AKP not only skillfully turned the referendum into a vote of confidence in Erdoğan's rule, but also read it as a positive sign to move Turkey to a form of quasi-presidential government.

43. For conceptual differences between hegemony and domination, see Gramsci (1971: 57–58).

44. For theoretical implications, see Poulantzas (1975: 163, 325; 1978: 140–43).

45. While the 10 percent national threshold remains, local Kurdish political figures continue to face police pressures and persecution. The government also remained silent about the closure case filed against the pro-Kurdish Demokratik Toplum Partisi (Democratic Society Party, DTP). The chief prosecutor of the Supreme Court of Cassation filed charges against the DTP for being "against the indivisible integrity of the state and the nation" and called for the party's permanent closure. As the Constitutional Court voted to ban the DTP in 2009, most of its members of parliament (MPs) joined the newly formed Barış ve Demokrasi Partisi (Peace and Democracy Party, BDP).

46. The Anti-Terror Law reintroduced clauses to curb individual liberties, but the government continues to support military operations against the PKK (Kürdistan İşçi Partisi, Kurdistan Workers' Party) in Turkey and northern Iraq. As a result of this grand return to aggressive strategies, the "low-intensity war" between the armed forces and the PKK that characterized the 1990s has been revived.

47. The "Solution Process" was comprised of three stages: first, the disarmament and withdrawal of the PKK and reintegration of combatants; second, constitutional and legal changes; and a third stage that would include political talks and normalization.

48. The demands include education in their mother tongue and the acceptance of Kurdish as a second official language; freedom for Kurds to organize under their own name (i.e., using expressions such as "Kurdish" and "Kurdistan"); the right of Kurds to determine their own future; and the safeguarding of these rights in the constitution.

49. Alevis are followers of a specific Shia strand of Islam and may be of different ethnic backgrounds, that is, Turkish, Zaza, Kurdish, Turkmen, and Azeri. An ongoing debate concerns whether Alevis have been discriminated against, persecuted, and deprived of political, financial, and organizational privileges enjoyed by Sunni Muslims.

50. Nor do *cemevi* places of worship enjoy the financial resources and state provisions afforded to mosques. Religious classes in schools are generally taught by graduates of İmam Hatip schools, which impose the Sunni tradition and explicitly discriminate against Alevi students. The AKP's open association with Sunni Islam is therefore anathema to the Alevi minority.

51. Between 2002 and 2007, 55 out of 537 laws enacted by the legislature were vetoed by the then president Ahmet Necdet Sezer. Sezer also vetoed more than 3,000 appointments. The Constitutional Court annulled quite a few of these laws on the grounds that they were incompatible with the constitution. Danıştay (Council of State, the highest administrative court in Turkey) blocked the privatization of a state-owned petroleum company (Petkim). In addition, university administrators, the president, and the military harshly criticized the law that allows İmam Hatip graduates to enter university on equal grounds with public high school graduates.

52. If the former strategy is interpreted in Gramscian terms as a *war of position*, it may not be too bold to argue that the AKP has been challenging the state in what appears to be a renovated *war of maneuver*.

53. These included the Ministry of Education, the Ministry of Energy and Natural Resources, the Ministry of Industry and Trade, and the Ministry of Public Works and Settlement. For example, Kemal Unakıtan, an executive board member of the Islamic

finance institutions Al-Baraka Türk and Family Finance Group, later became finance minister.

54. National Electric Distribution Corporation, Pipeline and Petroleum, Transport Corporation, and TÜBİTAK (Turkish Scientific and Technological Research Council) could be given as examples.

55. In addition, the university president appointments in the summer of 2008 put the AKP and universities at odds when President Gül refused to appoint nine of the twenty-one candidates who had won majorities in their universities' elections. Several academics, including deans, resigned to protest Gül's presidential choices.

56. The Contractual Personnel Regime passed along with the public sector reforms also allowed the AKP to appoint its own staff to the administration of public services.

57. In 2007 the police began an extensive operation against a secret organization named Ergenekon. Likened to the clandestine paramilitary Operation Gladio in Italy, the alleged Ergenekon members are accused of planning a secret coup against the AKP by paving the way for a military takeover. Since January 2008 hundreds of people have been charged in the Ergenekon case, including retired generals, some low-ranking army officials, ultranationalist lawyers, journalists, academics, intellectuals, a party leader, trade unionists, the head of the Ankara Chamber of Commerce, and over a dozen other suspected members of a shadowy group of right-wing nationalists. The detainments evoke the idea that the AKP has accelerated the clean sweep against its high-profile opponents, and this further alienates the liberal/pro-democratic wing of the alliance.

58. In 2010 the Turkish newspaper *Taraf* ran a story on a coup plot code-named Balyoz Harekatı (Operation Sledgehammer), which was allegedly devised in 2003. The article series was based on material (including cassettes and CDs) delivered to the editor of the newspaper by an anonymous individual claiming to be a retired officer. According to the allegations, the military was secretly planning violent acts to destabilize the government and pave the way for a military takeover. Despite questions on the authenticity of the material, they became the main pillar of the prosecution case. Since then some three hundred military officers were sentenced to prison terms. The case is to be appealed.

59. The initial protests were led by a number of environmentalists opposing the government's decision to redevelop Gezi Park (one of the Istanbul's few green spaces) into a massive complex consisting of a shopping mall and a cultural center. It is no secret that Erdoğan's chief preoccupation has been neoliberal gentrification under the guise of urban development. There have been other protests against ongoing projects such as the ones concerning the Emek movie theater, the third Bosphorus bridge, the historic Haydarpaşa train station, a new airport, and the hydroelectric power plants. What began as a demonstration against urban redevelopment has turned into a wider expression of anger against the government's authoritarian policies. The protests in Istanbul gained massive support from students, labor unions, NGOs, environmentalist groups, women's organizations, gay rights activists, football fans, and other groups such as the collective of Antikapitalist Müslümanlar (Anticapitalist Muslims), turning the demonstrations into a wider (antigovernment) popular movement throughout the country. The popular unrest concomitantly addresses other legislations that threaten the personal rights of citizens, including the recent curbs on alcohol sales, new antiabortion laws, and censorship imposed on mainstream and social media. While Erdoğan rallies to sharpen the divisions in order to consolidate his own troops, it is hard to argue that Gezi Park protests embody a new consensus in Turkish politics. In fact, neither the protests nor police brutality have ceased at the time of the writing of this chapter.

60. Both TÜSİAD and TOBB have expressed concern about the arrests, and Turkish media is also divided. While pro-AKP media hailed the operation, saying it is a step forward to enhance democracy, mainstream media seem perturbed that the Ergenekon operation was turning into a kind of "witch hunt" and being used by the AKP government to suppress its opponents. The tensions escalated when Yargıçlar ve Savcılar Birliği (Judges' and Prosecutors' Association, YARSAV) denounced the government and the police for the way they handled the investigations and detentions.

References

Akdoğan, Yalçın. 2004. *AK Parti ve Muhafazakar Demokrasi* [AK Party and conservative democracy]. Ankara: AK Parti Yayınları.

Bayramoğlu, Ali. 2008. "AKP Yalnızlık Arayışı İçerisinde" [AKP in search of loneliness]. *Yeni Şafak*, 1 May.

BSB (Bağımsız Sosyal Bilimciler, Independent Social Scientists). 2005. *On Economic and Social Life in Turkey in Early 2005*. Accessed 30 May 2007. http://www.bağımsızsosyalbilimciler. org.

———. 2006. *IMF Gözetiminde On Uzun Yıl 1998–2008: Farklı Hükümetler Tek Siyaset* [A long decade under IMF supervision 1998–2008: Different governments common policies]. Istanbul: Yordam.

———. 2011. *Derinleşen Küresel Kriz ve Türkiye Ekonomisine Yansımaları: Ücretli Emek ve Sermaye* [Deepening global crisis and its reflections on the Turkish economy: wage labor and capital]. Accessed 27 December 2012. http://www.bağımsızsosyalbilimciler.org.

Çınar, Menderes. 2005. *Siyasal Bir Sorun Olarak İslamcılık* [Islamism as a political problem]. Ankara: Dipnot Yayınları.

———. 2006. "Turkey's Transformation under the AKP Rule." *The Muslim World* 96, no. 3: 469–86.

Cizre-Sakallıoğlu, Ümit, and Erinç Yeldan. 2005. "The Turkish Encounter with Neoliberalism: Economics and Politics in the 2000/2001 Crises." *Review of International Political Economy* 12, no. 3: 387–408.

Cook, Steven A. 2007. *Ruling But not Governing: The Military and Political Development in Egypt, Algeria and Turkey*. Baltimore: Johns Hopkins University Press.

Dilipak, Abdurrahman. 1991. *Savaş, Barış, İktidar* [War, peace, power]. Istanbul: İşaret Yayınları.

Erdoğdu, Seyhan. 2006. "Sosyal Politikada Değişim ve Sosyal Güvenlik Reformu" [Changes in social policy and the social security reform]. *Mülkiye Dergisi* 30, no. 252: 211–36.

Ergil, Doğu. 1995. *Doğu Sorunu: Teşhisler, Tespitler; Özel Araştırma Raporu* [The Eastern Question: Diagnoses and evaluations; special research report]. Stratejik Araştrımalar Dizisi 1. Ankara: TOBB.

Gramsci, Antonio. 1971. *Selections from the Prison Notebooks*. London: Lawrence and Wishart.

Gülalp, Haldun. 1997. "Globalizing Postmodernism: Islamist and Western Social Theory." *Economy and Society* 26, no. 3: 419–33.

Gümüşçü, Şebnem. 2010. "Class, Status, and Party: The Changing Face of Political Islam in Turkey and Egypt." *Comparative Political Studies* 43, no. 7: 835–61.

Hamzaoğlu, Onur, and Cavit I. Yavuz. 2006. "Sağlıkta AKP'li Dönemin Bilançosu Üzerine" [The health sector during the AKP era]. *Mülkiye Dergisi* 30, no. 252: 633–59.

Heper, Metin. 2005. "The Justice and Development Party Government and the Military in Turkey." *Turkish Studies* 6, no. 2: 215–31.

İnsel, Ahmet. 2003. "The AKP and Normalizing Democracy in Turkey." *The South Atlantic Quarterly* 102, nos. 2–3: 293–308.

Jenkins, Gareth. 2003. "Muslim Democrats in Turkey?" Survival 45, no. 1: 45–66.

_____. 2006. "Symbols and Shadow Play: Military-JDP Relations, 2002–2004." In Yavuz, *The Emergence of a New Turkey*, 185–206.

Jessop, Bob. 1985. *Nicos Poulantzas: Marxist Theory and Political Strategy*. London: Macmillan.

_____. 1990. *State Theory: Putting the Capitalist State in its Place*. Cambridge: Polity.

_____. 2007. *State Power: A Strategic-Relational Approach*. Cambridge: Polity.

Jessop, Bob, Kevin Bonnett, Simon Bromley, and Tom Ling. 1988. *Thatcherism: A Tale of Two Nations*. Cambridge: Polity.

Kahraman, Hasan B. 2007. *Türk Sağı ve AKP* [The Turkish right and the AKP]. Istanbul: Agora Kitaplığı.

Keyder, Çağlar. 2004. "The Turkish Bell Jar." *New Left Review* 28 (July–August): 65–84.

Keyman, Fuat, and Ziya Öniş. 2003. "A New Path Emerges." *Journal of Democracy* 14, no. 2: 80–95.

_____. 2007. "Globalization, and Social Democracy in the European Periphery: Paradoxes of the Turkish Experience." *Globalizations* 4, no. 2: 211–29.

MÜSİAD. 2000. *Anayasa Reformu ve Yönetimin Demokratikleştirilmesi* [Constitutional reform and the democratization of the state]. Istanbul: MÜSİAD.

Onaran, Özlem. 2007a. "İşsizlik ve Alternatif Politikalar" [Unemployment and alternative policies]. *Türkiye'de İşsizliğin Çözüm Yolları ve Sendikalar Çalışma Grubu'nda sunulan tebliğ* [Paper submitted at the Workshop on Solutions to Unemployment and Unions in Turkey], 14 April. DİSK: Istanbul.

_____. 2007b. "Life after Crisis for Labor and Capital in the Era of Neoliberal Globalization." In *Neoliberal Globalization as New Imperialism: Case Studies on Reconstruction of the Periphery*, ed. Ahmet Haşim Köse, Fikret Şenses, and Erinç Yeldan, 171–95. New York: Nova.

Öniş, Ziya. 2003. "The Post-war Development Performance of the Turkish Economy: A Political Economy Perspective." In *Greece and Turkey in the 21st Century: Conflict or Cooperation?*, ed. Christos Kollias and Gülay Günlük-Şenesen, 165–78. New York: Nova.

_____. 2006a. "The Political Economy of Islam and Democracy in Turkey: From the Welfare Party to the AKP." In *Democracy and Development: New Political Strategies for the Middle East*, ed. Dietrich Jung, 103–28. New York: Palgrave.

_____. 2006b. "The Political Economy of Turkey's Justice and Development Party." In Yavuz, *The Emergence of a New Turkey*, 211–28.

_____. 2007. "Conservative Globalists versus Defensive Nationalists: Political Parties and Paradoxes of Europeanization in Turkey." *Journal of Southern Europe and the Balkans* 9, no. 3: 247–61.

Öniş, Ziya, and Umut Türem. 2001. "Business, Globalization and Democracy: A Comparative Analysis of Turkish Business Associations." *Turkish Studies* 2, no. 2: 94–120.

Özdemir, Ali M., and Gamze Yücesan-Özdemir. 2006. "Labour Law Reform in Turkey in the 2000s: The Devil is Not Just in the Detail But Also in the Legal Texts." *Economic and Industrial Democracy* 27, no. 2: 311–31.

Özel, Soli. 2003. "After the Tsunami." *Journal of Democracy* 14, no. 2: 80–94.

Pieterse, Jan N. (ed.). 1992. *Christianity and Hegemony: Religion and Politics on the Frontiers of Social Change*. Oxford: Berg.

Poulantzas, Nicos. 1975. *Classes in Contemporary Capitalism*. London: Verso.

_____. 1978. *State, Power, Socialism*. London: Verso.

Şenses, Fikret. 2003. "Economic Crisis as an Instigator of Distributional Conflict: The Turkish Case in 2001." In *Turkey's Economy in Crisis*, ed. Barry Rubin and Ziya Öniş, 92–119. London: Frank Cass.

234 | *Evren Hoşgör*

Şenses, Fikret, and Koyuncu, Murat. 2007. "Socioeconomic Effects of Economic Crises: A Comparative Analysis of the Experiences of Indonesia, Argentina and Turkey." In Köse, Şenses, and Yeldan, *Neoliberal Globalization as New Imperialism*, 197–223.

Sönmez, Mustafa. 2010. *Teğet'in Yıkımı ... Dünyada Türkiye'de Küresel Krizin 2009 Enkazı ve Gelecek* [The destruction of the tangent: 2009 debris of the global crisis in the world and in Turkey]. Istanbul: Yordam Kitap.

Tekin, Üzeyir. 2004. *AK Partinin Muhafazakar Demokrat Kimliği* [The conservative democrat identity of AK Party]. Istanbul: Orient.

Tepe, Sultan. 2006. "A Pro-Islamic Party? Promises and Limits of Turkey's Justice and Development Party." In Yavuz, *The Emergence of a New Turkey*, 107–35.

TOBB. 2000. *Anayasa 2000: Türkiye Cumhuriyeti için Anayasa Önerisi* [Constitution 2000: A constitution proposal for the Turkish republic]. Ankara: TOBB.

Tuğal, Cihan. 2009. *Passive Revolution: Absorbing the Islamic Challenge to Capitalism*. Palo Alto, CA: Stanford University Press.

Tünay, Muharrem. 1993. "The Turkish New Right's Attempt at Hegemony." In *The Political and Socio-economic Transformation of Turkey*, ed. Atilla Eralp, Muharrem Tünay, and Birol Yeşilada, 11–30. London: Praeger.

Turan, İlter. 2003. "The Justice and Development Party: The First Year in Power." TÜSİAD Washington Office. Accessed 12 November 2007. http://tusiad.us.

TÜSİAD. 1997. *Perspectives on Democratization in Turkey*. Istanbul: TÜSİAD.

_____. 1999. *Perspectives on Democratization in Turkey: Progress Report 1999*. Istanbul: TÜSİAD.

_____. 2001. *Perspectives on Democratization in Turkey: Progress Report 2001*. Istanbul: TÜSİAD.

_____. 2007. *Towards Full Membership to the EU on January 1, 2014: Deeper Democracy, More Stable Social Structure, Stronger Economy*. Istanbul: TÜSİAD.

Yalman, Galip, and Ergin Yıldızoğlu. 2003. "Responding to Financial Crisis With or Without IMF: A Comparative Analysis of State-Capital Relations." 2nd ECPR General Conference, 18–21 September, Marburg, Germany.

Yavuz, M. Hakan. 1997. "Political Islam and the Welfare (Refah) Party in Turkey." *Comparative Politics* 30, no. 1: 63–82.

_____. 2006. "Introduction: The Role of the New Bourgeoisie in the Transformation of the Turkish Islamic Movement." In Yavuz, *The Emergence of a New Turkey*, 1–19.

Yıldırım, Ergün, Hüsamettin İnaç, and Hayrettin Özler. 2007. "A Sociological Representation of the Justice and Development Party: Is It a Political Design or a Political Becoming?" *Turkish Studies* 8, no. 1: 5–24.

Yılmaz, Mehmet. 2004. "Darbeler ve İslamcılık" [Coups and Islamism]. In *Modern Türkiye'de Siyasi Düşünce* [Political thought in modern Turkey], vol. 6, *İslamcılık* [Islamism], ed. Yasin Aktay, 632–40. Istanbul: İletişim Yayınları.

Zubaida, Sami. 1996. "Turkish Islam and National Identity." *Middle East Report* 199: 10–15.

– Chapter 8 –

GLOBALIZATION, ISLAMIC ACTIVISM, AND PASSIVE REVOLUTION IN TURKEY
The Case of Fethullah Gülen
Joshua D. Hendrick

e⁓

Those who understand politics as political parties, propaganda, elections, and the struggle for power are mistaken. Politics is the art of management, based on a broad perspective of today, tomorrow, and the day after, that seeks the people's satisfaction and God's approval.
    —M. Fethullah Gülen

Introduction: The Turkish "War of Position"

On 27 April 2007, the Türk Silahlı Kuvvetleri (Turkish Armed Forces, TSK) intervened in Turkey's presidential nomination procedure by publicly expressing fear that a candidate nominated by the governing "Islamist roots" Adalet ve Kalkınma Partisi (Justice and Development Party, AKP) would threaten Turkish secularism. At midnight the TSK started a political crisis by issuing an electronic memorandum that stated the following:

> It must not be forgotten that the Turkish Armed Forces do take sides in this debate and are the sure and certain defenders of secularism. Moreover, the Turkish Armed Forces ... will make their position and stance perfectly clear if needs be. Let nobody have any doubt about this. ... The Turkish Armed Forces remain steadfast in their unwavering commitment to carry out in full the duties given to them by law. ... The public has been respectfully informed. (Turkish Mass Media Bulletin, 28–30 July 2007)

The next day, Turkey's Constitutional Court capitalized upon a loophole in the presidential nomination procedure by emphasizing that according to the 1982 constitution, 367 deputies were required to be present in the chambers of the parliament during the nomination. This resulted in a parliamentary vote in which the deputies from the two opposition parties did not attend. The AKP responded by calling for an early general poll to elect a new government. On 22 July 2007, the AKP was reelected in a landslide, taking nearly 47 percent of the electorate. Fearing a political backlash, deputies from the right-wing opposition Milliyetçi Hareket Partisi (Nationalist Action Party, MHP) attended the vote, and on 29 August 2007, the AKP foreign minister, Abdullah Gül, became Turkey's eleventh president.

Gramsci's concept of "passive revolution" refers to transformative social change that occurs gradually, without the overthrow of an existing political order. Passive revolutions occur when antithetical, "subaltern" social groups move patiently through the hierarchy of institutions that comprise the production centers of a society's "superstructure" (i.e., education system, the system of arts and culture, the media, etc.), for it is there that the dominant social group reproduces the conditions of their "social hegemony." By social hegemony, Gramsci refers to the degree of social power exercised by a dominant social group whereby, through the sophisticated mechanisms of cultural and moral authority, "spontaneous consent is given by the great masses of the population to the general direction imposed on social life" (Gramsci 1971: 12). By slowly redefining the contours of spontaneous consent (i.e., after taking over a society's superstructure), a passively revolutionary class/group wages a "war of position" in the institutions of social and political power until its leaders accumulate enough legitimacy to engineer a new social hegemony from the inside out.

The liberalization of the Turkish economy in the 1980s coupled with the relaxation of laws regarding the public mobilization of religious communities led to a shift in the country's state-society relationship whereby previously marginalized groups took advantage of opportunities in the market to patiently penetrate the hierarchy of Turkish institutions. As a case study, I explain the discursive and organizational strategies of the Gülen movement (GM), Turkey's largest and most influential Islamic activist movement and the primary power base in the AKP-led coalition. After introducing readers to the GM, I employ analytic categories from the social theory of both Antonio Gramsci and Max Weber to analyze Turkey's passive revolution by taking a step back to introduce the character and form of Turkey's state-managed development model. Before a transformative military coup in 1980, an oligarchic alliance of elites used the institutions of the Turkish state to reproduce the conditions of their social hegemony. Notwithstanding however crucial it is to understand the rupture of the 1980–83 military coup in order to understand why and when the GM emerged in Turkey, it is also necessary to appreciate the tradition of charismatic leadership in Turkey and its significance in regard to the mobilization of grassroots Islamic activism in general. For this reason, I emphasize the impact of Gülen's predecessor, Said Nursi (d. 1960), and the mobilization of the Nur movement, a nationwide phenomenon of which the GM is an updated offshoot.

The primary data used to develop this argument is drawn from field data that I collected in Turkey and in the United States to analyze the GM's impact as a faith-based identity and advocacy movement. In coalition with the governing AKP, the GM has emerged as Turkey's most influential nonpartisan, nonmilitary collective actor in an ongoing war of position for social hegemony. The GM leads this war of position by dividing the labor of the passive revolution between formal politics and market-based resource accumulation. The AKP mobilizes the "political march" in the parliament, the presidency, and the bureaucracies of the Turkish state, whereas the GM capitalizes upon its comparative advantage in education, business, media, and public relations to lead a corresponding "civilian march" through the institutions of Turkey's superstructure. As an alliance, these overlapping entities mobilize to affect a passive revolution in the interests of a new Anatolian bourgeoisie. For this reason, it is important to state that the war of position that characterizes contemporary Turkish politics is not an interclass battle between dominant and "subaltern" classes; it is an *intraclass* battle between old and new elites. Individuals recruited into the GM are not drawn from Turkey's working class, its disenfranchised, or its downtrodden; they come from an increasingly influential middle and upper class of social and economic conservatives. In other words, despite the conscious framing of the battle in cultural terms (i.e., "Islam" versus "secularism"), Turkey's passive revolution has emerged less as a reactionary movement against "Western materialism" than as a proactive effort to increase the Muslim share in Turkish capitalism.

The Gülen Movement in Turkey

"Hocaefendi" (esteemed teacher) M. Fethullah Gülen is Turkey's most famous religious personality. Born in 1938 (or 1941, depending on the source) in the northeastern city of Erzurum, Gülen started his career as a state-appointed religious functionary in the western coastal city of İzmir in the 1960s. There he attracted a small but devoted following of students who were drawn to his unique ability to synthesize a faithful identity within the dictates of twentieth-century Turkish nationalism. As his influence expanded, however, so did suspicion about his motives. During the 1971 military coup, Gülen spent seven months in prison for allegations that he was the leader of a secret religious community, and upon his release, he was briefly banned from public speaking. Over the course of the 1970s, Gülen's students took advantage of the latest developments in information and communication technologies and were successful at disseminating his teachings to a national audience. By the late 1970s, Gülen was attracting tens of thousands of people to his sermons, and it was not uncommon for people to travel hundreds of kilometers across the country to hear him, to meet with him, and/or to attend one of several "summer camps" that were organized by his disciples. In 1979, his community published the first edition of *Sızıntı* (Trickle), a monthly periodical that focused on the reinforcing relationship between divine revelation and scientific discovery, a theme that in many ways came to shape the GM's engagement with mainstream Turkish society.

During the military junta of 1980–83, Gülen's followers in İzmir and Istanbul consolidated a number of their foundational holdings into private education companies, and after the return to civilian governance, these first institutions provided a model for the emergence of similar learning institutions throughout the country. Considering Turkey's rigidity in terms of the role of Islam in the public sphere, the curriculum at these early "Gülen schools" was careful to follow the state's requirements in regard to keeping religion out of the classroom. Instead, math and science were emphasized, and a very conscious effort emerged to develop a network of private schools that could compete in Turkey's relatively young private education market. In 1991, the community expanded to Central Asia and the Balkans, and by the mid-1990s, the GM owned and managed schools in Russia, Southeast Asia, sub-Saharan Africa, Australia, the United States, Western Europe, and Latin America.

Adding another level of engagement to its initiative, in 1994 the Gülen *cemaat* (community) embarked on what was to become a permanent public relations campaign by bringing together a large number of Turkey's most influential journalists, academicians, and other public intellectuals for a meeting of the minds in the mountain resort town of Abant. The "Abant platform" collectively asserted that Turkey's rival political factions hampered the country's political and economic development, and that "tolerance" and "dialogue" were necessary to move the country toward consensus. During this period, Gülen formed close relationships with many of Turkey's center-right and center-left political leaders, he met with high-profile religious leaders, including the Armenian patriarch and Pope John Paul II, and his followers began to establish themselves as emerging players in media, finance, and trade.

Following Turkey's infamous "28 February process" in 1997 (see below), the GM became a target for reactionary state forces. In 1999, Gülen was charged with being the leader of a clandestine organization that directly threatened the integrity of the Turkish state. The primary evidence in the case was a video excerpt leaked to the press in which Gülen allegedly instructed his community to "move in the arteries of the system, without anyone noticing your existence, until you reach all the power centers. … You must wait until such time as you have gotten all the state power, until you have brought to your side all the power of the constitutional institutions in Turkey."[1] By the time the clip aired on Turkish television Gülen had fled to the United States. And while he cited health reasons, his critics lambasted him for leaving the country instead of confronting the allegations directly. Gülen eventually responded as follows: "[B]ecause of conversations which were edited and intentionally misquoted in written articles, I am facing execution without trial" (*Turkish Daily News* 1999). Gülen has lived in the United States ever since. In August 2006, he was acquitted of all charges against him in Turkey.

In recent years, the GM has attracted international media attention because of the "mild" and "liberal" alternative to political Islam that GM schools provide to the world's Muslims (*Economist* 2008a, 2008b; Rabasa et al. 2006; Rabasa and Larabee 2008; Tavernise 2008). Critics, however, insist that GM schools are really missionary outposts spearheading a religiously motivated project of Turkish imperialism (Balcı 2003), or worse, that they are educating soldiers for an imminent Islamic revolution (Yanardağ 2006; Çetinkaya 2007; Krespin 2007, 2009; Rubin 2008; Schwartz 2008). What factors explain the GM's mobilization, and what are its ultimate aims? In order to critically address this question, it is necessary to first introduce readers to the structure of political and economic development in Turkey, and to the unique characteristics of Anatolian Islamic activism.

The Laic Republic and the Politicization of Islam in Turkey

After militarily forcing a second treaty with the Allies, Mustafa Kemal "Atatürk" (Father Turk, 1881–1938) oversaw the formal demise of the Ottoman Empire and the formation of the modern Republic of Turkey (est. 1923). Together with a single political party, the Cumhuriyet Halk Partisi (Republican People's Party, CHP), President Atatürk's grand ambition was to politically, economically, and culturally reform Ottoman state institutions in accordance with a "modern" model of society and governance that was rooted in *Turkish* rather than Islamic civilization. The most controversial of his early reforms, therefore, was the implementation of a rigid form of Turkish secularism that sought less to "separate church from state" than it did to inhibit religion in the public sphere. Modeled after French *laïcité*, Turkish *laiklik* (laicism) was intended to dramatically reengineer social and cultural identity in line with a singular and indivisible Turkish nation. To protect the new republic from perceived internal threats, the regime granted the TSK the powers of political oversight, which laid the foundation for a number of successful and failed military interventions (the above-mentioned April 2007 "e-memorandum" being only the most recent).

To oversee the implementation of laic social reforms, the regime created the Diyanet İşleri Başkanlığı (Directorate of Religious Affairs, Diyanet for short, est. 1924), a sprawling state bureaucracy with a twofold purpose: (1) to provide religious services to Turkish citizens and (2) to define acceptable interpretations of Islam in Turkish society. The Diyanet's authority replaced the caliphate (abolished in 1924) and *cemaatler* (communities) and *tarikatlar* (Sufi orders) (both outlawed in 1925). The abolishing of the former ended a thirteen-century tradition of leadership in Islamic civilization. The outlawing of the latter two legally restricted organizational practices that under the Ottomans "offered a mystical, emotional dimension that was lacking in the high religion of the *ulema* and [that] … served as networks offering cohesion, protection, and social mobility" (Zürcher 2004: 192).[2] Thus, in addition to facilitating the emergence of a universal identity rooted in ethnic Turkish nationalism, the Atatürk-CHP regime also politicized Islam and created the conditions for unyielding tension for generations to come.

Corporatism

As Atatürk struggled to cultivate a "collective conscience" based on the secular notion of ethnic nationalism, he was hampered by a contradiction between his desire to construct a pluralist modern democracy and his perceived necessity to develop an effective vanguard state bureaucracy (Heper 1985: 67–68). What eventually emerged was a centralized system of political and economic power "around singular and compulsory corporatist structures whose purpose was to increase government regulation and control rather than promote associational consultation" (Bianchi 1984: 101–2). In this context, *corporatism* in Turkey referred to a development ideology that viewed "liberalism ... as overly atomistic and consequently disruptive of social equilibrium, and [that viewed] the struggle and warfare, if not the sheer presence, of classes ... as detrimental to the maintenance of the social system" (Parla and Davidson 2004: 28). In 1925, labor unions and other trade associations were outlawed and opposition newspapers were closed. In 1931, the regime passed a new media law that stated the government could monitor and/or close any press organ that "published anything contradicting the 'general policies of the country'" (Zürcher 2004: 180). Economically, industrialization was concentrated in Istanbul, in the western provinces, and on the western half of the Mediterranean coast, and was managed by an alliance of state economic enterprises and a small number of family-based holding firms. A rapidly developing urban bourgeoisie emerged against an agrarian Anatolian backdrop where the influences of underground religious communities remained strong, and where access to social, political, and economic mobility was severely restricted (Heper 1985; Mardin 1989; Jacoby 2004; Zürcher 2004).

In 1946 Turkey reformed its electoral system and allowed the formation of opposition political parties. In the same year, the ban on collective associations was lifted, which led to the development of the İstanbul Tüccar Derneği (Association of Istanbul Traders) and to a number of independent trade unions. Zürcher (2004: 217) explains that much of these reforms were conscious on the part of the one-party regime, which wanted to stymie a growing opposition movement that demanded the expansion of political and economic freedoms. These attempts, however, proved insufficient. In the 1950 national elections, the newly formed Demokrat Parti (Democratic Party, DP, est. 1946) won an impressive 53 percent of the electorate, and subsequently an overwhelming majority of seats in parliament (Zürcher 2004: 217). And even though the DP's economic policies closely resembled those of the CHP, its political platform linking Islam, free enterprise, and social mobility resonated with Turkey's Anatolian heartland. For ten years, the DP dominated Turkey's state apparatus, and ultimately succumbed to power's corrupting influence. In May 1960, the DP was forced from power in a military coup and its leader, Adnan Menderes, was executed. The TSK's official position was that the "popularity of the DP was not 'real,' but derived from the exploitation of religious feelings ... and from their bolstering of undemocratic patron-client relationships" (Heper 1985: 85).

In 1961, Turkey ratified a new constitution, which further pluralized the electoral system, expanded freedoms of the press and association, and created the conditions necessary for the rise of new collective actors (Bianchi 1984; Yeşilada 1988; Jacoby 2004; Zürcher 2004). Public debate, however, were quickly marred by a tendency toward ideological rigidity, and by the early 1970s, open conflict between left and right factions enveloped Turkey's major cities. This situation was overshadowed only by the fact that the TSK began and ended the 1970s with the country's second and third military coups.

Turkish Islamic Activism and the Legacy of Said Nursi

I define Islamic activism as the political and/or social mobilization of actors who deploy an Islamic discourse to express their aspirations for social change. By using the term "activism" I mean to include overtly political (i.e., parties, insurrectionary groups, etc.) and more culturally and economically active revivalist movements. In Turkey, Islamic activism emerged in its political guise in the cracks of the left/right divide of the 1960s and 1970s. In 1969, the Milli Görüş Hareketi (National Vision movement) emerged, and soon thereafter, its leader, Necmettin Erbakan (b. 1926), established Turkey's first "Islamist" political party, the Milli Nizam Partisi (National Order Party, MNP). In the context of the 1971 coup, the MNP was perceived as a threat and was closed by Turkey's Constitutional Court, a fate that three successor parties have suffered since. After the third MNP successor, Fazilet Partisi (Virtue Party, FP), was closed in 2001, a generational divide in the National Vision movement led to the emergence of two new parties, the Erbakan-led Saadet Partisi (Felicity Party, SP) and the younger-generation AKP (see below). The reasoning behind the split had to do with the National Vision movement's rigidity in terms of its Islamic worldview, which, despite being reformed in the 1990s, was still quite polarizing. Thus, despite his success in creating an Islamic political identity in Turkey, Erbakan's partisan strategies were less effective at fostering an individually oriented religious revival (Yavuz 2003a). This responsibility fell upon underground *cemaatler*, whose long-established connections were deeper and more diffuse than the party's, and whose stated objectives focused less on politics and more on social and cultural revival. Before the 1980 coup, the followers of "Bediüzzaman" (wonder of the age) Said Nursi constituted one of Turkey's most influential Islamic communities and set the stage for the emergence of Fethullah Gülen (Mardin 1989; Yavuz 2000, 2003a, 2003b).

Despite being a traditionally trained Islamic scholar, Said Nursi was an active participant in Turkey's nationalist project. In regard to the new Turkish government, however, Nursi became "dismayed to find a lax and indifferent attitude toward Islam and their religious duties among many of the deputies in the assembly" (Vahide 2005: 169). He called on the new government to account for the loss of the caliphate by assuring Turkish citizens that their sovereign nation was a Muslim nation. Aware of his influence, Atatürk tried to co-opt the leader by offering him a position in the Diyanet. Nursi declined. Instead, he reformulated a failed pitch he made to the Ottoman sultan in 1907 for government funding to construct a "modern Islamic university" in eastern Anatolia. His efforts were defeated in 1925 (Vahide 2005: 172). For the next twenty years, Nursi devoted himself almost entirely to study. Contrasting the "old Said's" life as a political activist and warrior, the "new Said" focused on the "greater *cihad*," which in Sufi Islam referred to the soul's internal struggle with the self (*nefs*). Drawing from his Nakşibendi roots, Nursi contended that Muslims had strayed from the straight path, and that it was necessary for the *umma* (community of Muslims) to return to Islam and to concentrate on the inner struggle against the corrupting influences of materialism, positivism, and moral decay. This message deeply affected an alienated Anatolian countryside that viewed its role in Turkey's modernization as marginal at best. The Nur community was, therefore, an influential collective supporter of the DP in the 1950s; but with the exception of this period, Nursi spent most of his adult life in exile and/or under house arrest. His teachings were banned, and shortly after his death in 1960, his tomb was moved to an undisclosed location.

Over the course of his life, Nursi authored a number of commentaries on Islam that his followers later collected into a volume titled the *Risale-i Nur Collection*. Recreating their identity through text, Nursi's followers began meeting in small groups to read and discuss the collection. Known as a *ders* (lesson), the Nur modified the Nakşibendi tradition of direct oral transmission from sheikh to disciple by disseminating knowledge at a dershane (lesson house, i.e., informal reading group).[3] Because the *Risale-i Nur Collection* was written in Ottoman Turkish, instead of in Arabic or in Nursi's native Kurdish, the *dershane* also provided an alternative foundation upon which to construct a modern *Muslim* identity in laic Turkey, an "embryo of civil society" that facilitated a shift from an Ottoman (universal) to a Turkish (national) sense of piety and belonging (Yavuz 2003b: 8).[4]

Although never having met Said Nursi, the young Fethullah Gülen was influenced by the Nur tradition, and in the late twentieth century the GM became Turkey's most influential offshoot of the Nur phenomenon. Gülen's followers, however, go to great lengths to distinguish their leader from his predecessor.[5] While misleading, such efforts are also practical, as GM followers strive to preempt attacks from their enemies, who consciously seek to slander them with titles such as "Nurcu," "Gülenci," and "Fethullahcı."[6] But if connections still exist, what factors distinguish Gülen from Nursi? The answer is found in the applied strategies that Gülen's followers employ to affect a twenty-first-century passive revolution.

Battling for Position: The Case of the GM in Turkey

From Islamism to Conservative Democracy

The 1980 military coup was a watershed event in Turkey's economic and political development. Responding to mass urban violence, the military arrested an estimated thirty thousand people in the coup's first month alone (Zürcher 2004). As an antidote to ideological conflict, the military government implemented a preexisting social policy that was developed by the conservative Intellectuals' Hearth Association. Its view was that in order to steer Turkey toward national consensus, the ruling elite needed to reform the outdated articulation of classless, laic Turkish nationalism, and replace it with a more carefully constructed ideology:

[One] aimed at overriding particularistic interests by stressing the dangers of anarchy and social divisions to the family, nation, and state ... a new ideology [created] out of Ottoman, Islamic, and Turkish popular culture ... that reinterpreted the state as being integral to the nation and society, [and that deployed] Ottoman-Islamic symbols to make the past seem relevant to the present. (Yavuz 2003a: 71)

This new brand of Turkish-Islamic nationalism was codified in a new constitution based on a "Turkish-Islamic synthesis," which created the foundation for a return to civilian governance in 1983 (Yavuz 2003a, 2006).

These new social policies coincided with new economic policies that sought to overhaul Turkish protectionism in favor of deeper integration with the global economy. This created the necessary preconditions for the emergence of a new, export-oriented economic elite in Turkey's rapidly industrializing interior. Unlike their counterparts in Istanbul, however, this new elite organized into regionally defined trade associations that received no subsidies from Ankara, and that relied primarily on the *global* marketplace for expanding their business model. Also unlike Istanbul's primary firms, most framed their enterprises in accordance with their religious leanings, which led to their collective recognition as Turkey's emergent "Islamic bourgeoisie" (Buğra 1994; Özbudun and Keyman 2002; Demir et al. 2004; Özcan and Çokgezen 2003, 2006; Yavuz 2006). Channeling Max Weber, this new cohort of Turkish entrepreneurs framed their professional life and business pursuits as somehow fulfilling the moral and ethical dictates of their Islamic faith. They redistributed their wealth through religious community networks, they invested profits in parallel social programs, private schools, and international lobbying, and ultimately they organized as a politically conscious interest group. Moreover, as Özcan and Çokgezen (2006: 147) explain, "the spread of Islamic companies and their promised moral economic revival took root in social institutions often under the guiding leadership of a paternal figure who had indisputable authority and recognition." By the early 1990s, it became clear that Fethullah Gülen enjoyed such authority and recognition (see below).

The political consciousness of Turkey's Islamic bourgeoisie was central to the National Vision movement's political success in the early 1990s (Gülalp 2001). By that time, Erbakan's Refah Partisi (Welfare Party, RP) had begun to downplay Islam and to promote free trade, democracy, and "moral values" in its stead. Nonetheless, despite its reformed discourse, the RP was still considered Turkey's primary

"Islamist threat," and in 1997, the TSK intervened in Turkish politics for a fourth time to force the RP from power in what was later dubbed the "28 February process." After the RP's overthrow and the banning of its successor, the FP, in 2001, a younger generation of National Vision politicians formed the AKP. These politicians were aware of the opportunities provided by Turkey's global integration, of its bid to join the European Union (EU), and of its continued economic growth through export. For these reasons, the AKP dropped its call for an "Islamic alternative" altogether, and advocated instead for something called "conservative democracy." According to the AKP leader, Recep Tayyip Erdoğan, conservative democracy is "a concept of modernity that does not reject tradition ... that accepts localism ... that does not disregard a spiritual meaning of life, and ... that is not fundamentalist" (2006: 335). By fusing progressive globalism with traditional conservatism, the AKP managed to win a parliamentary majority (34 percent) and to form a single-party government in 2002. It repeated its success by an even larger margin (47 percent) in 2007. The AKP did this by "keeping together both the winners and the losers of the neo-liberal globalization process," that is, by appealing across regional, class, and ethnic divides, and by insisting that however conservative, *it was not Islamist* (Öniş 2009: 2).

I contend that the GM mobilizes as the most significant power base in the AKP's new conservative democratic coalition, and is a direct contributor to the AKP's ability to "not stop and keep going" (*Durmak yok, yola devam*). Spearheaded by an alliance of new political and economic elites, I argue that together the AKP and the GM have mounted an effective campaign to gain control over the creation and manipulation of Turkish public opinion in education, media, and politics, and have thus managed to maintain their legitimacy by succeeding at accomplishing two goals: (1) bridging social conservatism with international neoliberalism (i.e., popular Islam with democracy, free markets, human rights, etc.) and (2) aligning the AKP's foreign policy of "strategic depth" (i.e., its policy to broaden Turkey's bilateral relations with its regional neighbors, and with developing countries in Africa and Southeast Asia) with the GM's efforts to deepen Turkey's cultural and economic relationships with developing countries the world over. As a coalition, the GM and the AKP constitute the leadership of Turkish conservative democracy, and via mutual support, they wage an effective war of position against the country's entrenched power elite.[7] Below I draw from field data collected from GM students, teachers, authors, journalists, bankers, and businessmen to illustrate the movement's impact in the new Turkey.

The Charisma of Fethullah Gülen

At the beginning of each of his books Gülen's editors write a brief hagiography about the author. In addition to these shorter pieces, there are a few larger hagiographies about him (Can 1996; Ünal 2005; Ergene 2005, 2008), a small number of available interviews (Akman 2004; Gündem 2005; Sarıtoprak 2005), an increasing number of internally produced articles and books (Ünal and Williams 2000; Yavuz and Esposito 2003; Sarıtoprak and Griffith 2005; Hunt and Aslandoğan 2007 Carroll 2007; Yurtsever 2008), and a small number of academic studies (Yavuz 1999, 2003a; Aras and Çaha 2000; Agai 2003, Balcı 2003; Turam 2004a, 2004b, 2006; White 2004; Park 2008; Hendrick 2008, 2009, 2011, 2013) that are focused on the GM's growth and impact. Considering the GM's influence in Turkish society, the success of GM schools around the world, and the growing international prestige of its leader, what factors explain the lack of an academically rigorous biography of Turkey's most influential living personality?

According to Max Weber, charismatic leaders are unique because they emerge in times of crisis. In the absence of crisis, charismatic figures tend to create the illusion of crisis "through their own actions by exaggerating existing deficiencies or threats to the environment" (Shamir and Howell 1999: 261). Unlike Gramsci's "organic intellectual," who must prove his worth rationally through verifiable facts and supportive evidence, charismatic leaders must prove themselves by performing miracles: "The charismatic hero derives his authority … by proving his power in practice. … Most of all, his divine mission must prove itself by bringing well-being to his faithful followers; if they do not fare well, he obviously is not the god-sent master" (Weber [1922] 1978: 1114). Gülen proves his powers by overseeing the GM's expansion, which is framed by his followers as evidence of his grace: Fethullah Gülen … possesses powers that an average educated person, an average person with average intelligence, could not possibly imagine. It is God-given. … If you find a more learned person in the world I would like to meet him. (field interview, July 2007).

In an effort not to reduce Gülen's appeal to subjective feelings of helplessness and frustration, Enes Ergene argues that "the Gülen movement did not rise upon the values of a past movement or period of crisis. The movement has produced its own appearance, structure, social and moral values, and institutions" (2008: 40). It is thus important that the world understands Gülen's appeal to be entirely original, and the GM to be neither reactionary nor a continuation of a preexisting project (i.e., the Nur movement). This is interesting when considering Gülen's account of modern Turkey:

> For several centuries ... our society has had the appearance of a wreck. It has been searching for an alternative system of order and thought in education, art, and morality. ... Now let me ask you earnestly how and with what we should overcome this moral misery ... and how we should overcome the crises which form an even stronger and deeper whirlpool in ourselves as the days pass? (Gülen 2005: 105–6)

Gülen's answer is to empower a "golden generation" (*altın nesil*) of "ideal humans" (*ideal insanlar*) who will emulate the perfection of the prophet Mohammad, and who will lead Turkey toward a brighter future. Such a generation will emerge thanks to the dedication of numerous "volunteers" under whose leadership humanity can prepare for the end of times:

> Not ordinary people, but rather people devoted to divine reality ... people who by putting into practice their thoughts ... dedicated spirits ... who wander like [the archangel] *İsrafil* ... on the verge of blowing the last trumpet in order to prepare dead spirits for the Day of Resurrection. ... This can be regarded as our final attempt ... nations that have been wrung with various crises have also been awaiting such a breeze of hope ... how fortunate are the ones whose breasts are receptive to this breeze. (Gülen 2004: 105–10)

Despite Ergene's claims to the contrary, Gülen both invents and embellishes upon the crisis that he purports to address. And typical of all charismatic leaders, he surrounds himself with a tight network of loyal lieutenants who promote and legitimize the larger charismatic movement.

Weber defines the cadre of the most devoted as a charismatic leader's "aristocracy," his "select group of adherents who are united by discipleship and loyalty and chosen according to personal charismatic qualification" (Weber [1922] 1978: 1119). Gülen's aristocracy is composed of individuals who were educated at the GM's original student dormitories in İzmir and Istanbul in the 1970s and early 1980s, and who are now highly successful authors, journalists, editors, and businessmen. Gülen's role vis-à-vis this inner *cemaat* (community) is to provide "advice" and "guidance" rather than management:

He says, "It would be good if it is done," he never says, "It must be done." For instance, he says, "In our age, media and television are of the utmost importance." Or he says, for example ... "Why don't you open a bank?" He never says "you." The person addressed may say there is no money. But a businessman can do it. ... So he might not have the money. But if he [Gülen] says something, we believe that it is very important, and we have to do it. (field interview, March 2007)

While I was in residence at the *Akademi* (Academy), the GM's central ideational node in Istanbul—an all-in-one think tank, publishing house, school, library, and mosque—I observed, interviewed, and became friends with a number of loyal lieutenants in the GM's inner *cemaat*. I interviewed editors, translators, writers, veteran teachers and administrators, and several of Fethullah Gülen's first-generation students who are now high-level authority figures in the movement.[8] It was from such people that I learned how and for what purposes the GM marketized its activities, how and why it expanded to Central Asia, and why, in the interests of growth, the movement transnationalized to Africa, Southeast Asia, Europe, the United States, and South America to proselytize "ideal humanity" by way of *temsil* (passive persuasion).

Competition and the Opportunity of Education

The GM's first private schools were founded in 1982 in İzmir and Istanbul. A first-generation aristocrat at *Akademi* explained that the vision for these institutions was a market rationalization of religious persecution:

[During the 1980–83 coup] Hocaefendi was inspired by a verse in the Koran. ... This shows that Hocaefendi acted in accordance with the primary sources of religion ... he changed the legal condition of the dorm and turned it into a school and registered it as private property. He gathered a board of directors consisting of businessmen. So that school wasn't taken by the military government because it was the property of a corporation. This school became a model for future schools. Anybody who wanted to open a [Gülen] school started a company and owned a school in the name of that company. It then spread abroad. (field interview, March 2007)

In its first year, the GM's Fatih High School in Istanbul sent over 85 percent of its senior class to a university and is now one of Istanbul's most reputable private education institutions, with six elementary schools, five high schools, and four dormitories.[9] Similarly, in 2008 students from İzmir's Yamanlar High School took home forty-five national and international science and math medals, including a gold medal at the thirty-ninth annual International Physics Olympiad in Hanoi.[10] Now operating ten institutions, Yamanlar's 2008 graduating middle school students earned more points on Turkey's high school placement exam than did any other middle school in Turkey, a fact that helps explain the GM's comparative advantage in the contest for Turkey's youth.

Indeed, the importance of Turkey's competitive education system cannot be overstated in regard to the GM's emergence. As of 2012, compulsory education in Turkey lasts eight years (raised from five in 1997), and high school and university placement are both regulated by a rigorous examination system (Aksit 2006; Şimşek and Yıldırım 2004; Tansel 2013; Tansel and Bircan 2003). First administered in 1973, the Öğrenci Seçme Sınavı (Student Selection Exam, ÖSS) has a tremendous impact on a student's prospects for social mobility. One's score determines the university s/he is eligible to attend, and if s/he performs poorly, s/he must wait a year to retake the exam. In 2003, 1.5 million students took the ÖSS, but only approximately 21.5 percent (311,498) scored high enough on the exam to place in a university (Tansel and Bircan 2006: 2). In 2009, 30,000 students scored a zero (Güngör 2009). In 2012, 1,895,478 students took Turkey's new Student Selection and Placement Exam, and only approximately 19 percent (360,140) made it to a university classroom (Tansel 2013: 12).[11]

Because of the ÖSS's primary importance, Turkey developed a private supplemental education system to teach to the test. Known as *dershaneler* (lesson houses, not to be confused with the Nur dershane), supplemental education companies in Turkey now comprise a highly profitable industry. In 2002, the total out-of-pocket expenditure for private *dershane* instruction was 650 million US dollars, nearly 12 percent of the country's personal expenditure (World Bank 2005: 21). In 2004, the average cost for a private *dershane* course was 4,711 US dollars (World Bank 2005: 21), despite a 6,700 US dollars per capita purchasing parity (CIA World Factbook 2004). Considering their competition, therefore, *dershane* companies go to great lengths to advertise their students' successes on billboards, bus and building advertisements, and in print media across the country. By 2007, the GM affiliated FEM Dershanesi (est. 1985) and its sister organization, Sevgi Çiçeği Anafen (Beloved Flowers, Primary Science) had become the country's market leaders.[12]

The market growth and success of GM-affiliated *dershane* institutions continued until late 2013 when, on November 17, GM-affiliated media published a front-page story detailing the AKP's efforts to close all *dershane* exam prep schools in Turkey.[13] Widely interpreted as evidence that the growing rift between the GM and the AKP was reaching existential intensity, as this volume went to press in July 2014 the future of Turkey's *dershane* system (and the GM's role within it) remained in serious doubt.

Social Networking and the Power of a Good Product

Lin defines social capital as "resources embedded in a social structure, which are accessed and/or mobilized in purposive actions" (1999: 35). Focusing on the saliency of social networks in regard to the generation of social capital, Passy argues that after being socialized into a movement, individuals "find themselves in an interactive structure that enables them to define and redefine their interpretive frames, [to] facilitate the process of identity-building and identity-strengthening, and [to] create or solidify political consciousness" (2003: 24). Only after strengthening one's collective identity, therefore, can actors in a network make use of the "structural connections" between institutions and individuals, and subsequently invest their accumulated social capital. In the GM, structural connections provide new recruits with access to a subsidized education, subsidized room and board, and a postgraduate network of professional opportunities.

In addition to its "official" education institutions (i.e., schools, *dershaneler*), extra tutoring is offered at GM *ışık evleri* (houses of light), subsidized apartments occupied by four to six university students who have been recruited into the "golden generation." While studying, visiting students are asked if they would like to participate in a *sohbet* (religious conversation), which in the GM constitutes a rearticulated Nur *ders* where participants meet regularly to recite and discuss the teachings of Said Nursi and Fethullah Gülen. Similar to the Nur *ders*, *sohbet* groups function as social networking sites that connect people and information within the movement. After scoring well on the ÖSS, GM-affiliated *dershane* teachers inquire about students' intended living arrangements when they attend a university. Freshmen students are offered a subsidized room at a GM *ışık evi*, and after moving in, they are asked to tutor younger students, to attend *sohbet*, and to participate in the community established at the house. When a student does this, s/he has been recruited into the GM network.

According to Gülen, ışık evleri are where "ideal humans" are conditioned to appreciate the challenges of the modern world and the role of faith in one's personal life. They are places "where deficiencies of people that may have been caused by their human characteristics are closed up ... sacred places where plans and projects are produced, the continuality of the metaphysical tension is provided and courageous and faithful persons are raised" (Gülen 1998: 12). In this way, *ışık evleri* function as primary institutions for GM socialization, as sites where individuals are conditioned to become a member of God's "cavalry of light":

> This cavalry of the light ... is now competing ... to turn those dry hearts that crave tolerance and love into the gardens of Paradise. ... They take such great pains to succeed in worldly affairs that people who see these valiant ones take them to be people of the world unaware of the Hereafter. When they see the love in them, however, they think of them as being of those of the highest rank. (Gülen 2004: 106)

Selim, an editor at *Akademi* who lived and worked at GM schools in Albania for seven years, explained how Gülen's concept of an *ışık evi* is intended to impact new recruits:

> Let's say a group of university students come together, stay together ... they have the same opinion, Hocaefendi's and Said Nursi's opinions ... you call it a "house of light." In such a place, for example, naturally, you don't watch everything on TV, like you know, obscene things ... or maybe you don't have a television at all ... you have, let's say, ahhhhh ... parallel opinions with your friends, you pray, nobody drinks ... when you compare it to a traditional, common house or apartment where students live ... they bring in their girl-friends, they watch pornographic movies, sometimes they have alcohol. Then you compare such things ... in one of them you pray, and you know, you read such books of Said Nursi and Hocaefendi ... you pray ... there is some spiritual pride. (field interview, January 2007)

In their ideal form, "houses of light" are sites where individuals learn to "succeed in worldly affairs" and where they are conditioned to exude themselves with "spiritual pride."

The above, however, is merely what Gülen and his aristocrats claim the GM should be, not necessarily what it is. I argue that on the ground the GM is a fluid and adapting organization of autonomous institutions that collectively "win" the allegiance of many by offering high-quality services in a competitive market economy. In addition to "sacrificing" individuality, young recruits also find access to potentially limitless professional opportunities. Moreover, even if an individual takes advantage of such opportunities, this does not mean that s/he is destined to become a devoted and loyal recruit. It does, however, mean that s/he will likely reap some sort of reward, and will thus likely come to sympathize with the GM's overall aims. As the below examples indicate, the GM's social network is organized via multiple spheres of belonging, from the most devoted to the only mildly affiliated.

Lale is a literature major who attended the GM's Maltepe Dershanesi in Ankara to prepare for the ÖSS. She explained that she originally did not want to go to Maltepe because she knew of its affiliation with the GM, and "did not want anything to do with them" (field interview, July 2007). Based on a pretest, however, Lale qualified for two tuition scholarships, one at Maltepe and one at another institution. She accepted the latter. Lale explained that after watching unmotivated students treat the course more like a social space than a study hall, however, she made the switch to Maltepe despite her misgivings. At the GM school, Lale said that there were always extra courses, extra help, and one-on-one lessons: "They force you to study ... there are intense interactions with the students. At other *dershanes*, people are not forced to study, it is up to them. At Maltepe, you are constantly watched and told to study" (field interview, July 2007). After scoring exceedingly well on the ÖSS, Lale earned a seat at Turkey's prestigious Boğaziçi University. Just before she moved to Istanbul, Lale received a phone call from one of her teachers at Maltepe, who offered Lale a spot in a GM *ışık evi*. After some thinking, Lale accepted because university dorms were very expensive and overcrowded, and because she had friends who had to leave school because they went into debt and she did not want to have a similar fate. For two years, Lale lived in a subsidized rental that was close to campus and that was "worth the sacrifice." And while she described her experience with the GM as "a really, really prolonged visit," she also said that living in the *ışık evi* was "good for her actually," because she was "never lonely" and because she enjoyed how much "everyone shared everything." When she began talking about the constant visitors at the house, however, Lale explained that her life with the GM was also quite troubling:

> There was one time when I did not sleep for over a week, but it was my own psychology. ... When they talk about "self-sacrifice," this is what they mean. Teachers work long hours for little or no extra pay, college students give free tutoring to [GM-affiliated] *dershane* students, people go out of their way to help others when it inconveniences them. I was the only person who had a problem with everyone coming and going all the time. (field interview, July 2007)

For Lale, participating in the GM had nothing to do with Islam; it was about opportunity, social mobility, and subsidized living. When she felt that her discomfort outweighed the rewards, she left. But despite her reasons for leaving, Lale made sure to let me know that she still had friends who lived at GM *ışık evleri*, and that even though she smoked cigarettes, drank alcohol, and was not a practicing Muslim, they regularly let her know that she was always welcome to return.

Yusef, a university student in Istanbul who was recruited into the GM network as a high school student in Azerbaijan, explained that reality on the ground is sometimes even further from Gülen's ideal:

> There are some students who use the movement for their own benefit. They try to appear better to their eyes. They are not the way they seem to be. They claim to be good people. I don't know, maybe they have some plans for the future. After graduation, if you ask for a job, *Hizmet* offers you one. (field interview, February 2007)

A similar trend of rational opportunism emerged with thematic regularity. For every "ideal human" who lived at a GM *ışık evi*, there was another who used the resources provided by such an affiliation for his or her own benefit. When I mentioned this observation to a GM aristocrat at *Akademi*, I was told that even if a person does not become totally dedicated, at least they will become socialized as a "friend" (*arkadaş*), and will look upon their experience as a service that deserves remembrance. When they become professionals in their own right, the hope is that the GM can rely on them as a potential client, financial supporter, or, at the very least, a sympathetic voice in the context of public suspicion/scrutiny.

Emerging Markets = Emerging Opportunities

Living at a GM *ışık evi* exposes individuals to a social and economic network that extends throughout Anatolia and, since the mid-1990s, throughout the world. In a process that began by funding schools in Turkey, in 1991 the GM expanded to Central Asia and the Balkans. Affiliated entrepreneurs in Turkey's emergent Anatolian bourgeoisie set up trade networks that used inroads established by GM schools and *ışık evleri* to facilitate the development of local trade relationships. Later in the decade, this model was extended to over one hundred countries. The companies formed to outfit GM schools led to the development of Kaynak Holding (est. 1983). While originally dependent on GM schools, by 2007 Kaynak had become Turkey's largest producer, distributor, and exporter of education products and is involved in publishing, information communication technologies, retail, paper, shipping, tourism, furniture, textiles, construction, and insurance. A Kaynak executive explained the holding's diversification as follows:

> Let's analyze a human being. A human has many needs. This holding developed in that way. The first occupation of the holding was books, then audiocassettes in İzmir. When the schools opened, there was [a] need for technical equipment and stationery. When there was demand, people started to manufacture these. I was visiting the schools since I saw them as the primary customers of this holding, and then I noticed that some publishers already started to publish [to] the needs of the schools. You see, this is a market, an economic sector. (field interview, March 2007)

The first of Kaynak's ventures was in cultural publishing and printing, which both started in İzmir in the early 1970s. Zambak Publishing later organized the corporation's academic publications (e.g., textbooks, etc.), and Sürat English Language Training (SELT) organized all English-language publication needs. Among its most successful brands was Sürat Teknoloji, a highly competitive ICT firm that became an IBM global partner and that has developed a diversified portfolio that includes completed projects for the city of Istanbul, the United States Agency for International Development (USAID), and the United Nations.[14] As a corporation, by 2007 Kaynak exported its products globally and managed offices in fourteen cities around the world.[15]

When I asked a long-time confidant of Fethullah Gülen about the logic of the GM's economic network, he explained as follows:

> You are a businessman, okay. Here are ten million people around the world, okay. If you are a businessman, you shall either sell something, or you offer a service. Okay. Out of ten million who will need your service, they will come to you first. Why? Because they know about your character. You are already two steps ahead of your competition with these people. (field interview, July 2007)

In Southeast Asia, GM followers set up the Pasifik Ülkeleri ile Sosyal ve İktisadi Dayanışma Derneği (Association for Social and Economic Cooperation between Pacific Asian Countries, PASİAD). Based in Istanbul, PASİAD centralizes the organization of GM schools in Thailand, Malaysia, Indonesia, and the Philippines, and has hosted and/or organized receptions for finance ministers and state elites from Singapore, Korea, Japan, Thailand, Indonesia, and Malaysia.[16] For Africa, GM loyalists started a similar organization, the Türkiye Afrika Ülkeleri Kültürel Sosyal ve Ekonomik İşbirliği Derneği (Turkey-African Countries Cultural, Social, and Economic

Development Association, AKSİAD), which, in 2007, coordinated trade, education, and social services throughout the African continent.[17] In 2005, 124 separate Anatolian regional associations representing over ten thousand businessmen came together to form Turkey's largest business-related NGO, the Türkiye İşadamları ve Sanayiciler Konfederasyonu (Turkish Confederation of Businessmen and Industrialists, TUSKON). TUSKON has since organized a series of trade conferences with Central Asia (September 2006), the Asia-Pacific (April 2007, June 2008), and Africa (May 2006, 2007, 2008), among others. At TUSKON's 2007 Turkey-Africa trade summit, Turkish and African businessmen signed two billion dollars in trade contracts, which equated to approximately one-third of Turkey's trade volume with Africa in the same year (TUSKON 2007). Two years later, a TUSKON trade delegation visited Kenya and Tanzania, and in two days Turkish and African businessmen signed over five hundred million dollars in trade contracts. Considering the AKP's policy to deepen Turkish interests in Africa, the former AKP deputy and current Turkish president, Abdullah Gül, accompanied the delegation. According to TUSKON's president, Rızanur Meral, Gül's participation during the trip was pivotal to its success, as it legitimized TUSKON's activities as having the full support of the Turkish state (*Today's Zaman* 2009). Meral has also noted on several occasions the crucial role played by "Turkish schools" around the world, which allow affiliated exporters to establish close relationships in foreign markets:

> Foreign trade is being conducted by graduates of these schools, who are integrated with the global world both culturally and economically. They are cooperating with Turkish businessmen or working in companies established by Turks [abroad]. I can securely call the graduates of the Turkish schools 'trade ambassadors'. (*Today's Zaman* 2007)

"Değirmenin suyu nereden geliyor?"

Since it began in 2005, TUSKON's primary sponsor has been the GM's Bank Asya (BA) (formerly Asya Finance, an "Islamic finance" institution that began in 1996 upon the advice of Fethullah Gülen: "Hocaefendi said it would be beneficial for [businessmen], for their future enterprises, and he asked them to pray. So people came together and [Bank Asya] started in this way" (field interview, July 2007). BA is now Turkey's largest "participation bank," with assets totaling more than four billion dollars. In May 2006, BA publicly sold

20 percent of its assets despite a demand that was 50 percent higher. When considering BA's growth and expansion, the answer to the ever-elusive question, "Değirmenin suyu nereden geliyor?" (Where does the water for the mill come from?) comes into view.

First, all individuals loyal to Fethullah Gülen donate some portion of their income to the movement's continuation. Donation is called *himmet* (voluntary religious donation), and is collected from followers and affiliates alike:

> I go to what they call *sohbet* … where we talk about religion and values. And you see a face come from another town, and they started a school. And they thought that they could finish with the budget they had, but it's not finished. … They go around once, and they count the money. The brother says that he will take anything, but that they need this much. In one round, short. Second round, this much more. Third round, this much more. He then counts how much he needs, and gives the rest back. Then they [the rest of the group] says, "No! You keep this, you keep the extra too, because you made the wrong calculations and now you may need it." This was my first experience. This happened fifteen years ago. (field interview, July 2007)

As mentioned above, *sohbet* groups are sites where GM loyalists meet to create community, to recruit followers, and to reproduce social networks. At higher levels, however, *sohbet* groups also function as pitch meetings for collecting investment/bailout capital for various GM projects. Like other social norms in the GM (e.g., attending *sohbet*, living at an *ışık evi*, tutoring younger students, and obtaining a working knowledge of Gülen's and Nursi's teachings), giving *himmet* is a signifier of one's dedication to the "community," which has both social and economic returns.

According to Osman Bey, a managing editor at *Akademi* who worked as a principal at a number of GM schools in Tajikistan in the 1990s, this model of redistributing wealth through social networks is best understood as a system of "friendship marketing." Within such a model, the tendency to seek guidance from a religious leader is an efficient way to assure who one's friends are:

> People from the Gülen movement have needs. … Someone has to fulfill these needs, and people want to do this business. Let's say the bank. How many banks went bankrupt in the last twenty years in Turkey? Many. A religious leader has to find a solution to these problems for the people. … He must give people hope and guide them. … [Gülen] said … "Only if some reliable businessmen come and found a noninterest bank, approvable by Islam." He only suggested this. After this, the listeners of these ideas … came together from Antep, Istanbul, etc., and decided to found a bank. … There was advice and it was carried out. … Schools are a different entity, Kaynak is a different

entity. … There's Sema Hospital, it's a different entity, too. Its management is separate. Do they make some contracts between them? Yes, they do, but it's a trade-based relationship. (field interview, February 2007)

The GM collects, invests, and produces value via a network of mutually cooperative enterprises. Once a school, company, or institution is self-sustaining, *himmet* funding is no longer required, and market rationality can take over. Social and economic ties between these institutions provide Turkey's conservative democratic coalition with an economic base from which it can draw to reproduce its influence and expand its position. These ties are promoted and reproduced, moreover, through affiliated media, which works to manufacture consent in the new conservative democratic Turkish republic.

Friendship Marketing and Media: Mapping the Conservative Democratic Coalition

The literature on Muslim politics agrees that when possible, Islamic activists focus on expressing themselves through media (Eickelman and Piscatori 1996; Mandaville 2001, 2006; Eickelman and Anderson 2003; Yavuz 2003a; Cooke and Lawrence 2005; Hefner 2004; Wiktorowicz 2004). With the rise of the AKP in 2002, however, a new era began. The AKP's victory coincided with a new law that allowed private media conglomerates to expand their enterprises into other sectors. Kaya and Cornell explain that this led to an environment whereby media moguls sought favors from the government, "given the expectation that their media outlets' attitude toward the government could influence their chances in privatization tenders" (2008: 2). This granted the AKP the ability to employ "soft state power" when deciding whether "to accord or not accord various companies the licenses and tenders they seek" (2008: 2). Lending evidence to this analysis was the ownership transfer of Turkey's second-largest media conglomerate, ATV-*Sabah*, which was seized by the Turkish government in April 2007 and sold to the GM-affiliated Çalık Group for 1.1 billion US dollars later the same year. In addition to its close relationship with the GM, allegations of nepotism over the ATV-*Sabah* deal reached a global audience, as Prime Minister Erdoğan's son-in-law was the Çalık Group's general director. This was compounded by an unprecedented 750 million dollars in state-administered loans that the AKP secured for Çalık to complete the deal in December 2007.

In addition to being Turkey's newest media mogul, in early 2008 the Çalık Group's CEO, Ahmet Çalık, was also the single largest shareholder in the GM's Bank Asya, and was Turkey's primary figure atop a 2.4 billion dollar corporation whose business spanned from textiles, power/electricity, and pipeline construction to mainstream news and entertainment media (Hayward 2007).[18] With a history dating back to the 1930s, it was not until the early 1990s, when Çalık expanded its operations into Turkmenistan, that it became one of Turkey's most influential corporate actors. There, Çalık funded a number of GM schools, supported the production and distribution of a Turkmen edition of Feza's *Zaman* newspaper (see below), and eventually became a close personal advisor to the Turkmen dictator Saparmurat Niyasov "Turkmenbashı" (Mamedov 2005: 58). After diversifying into energy in the mid-1990s, Çalık went global and became a major shareholder in the Trans-Anatolian Pipeline (TAPCO) project, which broke ground in April 2007. The TAPCO project will make use of preexisting passageways created by the 1,776 kilometer Baku-Tbilisi-Ceyhan pipeline, which was lobbied for heavily by Ahmet Çalık with overt support from the US government (Fried 2007; Roberts 2004).

Before the AKP's rise in 2002, the Çalık Group was relatively unknown to nonbusiness elites. Since 2002, however, Çalık has become a regular feature in Turkish media, especially since its 2008 takeover of ATV-*Sabah*. The most readily available coverage of Çalık's dealings, however, is found in one particular newspaper, the GM's *Zaman Gazetesi*. *Zaman* is the flagship brand under Feza Gazetecilik (Feza Media Group), a news corporation with modest beginnings in 1986 that by 2007 was overseeing Turkey's most circulated news daily (*Zaman*), Turkey's most widely circulated news magazine (*Aksiyon*), and Turkey's most widely read English-language news source (*Today's Zaman*).[19] In 2007, Feza's CEO, Ali Akbulut, was also Bank Asya's supervisory budget auditor and a majority BA shareholder. Together, Çalık and Akbulut emerged to rival Turkey's primary media moguls in the production of manufactured consent in Turkish society.[20]

Manufacturing Consent

A first-generation student of Fethullah Gülen explained the GM's initial interest in media as follows:

> A crowd of people consisting of students at the schools plus their families ... the people who listened to Hocaefendi's preachings in the mosques of İzmir and Istanbul, in Sultanahmet, Suleymaniye, etc. People overcrowded the mosques and not everybody could listen to him. And there was a need to inform people correctly. ... So, a more general medium was needed. Media fulfilled this. (field interview, March 2007)

While its original intent might have been to promote Gülen's teachings, in the mid-1990s, at Gülen's request, a handful of young GM recruits attended journalism school in the United States. Upon their return in 2001, *Zaman* underwent what one interviewee described as a "rebirth" (field interview, April 2007), and Feza's success since has been undeniable.

The group of men who managed *Zaman*'s rebirth met at a GM *ışık evi* while attending university in Istanbul in the early 1990s. Under the tutelage of their *ağabey* (elder brother), these young men formed the "*Zaman* Research Group" and put together news reports and opinion pieces that were later published in *Zaman*. Now in their mid-forties, these men are executives at Feza Gazetecilik and are considered by members of the inner circle to be the architects of the GM's renovated presentation (field interviews, March 2007, July 2007, August 2008). The primary intent driving this renovation is to present the AKP's conservative democratic coalition as collectively embodying the social mores of modernity *to a greater extent* than Turkey's oligarchic elite. It does this by publicly lambasting its adversaries, not for being "un-Islamic," but for being "undemocratic," "status quo," and/ or "fascist."[21] Just before the snap July elections of 2007, a *Zaman* columnist and founding GM brother who helped launch *Zaman* in the 1980s explained to both his Turkish and English-language readers that it was not the AKP that was running for reelection in Turkey, but "democracy" that was running for its life:

> July 22 is a moment of decision. ... Ask your conscience: Stability, peace and domestic integrity? Or tension, row, crisis and polarization? ... Democracy or status quo? ... Remain the inferior "other" or enjoy the protection of the fundamental rights under a civilian democracy? Ask your conscience: Ethnic nationalism or a brotherhood fostered through mutual tolerance and respect? (Gülerce 2007)

Despite its clear endorsement of and support for AKP policies and for the continuation of AKP power, however, according to the GM, democracy was the winner in 2007:

Everyone knows ... 95 percent of this community votes for the same party. But nobody articulates this. Even in their home, because we are far from politics. I know, for example, I assume, that 95 percent of our community voted for the AK Party, maybe 99 percent. ... But nobody talked about this at their homes, or in their *sohbets*. Unfortunately, in the last elections, since there was a huge conflict ... [the issue] was not supporting the party, but supporting "democracy" ... so people talked a lot more than expected. And also, *Zaman* newspaper and STV television, and some other friends blamed us for being more partisan now. But it is not partisanship. This is supporting democracy. (field interview, August 2008)

By demanding accountability in terms of "democracy," "peace," and "stability," *Zaman* journalism also projects the degree to which the categories of political and economic liberalism have expanded into Turkish society, and how "liberalism carries with it not the seeds of its destruction, but the seeds of its expansion" (Keck and Sikkink 1998: 205–6).

According to Feza journalists, Zaman and the GM's other print and broadcast media are "more liberal" and "more supportive of democracy" than other news sources in Turkey. This is because GM journalists and opinion makers realize that in order to "win" the discursive battle for public opinion, they must appeal to a global audience. That is, they must reframe "Islamic issues" like the ban on Muslim headscarves at Turkish universities as universal issues like individual freedom and human rights. Indeed, with a diversified public message, GM media constitutes the loudest and most consistent supporter of the AKP's "conservative democratic" republic. For this reason, when someone reads *Zaman*, they will not find a disclaimer announcing the paper's affiliation with Fethullah Gülen. Gülen never writes for the paper, and when asked, GM aristocrats insist with a straight face that *Zaman* is not "organically" a GM institution. Just as *Zaman* reporters and columnists do in regard to their coalition with the AKP, they simultaneously deny support when giving it and deny affiliation when affiliation is clear. Instead, they focus on alternative means to frame a story that seeks to avoid skepticism and to preempt criticism. The GM increases its legitimacy, therefore, by emphasizing the movement's national value for a skeptical Turkish audience, and by emphasizing its universal value for a qualitatively more forgiving global audience (*Economist* 2008a, 2008b; Tavernise 2008; Rabasa et al. 2006; Rabasa and Larabee 2008). The result is that "moderate Islam" à la Fethullah Gülen has become an eagerly sought after commodity in the world's intellectual marketplace, and is now second to none in receiving support and praise from influential opinion makers in European and American journalism, academia, and politics.[22]

Conclusion

According to Sydney Tarrow, "state structures create stable opportunities, but it is changing opportunities within states that provide the openings that resource-poor groups can use to create new movements" (1994: 18). In Turkey, changing opportunities provided openings for resource-poor Islamic activists to mobilize into resource-rich political interest groups. Neoliberal restructuring in the 1980s created opportunities for accumulation through trade. Openings in Turkish education, media, and trade, moreover, led to the mobilization of Anatolian social and economic networks that relied on each other rather than on the state for economic support. Such opportunities were compounded by a redefined state attitude toward Anatolian Islam, which subsequently freed Turkey's religious marketplace and allowed for an open competition for community allegiance. Adapting Said Nursi's influence to a post-Kemalist Turkey, the community of Fethullah Gülen took advantage of all such opportunities by expanding its networks in education, media, trade, and finance throughout Anatolia's transforming countryside, and in many ways set the stage for a national shift from Islamic activism to conservative democracy, from the National Vision to the AKP:

> The boundaries between these new elites and the Gülen movement supporters are blurred and it is the members of this Anatolian bourgeoisie who actually fund and establish Gülen schools. ... Many provincial Islamist politicians have also sent their children to Gülen schools. ... Gülen media is the largest in almost all Anatolian cities. (Yılmaz 2008: 914)

By promoting Gülen's teachings through social networks, through media, and through outreach, the GM is responsible for helping "a younger generation of Islamists to be comfortable as far as Islam and their minds and hearts are concerned" (Yılmaz 2008: 914), and is thus largely responsible for the success of Turkey's conservative democratic passive revolution. Considering its impact, how should observers of Turkish politics anticipate the GM's future?

According to Asef Bayat (2007), Egyptian Islamic activists are worth studying because they mounted a large-scale social movement without ever transforming the contours of state/political power. By contrast, in Iran a transformational political revolution occurred despite the absence of a large-scale Islamic social movement. Unique to both of Bayat's cases, in Turkey Islamic activists took advantage of the country's integration into the global economy to mount a (so far) successful war of position by dividing the labor of the passive revolution between civil/market activism and partisan politics. Spearheaded by the GM and the AKP, however, this collective effort seeks less to "Islamize Turkish society" than it does to manufacture a "Turkish-Islamic ethic of capitalism"—a socially conservative and economically liberal worldview that strives to increase and legitimize the Muslim share in Turkey's political economy. Despite the inclination toward passivity, however, the TSK's failed attempt to effectively influence the July 2007 elections, the Constitutional Court's failed attempt to close the AKP in 2008, and the constant attempts on the part of rival media to slander Gülen and GM followers together illustrate that (1) tensions within the Turkish elite are far from subsiding and (2) conservative democracy is winning. Moving throughout the networks of social power are new discourses of Turkish national identity, new companies accumulating resources, and new power brokers negotiating for influence. The GM is a primary collective actor in this contest, and its increasing influence is indicative of deep transformations already underway.

Notes

This chapter is republished for inclusion in this volume on invitation from the volume editors and with permission. The original article appeared as follows: Hendrick, Joshua D. 2009. "Globalization, Islamic Activism, and Passive Revolution in Turkey: The Case of Fethullah Gülen." *Journal of Power* 2, no. 3: 343–68. The version included in this volume is updated and slightly revised.

1. The full text and translation is widely published online and video is available for viewing at Youtube: http://www.youtube.com/watch?v=oNi3Z3qZ7Z4&mode=relate d&search.

2. *Ulema* (Turkish), more often recognized in English-language publications as *ulama* (Arabic), is a plural term (s. *'alim*) referring to the institution of religiously informed scholars, judges, and other legitimated authorities of Islamic tradition, philosophy, and law. The *ulama* traditionally constitutes a collection of scholars who are charged with the task of legal jurisprudence (*fiqh*) in accordance with one of four legal traditions in Sunni Koranic interpretation (*madhhab*). In both Ottoman and contemporary Turkey, the dominant *madhhab* and *fiqh* is Hanafi (Turkish, Hanefi). As a legally "secular" (*laik*) republic, the role traditionally filled by the Ottoman *ulema* is now fulfilled by the Directorate of Religious Affairs (Diyanet).

3. For the purposes of this study, Said Nursi is introduced to provide the reader with an overview of the Nur tradition, to which Fethullah Gülen and the GM are affiliated. The *Risale-i Nur Collection* is published by a number of publishing houses in Turkey, most of which are affiliated with one of the several Nur communities. The collection is divided into multiple volumes: *The Words, The Letters, The Rays, and The Flashes,* each of which are often found subdivided or abridged for easier access and publication. A complete e-copy of the *Risale-i Nur Collection* is available at http://www.nursistudies. com/. For a detailed account of Nursi's intellectual biography from a sympathetic perspective, see Vahide (2005). For a detailed account of Nursi's sociological impact on the formation and mobilization of Islamic political identity in Turkey, see Mardin (1989) and Yavuz (2000, 2003a: 151–78, 2003b: 1–18).

4. As with all formations in civil society, differences of opinion among the Nur led to divisions. The primary split occurred when a group of students sought to mass-produce the *Risale-i Nur Collection* (and thus to reform the text in accordance with the Turkish-language reform of 1928). In 1971, they published selections from the Risale-i Nur Collection in modern Turkish in a mass-produced journal called *Yeni Asya* (New Asia). A smaller group contended that the *Risale-i Nur Collection* was a work of art and spirituality and that its mass production robbed the work of its spiritual value. Known as the Yazıcılar (Scribes), this latter group sought to reproduce the *Risale-i Nur Collection* by hand in its original Ottoman script. While many smaller groups exist, the primary divisions in the larger Nur movement are as follows: Yeni Asya (New Asia), Yazıcılar (Scribes), Yeni Nesil (New Generation), Yeni Zemin (New Earth/Ground), Abdullah Yeğin Grubu, followers of Mehmet Kırkıncı, and the community of Fethullah Gülen.

5. While conducting research at the GM's *Akademi* in Istanbul, a group of editors, writers, and executives took a field trip to visit Mustafa Sungur, a living student of Said Nursi and the leader of the Abdullah Yeğin Grubu branch of the larger Turkish Nur movement (field notes, April 2007). This was a much-anticipated event. One informant shared with me that the objective of the visit was to pay their respects to the aged leader. They took photos with him and listened to a reading of the *Risale-i Nur Collection.* What was most curious about this meeting was that those who attended were told specifically not to share their experience with me, the American sociologist conducting research at the *Akademi.* Having already told me about the meeting before he was told not to do so, my informant considered that he had broken no rules, nor anyone's trust.

6. In Turkish, the suffixes, "-ci," "-cı," "-cu," and "-cü" are used similarly to the English suffix "-ist." To many, however, referring to someone as an "-ist" connotes an ideological orientation, and is thus understood to be derogatory. Fethullah Gülen comments as follows: "The word 'Nurcu,' although it was used a little by Bediüzzaman Said Nursi, is basically used by his antagonists to belittle the Nursi's movement and his followers and to be able to present it as a heterodox sect. ... I've never used suffixes like '-ci,' '-cu.' ... My only goal has been to live as a believer and to surrender my spirit to God as a believer." Many authors prefer to use "Nurcu" when discussing followers of Said Nursi. Out of respect for those who participated in my research, I do not invoke these terms to describe admirers or Fethullah Gülen, Said Nursi, or those who participate in the activities of either faith-identified community.

7. In the aftermath of the 27 April 2007 "e-memorandum," and less than a year after its reelection, the AKP came under indictment by a state prosecutor for being "an axis of antisecular activities," a charge for which it was narrowly acquitted in August 2008. While on trial, the AKP initiated a massive investigation into Turkey's so-called *derin devlet* (deep state), which has long been the most articulated conspiracy theory in Turkish society. Believed by some to be a remnant from Ottoman times, and by others to be a Turkish "Operation Gladio" created to stymie left mobilization in Turkey

during the Cold War, the existence of a *derin devlet* is unquestioned in Turkish society. When a Turkish journalist is assassinated (e.g., Hrant Dink in January 2007), when a foreigner is murdered (e.g., three Christian missionaries in Malatya in April 2007), or when a random act of violence disrupts a public event (e.g., five judges shot by a lawyer in May 2006), Turkish media and politicians erupt with conversations about *derin devlet*. In June 2007, Turkish police raided an apartment in Istanbul that was filled with weapons and explosives. This event sparked an investigation into the sources from which these weapons were obtained. This led to a still ongoing investigation into Ergenekon, the name given to a network of retired military personnel, political leaders, and journalists who are alleged to have conspired to instigate social/political tension in the interests of overthrowing the AKP. In the first indictment, eighty-nine people were accused of conspiring against the government. The Ergenekon trial began on 21 October 2008 when prosecutors started to read the 2,455-page indictment. The trial concluded in August 2013. Of 275 defendants, twenty-one were acquitted. Despite credible claims of falsified evidence, among those convicted included six retired generals, two retired colonels, a lifelong journalist, and the head of Türkiye İşçi Partisi (Workers' Party of Turkey, TİP), among others. Throughout the duration of the over-five-year trial, both supporters and opponents cried conspiracy, fabrication, ineptitude, and corruption. GM media covered the story as a top priority. In its English-language daily, *Today's Zaman*, for instance, the GM published on average 1.6 stories a day dedicated to Ergenekon, excluding hundreds more opinion pieces and editorials. From 29 January 2008 to 27 January 2009 (363 days), the daily published 580 stories related to the investigation and/or trial. Defending his paper's weighted treatment of the story, the editor in chief of *Today's Zaman* commented as follows: "Economic crises are temporary, but the troubles caused by shadowy Ergenekon-like networks will be permanent unless they are completely eradicated" (Keneş 2009). For more, see Hendrick (2011, 2013).

8. Of the nearly one hundred employees at the *Akademi*, nearly all are male, which highlights the survival of male privilege and conservative culture in the GM's inner world. In seven months at the *Akademi*, I observed four female employees, three who worked in children's publishing and one who worked in the kitchen, and who was thus employed by an affiliated catering company and not by the publishing house. See Turam (2006) for further discussions of gender dynamics in the movement.

9. See http://www.fatihkoleji.com.

10. See http://www.yamanlar.k12.tr/.

11. During the time of this research, the entrance exam for high school was called the Ortaöğrenim Kurumları Giriş Sınavı (High School Entrance Examination, ÖKS). The exam for university was called the Öğrenci Seçme Sınavı (Student Selection Exam, ÖSS). The latter was regulated by the Öğrenci Seçme Yerleştirme Merkezi (Student Selection and Placement Center, ÖSYM). The ÖSS was first administered in 1973 in response to rapid urbanization and a subsequent increase in student applications to university. The ÖKS was terminated in 2007. Starting in 2009, the Ministry of Education began a new program of testing that was envisaged to span three years of middle school. Beginning in 2010, the ÖSS was reformed and renamed the Öğrenci Seçme ve Yerleştirme Sistemi (Student Selection and Placement Examination, ÖSYS).

12. In 2007, FEM operated 45 branches in Istanbul and another 118 branches, totaling 163, across the country. Anafen operated 43 branches in Istanbul and another 55, totaling 97, across the country. By November 2011, FEM had expanded to 185 branches throughout Turkey (see http://www.femdershaneleri.com.tr/BranchList.aspx, accessed 7 November 2011). Other successful GM-affiliated supplemental education companies include Yeşilırmak Dershanesi in Bursa, Maltepe Dershanesi in Ankara, Nil Dershanesi in Erzurum, and Körfez Dershanesi in İzmir, to name only the most

famous. On the 2007 ÖSS exam, the majority of students in the top 1 percent on the ÖSS exam in each of the above cities attended these respective preparation schools and/or attended GM-affiliated private high schools (*Zaman* 2007).

13. The leaked information about the AKP intentions to close dershane schools in Turkey was published by *Zaman Gazetesi* (http://www.zaman.com.tr/gundem_dershane-kapatmak-hukumetin-politikasi_2168177.html) (Accessed 10 July 2014). An English language account of the story from a non-GM-affiliated English language news daily is available at http://www.hurriyetdailynews.com/debate-over-turkish-government-move-on-prep-schools-grows.aspx?pageID=238&nID=58131&NewsCatID=339 (Accessed 10 July 2014).

14. The city of Istanbul contracted the Kaynak subsidiary Sürat Technology to build a citywide surveillance system known as the Mobile City Information and Security System (MOBESE). In its first phase, seven hundred cameras were installed around the city and were all linked to a Cisco-developed GSM surveillance network. Sürat Technology developed the MOBESE Command Control Center, and is responsible for support and maintenance of the entire system. Kaynak worked with the USAID in its "Rebuild Iraq Project," supplying educational furniture and equipment, and with UNESCO in Afghanistan, to whom it supplied similar resources (see www.kaynak.com.tr:projects.references.asp).

15. See http://www.kaynak.com.tr/.

16. See http://www.pasiad.org/.

17. In 2010, TUSKON consolidated GM-affiliated trade relations underneath its umbrella.

18. In order to assure collectivity in the administration of BA, private shareholders are not permitted to own more than 9.99 percent of the total shares in BA. Through two subsidiaries, BJ Tekstil and Orta Doğu Tekstil, in late 2007, the Çalık Group owned more than three times any other shareholder (Bank Asya 2008).

19. According to Medyatava (2008), the average daily sales in June 2008 for Turkey's top five selling print dailies were as follows: (1) *Zaman*: 785,309, (2) *Posta*: 634,666, (3) *Hürriyet*: 521,100, (4) *Sabah*: 410,523, and (5) *Milliyet*: 209,318. *Posta*, *Hürriyet*, and *Milliyet* are owned by the Doğan Group. Between 2007 and 2013, Sabah was owned by the AKP/GM "friend company," the Çalık Group. In June 2008, *Today's Zaman*'s circulation was 4,101 a day. For current circulation statistics, see http://www.medyatava.com/tiraj.

20. As of the revision of this article (March 2012), pieces of the ATV-*Sabah* collection of media holdings that were acquired by the Çalık Group in 2008 were officially up for sale, including the company's two flagship brands, ATV and the newspaper *Sabah* (see http://turkishcentralnews.com/archives/5716, accessed 6 March 2012).

21. See opinions and editorials in *Zaman Gazetesi* and *Today's Zaman* in spring and summer 2007 during the presidential nomination process of Abdullah Gül, specifically Keneş (2007).

22. Since 2005, GM satellites in Europe, the United States, and Australia have sponsored a series of conferences dedicated to the mobilization of the Gülen Movement in Thought and Practice. Participants at these conferences include activists and affiliates directly related to GM institutions, as well as academicians who focus on the GM as a topic of scholarly research. The largest of such conferences to date was held in London in January 2008 and was cosponsored by the GM's London-based Dialogue Society in conjunction with the House of Lords, the British Parliament, the London School of Economics, SOAS, the University of Sussex, and the Middle East Institute. The first conference was held in Washington DC in 2002 and was sponsored by the GM's Rumi Forum in conjunction with the Center for Muslim Christian Understanding at Georgetown University. This was followed in April 2005 by a conference in Madison, Wisconsin, which was sponsored by the GM's Dialogue International, followed by another in Houston sponsored by the GM's Institute for Interfaith Dialogue (IID).

Following Houston, the IID sponsored successive conferences dedicated to the GM in March 2006 in Dallas (with Southern Methodist University), and two in November 2006 in San Antonio and Norman, Oklahoma (in conjunction the University of Texas, San Antonio, and the University of Oklahoma, respectively). Following the Dialogue Society's October 2007 London conference was a follow-up in Rotterdam, the Netherlands, and another in the United States sponsored by the Turkish Cultural Center in New York City. Both were held in November 2007. In November 2008, the Rumi Forum in Washington DC hosted its second GM conference at Georgetown University (www.gulenconference.us), and in March 2009, the Atlas Foundation in Louisiana sponsored a follow-up at Louisiana State University in Baton Rouge. At the writing of this chapter, the most recent conference was held at Potsdam University in Berlin and was sponsored by the GM's Forum for Intercultural Dialogue Berlin. GM-affiliated civil society organizations in the United States have received praise and support from such notable and influential people as former president Bill Clinton, former secretary of state Hillary Clinton, Madeline Albright, James Baker, and dozens of national and state congressional senators and representatives.

References

Agai, Bekim. 2003. "The Gülen Movement's Islamic Ethic of Education." In Yavuz and Esposito, *Turkish Islam and the Secular State*, 48–68. Syracuse: Syracuse University Press.
Akman, Nuriye. 2004. "Fethullah Gülen Interview with Nuriye Akman of Zaman Daily." Accessed 10 October 2008. http://en.fgulen.org.
Akşit, Necmi. 2006. "Educational Reform in Turkey." *International Journal of Educational Development*: vol. 27: 129–37.
Aras, Bülent, and Ömer Çaha. 2000. "Fethullah Gülen and His Liberal Turkish Islam Movement." *MERIA* 4, no. 4: 30–42.
Balcı, Bayram. 2003. "Fethullah Gülen's Missionary Schools in Central Asia and Their Role in the Spreading of Turkism and Islam." *Religion, State, and Society* Vol. 31, no. 2: 151–77.
Bank Asya. 2008. "General Assembly of Shareholders." http://www.bankasya.com.tr/en/about_us/capital_and_shareholder_structure.jsp.
Bayat, Asef. 2007. *Making Islam Democratic*. Palo Alto, CA: Stanford University Press.
Bianchi, Robert.1984. *Interest Groups and Political Development in Turkey*. Princeton, NJ: Princeton University Press.
Buğra, Ayşe. 1994. *State and Business in Modern Turkey*. Binghamton, NY: SUNY Press.
Can, Eyüp. 1996. *Fethullah Gülen Hocaefendi ile Ufuk Turu* [A tour of new horizons with Fethullah Gülen]. 13th ed. Istanbul: A.D.
Carroll, B. Jill. 2007. *A Dialogue of Civilizations: Gülen's Islamic Ideals and Humanistic Discourse*. Somerset, NJ: The Light Publishing.
Çetinkaya, Hikmet. 2007. *Fethullah Gülen, ABD, ve AKP* [Fethullah Gülen, the USA, and the AKP]. Istanbul: Günizi Yayıncılık.
CIA World Factbook. 2004. *Turkey Country Profile*. Langley, VA: Central Intelligence Agency.
Cooke, Miriam, and Bruce Lawrence (eds.). 2005. *Muslim Networks: From Hajj to Hip Hop*. Chapel Hill: University of North Carolina Press.
Demir, Ömer, Mustafa Acar, and Metin Toprak. 2004. "Anatolian Tigers of Islamic Capital: Prospects and Challenges." *Middle Eastern Studies* 40, no. 6: 166–88.
Economist. 2008a. "Beyond the Veil." 12 June.

_____. 2008b. "How Far They Have Traveled." 12 March.

Eickleman, Dale, and Jon Anderson (eds.). 2003. *New Media in the Muslim World*. 2nd ed. Bloomington: Indiana University Press.

Eickelman, Dale, and James Piscatori. 1996. *Muslim Politics*. Princeton, NJ: Princeton University Press.

Erdoğan, Recep Tayyip. 2006. "Conservative Democracy and the Globalization of Freedom." In *The Emergence of a New Turkey*, ed. M. Hakan Yavuz, 333–40. Salt Lake City: University of Utah Press.

Ergene, Enes. 2005. *Gülen Hareketinin Analizi: Geleceğin Modern Çağa Tanıklığı* [Tradition witnessing the modern age: An analysis of the Gülen movement]. Istanbul: Kaynak Kültür Yayınları.

_____. 2008. *Tradition Witnessing the Modern Age*. Somerset, NJ: Tuğhra Books.

Fried, Daniel. 2007. "U.S.-Turkish Relations and the Challenges Ahead." Testimony Before the House Foreign Affairs Committee Subcommittee on Europe, 15 March. Washington DC. http://2001-2009.state.gov/p/eur/rls/rm/81790.htm.

Gramsci, Antonio. 1971. *Selections from the Prison Notebooks*. Edited by Quintan Hoare and Geoffrey Smith. New York: International Publishers.

Gülalp, Haldun. 2001. "Globalization and Political Islam: The Social Bases of Turkey's Welfare Party." *International Journal of Middle Eastern Studies* 33, no. 3: 433–48.

Gülen, Fethullah M. 1998. *Prizma II*. Istanbul: Nil Yayınları.

_____. 2004. *Toward a Civilization of Love and Tolerance*. Somerset, NJ: The Light Publishing.

_____. 2005. *Statute of Our Souls*. Somerset, NJ: The Light Publishing.

Gülerce, Hüseyin. 2007. "The Meaning of This Election." *Today's Zaman*. 20 July.

Gündem, Mehmet. 2005. "Interview with Fethullah Gülen." *Milliyet Gazetesi*, 19 January.

Güngör, İzgi. 2009. "Mayday for the Turkish Education System." *Hürriyet Daily News*, 15 July.

Hayward, Chloe. 2007. "Borrower Profile: Çalık Builds Funding for Rapid Growth." *EuroMoney*, May.

Hefner, Robert (ed.). 2004. *Remaking Muslim Politics: Pluralism, Contestation, and Democratization*. Princeton, NJ: Princeton University Press.

Hendrick, Joshua D. 2008. "Islamic Activism in the 'Secular' Modern World System: Turkish Integration and the Civil/Cosmopolitan Movement of Fethullah Gülen." In *Islam and the Orientalist World System*, ed. Khaldoun Samman and Mazher Al-Zoby, 106–28. Boulder, CO: Paradigm Publishers.

_____. 2009. "Globalization, Islamic Activism, and Passive Revolution in Turkey: The Case of Fethullah Gülen." *Journal of Power* 2, no. 3: 343–68.

_____. 2011. "Media Wars, Public Relations, and 'the Gülen Factor' in the New Turkey." *Middle East Report* 260: 40–46.

_____. 2013. *Gülen: The Ambiguous Politics of Market Islam in Turkey and the World*. New York: NYU Press.

Heper, Metin. 1985. *The State Tradition in Turkey*. Northgate, UK: Eothen Press.

Hunt, Robert, and Alp Aslandoğan (eds.). 2007. *Muslim Citizens of the Globalized World*. Somerset, NJ: The Light Publishing.

Jacoby, Tim. 2004. *Social Power and the Turkish State*. New York: Routledge.

Kaya, M. K., and Svante Cornell. 2008. "Politics, Media, and Power in Turkey." Turkey Analyst, 4 June. http://www.silkroadstudies.org/new/inside/turkey/2008/080604A.html.

Keck, Margaret, and Katheryn Sikkink. 1998. *Activists Beyond Borders*. Ithaca, NY: Cornell University Press.

Keneş, Bülent. 2007. "Turkey: The Portrait of a Fascist Provocateur." *Today's Zaman*, 7 May.

_____. 2009. "The Media and the End of An Era of Impunity." *Today's Zaman*, 13 February.

Krespin, R. 2007. "The Upcoming Elections in Turkey (2): The AKP's Political Power Base." *MEMRI*, no. 375, July. http://www.memri.org/report/en/0/0/0/0/0/0/2301.htm.

_____. 2009. "Fethullah Gülen's Grand Ambition: Turkey's Islamist Danger." *Middle East Quarterly* 16, no. 1: 55–66.

Lin, Nan. 1999. "Building a Network Theory of Social Capital." *Connections* 22, no. 1: 28–51.

Mamedov, Nazar. 2005. "Ethnocultural Practices In Post-Soviet Kyrgyzstan and Turkmenistan: A Comparative Perspective." Master's thesis, Central European University.

Mandaville, Peter. 2001. *Transnational Muslim Politics: Reimagining the Umma*. New York: Routledge.

_____. 2006. *Global Political Islam*. New York: Routledge.

Mardin, Şerif. 1989. *Religion and Social Change in Modern Turkey: The Case of Bediüzzaman Said Nursi*. Albany, NY: SUNY Press.

Öniş, Ziya. 2009. "Conservative Globalism at the Crossroads: The Justice and Development Party and the Thorny Path to Democratic Consolidation in Turkey." *Mediterranean Politics* 14, no. 1: 21–40.

Özbudun, Ergun, and Fuat Keyman. 2002. "Cultural Globalization in Turkey: Actors, Discourses, and Challenges." In *Many Globalizations*, ed. Peter Berger and Samuel Huntington, 296–320. New York: Oxford University Press.

Özcan, Gül Berna, and Murat Çokgezen. 2003. "Limits to Alternative Forms of Capitalization: The Case of Anatolian Holding Companies." *World Development* 31, no. 12: 2061–84.

_____. 2006. "Trusted Markets: The Exchange of Islamic Companies." *Comparative Economic Studies* 48: 132–55.

Park, Bill. 2008. "The Fethullah Gülen Movement." *Middle East Review of International Affairs*, 12, no. 3. http://www.globalpolitician.com/print.asp?id=5355.

Parla, Taha, and Andrew Davidson. 2004. *Corporatist Ideology in Kemalist Turkey*. Syracuse: Syracuse University Press.

Passy, Florence. 2003. "Social Networks Matter: But How?" In *Social Movements and Network*, ed. Mario Diani and Doug McAdam, 21–48. New York: Oxford University Press.

Rabasa, Angel, Cheryl Bernard, Lowell Schwartz, and Peter Sickle. 2006. *Building Moderate Muslim Networks*. Washington DC: RAND.

Rabasa, Angel, and Stephen Larabee. 2008. *The Rise of Political Islam in Turkey*. Washington DC: RAND.

Roberts, John. 2004. "The Turkish Gate: Energy Transit and Security Issues." *Turkish Policy Quarterly* 3, no. 4: 97–125.

Rubin, Michael. 2008. "Turkey Turning Point: Could There Be An Islamic Revolution in Turkey?" *National Review*, 14 April.

Sarıtoprak, Zeki. 2005. "An Islamic Approach to Peace and Nonviolence: A Turkish Experience." In "Islam and in Contemporary Turkey: The Contributions of Fethullah Gülen," special issue, *The Muslim World* 95, no. 3: 413–28.

Sarıtoprak, Zeki, and Sydney Griffith. 2005. "Fethullah Gülen and the 'People of the Book:' A Voice from Turkey for Interfaith Dialogue." In "Islam in Contemporary Turkey: The Contributions of Fethullah Gülen," special issue, *The Muslim World* 95, no. 3: 325–47.

Schwartz, Stephen. 2008. "The Real Fethullah Gülen," *Prospect*. 26 July. http://www.prospectmagazine.co.uk/2008/07/therealfethullahglen/

Shamir, Boas, and Jane Howell. 1999. "Organizational and Contextual Influences on the Emergence and Effectiveness of Charismatic Leadership." *Leadership Quarterly* 10, no. 2: 257–83.

Şimşek, Hasan, and Ali Yıldırım. 2004. "Turkey: Innovation and Tradition." In *Balancing Change and Tradition in Global Education Reform*, ed. Iris Rothberg, 153–85. Lanham, MD: Rowan and Littlefield.

Tansel, Aysıt. 2013. *Supplementary Education in Turkey: Recent Developments and Future Prospects*. Discussion Papers 7639. Ankara: Middle East Technical University.

Tansel, Aysıt, and Fatma Bircan. 2003. *Private Tutoring Expenditures in Turkey*. ERF Working Paper Series 0333. Ankara: Middle Eastern Technical University.

270 | *Joshua D. Hendrick*

_____. 2006. "Demand for Education in Turkey: A Tobit Analysis of Private Tutoring Expenditures." *Economics of Education Review* 25, no. 2: 303–13.
Tarrow, Sydney. 1994. *Power in Movement*. New York: Cambridge University Press.
Tavernise, Sabrina. 2008. "Turkish Schools Offer Pakistan A Gentler Vision of Islam." *New York Times*, 4 May.
Today's Zaman. 2007. "Small Enterprises Star in TUSKON's Trade Bridge with Pacific." 9 April.
_____. 2009. "President's Africa Trip Yields $500 Mln In Business Deals." 26 February.
Turam, Berna. 2004a. "A Bargain Between the Secular State and Turkish Islam: Politics of Ethnicity in Central Asia." *Nations and Nationalism* 10, no. 3: 353–74.
_____. 2004b. "The Politics of Engagement Between Islam and The Secular State: Ambivalences in 'Civil Society.'" *The British Journal of Sociology* 55, no. 2: 259–81.
_____. 2006. *Between Islam and the State*. Palo Alto, CA: Stanford University Press.
Turkish Daily News. 1999. "Gülen: The Law Judges Deeds Not Intentions." 24 June.
TUSKON. 2007. *Turkey-Africa Trade Bridge Report*.
Ünal, Ali. 2005. *Geçmişten Geleceğe Köprü: Fethullah Gülen* [A bridge from the past to the future: Fethullah Gülen]. Istanbul: Kaynak Kültür Yayınları.
Ünal, Ali, and Alphonse Williams (eds.). 2000. *Advocate of Dialogue: Fethullah Gülen*. Fairfax, VA: The Fountain.
Vahide, Şükran. 2005. *Islam in Modern Turkey: An Intellectual Biography of Bediuzzaman Said Nursi*. Albany, NY: SUNY Press.
Weber, Max. (1922) 1978. *Economy and Society*. Edited by Guenther Roth and Claus Wittich. 2 vols. Berkeley: University of California Press.
White, Jenny. 2004. "The End of Islamism: Turkey's Muslimhood Model." In *Remaking Muslim Politics: Pluralism, Contestation, and Democratization*, ed. Robert Hefner, 87–111. Princeton, NJ: Princeton University Press.
Wiktorowicz, Quintan (ed.). 2004. *Islamic Activism: A Social Movement Theory Approach*. Indianapolis: Indiana University Press.
World Bank. 2005. *Turkey-Education Sector Study*. Report 32450-TU. Washington DC. World Bank.
Yanardağ, Merdan. 2006. *Fethullah Gulen Hareketinin Perde Arkası: Türkiye Nasıl Kuşatıldı?* [The Fethullah Gülen movement's hidden plan: How has Turkey been sieged?]. Istanbul: Siyah/Beyaz Yayıncılık.
Yavuz, M. Hakan. 1999. "Search for a New Social Contract in Turkey: Fethullah Gülen, the Virtue Party, and the Kurds." *SAIS Review* 19, no. 1: 114–43.
_____. 2000. "Being Modern in the Nurcu Way." *ISIM Newletter* 6: 7, 14.
_____. 2003a. *Islamic Political Identity in Turkey*. New York: Oxford University Press.
_____. 2003b. "Islam in the Public Sphere." In Yavuz and Esposito, *Turkish Islam and the Secular State*, 1–19.
_____ (ed.). 2006. "The Role of the New Bourgeoisie in the Transformation of the Turkish Islamic Movement." In *The Emergence of a New Turkey*, ed. M. Hakan Yavuz, 1–19. Salt Lake City: University of Utah Press.
Yavuz, M. Hakan, and John Esposito (eds.). 2003. *Turkish Islam and the Secular State: The Gülen Movement*. Syracuse: Syracuse University Press.
Yeşilada, Birol. 1988. "Problems of Political Development in the Third Turkish Republic." *Polity* 21, no. 2: 345–72.
Yılmaz, İhsan. 2008. "Beyond Post Islamism: A Critical Analysis of the Turkish Islamism's Transformation toward Fethullah Gülen's Stateless Cosmopolitan Islam." In Yurtsever, *Islam in the Age of Global Challenges*, 859–25.
Yurtsever, Ali (ed.). 2008. *Islam in the Age of Global Challenges: Alternative Perspective of the Gülen Movement*. Washington DC: Tuğhra Books.

Zaman. 2007. "ÖSS'de başarı arttı, dereceler Türkiye'ye yayıldı" [The results of the most successful students on the ÖSS are published]. 13 July.

Zürcher, Erik. 2004. *Turkey: A Modern History.* New York. I. B. Tauris.

– Chapter 9 –

THE LAIC-ISLAMIST SCHISM IN THE TURKISH DOMINANT CLASS AND THE MEDIA

Anita Oğurlu and Ahmet Öncü

Introduction

The current version of this chapter—apart from some minor additions—was written in late 2012, that is, almost one year before the Gezi Park Revolt. Thus, we had taken pen to paper prior to the 17 December 2013 corruption scandal that recently shook Turkey. These events not only undermined the political legitimacy of the Adalet ve Kalkınma Partisi (Justice and Development Party, AKP) government, but also revealed visibly how the media has been rendered subservient to the interests of the rising Islamist bourgeoisie through illegal means and maneuvers. As a result, some of our provisional arguments regarding such possibilities have become validated. We maintain that all these unexpected developments have not lessened but instead amplified the theoretical relevance and political significance of this chapter, which attempts to address two parallel concerns underscoring the class struggle between the laic and Islamist factions of the Turkish dominant class in connection with the neoliberal transformation of Turkish capitalism. In this regard we focus on the media sector, especially newspapers. First, the schism in the economically dominant class and its ramifications for the ideological supremacy of the bourgeoisie will be a focus for discussion. Second, how this schism is linked to the turf fight in the media sector will be analyzed.

In what follows, we first introduce a theoretical framework and elaborate upon the use of Ideological State Apparatus (ISA) and Repressive State Apparatus (RSA) in building hegemony by highlighting the implications of a schism in these apparatuses. Here we aim to combine the Gramscian notion of hegemony with Herman and Chomsky's (1994) Propaganda Model (PM) and how this model can be contextualized with reference to the peculiarities of the Turkish case. In the second section, in connection with our theoretical model, we focus on the media sector and the power struggle between the media corporations owned by the Islamist and laic factions. In the third section, instead of a conclusion, we argue that, although the lasting schism renders the building of hegemony an ever more difficult task for each faction of the dominant class, monopolization of the media remains to preserve the domination of the capitalist class as a whole and renew its oppressive power over the working masses.

Dominant Ideology, Media, and Class Hegemony

One of the well-acknowledged contributions of Althusser (1971) is that all capitalist class domination operates through the enforcement of Ideological State Apparatus (ISA) to retain hegemonic power over the masses. As the State is an "apparatus" in itself, it "interpellates," or utilizes for ideological purposes, all actors at all levels, be they economic, religious, educational, juridical, and cultural, to work within a bound and defined network, allowing little space for agency. In this imagery, media is but one arm of an ISA network with set strategies and tactics to maintain the supremacy of the economically dominant class. In order to interpellate individuals, the media as an ISA must be broad and far-reaching to ensure the authority of the dominant class. Most importantly, media must be cohesive and perform on behalf of a dominant class as a unitary force throughout society.

In the global context of media conglomerates, media as an ISA is predominantly operated by a handful of monopolistic corporations. In the Turkish case, we argue that although the media sector shares the main organizational features of the global context, there is a split in its respective dominant class position. An Islamist capitalist class, constituting a faction of the dominant class, which emerged in the 1990s, now challenges the ISA of the older secularist establishment that formed the nation-state with the bourgeois revolution under Mustafa Kemal Atatürk in the 1920s and 1930s. Ideological interpellation via the ISA has indeed brought a sizeable section of the subordinate and working masses in Turkey closer to believing in and adapting to the

Western laic nationalist ideology of the Kemalist ISA because of mass communication (Öncü 2014).

In its simplest and most straightforward representation, dominant ideology is supposed to play a double role. First, the working class must be told what is expected of them (i.e., rules to follow). Second, the existing relations of production must be reproduced. As Althusser puts it:

> I shall say that the reproduction of labor power requires not only a reproduc-
> tion of its skills, but also, at the same time, a reproduction of its submission to
> the rules of the established order, i.e. a reproduction of submission to the rul-
> ing ideology for the workers, and a reproduction of the ability to manipulate
> the ruling ideology correctly for the agents of exploitation and repression, so
> that they, too, will provide for the domination of the ruling class "in words."
> (1971: 132–33)

If there existed two factions with incongruent ideologies within the economically dominant class, then the question of which of these ideologies would tell subjects "what is expected of them" becomes a politically contested terrain, and thereby opens the ground for, in Gramsci's terms, a potential crisis of hegemony. Turkey's recent "media wars" are reflective of this very problem, which has attracted the attention of various scholars as well as political and media actors around the world.

Before continuing any further on the dominant class schism, we suggest that Herman and Chomsky's (1994) Propaganda Model (PM) is essential to understanding the key role of media as an ISA. Occasionally criticized as a "conspiracy theory,"—a model utilizing journalists as "gatekeepers" for corporations, or for referencing subjects as "dupes,"—the PM is a structural model, an analytic and conceptual framework to theorize the operation of power in relation to dominant structural elements (Klaehn 2003). The PM is embedded in capitalist social relations and constrained by the dominant ideology. Enough confusion, misunderstanding, and apathy in the general population must be created to allow elite programs to be administered, protective of a dominant class interest (Herman 2000). In defense of the model, Herman writes:

> The propaganda model does start from the premise that a critical political
> economy will put front and center the analysis of the locus of media control
> and the mechanisms by which the powerful are able to dominate the flow of
> messages and *limit the space of contesting parties*. The limits on their power are
> certainly important, but why should these get first place, except as a means
> of minimizing the power of the dominant interests, inflating the elements of

contestation, and pretending that the marginalized have more strength than
they really possess? (2000: 108, emphasis added)

Our purpose in the present discussion is to emphasize how the
Turkish dominant media has gone beyond the bounds of "inflating
the elements of contestation" and is jeopardized by the factional
schism that causes dysfunction of the PM. Compared with the
Turkish case, the media in the United States appears to be consistent
with the original Herman and Chomsky model. In the United
States the PM is administered from the ideology of one unitary
dominant class, which, for the lack of a better term, can be labeled
"Americanism" — understood as the unchallenged American claim to
global hegemony. Conceding the basic principles of this ideology, the
New York Times, together with other monopolistic media organs, for
instance, constructs and encloses a dominant discursive field for the
nation's media as a whole to perform within the limits of permissible
"differences of opinion."

In this respect, in the Turkish case, "flak," one of the five filters of
the PM, seems to be the most problematic. Herman and Chomsky
(1994) define flak as a certain permissibility of confrontation, actually
encouraged as a disciplinary measure but kept within manageable
parameters, between actors within an overall consistent and highly
oppressive structure. We consider that Islamist and laic ideologies
divide the dominant media space in Turkey into two disparate
discursive fields. These separate media spheres are antagonistic
and have by far overstepped manageable parameters, whereby
it is possible to gather vastly differing opinions on major issues in
the media — for example, the idea of national sovereignty. One
newspaper may print on its front page what another newspaper
may not consider newsworthy. Currently, as the factional schism
does not allow for a "one voice" dominant class, what occurs with
adverse effect is the slandering of two antagonistic ideologies, with
one side pitted against the other, sometimes discrediting both.
Contestation steps outside the bounds of permissible flak, and hence
the PM fails to function properly. In Turkey, neither side can gain full
"consent," nor does each lose their reputation in the public eye. As
we shall point out, this paradoxical discursive polarization in terms
of antagonistic ideologies is a central feature of Turkish capitalism.
An apparent Islamist versus laic ideological split is in effect the *façade*
against the actual class struggle within the dominant class between
the Islamist and the laic factions. The masses are left unclear of what

dominant class faction is in charge and what is expected of them, in the Althusserian sense.

The ascending Islamist dominant class faction aims to obtain full control over the media (i.e., means of mental production) and establish itself as *the* ruling class, to root out the old order of the Kemalist ISA and thus subjugate the laic faction of the dominant class to a version of Turkish Islamism fitting the requirements of the neoliberal context. The masses are invited to join this new hegemonic project by the Islamist dominant class, which claims to uphold democracy and order, supposedly incomplete under the previous Kemalist regime. The Islamist faction utilizes the media to present themselves as the "democratic ruling force" capable of superior governance to the Kemalists, and hence the laic faction of the dominant class. This particular "Islamist" contention against Kemalists obscures the ongoing backstage class war centered on weakening or outright removal of the laic faction from the commanding heights of the economy. Within this turbulence, the working masses and the oppressed are ideologically coerced to either reject or believe the "ruling ideas" of the Islamists or the laics.

The Islamist dominant class faction appears to aim to take over the laic dominant class newspapers in order to strengthen their class power in establishing hegemony over the masses and coerce them to adopt their values. Zizek, in his discussion on belief and how it functions in ideology, states that it is not enough to merely believe; "one has to believe in belief itself" (2006: 353). Whether an individual truly believes is irrelevant; what empowers ideology is that s/he thinks they believe, even when their practices are incongruent with what they claim to believe. The ISA has already set in its discourse rules of conduct and belief. As a result, the winner of the media wars will be better disposed to coerce the masses to believe in its ideology, which they do not necessarily believe in but are made to believe they believe in. In practice they merely exchange the ideology of one dominant class faction for another. Their subordinate class position remains unchanged whether they identify themselves with Islamists or Kemalists. Genuine working-class struggle such as protests, strikes, or walkouts are immediately met with reprisals from both dominant class factions, fitting the scheme of the Herman and Chomsky anticommunist filter; thus, both factions curtail and silence democratic struggles of the working masses.

Gramsci's notion of hegemony implies that the dominant class must possess a clear-cut ideology in order to coerce the working class to adopt its values in "maintaining the State":

The "normal" exercise of hegemony on the now classical terrain of the parliamentary régime is characterized by the combination of force and consent, which balance each other reciprocally, without force predominating excessively over consent. Indeed, the attempt is always made to ensure that force will appear to be based on the consent of the majority, expressed by the so-called organs of public opinion—newspapers and associations—which, therefore, in certain situations, are artificially multiplied. Between consent and force stands corruption/fraud. (Gramsci 1971: 80n49)

In considering the Turkish schism, each dominant class faction is struggling for complete access and control over "newspapers and associations" to ensure their hegemony, as media *is* one of the essential ISAs for controlling the masses; and, as Gramsci suggested, hegemony must be achieved through a balanced "combination of force and consent." In theory, Kemalists should willingly consent to Islamist hegemony, herein the importance of media in "maintaining the State." Nevertheless, the practice in Turkey sharply deviates from theory.

The security forces, army, and police (i.e., the Repressive State Apparatus, or RSA), educational institutions, cultural organizations, and, importantly, judicial institutions have all been Kemalist in heritage and been designed to recognize the state under laic hegemony. However, each of the above institutions has also long been subjected to the schism from within, including the army and police force. Islamists under the AKP government currently challenge with remarkable success: (1) Kemalist educational institutions (e.g., the debate over women being allowed to wear headscarves at universities or the sale of alcohol at universities); (2) Kemalist cultural organizations (e.g., the dispute over whether the AKM, the Atatürk Cultural Center, in Taksim Square, Istanbul, should be replaced with a new and renamed cultural center, or if Gezi Park, in the square, should be converted into a military museum); (3) Kemalist judicial institutions (e.g., the speculative court cases known as the Ergenekon trials, in which a clandestine organization comprised of a substantial group of prominent Kemalists allegedly planning a coup against the AKP are tried and jailed); and (4) Kemalist political institutions (e.g., the attempt to remove the reference to "Turkish" in the definition of citizenship in the Constitution). Essentially, this illustrates that should Islamists win against Kemalists, they must conquer outright three main spheres of power: the economy, the state, and the law— the three pillars of bourgeois hegemony.

Law written in the interests of the laic dominant class faction has its roots in the French model of *laïcité* (laicism) and remains contentious between Kemalists and Islamists; therefore, this is a weak link for Islamists. In connection with this, following Gramsci, it is possible to suggest that the school as a positive educative function and the courts as a repressive and negative educative function appear to be battlegrounds for hegemony. As parts of the ISA, these institutions lead the great mass of the population to a particular cultural and moral common sense (Gramsci 1971). Thus, the following questions gain central importance in the struggle for hegemony: Who shall control the Constitutional Court? Who shall administer the legal system of the state, for example, the High Council of Judges and Prosecutors? Who shall run the affairs of the Council of Higher Education? Will those in control be Islamists or Kemalists, considering the triumphant faction shall frame the rules/laws to protect specific interests and uphold the moral views of society? Here, control over media in general and newspapers in particular is an important objective, because these might enable Islamists to earn legitimacy in their struggle for moral and cultural leadership: to be represented in the media as true and just, thus gaining consent of the masses to change the most contentious sphere—law. Without absolute control over media, Islamists cannot establish a complete hegemony throughout society. In that sense, until reaching that position, their struggle for hegemony represents a kind of reformist strategy or, in the Gramscian sense, a "passive revolution" whereby the old order of Kemalism should not be completely swept away (as it would with a revolution); therefore, a slow and gradual transition within the existing state order toward Islamist hegemony occurs (Tuğal 2009). Gramsci's following analysis resonates closely with the current situation in Turkey:

> There is a passive revolution involved in the fact that—through the legislative intervention of the State, and by means of the corporative organization— relatively far-reaching modifications are being introduced into the country's economic structure ... without however touching (or at least not going beyond the regulation and control of) individual and group appropriation for profit. (Gramsci 1971: 119–20)

Indeed, Kemalists react in a "passive counterrevolution" against Islamists within the overall resiliency of capitalism. In effect, Islamists seek to pacify Kemalists through making a transition in all domains whereby everyday practice changes but is accepted as normal—a shift in worldviews. It is a "war of position" that is continuously fought between Islamists and Kemalists in obtaining ideological legitimacy in civil society within universities, cultural and entertainment institutions, and especially the media. No matter what economic power each dominant class faction holds, without securing ideological supremacy it cannot transform itself into a ruling class.

Dominant Class Schism in the Turkish Media

Newspapers were first printed in the Ottoman Empire in the midst of nascent independence movements between the mid- to late nineteenth century. Nation-states structured themselves on language through print capitalism. A nation's dominant language became the language with access to the press (i.e., means of language production), with the ability to control and distribute language, thereby overshadowing and marginalizing other existing languages. Hence, France was the quintessential nation to emulate. For this reason, newspapers emerged promising national independence, an essential element of such struggle. Historically, the newspaper is viewed as a potent political and ideological tool. Television was not as easily accessible to Turkish society in its entirety until after 1980; thus, a cultural habit and belief remains even today that newspapers are the main source of information. A vast difference in media penetration once existed between western Turkey and the provincial towns of central, northern, and southeastern Anatolia. Today, popular TV series, newscasts, and newspapers find their way into most homes across the nation. Despite rapid media development over the last fifty years, a tradition of reading the newspaper to foster political awareness is still habitual. Newspapers are read with a certain sincerity and seriousness, even when the reader may partially accept what they read as manipulated for some political party benefit. Often newspapers are viewed as specific voices to either slander or praise a certain leader during an electoral process.

Secular founders of the Republic instilled their beliefs in the working masses via the newspaper. Under Atatürk's modernization scheme to mass educate the peasantry, reading and language essentialized the importance of literacy. Reading the newspaper was a privilege and afforded one status. When uninformed about an issue, a typical response in Turkey might be expressed, "Did you not *read* the newspaper?" In the United States, a similar response might be expressed, "Did you not *watch* the news?" This is indicative of a culture driven by television and visual media. In Turkey, daily circulation of nearly four million newspapers, for the most part, is split along laic or Islamist lines, representing either the interests of the laic or Islamist dominant class factions. Issues that make headlines in one newspaper might be expressed differently or omitted in another, implying a schism in the social construction of reality.

Freedom of speech and the press, especially since the coup in 1980, has been cause for much contention. Journalists were killed, persecuted, and incarcerated. Newspapers were closed. Islamists manipulated public resentment about repression of the media as justification for their alleged "redemocratization" of Turkey to gain hegemony, as in the spectacular Ergenekon trials mentioned earlier. After the AKP's third period of rule, however, defensive strategies to protect freedom of speech and the press shifted to laic newspapers. In this context, the concept of a "deep state" gained additional importance in disputes over freedom of expression and the press. Over the past few years, the AKP has been mentioned as having its own "deep state."

In the last five years, media wars have played out in sensationalist newspaper headlines. Becoming ever more visible, they are continued cause for skepticism and disgust. Below we provide statistics regarding the top ten newspapers. As newspaper sales can be accurately monitored, they provide a benchmark for understanding how the schism between laic and Islamists fares in terms of rallying the public to their respective agendas. We have chosen three one-week intervals for observation in the years 2002, 2009, and 2012 from the reputable source Medyatava, which tabulates and annals media sector information. Approximately 3,634,004 newspapers were sold across Turkey in 2002, while total sales in 2009 were 4,816,761 and 4,688,522 in 2012, down slightly from 2009. The top ten selling newspapers in December 2002 for one week were as follows (listed beginning with largest sales): *Hürriyet, Posta, Sabah, Star, Zaman, Milliyet, Vatan, Akşam, Fanatik, Fotomaç*. Except *Zaman*, all newspapers were owned by laic businesses. Substantial readership placed *Zaman* in the number five rank in the top ten. Media tycoon Aydın Doğan, whose daughter was once former head of the laic business association Türkiye Sanayici ve İşadamları Derneği (Turkish Industrialists' and Businessmen's Association, TÜSİAD), is popularly referred to as the Rupert Murdoch of Turkey. In 2002 he held a lion's share of the market (*Hürriyet, Posta, Milliyet, Vatan*, and *Fanatik*). By 2009, Doğan was the only laic figure remaining in the top ten. In 2009 Islamist-owned newspapers had a readership of 1,852,021 in weekly sales, substantially higher than Doğan, with 1,551,290 in weekly sales. Comparing 2002 figures, in which laic newspapers had 2,697,073 weekly sales and a mere 301,694 were sales from the one Islamist newspaper, *Zaman*, it is evident that a leaning toward the Islamist faction of the dominant class occurred.

Between 2002 and 2009, *Akşam* and *Star* fell behind in sales, no longer in the top ten. *Sabah* was sold to Islamists, and a newly launched newspaper, *Habertürk*, owned by the Islamist Ciner Group, entered the market and took fifth place almost overnight. By mid- to end of 2009, the Islamist dominant class faction exceeded the laic dominant class faction in the top ten, not only by ownership but also with overwhelming readership. In May 2009 the top ten newspapers, with *Zaman* in the number one spot, were as follows (listed beginning with largest sales): *Zaman, Posta, Hürriyet, Sabah, Habertürk, Fotomaç, Milliyet, Fanatik, Vatan, Takvim*. This occurred for two main reasons. First, there was an aggressive takeover by the Islamist Çalık Group of the *Sabah* newspaper and the ATV channel after an "early-morning raid" in April 2007 by Tasarruf Mevduatı Sigorta Fonu (Savings Deposit Insurance Fund, TMSF) for alleged tax evasion. The AKP government recouped debts totaling 900 million US dollars by the previous owner, Dinç Bilgin of Merkez Yayın Holding. When the newspaper was seized, it was immediately put up for tender, and the Çalık Group purchased it as the sole bidder for 1.1 billion US dollars and took over in September 2007. There was considerable controversy in the public sphere over the financing of this acquisition. According to well-documented sources in the mainstream media, 750 million of the 1.1 billion dollars was obtained as a loan from two state banks, Vakıf Bank and Halk Bank, by using the political clout of the Prime Minister. Under new management, Çalık swiftly fired most of the employees at *Sabah* and ATV, replacing them with a majority who held an Islamic worldview. Acquisition of *Sabah* and ATV added substantial market share to the media of the Islamist dominant class faction.

Second, *Zaman*, owned by Ali Akbulut of the Feza Media Group, is a staunch supporter of the AKP government. Tunç (2008), in the *KAS Democracy Report*, stated that *Zaman* has connections to and the financial support of Fethullah Gülen, who resides in the United States and utilizes the newspaper for his propaganda in the Nursi community. He is the leader of a religious cult, part of the Nur sect, *nur* meaning "light" in Arabic. Where Gülen obtains his financial support is questionable. When investigative journalist Ahmet Şık tried to publish his book, *İmamın Ordusu* (The Army of the Imam, 2011) in an attempt to expose the workings of Fethullah Gülen in Turkey, he was arrested for allegedly being a member of the Ergenekon "gang" and was swiftly jailed. *Zaman*, established in 1986 during Turgut Özal's neoliberal government, grew tenfold over the past twenty-five years. During this period, Islamist-influenced newspapers blossomed.

Profitable and propaganda-driven media steadily strengthened the Islamist dominant class faction. The Islamist capitalist class was direct witness to the possibilities of media, having experienced over thirty years of laic right-leaning conservative party use of propaganda. Backed by the AKP government, Islamist media corporations have grown increasingly powerful. *Zaman* has won over forty awards for its design and journalism, uses the best-quality newsprint, and attracts non-Islamist journalists and columnists to its workforce. The newspaper is published outside Turkey in Azerbaijan, Romania, Bulgaria, Kazakhstan, Kyrgyzstan, the United States, and Europe.

It need not be assumed that Islamist newspapers always harbor radical agendas. Tunç (2008) points to the depoliticization of radical Islam in the press. While *Zaman* has not ever represented radical Islamist ideals, some of the smaller Islamist newspapers favored radical Islamism at one time. *Yeni Şafak* used to be such a newspaper. When it ran into financial difficulty it was bought up and taken over by a more moderate Islamist business family, Albayrak, who shifted it away from radical Islamism, whose manifesto once proclaimed "the worthless order of the West." Sadık Albayrak, a columnist for Yeni Şafak, married into Prime Minister Erdoğan's family, thus making the paper a staunch supporter of the AKP and a moderate Islamist voice. When Ahmet Taşgetiren, *Yeni Şafak*'s head columnist, wrote an article stating Erdoğan was out to create his own media conglomerate, the paper promptly rejected the article and Taşgetiren resigned (Tunç 2008).

Events in 2009 revealed an ever-increasing tension between Islamists and laics. Doğan, who once boasted he paid the greatest amount of tax, was charged with a fine for tax evasion in September 2009 to the hefty sum of 3.76 billion Turkish lira (1.74 billion euros), approximately equal to 80 percent of Doğan Media's standing value. Declaring the fine to be politically motivated, Aydın Doğan attacked Erdoğan, claiming he was out to destroy the free press in Turkey. Erdoğan reported to the *Wall Street Journal* (2009) that the fines had nothing to do with stifling the media and likened Doğan to a gangster: "The issue here is a routine tax examination. ... In the U.S., too, there are people who have had problems with evading taxes. Al Capone comes to mind. He was very rich but then he spent the rest of his life in jail. ... Nobody raised a voice when those events happened." In December 2009, at the World Association of Newspapers and Newspaper Publishers (WAN-IFRA) annual conference held in India, Bülent Keneş (*Zaman*), Suna Vidinli (*Sabah*), and Ergün Babahan (*Star*) spoke out fervently against a report that suggested that the

AKP government campaigned strongly against Doğan Holding. They argued that the report was biased and stated the following in *Today's Zaman* (2009):

> We had expected a more objective and unbiased position by such internationally acclaimed platforms as WAN and the WEF [World Editors' Forum]. We find it misleading on the part of WAN and the WEF not to consult Turkish members of WAN, apart from the Doğan Group, while preparing an overview of the status of media freedom in Turkey. ... Equating a tax evasion case [which is under judicial review—with the accused party seeking settlement] with media freedom is an oversimplification of the matter. We hereby request our statement of dissent to be published at the end of the WAN statement concerning Turkey.

Returning to newspaper sales, by 2012 another shift had occurred. In the struggle for dominance over the discursive field in the media, the laic dominant class faction, together with emerging newspapers, entered a period in which they made slight gains. From 2012 onward, *Sözcü* (regarded as center right), owned by Burak Akbay, which is not only a laic but also an overtly Kemalist newspaper openly critical of Islamists, entered fifth in the top ten. Top ten selling newspapers for one week in August 2012 were as follows (listed beginning with largest to lowest sales): *Zaman, Posta, Hürriyet, Sabah, Sözcü, Fotomaç, Fanatik, Habertürk, Star, Milliyet.* Islamist-owned *Zaman, Sabah, Fotomaç,* and *Habertürk* (*Zaman* comprising 897,881) had a total of 1,653,501 in newspaper sales. Despite penalization of Doğan by the AKP with heavy fines, sales began to increase compared to 2009. In 2012 the Doğan-owned laic newspapers *Hürriyet, Posta,* and *Fanatik* remained in the top ten.

In addition to these quantitative changes, from 2010 onward, analysis of the media space became increasingly complex as some qualitative transformations emerged. Amid the laic/Islamist conflict in the media space, some laic newspapers prefer to remain silent or openly support the Islamist agenda of the AKP and maintain an ambiguous identity. *Star* is one such laic newspaper. Founded by Ahmet Özal and Cem Uzan in 1999, Star is currently marketed as a liberal-conservative center-right newspaper. In 2004 it was sold to a Cypriot businessman through the use of the TMSF methods explained above in the context of *Sabah* and ATV. In 2009, Ethem Sancak, founder and chairman of the board at Hedef Alliance Holding, bought a sizeable share of the newspaper. Ethem Sancak does not have an Islamist past but is regarded as a "close friend" of Prime Minister Erdoğan. A similar case is the Demirören-Karacan Holding.

This laic business group purchased *Milliyet* and *Vatan*, formerly Doğan newspapers, in 2012. At that time there were rumors that Akif Beki—a well-known journalist who used to be an advisor to the Prime Minister—would be the general manager of these two newspapers. Thus, the perception created was that they would "get along" with the AKP government. Indeed, this perception was justified by the forced resignation of the well-known and long-standing laic journalist Hasan Cemal at *Milliyet* in early 2013. The case of Hasan Cemal created an earthquake effect, so to speak—the beginning of a new trend in the media. Hereafter in the media wars, some laic journalists forced to resign from their posts by the government may be willing to work at smaller and less prestigious laic newspapers or may choose to broadcast on social media on their own in order to get their voices heard. All these developments have led to the emergence of a new terminology for categorizing newspapers. Nowadays, *Sözcü*, taking over as the leading representative of the laic opposition, has earned a new identity and given a new "voice" to the laic subdiscursive field in the media space. Therefore, while *Sözcü* is given the title "free press," other laic newspapers are described either as "those who subjugate under pressure" (i.e., *Hürriyet*) or as "direct supporters" of the AKP (i.e., *Star* or *Milliyet*).

As rhetoric between the Islamist and laic factions grows ever more antagonistic, both begin to lose legitimacy. Working and middle classes, who follow headlines like a daily opium fix, become disgusted with both factions as neoliberal policies impinge directly on their lives. As firing and jailing of journalists continues to threaten freedom of speech for all, as students and parents become alarmed about education reforms, or neighborhoods brace themselves against eviction for urban gentrification projects, contention spills over into the streets, derailing order, culminating in the Gezi Revolt. Prime Minister Erdoğan's response to Gezi with repressive measures (RSA) challenges his legitimacy and further sharpens laic/Islamist contestation, as Islamist media outlets slander laics as alleged perpetrators of the revolt. As mentioned earlier, if the battle is won in the Gramscian sense, and the audience adopts the values set by the dominant class ideology as understood by Herman and Chomsky's Propaganda Model, there can only be "one voice" to constitute "consent." Currently, the ideological shift from laic to Islamist, if it can be called such, has been disrupted and derailed by too much antagonism between worldviews, propagating disorder. Turkey, therefore, is suffering from disorder in the order of consent.

Discussion and Concluding Remarks

As we have explained throughout the chapter, the contentious media wars in Turkey represent the struggle for hegemony over the media and the commanding heights of the economy. In other words, what appears to be a political and ideological battle between the Kemalist establishment and the allegedly democratic Islamist government is indeed integral to the processes of capital accumulation on behalf of one or the other faction. Media wars serve several important functions for the reproduction and legitimization of capitalist social relations. First, under the neoliberal regime, these wars must obtain the consent of the working class and oppressed—whose everyday lives are full of troubles and difficulties like debt, rising prices, and reduced wages—according to each faction's struggle to establish its ideas and values as normalcy. Yet this involves a major shift in the political discourse of capitalist governance from one version of citizens seen as abstract individuals within the framework of a constitutional nation-state to that of conceptualizing citizens as members of a community of believers.

Second, it is essential that Islamists implement "one voice" in the media in order to ensure the advantages and privileges of the Islamist dominant class faction remain intact. In the case of any serious defamation of liberal Islamist values throughout the society, the political and economic agenda of the Islamist dominant class faction will be decisively disrupted. Thus, the program to limit and eventually eliminate any oppositional media outlets is, unquestionably, in the best "business" interest of this rising Islamist capitalist class. In doing so, they aim to remove or silence the voice of Kemalists.

Third, as Herman and Chomsky mentioned of the Propaganda Model, flak must be kept at a standard minimum. Dominant ideology cannot function effectively when two antagonistic ideologies exist where there should be only one dominant class with one coherent worldview. This renders the media incredulous and this incredulity harms the reputation of the AKP in the eyes of its supporters.

Fourth, under the conditions of the current global crisis, as this war between the factions of the dominant class continues, the further exploitative and harsh oppressive conditions that prevail over the poor and working masses will have difficulty finding a voice in the media. Under the Turkish bourgeoisie, protest against class oppression and desire for legitimate change (for the betterment of the lot) is severely reduced and curbed. The elimination of issues pertaining to the class interests of the working masses leaves large proportions of society silenced and their needs unheard and unaddressed.

Our observations regarding the notion of freedom of the press and monopolization of media space are bleak. Our analysis above proves there is no freedom of press and the media will remain monopolized by the capitalist class; whether the dominant faction will be Islamists or laics is yet to be determined. Public access to information is and will be curtailed further.

In sum, the ideology of capitalist Islam is finding a new footing. Capitalism continues in the form of a neoliberal Islam, strengthening itself in crisis against what might have been a laic backlash. Capitalism works in tandem with Islam. The umbrella ideology of capitalism remains intact when media wars between Islamists and laics serve to remove any critical opposition to ever-growing inequities of capitalism. What is most disturbing behind the façade of the media wars remains a capitalism hard at work—a capitalism that makes for a fragile democratic environment in Turkey.

References

Althusser, Louis. 1971. *Lenin and Philosophy and other Essays by Louis Althusser*. New York: Monthly Review Press.

Champion, Marc. 2009. "Turkish Premier Defends Media Tax Battle." *Wall Street Journal*, 5 October. Accessed 26 December 2009. http://online.wsj.com/article/SB125469621389762827.html.

Gramsci, Antonio. 1971. *Selections From The Prison Notebooks*. Edited and translated by Quinton Hoare and Geoffrey Nowell Smith. London: Lawrence and Wishart.

Herman, Edward S. 2000. "The Propaganda Model: A Retrospective." *Journalism Studies* 1, no. 1: 101–12.

Herman, Edward S., and Noam Chomsky. 1994. *Manufacturing Consent: The Political Economy of the Mass Media*. London: Vintage.

Klaehn, Jeffery. 2003. "Behind the Invisible Curtain of Scholarly Criticism: Revisiting the Propaganda Model." *Journalism Studies* 4, no. 3: 359–70.

Öncü, Ahmet. 2014. "Turkish Capitalist Modernity and the Gezi Revolt." *Journal of Historical Sociology* 27, no. 2: 151–76. First published online 30 August 2013. doi:10.1111/johs.12036.

Today's Zaman. 2009. "Three Turkish Newspapers Suspend Membership in Int'l Press Body." 4 December. Accessed 26 December 2009. http://www.todayszaman.com/newsDetail_getNewsById.action? load=detay&link=194508.

Tuğal, Cihan. 2009. *Passive Revolution: Absorbing the Islamic Challenge to Capitalism*. Palo Alto, CA: Stanford University Press.

Tunç, Aslı. 2008. *KAS Democracy Report April 2008*. Berlin: Konrad-Adenauer-Stiftung e.V.

Zizek, Slavoj. 2006. *The Parallax View*. Cambridge, MA, and London: MIT Press.

NOTES ON CONTRIBUTORS

Erol Balkan earned a PhD in economics from the State University of New York at Binghamton and joined the Hamilton College faculty in 1987. His current research focuses on the formation of middle classes through education and financial liberalization in developing countries. He teaches economic development, international finance, and political economy of the Middle East at Hamilton College in New York. Balkan's recent book on the formation of the Turkish middle class and education, *Reproducing Class: Education, Neoliberalism, and the Rise of the New Middle Class in Istanbul*, was published in January 2009 by Berghahn Books.

Neşecan Balkan earned her PhD in economics from Istanbul University. She is currently senior lecturer in economics at Hamilton College. Her academic interests include crisis theories, sustainable development, and gender issues. She is the author of *Capitalism and the Debt Crisis* published in Turkish in 1994. Balkan co-edited with Sungur Savran two books published in both English and Turkish in 2002: *The Ravages of Neo-Liberalism: Economy, Society and Gender in Turkey* and *The Politics of Permanent Crisis: Class, Ideology and State in Turkey*. She has also written for various US and Turkish journals.

Burak Gürel is a PhD candidate in sociology at Johns Hopkins University. His research is focused on political economy and historical sociology.

Joshua D. Hendrick earned his PhD in sociology from the University of California, Santa Cruz, in 2009. He currently teaches courses in sociology and global studies at Loyola University Maryland in Baltimore (USA). Professor Hendrick is an associate editor and book review editor for the *Sociology of Islam* journal and is the author of the book *Gülen: The Ambiguous Politics of Market Islam in Turkey and the World* (NYU Press, 2013).

Evren Hoşgör is assistant professor at the Department of Business Administration in Istanbul Bilgi University (Turkey). She earned her PhD from the Department of Sociology in Lancaster University (UK) in 2009. Her PhD thesis was entitled "AKP, State and Capital: A Class-theoretical Re-interpretation of the Conflict between 'Centre' and 'Periphery' in Turkey." Her key research areas are as follows: state-business relations, business history, political economy, sociology of work, and culture industry.

Anita Oğurlu is a PhD candidate in humanities and cultural studies at Birkbeck College, University of London. She completed an MA in cultural studies at Istanbul Bilgi University and BA in visual communications at Ryerson University, Toronto, Canada. Her research interests include culture and economy, film and media studies, autobiographical literature, and labor and social movements. Oğurlu taught film and television studies at Istanbul Bilgi University. Before returning to academia in 2005, Oğurlu worked as a creative director in multinational advertising agencies in Istanbul and Toronto.

Ahmet Öncü is professor of sociology at Sabancı University, School of Management, Istanbul. He completed his PhD in sociology at the University of Alberta in 1996. He obtained his MSc and BSc in economics from the Middle East Technical University. His academic interests include social theory, political economy, and political sociology. His articles have appeared in such journals as *New Perspectives on Turkey, Journal of Historical Sociology, Cultural Logic, Science and Society, Citizenship Studies, International Review of Sociology,* and *Review of Radical Political Economics.*

Özgür Öztürk is a lecturer of economics at Ondokuz Mayıs University. His research interests include the economics and politics of imperialism, value theory, financialization, and the capitalist development process in Turkey. He is the author of *Türkiye'de Büyük Sermaye Grupları* (Big Business Groups in Turkey), published in 2010.

Sungur Savran is a writer and political militant based in Istanbul, Turkey. He received his BA from Brandeis University in Massachusetts in politics and completed his PhD in economics at Istanbul University.

He has taught at various universities in the United States, including the New School for Social Research in New York City. He is the author of several books in Turkish and coeditor of two volumes on Turkey in English: *The Politics of Permanent Crisis and The Ravages of Neo-Liberalism* (2003). He has written for various US and British journals, including the *Monthly Review* and *Capital and Class*.

Kurtar Tanyılmaz is assistant professor at the Faculty of Business Administration, Marmara University. His research interests and several articles are focused on theoretical and empirical issues concerning industrial restructuring in developing economies, capitalist development in Turkey, and Marxist analysis of contemporary capitalism. He is a member of the editorial board of the Turkish political journal *Devrimci Marksizm* (Revolutionary Marxism) and also a member of the advisory board of the Turkish academic journal *Praksis*.

INDEX

DISLOCATIONS

General Editors: August Carbonella, *Memorial University of Newfoundland,*
Don Kalb, *University of Utrecht & Central European University,*
Linda Green, *University of Arizona*

www.ingramcontent.com/pod-product-compliance
Lightning Source LLC
Chambersburg PA
CBHW060027030426
42334CB00019B/2215